Lifenotes

A user's guide
to making
sense of life
on
planet Earth

Peter de Ruyter

Also by Peter de Ruyter

Books

- Understanding Candida (Nature & Health Books, Australia, 1989)
- Living with HIV/AIDS (Allen & Unwin, Australia, 1996)

Lifenotes

A USER'S GUIDE

TO MAKING

SENSE OF LIFE

ON

PLANET EARTH

Peter de Ruyter

Copyright © Peter de Ruyter 2009

Copyright © Cover design and diagrams - Peter de Ruyter 2009

Published by Peter de Ruyter

All rights reserved. No part of this book may be reproduced by any mechanical, photographic or electronic process, or in the form of any audio format, nor may it be stored in a retrieval system, transmitted or otherwise copied for public or private use – other than for 'fair use' as brief quotations embodied in articles and reviews – without prior written permission of the author.

Please be advised that no part of this book is intended as a form of diagnosis or prescription on physical, mental or emotional levels. If, after reading this book, the reader decides to instigate a change in their present therapeutic regime, then it is imperative they also seek out the professional advice of an appropriate specialist – be they natural or medical.

The intent of the author is solely to provide information of a philosophical nature in the reader's quest to seek a greater understanding of the human condition. In the event the reader uses any information from this book with which to change their lives in any manner whatsoever, the author and publisher assume no responsibility for your actions.

Printed and bound in Australia by BookPOD

National Library of Australia Cataloguing-in-Publication Data:

Author:	de Ruyter, Peter, 1951 –
Title:	'Lifenotes – a user's guide to making sense of life on planet earth / Peter de Ruyter.
Edition:	1st ed.
ISBN:	9780646522401 (pbk.)
Notes:	Includes index. Bibliography.
Subjects:	Life. Spiritual direction. Philosophy. New Age movement.
Dewey Number:	128

Typesetting and cover design by BookPOD

Author photograph by Ross Gardiner

*This book is dedicated to Amma,
who has hugged the world and been a major
guiding Light in the creation of this book*

*Also to Arv,
whose Presence deeply touched my Heart, crumbled its
walls and then held the Energy as I dared to love again*

*To Zus,
my deceased aunt
whose conversations and letters inspired
me to keep searching*

ACKNOWLEDGMENTS

Where does one start when wanting to thank specific people for their help in the monumental task of preparing a book? Inevitably, such a project involves a huge amount of input via numerous friends, professionals, as well as the many authors who have inspired me on this Journey.

I had known for years that there was one particular book bubbling away within me. However, during a psychic reading by Sally, it became clear that writing this book was something of a 'pre-incarnational assignment', which I knew I was avoiding, but which she made clear I would eventually have to attend to.

Then, some years later, I met a remarkable man, Michael, who did a profound astrological reading for me, which once again put me on notice that this project needed to be done... and to stop procrastinating! Without his powerful but compassionate push, this book would most likely still be slumbering somewhere in my neural network.

So many dear friends have encouraged me in this enormous task, as well as offering practical help in reassessing the various manuscript drafts, and providing constructive feedback. To Ross Forman, my main thanks for his meticulous, perceptive and constructive editing of the manuscript. Without his invaluable insights and help, this book would not be what it has evolved into. He created a sparkle and shine to what was a very rough diamond indeed.

Also, my thanks to all those who so kindly gave of their time, providing valuable feedback after 'test-driving' the manuscript:- Greg Ockenden (for advice on cover design); Harry Binder; Greg Trutza; Sieglinde Leferink; Carl & Linda Childs-van Wijk; Ron Mateljan (for the exercises and summary suggestions); Gerda Hawke; Chanelle McKellar; Ross Gardiner & Anita Patel; Anne Wyatt.

Further thanks go to some very special people in my life, without whose help and loving support, my Journey at times would have been difficult to get through. Again, to Ross Forman for his unwavering and kind assistance on so many levels, especially over the last few years when my life Journey became rather 'challenging'. To Harry Binder for his constancy of friendship and care down the many years; to Carl and Linda Childs-van Wijk, whose ever loving support has sustained me in a multitude of ways; to Greg Ockenden and Michael Hing for keeping me sane and grounded during some trying times, acting variously as father confessor, mentor and advisor; to my deceased aunt, Jana (Zus) de Korte whose inspiring conversations nourished my soul as it searched for answers to Life's conundrums, and to Mark Phillips for sustaining me with Healing and Caring Acupuncture Therapy during some problematic health issues.

Then comes the time to turn a manuscript into a finished book; no mean feat, and something I found to be rather overwhelming. Writing a book is quite demanding enough, but to understand all the technicalities of transforming a rough manuscript into a finished product is something else again. Here I have so much gratitude to 'BookPod' for helping make this transition in such a painless manner.

And finally, to you the reader, my thanks for being willing to explore the concepts presented within this text; that takes courage. May you be empowered to transform your Life in many positive and Healing ways.

ABOUT THE AUTHOR

Peter de Ruyter was born in South Africa in 1951 of Dutch migrants. In 1964 he moved with his family to Sydney, Australia, where he did his secondary schooling before going on to study at Sydney University. In 1975 he graduated with a Bachelor of Science Degree, which was used to obtain entrance to a specialized Nursing Course offered by Prince Henry Hospital. He graduated as a Registered Nurse two years later.

He worked in several major teaching hospitals in Sydney, and did a second Certificate in 'Nursing Unit Management' at St. Vincent's Hospital. He then worked in Pathology, which provided an in-depth experience in a multitude of orthodox diagnostic procedures. This background produced an excellent base from which to enter the Naturopathic arena.

It was during the latter years of his Nursing career that Peter became increasingly interested in Alternative or Complementary approaches to true healing. This desire lead him to undertake courses in Reiki, Homeopathy, Iridology, Bach Flower Therapy, Tissue Salt Therapy, Diet, Massage and finally to major in Medical Herbalism, having studied this in a Diploma Course at the Southern Cross Herbal College, under the renown herbalist, Denis Stewart.

Peter started practise as a Natural Therapist in 1982, specializing in Medicinal Herbs, at the 'Village Healing & Growth Center' in Paddington. He consulted from there for two years before being invited to practise at the former 'Euroa Center' in Balmain. He ran a highly successful practise from this Center for 12 years; between 1984 – 1996. Presently he operates from Randwick.

From the beginning of the HIV/AIDS epidemic, Peter was involved in helping people deal with this health challenge, using a wide range of natural therapeutic techniques. Although no cures have been achieved, these protocols provided immense benefits to many people, frequently stabilizing them for long periods of time, as well as greatly increasing quality of life. Over the years, about 25% of Peter's practise involved dealing with HIV/AIDS clients. The remaining 75% of his clients came for a range of ill-health conditions, including cancer.

Peter has presented his work at local and national conferences, and lectured to a host of lay groups. In the early days of the AIDS epidemic, he organized and facilitated many intensive workshops, and several self-help groups in which people learned a range of techniques through which to help regain their health. In a number of radio and TV appearances, similar topics were addressed. He is author of 'Coping With Candida', which went to a second edition. His next book, titled 'Living with HIV/AIDS – a practical guide to staying well' was published by Allen & Unwin in 1996.

After 28 years of consulting with thousands of clients, Peter has recently taken a Sabbatical, during which time he finished this, his third book. Peter now offers a range of training workshops in the area of natural health. Drawing on both orthodox and complementary methods, he finds himself well placed to continue being of service in a truly Wholistic manner.

CONTENTS

ACKNOWLEDGMENTS 1

ABOUT THE AUTHOR 3

PREFACE 9

CHAPTER 1
Some background data to set the scene 17

CHAPTER 2
Reality can be fickle 31

CHAPTER 3
Thoughts are reality-creators 45

CHAPTER 4
Meaning of life 71

CHAPTER 5
How does religion fit into all this? 113

CHAPTER 6
Suffering issues 133

CHAPTER 7
Incarnational metaphors 175

CHAPTER 8
Being in the Now 195

CHAPTER 9
Meditation 221

CHAPTER 10
Co-creativity – what is it? 243

CHAPTER 11
Co-creativity – further explorations 279

CHAPTER 12
Co-creativity – techniques 317

CHAPTER 13
    Co-creativity – blockages 351
CHAPTER 14
    Multiple realities 363
CHAPTER 15
    Once you've opened Pandora's Box…... 387
APPENDIX I
    Book list 405
APPENDIX II
    'Fountaining' protocol 407
APPENDIX III
    EFT.. 411
INDEX... 415

ILLUSTRATIONS

DIAGRAM 1
    Oversoul setting up the incarnational game 181
DIAGRAM 2
    How the oversoul concept can help explain past and future life
    experiences obtained via rebirthing, hypnosis, etc. 188
DIAGRAM 3
    Our mind as a movie projector 293
DIAGRAM 4
    Humanity's thoughts and beliefs determining the most probable
    reality from a range of multiple realities. 366
DIAGRAM 5
    How small changes in belief can result in considerable change in
    life-direction, over time. 368

The gods did not reveal from the beginning,

All things to us; but in the course of time,

Through seeking we may learn and know things better.

But as for certain truth; no man has known it.

Nor will he know it; neither of the gods,

Nor yet of all things of which I speak.

And even if by chance he were to utter the final truth,

he would himself not know it.

For all is but a web of woven guesses.

Xenophanes of Colophon, 500 BCE.

PREFACE

The real voyage of discovery consists not in seeking new landscapes, but in having new eyes.

Proust

No doubt there have been times when you've asked yourself *the* most fundamental human question... 'What is this life all about'? 'What am I doing here'? 'Where am I going'?

Does your life seem to be spinning in endless grey loops towards nowhere? Are you still wondering what your 'path' is – searching for a life direction and focus which gives you a sense of real purpose, and a spring to your step when you get up in the morning? Or perhaps you feel as if your entire life is slowly but surely unraveling, with no sense of what to do or where to turn? Maybe your usual strategies just aren't cutting it anymore?

Welcome to the human condition on planet Earth!

There are a plethora of guidelines, 'road maps', life strategies, philosophies and religions to supposedly guide us on what can be a most confusing experience – a human existence. One problem is that so many of these allegedly infallible 'solutions' being offered out there also seem to contradict each other, thereby only adding to the confusion. Now what! Who's right? Who's wrong?

So why this book?

The short answer is that I needed to find a more rational and sane way of dealing with day to day existence on planet Earth myself. Certainly the Catholicism of the early '50s I was born into left me with little else than huge amounts of guilt as well as a deep sense of disempowerment. The other religions I explored also felt too disempowering to me, mainly because the 'solutions' they offered were inevitably coming from an external authority, rather than being derived from within me, or more importantly, from my own experiences.

And so the quest began to find a system; some sort of viewpoint which could provide more than just guilt and a feeling of how insignificant we humans were. I needed to find a philosophical model which could provide a means of explaining and dealing with the many inconsistencies life seems prone to throw onto our Path. I was also searching for techniques capable of providing a platform from which to live a more self-empowered life.

As a child, my existence was definitely not devoid of rules and regulations – 'guidelines' – as to what this life was all about, and how it needed to be lived. The Catholic family background I was born into saw to this in no uncertain terms. I had been given a strong foundation, but it was confined to a particularly narrow 'style' of religious belief.

Yet, as time went by, increasingly the Catholic guidelines and 'maps' meant to help navigate me through life weren't making sense. Even as a youngster, they just didn't tally with what I was already starting to understand about the human existence. This was especially so during my teenage years. Here, life can be experienced as a rather chaotic time anyway, as one struggles to create a personal identity, plus make sense of one's reality.

I was also dealing with some major issues about who I was. The expectations of both my culture of that era, as well as my religion were at odds with whom I felt myself to be. And so my own Journey began: reading books, endlessly pondering, as well as attending a plethora of New Age workshops, many claiming to offer instant Enlightenment.

Well, the Enlightenment hasn't happened yet! But what I can say is that as the years pass by, I've managed to create a clearer understanding of what does and doesn't seem to work within this human reality. At least for me. I have definitely not found 'The Truth', and the concepts I'd like to explore in this book are only some ways of looking at life's mysteries. Nevertheless, the aim is to use such concepts in as empowering and effective a way as possible, enabling us to respond more positively to the inevitable challenges life throws at us humans.

Authors and authorities who have inspired me

It is also important to realize that most of what I have to say has already been said by many before me, and in many different ways. My own Journey has been inspired for at least three decades by a host of amazing people. They have shared their insights and wisdom via their books, lectures, workshops, CD's or DVD's, thus helping me see my own Journey more clearly. People like Gregg Braden, Eckhart Tolle, Neale Donald Walsch, Deepak Chopra, Frederick Bailes, Shakti Gawain, Dr. Carlson Loke, Petrea King, Bernie Siegel, Stephen Levine, Serge King, Lynne McTaggart, Ram Dass, Jack Kornfield, Wayne Dyer, Lazaris, Jane Roberts and the 'Seth' books, Bartholomew, Jean Houston, Carolyn Myss, Zechariah Sitchen, and so many more.

A list of books is provided in Appendix I, which you might like to explore or even re-visit if it's been some time since you've read them. I owe so much to these wonderful Guides, as their books and other resources held me by the hand, and encouraged me to continue exploring this odd, amazing, baffling, wonderful, often painful, yet exciting experience called life.

This book will be very eclectic

Investigating life perspectives through the eyes of so many authors has had the effect of making me eclectic in what I choose to believe or use in my own Journey. This book is therefore inevitably going to reflect that personal voyage, and draw on a diverse range of ideas and concepts. From where I stand, no one system seems to have *all* the answers. Therefore, the major yardstick used is simply to gauge to what extent a particular idea or concept gives meaning to life, and how much it provides a significant measure of empowerment to deal with the confusion, idiosyncrasies, and often, what can only be described as the insanities of life.

Some of the exciting ideas we'll explore include:-
- the reality that Creative Visualization is ultimately a Journey into Spirituality, not materiality
- how we are Co-creating reality all the time; albeit mostly unconsciously, and hence the level of chaos in our earthly dimension
- that reincarnation of an individual Spirit is not necessarily a *sequential* phenomenon, but rather something that may actually be happening *simultaneously*
- how religion's dark side has been disempowering to humanity, despite all the good it has also achieved over the centuries

- how suffering can be put to good use, especially as a means to training us to access our Higher Self – a crucial ability if Creative Visualization is to work
- the fact that contrary to popular promotion by some New Age practitioners, Creative Visualization is not something everyone can instantly be 100% successful at accomplishing. It's a skill which has to be learned and much practised
- how your level of success at Creative Visualization depends on where you happen to live on planet Earth; another concept so often not mentioned in most books on the subject
- the notion that we are *primarily* and *fundamentally* Spirit in a body; not a body with a bit of Spirit thrown in. This crucial twist has powerful ramifications within our lives
- the perspective that *external* change can ever only occur successfully if we first create *inner* change. This fact is another decisive aspect to successful Creative Visualization
- how each incarnation may be planned by an Oversoul in collaboration with other Spirit 'friends', and how this concept can provide Healing of so much of our suffering and bewilderment experienced here on Earth
- how the 'currency' of Awareness may be a far more realistic way through which to pay off our Karmic debts.

Realize too that in writing this book, my primary aim has not been to create some sort of marvelous literary work. Rather, my desire is to engage you, the reader, in a sincere, meaningful and empowering conversation which you can stop and start as you wish. Hence the conversational style in which the ideas will be presented. What I'm hoping to achieve is for this book to act as a substitute for you and me sitting down over a 'cuppa', and having some intriguing discussions on the nature of life and this earthly reality.

You'll also notice an atypical usage of capital letters for certain words, indicating a Higher Dimension to what is being discussed. In other words, such capitalized words are being utilized to alert the reader to a concept which is being described from a Higher level of Awareness or Consciousness.

Preface

I am definitely not 'the answer'
It needs to be clearly reiterated that I certainly don't profess to have all the answers. Indeed, as stated earlier, I'm still very much on the Journey myself. Keep in mind... *they teach that which they most need to learn themselves.* How true!

Why accept this book when there are so many other guides out there?
But a very valid question would be... 'Why would you then automatically believe anything written in this book'? The answer is an emphatic... *you absolutely shouldn't!* Only accept whatever you read here if it resonates somewhere deep inside you; almost on a cellular level. If you come across anything in this discussion which you feel to be rather weird or irrational, then you have a choice: either toss it - or file it for future use. The latter is a worthwhile strategy, because what may seem absurd now may nevertheless make much more sense when extra 'pixels' are added to the 'picture'. This is especially likely to happen as time goes by, and as you do further reading and exploration in these realms. It's just that at the moment, certain individual 'pixels' may still be out of context from the rest of the 'picture'. It's a bit like trying to imagine an entire puzzle by just looking at one small jig-saw piece, which by itself seems pretty meaningless.

Over time, however, you'll accumulate more of these individual, 'filed away concept-pixels'. Then along comes that one, specific, new piece of information; that one new 'pixel'. Suddenly, those 'filed away' collection of individual, nonsensical pieces of the jigsaw puzzle of life *do* make a bit more of an understandable picture. It still won't be the full picture, but enough can be seen which is suddenly identifiable, and actually has got a feel of rationality about it. More importantly, it resonates deep within you as making sense at this point.

But how can you really trust this impression of inner 'resonance', and what does that feel like anyway? Let's use another example which no doubt everyone has experienced at some time. Let's imagine you've just left home on your way to do the shopping. As you're driving along, you have this nagging awareness you've forgotten something. Try as you may, you just can't seem to figure out what it might be. You mentally go through a long list of possibilities – do you have your shopping list? Yes. Your money or credit card? Yes. Your recyclable bags? Yes. Nothing 'pings'.

But all of a sudden you've got it – you forgot to bring your jacket for dry-cleaning! Every fiber of your being absolutely, definitely *knows* that this is what you have forgotten. You simply don't need anyone or anything else to vindicate you've now 'got it'. So too, with this issue of 'resonance'. It's exactly that same sense of almost 'cellular/body knowingness'; a feeling often experienced deep in your gut, which happens when you hear or read something which may be quite 'new', yet you just *know* to be correct.

Accepting certain information, based on a 'gut feeling', may appear to be rather irrational if you were coming from a more 'scientific' or left-brained approach. After all, where is the 'proof' that this is a valid piece of information; of understanding? Yet, *intuitively* you absolutely know that it is correct. It's that sort of *experiential* knowingness we are talking about here.

As a Science graduate myself, I'd like to pre-empt certain 'scientific' critics, who might like to discredit this type of approach. For we need to remember the manner in which many of science's most dramatic discoveries and insights have occurred. The greatest scientists, with Einstein a prime example, are known to have had insights explode into their Awareness through intuitive hunches, dreams and other 'less-than-scientific' means.

Intuition was their starting point. From there they applied scientific methods to move to a more formalized level of understanding. We also need to remember that there are many things in science which we still don't fully understand, but which we have no hesitation in applying to our daily life situations. Time and Gravity are two good examples.

Hence, it's that Inner, intuitive resonance that needs to happen before you take on board anything at all from this book – or from anywhere else for that matter. As I've suggested above, if such a sense of resonance doesn't occur, you could just 'file it', never mind how weird it seems. More likely than not, in the future you'll come across other bits of data, allowing what presently seems quite ridiculous to then suddenly fit into the overall puzzle... and to make perfect sense after all.

This is just how life is. We are not automatically presented with the full, understandable picture in one single instant of time. It would appear that the Journey of life is more about constantly accumulating one bit of new information after another. Eventually, as we've put enough of these bits together, we create a much clearer image of what we are trying to investigate or understand. Another choice while reading this book could be to simply dump the entire topic, and move on to the next chapter – or book!

However, what I would also say is that if even a smidgen of what we'll be discussing and exploring does somehow resonate within your own heart, at least be willing to play with these ideas. And if you do, then give it a fair go. Remember the old saying... 'what you put in is what you'll get out'. *Personal experience is truly the most unequivocal way to confirm something for yourself*; not because 'so and so' said it - no matter how authoritatively. In this Journey you're about to go on, you don't need to convince or change anyone... except yourself. But you may find, especially if this sort of information is rather new to you, that re-reading this book every 2-3 months, will be a powerful and productive way of helping transform your life. You'll find that each new reading provides yet another layer to your understanding of life situations, which was not apparent before.

There will also be one golden rule underlying this entire book, which will be hammered home ad nauseum... 'don't get hung up on whether something is '*The Truth*' or not. Only ask yourself... 'is it *useful*'? The sad reality is that 'Truth' has become a very diverse and dangerous thing to us humans, being the instigator of much misery along the way.

Lifenotes - A user's guide to making sense of life on planet Earth

CHAPTER 1

SOME BACKGROUND DATA TO SET THE SCENE

Argue for your limitations and they are yours.
Argue for your possibilities and they are yours as well.

Various Authors

How my work aided my own journey of understanding

As far as my professional life is concerned, I come from a rather eclectic background, having originally studied Agricultural Science, majoring in horticulture. Then, due to a whole range of life events, I made a huge U-turn and studied nursing, graduating from Prince Henry Hospital, Sydney, in 1979. I did several post-graduate nursing courses, worked in Pathology for a while, yet continued to feel rather out of place. My family origins were steeped in medicine, dad having practised many years as a medical doctor. With his European background, he had also studied homeopathy. As a child, therefore, alternate ways of dealing with health issues were a normal and fundamental aspect of treating illness.

But the science and nursing I'd studied and explored thus far still left me feeling out of alignment with life's purpose. So I drifted into studying homeopathy, thinking I would simply focus on becoming the third generation Homeopath in the family – dad's father also having been a homeopathic doctor, while his mother was a homeopathic dentist. But after attending a talk by renowned herbalist Denis Stewart, I came out of that experience feeling 'on fire'. I absolutely knew I had finally found my Path. Herbalism!

Now, nearly thirty years later, I find myself still involved in the field of wholistic healing, working – according to one friend's view – as a 'healing tour-guide'. I love this label, as I frankly don't believe many people, including myself, are true Healers. I'd much rather see myself as a 'healing facilitator'. From my perspective, true Healing occurs from Higher levels, as well as via the inherent body-wisdom of the person seeking help. All any therapist can really do is to catalyze or facilitate that Inner Healing capacity which every person does have within themselves.

My experience of dealing with thousands of patients over more than a quarter of a century has provided a rich resource from which to learn much about the human condition. It has helped me discover what works; what doesn't seem to work; and how to manage one's day to day existence on planet Earth in as empowered and productive a manner as possible.

Healers and authors are not automatically fully Enlightened

Over the many years of attending workshops given by various New Age 'Gurus', I've noticed a disturbing phenomenon. Too many participants tend to have an almost unquestioned belief about the status of such presenters. There seems to be an acceptance that these leaders truly have it all 'together'; that they have reached the final goal of Enlightenment, and thus live their lives in a state of complete health, fulfillment and happiness. But this is both an unrealistic, and an unfair expectation to put onto them. If Enlightenment was indeed a requirement before they could start being a Healing catalyst to others, then they would have to be J.C himself! Obviously ludicrous.

Healers, therapist, workshop leaders – they all have their own Journey to travel. Ironically, this frequently involves some rather challenging health or life issues as well. Often these are precisely the factors which got them into the field of Healing and teaching in the first place. Such challenges, therefore, were the situations which provided them with powerful means through which to do their true 'apprenticeship'. It became their 'school of hard knocks', facilitating that deeper learning so necessary in creating better understanding, empathy and compassion. Attending University or College is all very well – and important. But the 'school of hard knocks' is the one which ultimately provides the greatest learning - although one doesn't end up with a piece of paper, a Certificate or Diploma, indicating you've attended this much harder 'School'!

Chapter 1 - Some Background Data to Set the Scene

Life - enjoyable for many… if incarnated well

To any casual observer of life on planet Earth, it would seem that for numerous people, life here is a bundle of fun. This is something which many who live in the Western, more developed and technologically advanced cultures almost expect as their 'birthright'. By the same token, this is not to say that people can't experience happiness in other than Westernized cultures; far from it. But in the West, all too often we do tend to believe our culture somehow 'owes' us the maximum opportunities to play, explore and have fun. Indeed, many people do so with gusto and abandon, but often also conveniently forgetting the costs such desires do extract from others on this 'Earth-ship' planet of ours.

However, along with a propensity to want to maximize their own experience of fun and good times, there can be a tendency within too many humans – whatever their cultural background - to try and ignore the suffering of others. A bit of the… 'I'm alright Jack' syndrome. A clear example of this would be the outrageous level of luxury with which Mugabe of Zimbabwe and his cronies live their lives, compared to the people he is supposed to rule and be guardian over. But he definitely isn't the only example that could be highlighted! Many such abuses occur within the West, and all over the world in every culture.

If we were to believe what our Western culture promotes about itself, then one could expect to find a greater degree of happiness for those who have incarnated into these relatively safe and trouble-free Time/Space co-ordinates. This is especially so if one considers the many other areas on Earth a person could have been born, such as Somalia, Nigeria, Rwanda, East Timor or Iraq, where life is not quite as smooth. But one thing my 28 years of experience as practitioner has clearly shown me is that even those people whose desire is *not* to experience suffering, do eventually hit this ubiquitous human experience within their own personal life journey.

Most humans do try to enjoy themselves here on planet Earth, and if things get a bit rough, they put on a brave and cheerful face. Yet, get them to sit in my clinic room, and really open up as to what is actually happening in their reality, and a far different picture appears; one often of quite deep suffering. I'm sure this will resonate for anyone who is a practitioner – medical or natural - who allows themselves to get to know their clients on a deeper and more heart-felt level.

For others, although planet Earth itself is a most beautiful and fascinating place, they can't help but see that it also is a plane of reality steeped in much pain and misery. It's all very well to sit comfortably in our Western home; with a good Western job which provides food for the table; a roof over our heads, and in fact so much more than just the basic needs for survival. But life may not seem so rosy to those who live in Third World countries; starving; ill; living under dictatorships; having to deal with constant war and chaos. How do we then make sense of such disparate experiences; such realities – as remote as they may seem to our own daily lives?

There are many ways in which we can try to ignore or distance ourselves from our own and others' suffering. One effective method is to keep ourselves distracted from reality via a wide range of materialistic diversions. 'Let's do some retail-therapy'; 'let's just go to the footie'; 'see a movie'. Actually, let's do anything at all, as long as we don't need to dwell on the very real distress which is so much a part of the human experience. It's precisely this side-stepping which a lot of people tend to do in the West, which then becomes an important basis for the continuation of these very same miseries we see within the human family.

For those who already find life fraught with pain, it becomes vital to have some sort of construct through which to be able to survive or manage this suffering as productively as possible. And humans, with their insistent and insatiable desire to understand things, do need to formulate a workable way of dealing with the suffering which is a reality to billions of lives here on Earth.

Life can be a challenging ride for countless people. How do we make it a much smoother, more joyful and more fulfilling experience? How can we maximally empower ourselves, despite many life situations which often leave us feeling quite powerless? How can we find a sensible format which helps to see ourselves as so much more than just a lump of flesh? How can we view ourselves as more than human beings who are pathologically focused on only accumulating as much materiality as possible, hoping or expecting that this will make life more worthwhile and enjoyable?

Yes, we can get involved in fascinating jobs; raise a family; accumulate a lot of money or power. But is any of this ultimately enough to satisfy that inner psychological itch, which for numerous people is constantly seeking attention; needing to be scratched to a point of satisfaction? How then does one create a world-view or structure, which gives support if not meaning? Enter philosophy... and its more problematic cousin, religion.

Chapter 1 - Some Background Data to Set the Scene

Need for guidelines

Guidelines we certainly do need to enable us to navigate our way through the many ups and downs of life; its countless inconsistencies and confusions. For many, such guidelines are still provided by religions. As narrow and restrictive as religions can be, they nevertheless do offer a means of holding on to one's sanity for the duration of a human life.

The issue is not that we've come into a world where there aren't any fundamental set of rules by which to live. The guidelines themselves usually seem simple and straight-forward, but the interpretation and subsequent dogmatic *enforcement* of such rules is where the distortion and confusion sets in. The end result is that even though religions provide some basic and useful guidelines to living life as a human on planet Earth, the organizations promoting them are all too frequently hypocritical in their execution. In recent times this has particularly been seen in some of the 'televangelists', as well as other Church leaders. Again and again they are found not to be 'walking the talk'.

Those overly immersed in these religious situations, and who don't question what they are told, are also the most likely to be blind to such discrepancies. One fascinating and most refreshing book which explores this phenomenon is 'The Scandalous Gospel of Jesus', [1] by Peter Gomes, a book you are highly encouraged to read and take to heart. The reality is that most religions have strayed from their original teachings as given by Christ, Mohamed or Buddha for instance, and become increasingly hypocritical and lacking integrity. Hence the crucial need for religions to be questioned and assessed as to what they are actually putting on offer. This assessment of religion can be best perceived if one is coming from *outside* the religion, looking *in*.

Interestingly, in parts of Western societies, we've now had several generations with very few guidelines. We've had a situation where it's been more of a free-for-all attitude on many levels – political, economic, religious, societal, and personal. Some would say that this appears to have only increased the chaos and disquieting lack of life-direction. It makes one realize that some form of structure or ethical worldview would seem a pre-requisite to support us through the human Journey. Humans need a sense of meaning to what so often seems meaningless; to be given courage to go on when suffering enters our life; to have a sense of purpose, which also provides collateral value to those around us; to receive guidance when critical forks in the road of life occur, where we need to make vital decisions.

God not so certain now; less guidelines; more mystery

In former days, religions in a sense provided a set of truths, constructs or guidelines that seemed to be absolute, clear, certain and well-defined. The God of that time was far more black and white; a God of very strict laws and clearly defined regulations as to what was to be considered a righteous life.

Nowadays, a lot of those constructs or securities have been ripped away. We're left with a God who is far less certain, and a life situation that seems far more complex and confusing. For many people, today's God seems less well defined or knowable. The God of yesteryear was understood more within human terms. God was a 'He'; God was very demanding; God could get angry; God could become very jealous... strangely, God was almost human in so many ways. It's said that God made man in the image of God. It would appear that far too often, man has made God in the image of man... not a good idea!

Nowadays, we do seem to deal with a God who is more of a mystery, in a life that is less certain. Perhaps the challenge in today's world is to live within a plethora of such uncertainties, and yet to live a life fully, productively, with much joy and strength. Perhaps it is high time we find a way to connect to our own Inner Spiritual Center, capable of sustaining us despite the mystery and uncertainty of life, rather than necessarily having to find it *outside* of ourselves.

Today, many more pertinent, searching and often unanswerable questions are being asked of religion, particularly as the power and strangle-hold such various religious organizations have had over people's ability to think for themselves appears to be declining. Alternate paradigms through which to understand and live our lives need to be explored, which may previously have been actively discouraged or prohibited.

How else can we gain a sense of guidance?

Other ways of achieving an ability to re-empower our own life Journey do exist, and one example is via the concept of Creative Visualization. Much has already been written about this subject, but hopefully this book will allow you to discover nuances and angles to this potent way of living your life which haven't been expressed in quite the same way before. Sometimes we simply

Chapter 1 - Some Background Data to Set the Scene

need to hear a message from different perspectives till the penny finally drops and we've 'got it'.

Suddenly it all makes sense, and we can see how to apply a new perception to our lives. Such insight allows us to become less the victim to our circumstances, and more empowered in how we can respond to our life challenges. Ultimately, Creative Visualization is truly a Spiritual Journey, although for many people their initial focus may be more on how the *material* aspects of this process can enrich their lives. In fact, and strangely perhaps, either way is O.K. And we'll explore the reasons why as the book progresses.

One major thread therefore of this book will be to investigate how the essence of Creative Visualization ironically forces us into Spiritual mode, whether we initially understand this or not. A major reason for this lack of understanding is precisely because we ultimately have much too narrow a perspective on what it means to be Spiritual. In so many books and workshops on Creative Visualization, what's often left out, or just not understood is that this process can only work by going via a Higher, more Energy-based or Spiritual Dimension.

We can visualize all we want, but it is only when we allow ourselves to become congruent with what it is we desire, that it can then manifest into this material reality on Earth. So the end result is that this process forces us to grow in Consciousness, to the point where we first need to manifest inside us precisely that 'State of Being' which is resonant with what it is we desire - but then are also already living and experiencing *within* our being.

Confused? Let's re-phrase it then: we first need to create an *Inner* change before we can effectively create an *outer* manifestation of our desire. This is an extraordinarily crucial, yet very subtle point when dealing with the process of Creative Visualization, and one we'll explore in more depth as we progress further into this book.

What's all this 'resonance' about?

Perhaps some of the issues raised in relation to Creative Visualization seem at this stage to be more like double-Dutch. But a quick example may help to clarify the point. Imagine that you want to have a relationship. Your ideal partner is someone who is not only kind, considerate, romantic and good-looking, but also loves you deeply, with great commitment. Sounds good? Mind you, feel free to embellish this basic visualization as you wish!

But here comes the crunch... are you, deep inside your soul; in the very core of your Being, *resonant* with allowing such a wonderful person into your life? Or are there aspects – obvious or subtle – within your mind and emotions which might just feel a bit unworthy of such a gorgeous creature becoming your life-partner? Do you feel you are good enough? Lucky enough? *Lovable* enough? Because unless the answer is an emphatic 'YES', you are not *resonant* with the Energy of what it is you desire. And it's precisely this lack of resonance which acts like the reverse side of a magnet, more likely to actually push away or keep at bay what it is you desire.

Making change outside is first about making change inside

So, to allow our desire to manifest through the process of Creative Visualization, we also need to work on *ourselves*. We need to learn to come from a Higher Dimensional perspective; a more Loving Plane of Reality - and *then* our desire is also more able to manifest. But that entails becoming more Spiritually aligned within ourselves. Hence, this whole play with Creative Visualization is ultimately a Journey of growing in Consciousness or Spirituality - something that is often glossed over or not mentioned at all within some New Age circles.

One of the criticisms often thrown at the concept of Creative Visualization is that its entire focus seems to be on materiality. Yet, as noted above, ironically the outcome is the opposite. It's only by increasingly learning how to access the Higher level of who we are - shall we call it 'Higher Self' - that we then can truly be successful in our Creative Visualization.

The reality therefore is that something happens to us as we progress along this Journey of Creative Visualization. Eventually, we realize that although there is nothing wrong with material 'stuff', neither is it the answer to our life dilemmas, nor does it fill that sense of emptiness and lack of connection which so many Westerners seem to carry around within themselves. That's why it was stated a little earlier how it was alright to solely focus on the material aspect of Creative Visualization, as we initially play with this process. Eventually, people will get to the more Spiritual aspects, once they've burnt through being so enamored with the material aspects of the process, and are ready for the next phase.

Creative Visualization therefore is an invitation to re-connect with Higher levels of who we are, beyond just the physical body – never mind whether we call this Higher Self, God-self, Universe, Source, The Matrix, etc. So it is by working through this level of Higher Consciousness that we ultimately become more skillful creators on this physical dimension of planet Earth. Hence the ultimate goal of Creative Visualization is actually to transcend beyond materiality, into Spirituality.

From personal observations of life, it seems that a fundamental source to our human woes is really our disconnection – experientially – from Source; from God. What Creative Visualization asks of us is to learn, one step at a time, how to re-connect back to our Source. And hopefully out of that, we will become increasingly able to choose manifestations of a Higher and Higher level of Consciousness, as we amplify the Spiritual Awareness inside ourselves.

Humanity's inherent empowerment neutered

What is a problem is the reality that although we can all inherently do Creative Visualization, our awareness of this fact remains so elusive. This has been the case for the greatest majority of people, for most of human history. It's a sad fact that an important way in which humans could have empowered themselves into a Higher level of Consciousness has been denied them. This seems incredibly unfair.

Indeed, books abound which do explore some of these Creative Visualization concepts. Even Christ taught it, as will be explained in greater detail in chapter 10. However, in the past, this knowledge was inevitably couched in such mysterious terms, that generally speaking only those who already understood the process could make any sense of it. This powerful technique has been actively stifled, and kept hidden from the masses. This was even the case within religion. Some of these Creative Visualization messages are indeed found within the various Holy Texts, but are well and truly glossed over or ignored, or their religious interpretation so distorted as to neuter them.

The other problem has been the contradictory ways in which this information has been presented – when made available at all. These are some of the reasons why Creative Visualization concepts could seem so unclear and confusing that the average person would have just shrugged their shoulders and ignored what basically seemed an unfathomable concept.

Only do what seems easiest to start with

In this book, you don't need to do everything being suggested. Just start with whatever process most appeals to you. Focus on that till you feel more skilled or at least have made some headway. Then go to the next stepping-stone. It's all about being on a Journey, made up of many individual steps.

The aim of this book is to provide a series of such stepping stones. Individually they may not seem so rational or make immediate sense. Nevertheless, by the end of the book, and when seen as a whole, hopefully these 'stepping stones' will generate a usable 'picture' or world view for you - one which does somehow hang together, providing a powerful platform or construct. This world-view can then be used as an empowering guideline to living life on planet Earth, and dealing with its many challenges along that Journey.

Perhaps this book can become a starting point for those who have not really been that interested in the Metaphysical aspect of life, or who felt Metaphysics was all just a bit too hard or weird to comprehend. Hopefully those already well on the Path will also gain further insights as to how they can refine and hone their skill in this life arena. See this book more as a series of 'seed-thoughts' or concepts, around which you can now develop *your* own personally appropriate 'pearl'.

Life rarely offers instant, magical answers

But it does need to be understood that in a person's search for meaning there may not be any quick, instant answers. In other words, the search for meaning to life, is itself a Journey within a Journey – the latter being that voyage of physically living life itself, day by day. The search for meaning may even take an entire lifetime; in fact I think it does. That search just alters and evolves from one level to another. Also expect that a purpose or meaning which may have been workable at one stage, may not be right for the next stage. As much as most of us don't want to hear this... life is anything but static!

Such changes in our beliefs and sense of meaning to life should be seen as OK. Not a judgment of failure, but rather a sign of progression in the Consciousness evolution of who we are. Some of the things you believed as a child may not serve you as an adult either; that is just the nature of life. Ultimately, it can be said that whatever meaningful metaphor or protocol we choose doesn't really matter, as long as it allows us to intrinsically work through the 'lens' of expressing Love on as High a level as we possibly can. So if your calling is to be someone in the money market or advertising world or selling cars or... whatever, then do it from as High a Love-Space as you can, with great integrity and honoring of other people. By doing so you are nevertheless living your life from a very High Consciousness perspective – never mind the exact format you might be using at any particular point in time.

Need to find our own purpose through our own choices

Finding a meaning and purpose to life is therefore about you searching amongst all the various options as to what suits you best, and gives you the deepest sense of value. That doesn't mean the purpose you might choose now is going to suit you for the entire length of your life here. But for the time that it does serve you, it needs to be honored, even if it is perhaps the pursuit of money, sex, drugs or power as some examples.

To an outsider, such choices may be judged as less than constructive or ethical. By the same token, there are some people who still have to go through these type of experiences in order to ultimately learn the emptiness of such life choices, and thereby finally burn those desires out of their system.

So, let this Journey of exploration begin... and may it be a fruitful and empowering one for you.

Some people love doing exercises to help them focus and clarify a concept. For those of you who do find this method useful, a series of questions will be provided at the end of each chapter. For those of you who don't like doing such exercises... please feel free to skip them, and go to the next chapter!

Exercises

- Make a list of 5 things that give you a sense of purpose in your life.
- Write a brief description of how you would describe the God/Source/Universe in your life

Summary of thoughts thus far
Preface and Chapter 1

- Focus more on something being *useful* versus *'The Truth'*.
- Learn to resonate 'truth' within yourself, and trust that inner, intuitive knowingness', rather than automatically and solely accepting external 'authorities' as to what is 'true'.
- Understand that such intuitive wisdom is not incompatible with science. Many of science's greatest breakthroughs occurred initially through intuitive hunches.
- Be curious; dare to ask questions, and expect to receive answers that make sense.
- Wisdom obtained via personal experience is inevitably more powerful than 'wisdom' achieved via externally dictated dogmas or rules.
- Healers, Authors and workshop 'Gurus' are not necessarily or automatically Enlightened Beings. They inevitably have their own 'stuff' to contend with.
- Due to the ubiquitous nature of suffering, there is a critical need to have a workable system through which to deal with life's suffering – personally and globally.
- There is a great need to not only acknowledge the value of organized religion, but also its limitations.
- The reality is that self-empowerment has been so often actively suppressed – not just by political systems, but far too often by many religions too.
- One potent way of empowering our lives is through the concepts of Creative Visualization.
- The reality is that Creative Visualization is ultimately a Journey of Spirituality – not just materiality.
- In Creative Visualization, it's all about creating *Inner* change before we can have any hope of creating *outer* manifestations of our desires.
- It is vital to be in 'resonance' with our desires before they can manifest.
- The Journey of Life is more often made up of many small steps, rather than the quantum leaps so often promised by the New Age.

REFERENCES
1. P. Gomes, *The Scandalous Gospel of Jesus – what's so good about the good news?* Harper One, NY, 2007.

Lifenotes - A user's guide to making sense of life on planet Earth

CHAPTER 2

REALITY CAN BE FICKLE

The greatest enemy of any science is a closed mind

Dr. J. Rozencwajg

Hopefully the Journey this book has taken you on so far hasn't been too arduous or confronting. The road we're about to explore may be a bit more taxing, but every effort will be taken to ensure you are supported along the way.

Dealing with ill people on a daily basis has certainly brought home to me how much suffering and pain does exist on planet Earth. There is a crucial need to find productive ways in which to more effectively deal with what can often be almost overwhelming suffering. The next few chapters, therefore, are primarily borne out of my own life experiences, and based on many years of observing the life experiences of thousands of clients. But they are also echoed in the writings of a multitude of other people, who have come to similar conclusions.

Growth can be through joy – not just pain

A predominant belief on this planet is that of 'no pain, no gain'. It is indeed true that the stimulus of pain or suffering can be a most potent motivator for change. Yet, it should be feasible to grow in Awareness through joy as well. However, this does require us to be more self-motivated in our Journey. Hopefully we will opt to do this before the prod of life comes along to poke us into action - a concept which will be explored in greater depth later.

When we start to venture into this new dimension of reality, we will encounter experiences, and see 'views' for which our language does not yet have the appropriate words. In such a situation, words need to be used in a different fashion. Here, rather than trying to understand the literal meaning of the language used, it becomes important to try to tune into the message transmitted *beyond* the words themselves.

Analogies are wonderfully useful here, because they provide a means of bridging that which we know and understand with that which is largely unknown. In this way, by tying in the new with the old concepts, it's possible to create stepping-stones. These then provide the actual Path on which we can Journey forward into largely unexplored territory. So it is not so much the message *in* the words as the message *beyond* the words which takes us forward.

Beliefs versus facts

On reading this section, a person with a scientific, left-brained approach to life may feel that what's being presented is nothing more than a series of 'belief systems', rather than so-called hard 'facts' which scientists normally prefer to play with. However, within science there is often a seemingly invisible propensity to allow theories, over time and endless promotion, to achieve the status of 'fact' – even when in reality they are still only theory. There is another layer to this situation. Many researchers have made a huge reputation for themselves from those theories; 'their' theory. Such theories may now also be underpinning an entire research industry, often worth billions of dollars. These scenarios have much to lose by new, alternate ideas. Thus, a major defensive is inevitably set off by those who now understandably have much to lose if their theory is discredited or replaced. Status and power will go elsewhere, immediately followed by the almighty research dollar. Truly, much is at stake!

Science and medicine are littered with examples of how what was absolute 'truth' at one stage was later found to be nothing more than a distorted or limited view of 'reality'. Indeed, as further information came to light, certain 'truths' were found to be utterly incorrect – not just distorted. Yet, people who opposed any contemporary and commonly accepted perspective or 'truths' were often persecuted, even killed, because they dared to present a different viewpoint on a topic.

Look at the 'theory' of evolution for instance. In as far as where we, and the entire physical cosmos ultimately came from, there is much that is still only theory, even though there is also a great deal of scientific data which does substantiate an evolutionary process occurring. The latter point is not in dispute. However, especially within this theory it's surely rather pertinent to at least continue asking that really fundamental question, crying out for an answer... 'but where in turn did *that* come from'?

In other words, evolution conveniently starts with a Universe, as well as matter from which the various planets were subsequently made, *upon* which life then evolved from some primordial slime, zapped by lightning, thus supposedly 'creating' the next level of evolved life. Yet, when it comes to responding to such vexing questions as... 'in the final analysis, where *does* all of life, this material universe and humanity come from'? – scientists' only real answer is... 'the Big Bang'.

Ultimately though, is it stretching the mind any more, or less, to ask us to believe that everything came from some mysterious 'Big Bang'... or from a mysterious 'God'? In the end, neither answer really explains where *that* mysterious 'First Origin' came from. In both situations, humanity is still left with an un-answered question, and having to depend on a degree of *faith* when believing in anything built upon *either* 'foundation'!

So we find that science and medicine are not immune to the phenomenon of how what started off as theory, can over time, and with sufficient reiteration, often assume the status of 'Truth'.

The problem is that science and medicine can be rather blind to this tendency within their own ranks. Yet, these disciplines have no hesitation in becoming stridently critical when it comes to anything even slightly Esoteric or Metaphysical, where it is true that things are inherently harder to measure, and thus 'validate'. It is not the case that these more Metaphysical issues are intrinsically un-measurable. Rather, it's more about science all too frequently not yet having tools of the required sensitivity or sophistication with which to make the necessary measurements. This is a totally different issue.

Remember, there was a time when the idea that matter was composed of infinitesimally small 'bits' was ridiculed. 'Prove it by showing them to us' was the retort. But it wasn't till science at last caught up with the concept, via the creation of machines with the required sophistication, that finally what had seemed absurd was in fact proven true.

A similar situation exists when science tends to point the finger at many Metaphysical ideas, declaring such concepts to be nothing but wild daydreams or illusions, with little to back them up. However, and this may come as a shock to some, we need to realize that science also is *primarily* composed of a series of belief systems or ideas, as much as some scientists may like to think otherwise.

In the autumn of 1927, physicists working on the frontier of science met in Brussels. Their aim was to clarify exactly what Quantum Mechanics described, and their decision became known as the 'Copenhagen Interpretation of Quantum Mechanics'. Although further interpretations have been developed since then, this was the beginning of a new way in which science started to view the world, which Gary Zukav explores in his book 'The Dancing Wu Li Masters'. [1]

The essence of the Copenhagen Interpretation is the notion that it is not necessary to always understand exactly what Quantum Physics is about, as long as the concepts within this system of thought are able to produce consistent experimental results. In other words, it's not so much about proving the ultimate truth of a particular scientific idea, but rather, how consistently the theory can be applied to real life.

These understandings are priceless! Scientists found themselves having to formally admit to a fundamental enigma about this reality. In trying to devise a consistent type of physics, their own findings are forcing them to conclude that a total understanding of reality, certainly at present, actually seems to lie beyond the capabilities of *rational* thought.

What is true today is false tomorrow

Beliefs can become like blinkers which narrow our view, and can effectively cut out parts of the world from our consciousness. And one big belief that humanity has so powerfully embraced is this absolutely foundational criterion by which things are measured... *'But is it True'?* And if it can't be proven True, then often a very useful concept will be discarded and thrown aside.

A similar process happens in science where the 'blinkers' are... yes, but has it been proven via the double-blind placebo controlled trial? It never ceases to astonish me how within the health arena, so many things which are obvious, and *clinically* visible to a carefully observing practitioner, nevertheless are hotly denied by many doctors and scientists. Such an attitude persists, despite clinicians being able to observe things in their patients which are actually quite obvious to any enquiring intelligence.

We need to keep in mind that a *genuine* scientist is one who is fundamentally curious, and willing to look at phenomenon, experiences or data *even if they don't seem explicable or possible within the existing framework of knowledge*. Sadly, many self-proclaimed scientists fall short of this capacity.

It's important to bring up such points, not necessarily to point the finger, but rather because of the wasted opportunities such attitudes create. For instance, having *clinically* observed a reality, a phenomenon, within a person or group of people, also allows us to then create at least a potential 'game plan' through which to deal with such cases.

Let's just explore this sort of situation in relation to spina bifida. Here, the initial medical perspective, many years ago, was that it had absolutely nothing to do with a deficiency of folic acid – despite early evidence suggesting such a connection. But as there were no double-blind trials in the literature - at that stage - to 'prove' this connection, it was therefore ignored and scorned for many years. Besides, how could a few milligram of something as insubstantial and unglamorous as a B-complex vitamin possibly have any ability to prevent such an awful health condition?

Fifteen years went by before someone finally bothered to do the research, and lo and behold there *was* a connection! Yet for 15 years, pregnant women were not advised to take this very cheap and already known-to-be-safe vitamin... because there was no research to 'prove' its association with spina bifida. And this is the painful bit: over those 15 years, how many cases of this dreadful condition could have been prevented by such a truly innocuous nutritional intervention?

It's not about now suddenly throwing out scientific method. But it equally shouldn't be about ignoring *clinical*, real life situations which are staring us in the face. We need to at least be willing to 'connect the dots', even if the supposedly ultimate scientific validation is not yet available. Equally, we need to consider the reality that at this stage of our scientific 'sophistication', validation may not be possible for a whole range of issues, simply because we haven't been clever enough yet to have devised the appropriate 'measuring tools'. Many situations do constantly occur in life – like the example of spina bifida and folic acid – where simple, already-known-to-be-safe, apparent solutions seem to exist. We should be willing to at least try them out, rather than refusing to budge till science can ultimately prove – or even *attempts* to prove their validity.

Obviously, where totally new substances, about which we know absolutely nothing, are suggested for various therapeutic means, then these do need to be approached with a judicious and rightful caution. But when such therapeutic suggestions involve already long-known nutrients, herbs or even existing drugs, with an equally long history of safe usage in other health conditions, then these substances should not have to wait for years of trials before being utilized in an apparent unconnected situation. By all means do the trials, but meanwhile just keep very accurate, *clinically* based records to provide evidence of efficacy – or lack thereof. The latter approach may save a lot of 'spina bifida' repeats, with all the attendant, yet preventable suffering.

Molecules of emotion

Another example of how humans can remain blind to what is staring them in the face is the concept of the mind:body connection within disease. Once again, medicine and science initially saw this assertion as ludicrous. Yet once the research was actually instigated – elegantly elucidated in Candice Pert's book 'Molecules of Emotion' [2] – we were able to fully and very specifically understand the connection between the mind and the body. It was discovered that a vast range of hormonal and other molecular substances were in fact the 'common language' between these two apparently separate parts of who we are as humans – the brain and the immune system.

Nearly thirty years ago, right at the beginning of the HIV epidemic, we as natural therapists were already teaching people how to visualize and *imagine* their immune cells working better, thereby empowering people with HIV to stay alive much longer. Yet science turned up its nose at such 'therapeutic' suggestions, declaring them nonsense, or at best, 'placebo effect'. It took many years for scientists to even bother to do any research, and when they did, it only vindicated yet again what we had already understood *clinically*; observationally. Now all of a sudden, the mind:body phenomenon *does* exist. It was even given a grand name... 'psychoneuroimmunology'. Thank you, scientists!

There is a powerful and crucial reason for bringing up all these points. The problem is that if we insist on having such extraordinarily strict and *restrictive* criteria through which to see life, then this will also strongly inhibit our ability to *respond* to life's challenges. Double-blind trials are good; this is not being denied. But when they become the sole and *ultimate* version of reality, then they can but hinder, rather than enhance one's Journey of life. Similarly with the idea that any particular religion is absolutely the one-and-only True one.

Commenting on all this is not just sour-grapes from some of us who have had to endure skepticism from many doctors and scientists over the years. Well... perhaps to some degree there is a measure of sour-grapes! But it is also about clearly delineating a tendency within science, medicine and human thinking which can be dismissive of certain ideas, concepts or processes, which nevertheless *do* have value and effectiveness, although they may not have been researched in the ways scientists believe valid. For those people who rely too much on scientific opinion, they may also end up dismissing opportunities for powerful and positive change in their lives.

Maybe there is at least one advantage to becoming an older and increasingly experienced therapist who is thus accumulating mounting 'mileage' in the field! Those years give one a perspective, a history, a time-line of what was understood and *intuited* and yet for which we were ridiculed or ignored. Nonetheless, usually after many more years passed by, we were so often vindicated - although inevitably not acknowledged for our earlier insights, understandings, and resultant therapeutic protocols.

Need to also honor our intuition

The whole point of this part of the discussion is that we often see things in our reality which do create a pattern. When we start to see these patterns, we need to find the courage with which to at least start using that awareness, albeit carefully and with adequate and frequent further evaluation. 'Connecting the dots' between observations and intuition can help empower our life Journey in many ways, and this approach should not be so easily dismissed as it all too often is by science. If at some later date, science can 100% vindicate that those perceptions or intuitions were in fact correct, well... bully for them.

But think of how much more can be done, so much sooner, by also honoring those *right-brain* perceptions and validations of reality, rather than as Westerners, where we tend to over-focus on the use of left-brain techniques through which to live our lives and perceive our reality.

It's not a matter of either/or. It's a matter of honoring *both* ways of seeing reality, thus providing a much broader platform from which to respond to life's situations. Just using the left-brain; the double-blind trial style of approach; the concept of 'yes, but is it *The Truth* or not', all these incredibly limit how we could live our lives.

In regard to the use of the 'scientific method', we therefore need to clearly understand the tendency scientists have to fall into a rather predictable pattern when confronted with something quite new. All too often their knee-jerk response is that the proposed new idea or technique can't be real or worthwhile, because... 'there is nothing in the literature' to validate it. What needs to be understood is that 'lack of data in the literature' is not automatically a form of *evidence* that something doesn't exist or isn't true. It usually only means no-one has yet bothered to *investigate*, let alone report on it within the literature. This is quite a different kettle of fish.

What was seen as nonsense often becomes fact

Initially, some of the concepts presented in this book may seem bewildering. It does take time to adjust to new data, especially when these are of a philosophical nature, seemingly intangible, and therefore all the harder to grapple with. Look at the environmental movement for instance. As recently as ten years ago the 'Greenies' were seen by many people as little more than misguided eccentrics. Now planetary awareness has increased, and it is self evident that our planet – and ourselves! - are in deep trouble.

What about cigarettes? When I started practise 28 years ago, those of us who warned of the dangers of smoking were all too frequently ignored as health-nuts. Now, the entire might of modern medicine is validating those dangers, and our earlier concern. This has also been the case with many 'facts' espoused by science, for example, that lead - added to petrol and paint - was safe; that asbestos was physiologically inert and therefore harmless; that bottle-feeding versus breastfeeding was the only sensible way to give nourishment to a new baby. Seems unbelievable now, but these were 'Truth' fads in the 50's and 60's.

Mention the word 'Global Warming' and see the response now, compared to even a few years ago. How quickly the mighty skeptics have fallen! So too with many other *beliefs* - not *facts* - held by science. Each one was ultimately proven to be simply a 'belief system'; supported so ferociously at the time as to be given the status of 'truth'. Ironically, often science has acted more like a rigid and uncompromising religion, with its *theories* and *hypotheses* presented all too frequently as dogmatically declared, 'self-evident' *reality*.

As Arthur Shopenhauer said... *all truth passes through three stages. First it is ridiculed. Second, it is violently opposed. Third, it is accepted as being self-evident.*

Chapter 2 - Reality Can Be Fickle

Climbing the 'mountain' creates different 'views'

This Journey can be likened to climbing a very large, high mountain. It takes time to get to the top, and perhaps not everyone even wants to climb that high. Yet, what has to be realized is that the view you get on such a climb depends very much on where you stand on that mountain. Wherever you climb, you will have a view of the plains below, the distant horizon and the mountain itself. Each view is 100 per cent valid from that particular vantage point. Yet, to someone who has climbed higher, the view, although similar, may now also be spectacularly different. That doesn't make the view from lower down the mountain invalid, bad or wrong. What needs to be realized however is that the first view certainly was more *limited*.

So, let's assume you happen to be walking along that Path, but twenty kilometers ahead of someone else. Your view is obviously going to be quite different to what they are able to see from *their* vantage point. Not only are they way below where you are on the track, but they are also on quite a different flank of the mountain, facing an entirely different direction back to the plains.

Let's assume that from your particular position on that mountain, you can see a major fire burning on the plains below. Let's suppose you both have walkie-talkies, so you radio that information to your traveling companion twenty k's away. Yet, they reply that you must be imagining it, because look as they may, there's no fires to be seen at all. When you keep insisting that there definitely is a fire out there, they'll eventually either get annoyed at your persistence or think that you have gone crazy. In turn, you might get equally annoyed - or think they have gone blind!

The perception of neither party is right or wrong. In fact *both* are correct, and the difference is simply due to seeing the huge plains below from a totally different perspective. And that perspective - *from where you both individually are on that path* - is so fundamentally different, that you simply can't see what the other is seeing. At least... *not until you are both standing on exactly the same spot, on that same path, looking out at exactly the same view as each other.* Then you can both see the fire.

In the meantime, as long as you are still separated on the path, on that mountain, facing different views, so too will you also not be able to fully understand what the other is seeing. At least, not until you 'get it' that you are actually both describing a different aspect of that same huge plain, but due to your different points along the path, your perspectives also don't – and *can't* match each other.

At that point of 'ah-hah'; of comprehension, both parties finally understand one another. By that 'ah-hah', you can stop making yourself 'wrong'... or indeed, thinking the *other* 'wrong', as more usually happens. Everything is as it should be on this journey up the mountain path. Both are 'right' - from *their* own aspect on the path.

What a simplistic analogy, you may think. Yet, the bottom line is that so often in life, when people are trying to make each other 'wrong', it is precisely such different 'views', from different 'points on the path' which are the cause of the confusion and contradiction. Neither party is automatically or necessarily wrong; they both hold 'views' of the same vast 'plain'... but from different perspectives. The problem is that in religion, many would use such discrepancies of 'reality' as enough reason to then maim, torture or kill each other. History is full of such examples.

Double vision and Life's duality

Think of a very still pond, the bottom of which is covered with pebbles. On the surface you have the reflections of the surrounding trees, sky and clouds. Now, imagine you are standing by the side of the pond, and are looking at the surface, seeing the reflections of those surroundings. Then all of a sudden, without moving an inch, you realize you are looking *beyond* the surface reflection, and seeing the pebbles on the floor of the pond. Again, without moving, you can now see the surface reflections only. You haven't done anything else but *shift your focus*.

The issue is that two distinct realities exist here at the same time - the superficial reflections, and the view of the deeper pebbles. Both exist, although you can only see one at a time, and which one you see depends on how you *choose* to focus on the reality presented to you.

*Hence the view of reality you experience is determined by a shift in perception you create - **within your mind**.*

The sole aim of the discussion in this book is to help present alternate theoretical models, which hopefully can broaden your knowledge and understanding of yourselves and your reality. By putting as many of the individual pieces of the puzzle together as possible, this will with time allow for a fuller and more understandable picture of these models to emerge. What may at first have appeared to be outrageous, in fact becomes self evident.

As Margaret Mead put it... 'to believe without questioning *or to dismiss without investigation*, is to comport oneself unscientifically' (emphasis added).

Reality is dynamic and flexible

The other point to remember is that the higher we climb the mountain, the more changes occur. On the plains it was hot and you wore light clothing. You were accustomed to sea-level air density, and had no problems breathing. Yet, as you climbed higher and higher, not only did the views change, but the circumstances you found yourself in also changed - sometimes drastically. No longer was a light T-shirt enough to keep you warm. No longer was the oxygen content of the air sufficient to provide for your laboring body's needs. No longer did water boil at exactly 100 degrees Celsius.

In the 21st century, even the so-called rules of science seemed to be altering. Similarly with this Metaphysical – beyond the physical – Journey we're about to embark upon. All that you, as reader, can do is to 'feel' out this information. If it somehow sits right with you, even if you can't exactly explain why, then perhaps allow it to be, and see where this Journey takes you. Regard it as an adventure with absolutely no commitment required of you. No signing on dotted lines; no dogmas to bow down to; no religion to join. Remember, no one is forcing you to go anywhere you don't want to go, and you can leave the 'trip' at any stage. Only do understand that it could be quite easy to resist the following discussions, simply because they are unusual or possibly even confronting.

Therefore, your conclusion about this book, the ultimate judgment given it, should perhaps be based not so much on whether what is being discussed here is 100 per cent 'Truth'. Rather, judge it on *whether it is useful*. Does it provide a *model* of reality; an explanation for your own life experiences and observations? Does it help to empower you rather than drag you down into inertia, because so much of what life presents to you seems too negative or painful?

Metaphysics can blow the circuits

But this Journey also comes at a price. Once upon a time, this Esoteric Knowledge was only available to a chosen few. People were pre-selected through the use of various processes, and if shown to be ready and able, then had this Knowledge given to them piecemeal. In turn, this enabled them to slowly but surely acquire the necessary skills to *become* this Knowledge.

It needs to be understood that this Knowledge is very much like an electrical current. If the fuse wire is not strong enough to handle the charge, it could potentially blow that fuse. So too with humans. The Power that is unleashed by using this sort of Esoteric Knowledge is extraordinarily powerful, and could equally 'blow' the 'circuitry' in a human, if that 'circuitry' isn't yet strong enough for the 'Current'.

Going for a space flight

It's a bit like wanting to become a passenger in a futuristic space flight. This reality is virtually on our doorsteps, but at the moment, it is not like boarding a train, or even a plane for that matter. Much preparation will be necessary before a passenger can board a space rocket of the vintage we're presently capable of launching. That potential passenger will need a certain level of physical health and strength, as well as training, before it would be safe to board such a rocket and take off into space.

So too with humans who wish to 'board' a 'flight' into these 'Other Dimensions'. To do so in an off-handed way, and to tap into this Power unprepared, could be courting potential disaster for our 'circuitry'; our physical and mental well-being. By the same token, this possibility should not give cause to then never start any exploration into the Metaphysical realms. For the greatest majority of people, this Metaphysical Journey is utterly safe and exciting. However, people with severe mental problems; a past history of psychosis; or other serious psychological issues, may want to draw upon the care of a more seasoned 'trail-blazer' or therapist.

The reality is that exploration and growth are inherent, deeply driven needs within humans, and must be allowed and encouraged. But this needs to be done one step at a time and with due care, rather than in a cavalier manner which could court potential problems.

Exercise
- Think back and describe three recent examples where intuition played a big part in how you responded to a life situation.
- Discuss with a friend whether the reality is that you find yourself growing more through pain... or joy?

Summary of thoughts thus far
- We need to understand that Consciousness Growth can be through joy – not just suffering.
- Theories can – over time – all too easily drift into a status of 'truth'.
- Quantum Physics in fact vindicates the approach of using concepts even if they are not yet proven 'true', but do provide practical use.
- Medical and scientific stubbornness in refusing to utilize so many concepts, unless they've been proven beyond doubt, can lead to much suffering; for example, 15 years of refusal to use folic acid in helping prevent spina bifida.
- We need to understand and acknowledge how blinkered we humans can be when it comes to investigating, let alone accepting new ideas.
- The problem is that the more we *can't* see this pattern in ourselves, so too the more we sabotage our ability to grow in Awareness or Consciousness.
- Any particular perception about this earthly reality can be very subjective. Bring to mind the metaphor of the different 'views' obtained as one climbs a 'mountain'.
- Any view of reality you experience is determined, and can be changed by a shift in perception you create within your mind. Think back to the example of the pond; its surface reflections and the pebbles deeper down.
- Reality is dynamic, and much more flexible than we generally give it credit.
- The mind:body connection is now scientifically validated, and the ramifications of this reality need to be urgently incorporated into medical approaches to our health issues.
- Esoteric or Metaphysical knowledge is very powerful, and needs to be used with care and wisdom.

REFERENCES
1. Zukav, Gary. *The Dancing Wu Li Masters,* Flamingo Fontana, USA, 1979.
2. Pert, Candice. *Molecules of Emotion – the science behind Mind-body Medicine,* Scribner, NY, 1997.

CHAPTER 3

THOUGHTS ARE REALITY CREATORS

The greatest revolution of our generation is the discovery that human beings, by changing the inner attitudes of their minds, can change the outer aspects of their lives

William James, Harvard Psychologist

We live in a time and culture with rather unusual indoctrinations and perceptions of what is real. We tend to find it very difficult to see connections between our all too obvious outer physical reality, and our more subtle inner reality. Ironically, there are many people who don't realize that this deep and fundamental connection even exists. Not having experienced or heard of such concepts can be an enormous stumbling block when it comes to taking on board the sort of issues we'll be exploring in this book.

The importance and validity of intuition

The problem with modern humanity is that we have become disconnected from Mother Nature. As 'civilized', modern people, often stuck away in densely packed cities; locked up in concrete towers stretching far into the sky; living with our artificially created rhythms, we seem so superior to, and independent of Nature. Our technology has allowed us this lifestyle, dictated by our whims and desires rather than by natural cycles. But there has also been a very high price tag associated with this disconnection and isolation from Mother Earth. [1]

In fact, it has meant a disconnection from our Inner Source, and hence a lot of 'intuitive knowingness' has also been lost. This is why it could be argued that concepts entailing a Metaphysical – beyond the physical – explanation to what happens in our lives, have become such seemingly foreign and difficult ones to take on board. Interestingly, Jung came to the same conclusion many years ago, noting that we become disconnected from the Earth, literally, by the style of buildings in which we live and work.

Equally, we have become disconnected Metaphysically by our immersion in the artificial rhythms we've established in our society, such as night shifts, 24/7 shopping and living. Somehow this has severed us to some degree from a source of nourishment and replenishment normally received through Nature. Such recharging or nurturing was seen by Jung as vital for a deeper state of inner balance and harmony.

In fact, many people have become so disconnected from their Source, that they can't even fathom why people do feel recharged by going out for a walk into Nature; or sitting under a tree and allowing oneself to merge in with the Natural surroundings; or spending some time in the garden digging, weeding, watering or simply 'being'. However, it is the experience of many people that if they feel stressed, or in a state of disharmony, reconnecting with Nature can be a most soothing and healing event.

One other reality we as 'civilized' people have become disconnected from is the concept that thought is in fact a very potent form of energy, rather than just the flimsy, ephemeral consequences of certain neuronal activity. Let's take a flight into fantasy; play with a few concepts and see where they take us. Remember, in this section we're not worried so much about the ultimate, provable truth of something, as much as whether it is *useful* if applied to our daily lives.

Morphogenetic Field theory

Rupert Sheldrake hypothesized the existence around planet Earth of what he called a 'Morphogenetic Field'. He saw each person as an individual 'Energy generator', producing Energy of either a positive or negative nature. The Morphogenetic Field was seen as the sum total of all these individual Energy generations. His next hypothesis - strongly supported by experimental results [2] - suggested that this surrounding field in turn affects each one of us. So there is a definite two-way flow or Energy exchange, each profoundly affecting the other.

This Field could also be likened to what some ancient cultures called the Akashic records. In other words, these records are like a cumulative register

Chapter 3 - Thoughts Are Reality Creators

of every iota of thought and experience ever manifested through the mind of humanity, on individual as well as general levels. If this is indeed so, then observation of this world with all its pain and suffering would tend to suggest that the Morphogenetic Energy Field is being composed more from negative thoughts than positive ones.

That in turn leads to an interesting and promising conclusion. We certainly know that each of us generates thoughts. Just for a moment, let's conceive of these thoughts as a form of Energy. From physics we know that Energy cannot be destroyed; only transmuted. These thought-Energies therefore, once generated or transmuted by our mind, could be speculated to have the property of a continued existence within a type of Energy Field.

If in turn, this Energy Field directly influences our way of being, then we need to make a choice. Do we add our own personal destructive thought Energies to this already negatively biased Energy Field? Or do we choose to build up positive Energies by responding more constructively to our own personal life circumstances? This latter scenario will in turn ultimately affect our total reality more positively. It may seem as if everything we do as individuals is so terribly insignificant. Yet, the fact remains that everyone could *choose* a positive way of responding to life's situations, be they painful or not, *by the thoughts they choose to focus on*.

Again, this ability of humans to *choose* what they focus on is the essence of Free Will, and may be one of the few arenas within the human experience where we truly can exercise choice. This doesn't automatically mean our choices are always easy to make; far from it. But the more we can make a choice to respond positively to a life situation, then over time, profound Energy changes would also be created within this Morphogenetic type of Energy Field. This in turn would generate a completely different feedback effect onto all of humanity. Pie in the sky? Perhaps; but certainly not impossible.

This ability we as humans do have, to choose which thoughts we focus on in response to a particular situation, could be seen as our primary point of empowerment, not only as individuals, but also by the effect this would have on the entire planet. Choosing positive, constructive responses to life's situations, however painful or confronting they may be, will not be automatic or easy for the majority of humanity. It will demand a certain degree of maturity, self-discipline and patience. But inevitably, if only for the outcomes such positive choices allow us to manifest into our personal lives, it would be worth trying to live by these concepts.

Inner change is more potent than externally imposed change

The point of power for change certainly does not lie in enforcing specific philosophical, religious or political 'solutions' onto the masses. Instead, individuals should understand how the point of power for personal and planetary change lies within *themselves*, in as far as how they choose to entertain or create particular thought patterns, with their subsequent and inevitable effect on our actions.

Perhaps at this point some people may be finding these ideas a bit too 'far out'. However, even if we assume that so far these ideas are nothing more than fantasy, maybe they are nevertheless starting to trigger vague and subtle nuances within our ever so real cerebral synapses!

From our earlier discussion, we also know that thoughts - whatever they ultimately are; simply forms of Energy or otherwise - do have a definite effect on our physical bodies. Let's do a simple experiment. Imagine that you have a very ripe and juicy lemon in your hand. You cut it in half, and start sucking on the tart, sour juice. You let that juice fill your entire mouth, puckering the membranes and making your mouth feel as if it is shriveling up with the sharpness of the juice.

Now, if you were to continue this experiment for just a few more minutes – *albeit solely in your imagination* - then before long you will probably find yourself starting to salivate. How interesting! Because you are not even sucking that lemon. You are only *thinking* about sucking a lemon, and yet you are also experiencing incredibly *real* salivation. The very nebulous, ephemeral thought of a lemon is affecting your very real salivary glands.

Similarly, if you were to think of the worst thing that ever happened to you, and if you were to really get into that memory, before long you would notice certain sensations in your tummy: your pulse rate would go up or you might feel sweaty. Again, simple, non-material thoughts are having quite a real effect on your body.

So, if these type of thoughts affect us biochemically or physically... *why not all thoughts?* Then there is PNI, psychoneuroimmunology, which has scientifically validated that thoughts trigger certain emotional states, which in turn result in the release of various bio-chemicals. These are known to slot into specific components of the immune system, amongst other areas, either activating them or switching them off.³ So could it possibly be stated therefore, that 'thought is creative' – or destructive! - at least on those levels of the body?

Let's go back briefly to some points made earlier in this discussion. The issue is not that perhaps 'thought is creative', but ultimately what is more important is the fact that we do choose how we perceive our reality. The problem is that most of us 'choose' how we react to life in a very knee-jerk fashion. Someone says something nasty to us, and we react by hitting back in various ways. This is usually the easiest form of response. After all, they hurt us, so we now have a right to hurt them. Even the good Book says 'an eye for an eye'.

Yet, where does such an approach ultimately take us? Let's assume it's true that each thought is an alive and powerful form of Energy which gets added to the general Morphogenetic Field. Remember, this Field in turn potently affects us, individually and collectively. Then from a deeper level of awareness, the 'eye for an eye' approach could be seen as a vicious cycle, with the sole capacity to spiral into further negativity, pain and suffering - not only for you in that particular life situation, but ultimately for all of humanity in the end, via the Morphogenetic Field. Some life examples would include the recent conflict in Ireland between Catholics and Protestants, or the continuing strife in the Middle East between Israel and Palestine.

On one level, you may have every valid reason for reacting to someone's nastiness by hitting back. Nevertheless, a more mature and compassionate response is possible too. You could *choose* a response where you're still able to acknowledge your own pain at what's happened, but you can also choose to try and understand the other person's inner wounding, which drove them to do something hurtful to you.

Perhaps you even 'deserved' the hurt because of something you had done to them previously. The mature choice would be to accept the situation without fuelling it into a further negative spiral. This may be what one great Teacher once meant when he said to 'turn the other cheek'. Or as Nelson Mandela said... 'resentment is like drinking poison, and then hoping it will kill your enemies'.

This is not a matter of white-washing what people do. Far from it. But it is a matter of choosing how we *respond* rather than how we *react* to any event. Thus, by not returning anger for anger, hurt for hurt, there is at least the chance of breaking this cycle of strife humanity finds itself in. Instead, using the concept of the Morphogenetic Field, and how our choice of thoughts does rebound upon us, we could create more harmony not only for ourselves, but for the entire planet by choosing positive, compassionate responses to our hurts. Understand however, that this scenario totally revolves around thought... and choice. What thought will you choose to manifest or entertain in your mind, realizing that for every action there is a reaction?

Cultivating the 'Witness State'

Choosing a more constructive and Conscious response does take a lot of Inner Awareness and maturity. To this end, the ability for us to develop what is called the 'Witness State' becomes increasingly important. Based on this concept of choice, we can choose to either live on 'automatic mode' or we can encourage a part of our consciousness to stand back a little and allow for a more discerning perspective of any particular event that is occurring. With this more objective view, it becomes possible to see the various layers associated with an experience, in turn allowing us to deal with or respond to the situation in a more productive manner.

This is especially so when emotions cloud the issue. We either choose to allow the emotion to overcome us, or we stand back from the emotion. Allowing our emotions of perhaps anger, fear or guilt to consume us would also minimize the possibility of responding in more constructive ways.

If we are to achieve a platform of compassion from which to operate in this life, it becomes crucial that we, as individuals, can come from a more centered and calm Inner space. A powerful way of achieving this centeredness or balance is to be in a state where we feel whole inside because we feel adequately nurtured and loved. From this space of fullness, we can in turn give nurturing or compassion to others, even under very difficult or painful circumstances.

Many of us are not in such a space, or at least not very often. Most of us also feel that unless we have that special partner or relationship, we are but an incomplete half, waiting and searching for fulfillment by finding our 'other half'. However, we need to realize that a relationship is only meant to *complement* - not *complete* us. It is indeed true that when we fall in love, we shine with an energy beyond this mortal realm. But if this energy or light is dependent on the existence of the 'other half', then we automatically also set ourselves up for potential pain and loss. The idea is to reach a stage where we are able to nurture ourselves to the same point where we start to radiate out that certain 'glow' often associated with the state of being 'in love'.

Voice dialogue, and working with concepts of the 'Inner Child' [4] provide some powerful tools for achieving this state of self-nurturing. Such enhanced self-acceptance and recognition is totally beyond the ego concept of self-love, and allows us to achieve an Inner state of harmony. From here it then becomes much easier to make more conscious, positive, nurturing and compassionate choices to life events.

Again, the point isn't whether we have 'Inner children' or not; whether thought truly is a form of Energy; or even whether Rupert Sheldrake's Morphogenetic Field exists. The issue is simply whether these concepts do somehow hang together, even if on some weird level. At least they may serve to create a picture which allows us to feel more empowered in our lives. Hence, how we experience our lives - our reality - does depend on how we choose to perceive or interpret that same reality.

And so, using the above points of discussion, we could choose to accept that we do influence our reality by the type of thoughts we choose to generate in response to certain events.

Left brain:right brain concepts

To help explain the phenomena known to occur through the use of Creative Visualization, it would be useful to look at Tansley's hypothesis of Dimension I and Dimension II. [5] His interpretations of these two Dimensions correlate beautifully with the different functions of the left and right brain hemispheres respectively. Studies done on brain-damaged people reveal the left and right brain having very different roles. Following is a brief and rather basic summary of some of the key functions and characteristics of these two brain hemispheres.

Left brain

Just one important role of this side of the brain is involved with logical, analytical thinking, where we work out mathematical equations or use our language functions. The scientist Carl Sagan states that the left brain processes information in a sequential manner, much like a computer does. It's that part of the brain which deals with this physical reality of ours. It is also governed by time, and could be seen as the concrete, lower mind.

Right Brain

The right brain, in contrast, works in a more wholistic manner, whereby it is able to process a whole range of data input at the same time; this part can be likened to an analog computer. It gets more complex than this, but for simplicity's sake, it's this right brain area which recognizes patterns, and allows us to be orientated in our space:time reality.

It deals with transcendent reality, that is, Metaphysical reality. Herein lies the domain of our creative, artistic, intuitive thoughts or capabilities. Using the right brain, things are perceived in a wholistic, simultaneous way, which goes beyond time. The right brain can be seen as the home of our abstract or higher mind. It is from here that Creative Visualization would appear to become a concrete manifestation in our daily lives.

Life is more than what we can perceive directly

Our modern Western culture is very left-brain biased, compared to many traditional Eastern or Native cultures. Just about everything we do or judge is via the characteristics or specifications as seen through the left brain. This way of dealing with our reality can however, invalidate or discredit much of the information obtained through right-brain avenues. Tansley eloquently describes this phenomenon in his book 'Radionics: Science or Magic',[6] where he points at the way we tend to use language to dismiss anything we might imagine in our mind, as being not real, through phrases such as…'oh, you're just imagining things', or… 'it's all in your mind'.

The reality is that we are not just a left brain or right brain alone. We have two hemispheres, and we function - whether we know it consciously or not - through the use of both sides of the brain. These two very different types of brain functions, and their resultant different ways of explaining our reality are known, scientific fact. No need to hypothesize here. But what Tansley then did, was to use this known and proven concept as the basis for providing a model which allows for a very different way of looking at our reality experiences. Through this model he gives us an explanatory 'tool' for so much of our observed phenomena.

Tansley proposes that we actually experience two dimensions of reality, although we are generally only aware of one. He calls these Dimension I and Dimension II, which, as indicated before, correlate in broad terms to the left and right brain respectively. Think back to the example of the pond – seeing surface reflections *and* the pebbles; two realities co-existing, yet we're normally only aware of one. The characteristics of Dimension I are those of our daily,

Chapter 3 - Thoughts Are Reality Creators

physical reality, where life is experienced from a very physical perspective, governed by the known laws of science.

Dimension II however, is quite different, being the domain of transcendent, wholistic reality as experienced by our consciousness. It lies outside of time. Time has no power or control here, and because of that, it is the realm of simultaneity, where there are absolutely no limits.

This often doesn't make sense to the left brain, which sees things in a two-dimensional way as it were, while the right brain sees reality more from a three-dimensional perspective. So obviously, from the limited, two-dimensional frame of reference of the left brain, many right brain events or phenomena will be totally inconceivable, simply because reason and logic, while essential to orderly functioning in Dimension I, do not necessarily apply in Dimension II.

In Dimension II, anything can happen, due to it functioning as a limitless, infinite reservoir of creative forces, freely available at all times. It is from this Dimension that all the power and Energy needed to sustain the reality of Dimension I originates, and is therefore the source of all events occurring in Dimension I. In other words, the thoughts you choose, based on the beliefs you hold, selected from Dimension II's infinite possibilities, then become the events you experience on Dimension I. Tansley's hypothesis is therefore that whatever you see in Dimension I as a physical reality, first existed in Dimension II as a thought, powered by an emotion.

The analogy Tansley uses to clarify the concepts of these two dimensions is to see Dimension I as a TV set. The program viewed on this very physical set is the ultimate product of Dimension II, where a very complex series of events had to occur to produce the images seen on the screen. The program required a vast array of complicated technology, as well as many different people to write the script, produce the stage on which it was then filmed, directed, edited and finally beamed through further sophisticated wizardry to your TV.

When you sit in front of your set, you normally take for granted the immense amount of work and organization needed for you to see the final images on your screen. So too with Dimension I. We take it very much for granted that events 'just happen', whereas in reality, there is quite a complex process which occurs in Dimension II before any particular event finally manifests into our lives, or into Dimension I.

'Thought is creative' is a dynamic, not rigid concept

The concept of 'Thought is Creative' is an inherent, primary Law which affects humans wherever they may be. But it is true that the *application* of this Law will vary from place to place on this planet, and from person to person. Even at a cursory glance it is obvious that a multi-millionaire in the West has a far better chance of creating their reality on a much greater scale than a peasant in Biafra, who along with a million others is homeless and starving. After all, how extensively could their environment allow them to actualize their potential of 'creating their reality'?

An analogy may better explain this apparent contradiction. The Laws of electricity remain the same wherever you might go. However, their application and ultimate manifestation through a certain object or machine which utilizes electricity will vary from place to place. If I wanted to build an electrical device in the West, the know-how, and the individual components needed for the manufacture of such a device would be available. Even a ready-made source of electricity would be there to plug the end product into.

Yet, here I am in the middle of Biafra, where I can barely find enough wood to light my fire on which to cook my meager rations. What are the chances of getting the right components, like wire, microchips, transistors, and whatever else is needed for the building of my device? Pretty slim indeed! Despite the lack of easy accessibility to raw materials, from which to build an electrical device, the *knowledge* of how to build this gadget is stored and available within my mind. Equally, the Laws of electricity are just as applicable in the middle of desolate Biafra as they would be in 'Silicon Valley', in California.

The *potential* for creating or manifesting such a device in Biafra would be there. However, it would also need much more effort to import all the necessary components for the device. Then, once it is built I would also have to obtain at least a small generator to provide me with the electricity needed to actually run it. So yes, it is true that the essential Laws with which I would be working remain the same. Yet the *application* of such Laws would not only require the knowledge necessary to create or build that machine, but also a lot more effort, organization, and access to the appropriate materials.

You might say 'that's not fair'. Why should a Biafran have less chance of manifesting electrical gadgetry compared to a Westerner? And indeed, on one level you have every right to your judgment. But if you can step back from the rights or wrongs of the situation, you can also choose to see that beyond the fact 'it isn't fair', does lie the very simple reality of... 'that's just how it is'. The opportunity to manifest or create certain things in the West is definitely quite different from trying to achieve the same thing in places like Biafra. That's how this world happens to be in any particular moment.

However, the most critical point to emerge from this discussion is that the Laws of electricity do not vary from place to place. Given the know-how and basic components necessary, a Biafran could potentially create the very same device you might choose to create in the West. So too with the Laws of 'Thought is Creative'. That Law is fundamental, never mind where you might be on this planet. Its usability or application though, does vary depending on where you are. This is not dictated by some whim of Nature, but by the fundamental basis of the nature of the human condition on this Earth. At this time in the evolution of our species, there are gross inequalities present on so many levels, including the level of 'Thought is Creative'. However, this doesn't mean the situation can't change.

Beware guilt or blame

The fact that a Biafran can't manifest an electrical gadget, let alone use it as easily as someone in a developed nation, has absolutely nothing to do with blame or guilt in any sense whatsoever. It has to do simply with 'how it is' in any particular area we choose to focus on. So too with someone perhaps dying of cancer, AIDS... or whatever.

'Thought is Creative', and the knowledge of these fundamental Laws of reality have allowed profound 'miracles' to occur. This is certainly the case for the many who have been lucky enough to know about them, and who have had the courage and ability to do the necessary work in applying them. But what about someone who doesn't even know about the possibility of such things, let alone the techniques for manifesting them? Can they then be judged or blamed for their illness and possible decline, resulting in death? Of course not!

Blame as a major block to accepting the concept of Co-creation

Probably the biggest stumbling block to the entire topic of Co-creation is the strong, negative, knee-jerk response so many people have to the concept that 'we create our own reality'. Immediately, the doors slam shut with a resounding thud. End of discussion. Why? Because many people – especially those coming from a more religious background – feel such a statement implies blame for whatever may be in their reality. Not only does such an ostensible accusation sound outrageous, but it also pushes a lot of uncomfortable buttons in our psyche, simply because deep-down, almost subconsciously, many do realize there just may be a grain of truth to the fact that we do play a role in manifesting things into our reality.

But it is not about blame

People can become irate when they misunderstand the essence of 'thought is creative', and feel they are being *blamed* for creating their suffering. For many people, their response to being told they are Co-creating their own reality is to not just feel blamed, but also feel stunned that anyone could possibly believe 'such obvious rubbish; it couldn't possibly be true'! Who would want to do something so utterly foolish and irrational? As if a person with cancer, multiple sclerosis or AIDS would wish to consciously create their disease.

What is needed here is a reversal of a deeply entrenched, destructive mind-set. What we truly need to be able to understand is that the concept of 'thought being creative' *has absolutely nothing to do with blame.* Ironically, it has everything to do with empowerment!

Based on the fact that far too many of my clients, friends – and even colleagues - have found this point to be so extraordinarily difficult to grasp, let's re-emphasize this line of reasoning potently and repeatedly... it has absolutely nothing to do with blame! One more time... it has absolutely nothing to do with blame! Have you got that then? 'Yes, but...' would come the immediate and inevitable response from many clients.

Sooooooo, let's say it again:-

> *...The 'thought creates reality' concept has absolutely nothing to do with blame!...*

Please... just let that one in, and accept it! Being told you are a Co-creator to your own reality is *not* about blaming you for all the woes and sufferings that may be in your life – past or present. It *is* about being offered an incredibly powerful opportunity to break out of that previously **unconscious** Co-creative cycle.

Chapter 3 - Thoughts Are Reality Creators

For now, just hang in there! As the discussion progresses, hopefully this seemingly outrageous proposition will make more sense.

It's not about guilt – it's about empowerment

It is indeed true that for every choice and action – even if made unconsciously - there is a consequence. That's just how this reality works on planet Earth. But as Dr. Bruce Lipton states... *You are* **personally** *responsible for everything in your life...* ***once you become aware that you are personally responsible for everything in your life!*** [7] (emphasis added).

Not before.

However, for those who strongly dismiss these Creative Visualization concepts, some worthwhile questions may be... 'O.K, so is your present explanation of why myriads of things "keep happening" in your life really satisfactory to you'? 'Does it truly provide you with an *empowering* and realistic explanation to your sufferings'? 'Or is it all just bad luck which has nothing to do with anything you might be doing'?

Perhaps, if you think about it, affirmative answers to these questions might be seen to be rather disempowering, because what is it then going to take for you to break through this run of 'bad luck'? If it is God doing this to you for some reason, does this mean you are basically stuck till God decides to have a 'good day', and changes Its mind as to whether to continue torturing you? Or, if it is all just a roll of the dice... then this way of looking at your suffering is even more disempowering!

At least with a God in the equation, you could argue there is still a possibility that It may be persuaded, cajoled or even blackmailed into reversing Its attitude to you, and allowing some good things to happen in your life for a change. Particularly if this God is supposedly Just and Loving. However, if it truly is all simply a matter of 'bad luck', totally unrelated to a God, then the chances of such a run of 'bad luck' suddenly changing, is about as good as you finally winning the Lottery. I wouldn't hold my breath if I were you!

But what if we are indeed generating a lot of this suffering into our reality – *albeit unconsciously*? Then, if this is so, doesn't this at least provide us with the *possibility* – however vague – of actually having the power to change this run of 'bad luck' *ourselves*?

Again, we need to invoke this primary concept of... 'it doesn't ultimately matter if these ideas are 'The Truth' or not; simply ask yourself... are they useful'? Could they possibly provide you with a point of leverage through which to then try to change your 'bad luck'? After all, the way you are presently looking at, and dealing with this reality doesn't seem to have changed it much. And how empowered are you therefore feeling? Or is it perhaps – on some deep, barely conscious level – you actually like being in victim mode? Does feeling the 'victim' truly provide you with the only way of getting some attention, 'love' or sense of empowerment? But what a distorted version of empowerment! And what a price to pay in suffering.

Surely, if you really are complaining about your life being not as comfortable, productive or happy as you'd like, wouldn't it be better to investigate other options and concepts, rather than remaining stuck in your sense of disempowerment - or possibly victimhood? Never mind how 'sort-of-comfortable' this state of disempowerment may be on one level? It's interesting to note that remaining in victim status can definitely also get us 'off the hook' from so many things occurring in our lives.

After all, if we buy into this perspective that we have absolutely nothing to do with how our life is playing itself out, then it could also be seen that we don't have to do anything ourselves to alter our life reality. In the end, it is up to God to be kind to us; for the dice of life to roll differently; for that boss to stop doing what they are doing; or those neighbors... or those friends... endlessly!

Dr. John Harrison, in his book 'Love Your Disease – it's keeping you healthy', [8] explores this largely unconscious tendency we humans at times can have to use our 'ill health' or 'bad luck' as a bargaining tool through which to obtain love and attention. But this inevitably comes at a terrible price on other levels.

Yes, these are challenging ideas – but can also be empowering

These concepts we're starting to explore here may not necessarily be immediately comfortable to the mind and ego. But they can definitely be empowering, if only we can get beyond feeling discomfort or guilt, and see them more as an amazing chance to do things differently. Making that internal shift in perspective is also that point of power in being able to constructively change our life. Yes, it will – like everything else in life – take effort and skill. But it is achievable. Yes, some will do better at it than others, just like some people who have never sung or skied or attempted any one of a myriad possible skills will learn that skill faster and better than others. But that shouldn't stop us at least trying.

Chapter 3 - Thoughts Are Reality Creators

This is so incredibly important. Unless we can break through this deeply engrained, negative worldview which believes that we don't really have much influence over what happens to us, then we also can't get to the flip side of this whole situation regarding visualization - which is that it is so incredibly self-empowering. That's the irony.

There have been many concepts and dogmas, however dysfunctional, which countless people were prepared to continue believing in, rather than abandon their illusions. These were concepts often believed so passionately and so earnestly that people would hang in there even if it meant self-ruin. As Arthur C. Clark says in '3001 – the final odyssey'... *That's a good operational definition of insanity.*

Ironically, sometimes it does take a series of life situations to culminate in such a strong sense of suffering that something snaps inside us. We become so angry at the injustices being perpetrated on us by life; by God; by - whoever or whatever - that something inside us shifts. At this point, we can then either fall into a state of inertia and internal collapse, or we can feel an anger that actually outweighs our resistance to change. This emotion can then act as a catalyst and motivator instead.

The Laws governing Co-creation are beyond morality issues

Let's play with a few analogies to help clarify all this. There's a lot of correlation between the concepts of Gravity and those of Creative Visualization. Gravity simply exists - whether we like it or not. And to someone who has decided to step off their 20th storey balcony because they wanted to get to the ground floor faster than by using the stairs, Gravity is not going to be kind! To humans, Gravity for so long 'just was'. People weren't aware such a Force even existed, which kept them to the Earth's surface; made them fall if they tripped; caused things to plummet to the ground if dropped from a height. There was no name for it, let alone an understanding that knowing the existence of such a Force would also allow people to start using it to their advantage. The capacity to keep satellites whizzing around Earth, or our ability to now send space probes to the outer fringes of our solar system are all based on an ability to utilize the Laws of Gravity.

Gravity, for so much of our human Journey, and until fairly recently, was nothing but a background level of reality; something we were utterly ignorant about. So too with the Laws of Creative Visualization. For the majority of humanity, and until recent times, this phenomenon just wasn't even known to exist. It had no name, let alone having the capacity to be consciously utilized.

Nowadays we acknowledge and utilize the concept of Gravity – despite still knowing little as to exactly what it is or precisely how it is generated. But we know the *effects* it has on the human system, and everything else on this planet. So we have learned to respect it, and live within its constraints. Or we have learned to use it to our advantage, for instance, when we create water storage on a higher level to a city, thus providing adequate water pressure to feed pipes to each home in that city.

Similarly with Creative Visualization. It is a fundamental Law of reality that simply exists – whether we like it or not; whether we know about it or not, and even whether we know how to use it or not. The reality, *and the problem*, is that all of us are Creatively – or destructively! - Visualizing all the time. But the greatest majority of us are also doing it *unconsciously* most if not all of the time. Yet, our lack of awareness around what we are doing doesn't lessen the effect of such unconscious Visualization. It's just that the process becomes a highly random and often chaotic one.

It's a lot like someone who has stepped into a car; has absolutely no idea of how to drive it, yet attempts to do so. Such efforts would only result in a wild careening of the vehicle, crunching of gears, and a possible accident waiting to happen! Certainly, during this phase of unconsciousness about our inherent powers of Creative Visualization, there can be no blame attached to our unwitting outcomes. In the same way, we wouldn't blame a passenger on a small plane for the final outcome of an emergency landing they're suddenly forced to make because the pilot is having a heart-attack.

Concept of Karma can sometimes explain the unexplainable

Then there are the karmic levels to what happens to us. This can be an especially useful concept to help explain the many absolutely horrible or sad things that happen to humans, particularly the young, who would appear to have so little power over what happens to them in such early stages of their lives. How do we explain the dreadful situations of young children with cancer? Those babies who are born grossly deformed or severely intellectually handicapped? However, if our living reality and experiences on Earth are seen through the lens of karma or incarnation, explored more fully in the next few chapters, then another interpretation becomes possible.

Chapter 3 - Thoughts Are Reality Creators

The concept of Karma is well described in many books, with one notable volume being 'Journey of Souls' by Michael Newton.[9] Here, Newton speculates that we come down to 'Earth School' with a very specifically designed 'curriculum', through which to learn certain things. Via this perspective, there is at least the option to say that it was the conscious pre-decision of these young ones to incarnate to parents… for *whom* they were then going to be the source of 'learning'! As mentioned, we'll soon explore this delicate and problematic concept in greater depth, trying to make sense out of the reality of suffering so endemic to planet Earth.

However, even these explorations into finding plausible answers to this ubiquitous phenomenon still don't explain why God set up the system in such a painful way in the first place, allowing this level of suffering to occur to humans - even if there ultimately is a possibility to learn from it. Nevertheless, the explanations we can conjure up, do at least help provide some sort of framework through which to make a bit more sense out of the otherwise senseless suffering seen so often on this planet.

These ideas hold within them the potential for a slow 'awakening' within us to the reality that we have more say in what is drawn into our experience than we give ourselves credit for. Ideas like this suggest that the phenomenon of Creative Visualization does exist – just like Gravity does.

So too with the Law of Creative Visualization. It has always been such an unquestioned background to our lives that we didn't even know to single it out for naming; let alone manipulating or using it.

Once again, we need to be very careful not to go into blame around any of the Creative Visualization situations – implied directly or indirectly. It has far more to do with simply acknowledging our level of *skill* at being able to use it. Think back to the example above of a person, quietly enjoying their flight as a passenger in a two-seater Cessna, and the pilot suddenly having a heart-attack. The flight ends in disaster, despite their most earnest efforts to land safely.

So it is with us too, when it comes to the *unconscious* use of our Creative Visualization abilities. And if we really insist in going into blame mode, then let it be against the Maker of us humans. One could legitimately ask why we weren't installed or hard-wired with very clear and specific instructions on how this Force can be utilized with skill and positive effects.

Life – like working a computer if you've never known one

Wouldn't it make so much more sense if we came into this reality with some sort of inherent, built-in knowledge? Knowledge which then automatically provided us humans with a clear outline of how the system operates on planet Earth? At least it would be a starting point. Presently, the human situation is a lot like trying to teach someone about computers by simply sitting them down in front of one. But the person has never encountered a computer, and has absolutely no idea what this weird 'plastic box' in front of them is all about. Yet, the expectation is that not only should they be able to figure out what this gizmo is, but to also become skilled at productively running all the programs inherent within it!

No-one from our earthly reality would find such a scenario productive, let alone compassionate. Yet in many ways, it would seem that this is what God has done to us. We are plonked into a reality, governed by definite laws which dictate how things work, and then we're expected to somehow figure it all out without causing ourselves or the environment any damage or dysfunction. How unrealistic! As an author, writing about such idiosyncrasies, I have no answers to this conundrum... but at least it can be stated.

Even the animals seem to know more

It's ironic how animals of all kinds have had their fundamental 'instructions and guidelines' hard-wired into them. Rabbits intuitively know how to burrow. Hatchling turtles know within minutes that they need to head for the ocean, rather than wander off deeper into the sand dunes. Birds automatically learn to fly, and inherently know how to migrate over astounding distances, never missing their destination.

Yet as humans, although it is true that most of us have an instinctive drive to search for a deeper meaning to Life, finding truly workable answers seems amazingly difficult – or blocked in many of us. So instead of blame, we first need to accept that this is just how it is for us humans on Earth. Then we need to focus on how we can most effectively become skilled at further understanding this 'Thought is Creative' Force of Nature, as well as how we can subsequently learn to utilize it for good in our lives.

But we also need to acknowledge and respect that not everyone wishes to include such perceptions into their reality. Certain beliefs just aren't appropriate for everyone. Just like certain diets don't work for some people. As natural therapists, a major foundation upon which we operate is to accept that there is no general treatment that 'does it' for everyone. Instead, there is a great need for being highly specific in our prescription. And so too with the use or application of the concepts surrounding Creative Visualization.

No proselytizing!
Hence, there is a need to use these highly Metaphysical concepts with compassion, appropriateness and specificity – not ram them down everyone's throat. It would be important to assess each individual as to whether they can in fact 'digest' or process this particular level of reality. If we sense not, then don't share this concept with them! Simple as that. Ask yourself first, would sharing these ideas empower or dis-empower them? If the latter, they will inevitably see these concepts as a 'blaming'. And this doesn't serve well. So then, it would be better not to share this concept with such people at this stage of their human Journey.

We also need to recognize that there is no 'right' or 'wrong' stage on this Journey of life. There is nothing wrong with a human attending pre-school. There is nothing inherently better about another human attending University. These simply represent different stages of knowledge accumulation, consistent with different stages in a human's development. Nothing more; nothing less. This is not a moral issue. It's just 'how it is' to be a human.

This is something that many in the New Age fraternity still very much need to learn. Proselytizing to all and sundry – never mind how sure you are that a new concept works - is arrogant, and may be damaging to those not yet ready to handle this level of knowledge. Yet, for those who can digest or process these concepts of reality, it can also be found to be extraordinarily empowering, resulting in huge, positive shifts occurring in their lives. Again, the issue is not whether all this is true or not. The only question that needs to be answered is…'is it useful'? It's ultimately all about allowing each person their own Path. If it serves… good! If not… then leave it alone.

Don't throw the baby out with the bathwater
It is therefore important to understand that the whole topic of Creative Visualization, and any discussion of it, needs to be within the context of the

above points or caveats. If you – the reader – are finding these concepts utterly frustrating or unacceptable, then simply skip along.

However, if you have voluntarily chosen to read this book, or it has come into your hands in some weird or wonderful way, then more likely than not you are indeed ready to handle the style of 'vista' presented here. This may be especially so if some of these ideas do resonate as real, despite them being confronting, and possibly contradicting your present opinion or belief about a range of human issues. At least start to play with them, keeping constantly in mind - at the risk of being repetitive - that it's not... 'whether this is all true or not, only whether it is useful'.

The fundamental issue here is that these Laws exist, and do work, and do affect each and every one of us, even if we don't know about it. It also must be clearly understood how the Laws governing 'Thought is Creative' go totally beyond morality. The aim in this discussion, therefore, is to see us as a species constantly evolving on many levels, with the emphasis being on our ability to influence our reality through the process of Creative Visualization. Humanity seems to be coming closer to some critical point in that evolution, where these Laws are going to be used and understood on a far wider scale than ever before. More about this in the final chapter.

Knowledge gives us response-ability

'Response-ability' is about the capacity to respond to any particular situation. How we respond is the crucial issue, and it is precisely around this pivotal point that we can choose to connect with our own innate power. Being negative about our ability to respond is more a statement about possibly being in a victim mind-set. The alternative is to act in a more self-empowered way, choosing to respond positively – i.e. we latch onto our response-ability.

The problem is that although this knowledge can greatly empower people, it also definitely presents them with a much higher level of *accountability* within their lives. This is confronting, and often rather uncomfortable for many people. Hence, instead of taking up their new power and responsibility, it may initially be easier for them to simply deny it or discredit this 'new' knowledge.

Just as a long-caged animal might refuse to move from its opened cage into freedom, so do we humans all too frequently stubbornly refuse to move on to the next stage of our Journey of freedom or empowerment. Until perhaps life comes along and starts to prod us into action. This usually manifests for us humans as some form of so-called suffering. It may be a life-threatening illness; a painful relationship break-up; being fired from a job we may have felt secure in - but perhaps one in which we were nevertheless also growing very stale or dissatisfied!

On one level, the pain and suffering such events create must be acknowledged and honored. But it is by choosing to go beyond the suffering - whatever form it may be in – that provides us with an opportunity for change and growth. Here, we can choose to see such events as the 'prod of life' coming to tell us that a greater freedom could lie ahead, and it might be best to move along. Then we truly can grow and gain from such 'suffering'.

After all, here we are with our suffering; this ubiquitous phenomenon within the human experience. And as much as we might want to argue about or try to understand why a supposedly Loving God would want humanity to suffer so much, the point is that we can at least choose to *use* suffering, in all its many forms, as a reason for learning and growing in Consciousness. If in this process the suffering or disease is eradicated, that's great. However, the primary goal in this whole experience is not necessarily to get rid of the 'problem', but rather, to choose to use it constructively. This therefore empowers us to shift ourselves out of possible victim roles.

The point of power is in the moment

We connect with that point of power when we become aware of the choices we have as to what we are able to do. All we then need is the courage to activate those choices. There is, however, a difference between *'Thought is Creative'* and *'we create our reality through our thoughts'.* The former is a statement of absoluteness: within the context of Creative Visualization, every thought simply is creative. However, the latter is more a statement of variability, dependent on our level of skill and knowledge about the Laws governing this process; how they work; what type of environment we're in, and therefore how we can utilize these Laws. It's really the same as learning about any form of energy.

It seems to be the nature of this reality we call life that we constantly learn and grow, and in that process some of us may get hurt. That is no reason, however, for then invalidating the further exploration and use of this Energy. In other words, on this plane of reality certain things just happen: it rains; it shines; volcanoes erupt; earthquakes occur; asteroids can hit Earth. It's as if there is an inherent background level of activity or experience that constantly occurs. What the concept of 'Thought is Creative' or Creative Visualization is offering us is the ability to have a far greater potential to *influence* our own personal reality within these generally occurring events than we've ever been led to believe. But first we need to actually know this, and then we need to do a lot of practise in learning this skill, and from that, allow more positive changes to occur in our lives.

Visualization – much we still don't know
It's also important not to look at Creative Visualization from too black and white a perspective. No doubt, there is still much we don't know about this process. Not every human experience will neatly fit into it; nor is it for everyone, especially those who can't get beyond the idea that this model of reality is perceived to then blame them for their life situations, rather than realizing that our realities are by and large created *un*consciously.

The whole aim is to become more conscious of how unconscious we've been at Creatively Visualizing our reality! A good definition of Consciousness could be expressed as… 'the awareness of being Aware'. And as that occurs, and as we gain skill at managing this fundamental Law of reality, so too will we get to increasingly understand the process. We'll also learn where we've perhaps not been doing it as productively or as accurately as we first thought. But that is of course the fundamental way all of life is lived. We're always learning more; refining more; throwing out ideas which initially seemed perfectly reasonable or workable. But as our understanding grows, so too do we need to replace these outmoded concepts with new and further evolved models of reality.

Beliefs can become our prisons – or our liberation
Let's bring all this back to the issue of our general lives. What is being said here is that it is possible to use all these sort of concepts through which to positively alter our day to day existence. These concepts also allow us alternate ways of looking at, and treating a multitude of ill-health matters. You may have any one of a range of diseases or demanding life situations. You could choose to see yourself as a suffering victim with total validity. You could however, also choose to use your illness or life situation to open yourself up to other ways of experiencing your reality. In this process, the concepts you may choose to play

Chapter 3 - Thoughts Are Reality Creators

with could greatly enhance your ability not only to increase your Awareness or Consciousness, but to heal yourself too.

How effective you are in being able to use these new tools is in no way a judgment of who you are on some fundamental level as a person. Certain people can sing like Pavarotti; others just croak and warble. That doesn't make the one good or the other evil. Simply, more or less *skilled*. There can be no morally based judgments here. Please understand how this entire area of discussion, and its ramifications, are totally and utterly beyond morality!

All that each and every one of us can do is to use this knowledge as best we can. What can be judged however is not so much the results, as our *intention* backed up by our *efforts*. It is beyond whether we achieved our goal, and has more to do with the impeccability with which we traveled the Journey *towards* the goal, and how much we grew and learned through this process. What the illness or painful life situation may have done, though, is bring such issues more into focus for us, thereby allowing us to use and experience each moment of our lives with greater Awareness and productivity. In that sense, our life circumstances can also become our greatest gift or opportunity. But again, that is a choice only we can make.

In this way, all these concepts fit in with the idea of thought being a form of Energy, which has the ability to be creative. Whether we are conscious of it or not, these thoughts do influence the manifestations of reality as we experience it in our lives. The first thing to create is an Awareness of such concepts, because without that Awareness or Consciousness, there can also be no choices. Choices to empower ourselves.

Exercise

- Next time someone says something nasty or hurtful, choose to respond from Higher Self. List three characteristics of how such a response would differ from an ego based reaction.

- List two concepts in this chapter you found challenging. Then reframe them to see how they could also empower you. Write a few paragraphs on your new perspective.

Summary of thoughts thus far

- Many humans, because of the way we now live our 24/7 lives within our concrete jungles, have become disconnected from so much of our innate, intuitive knowledge.

- Western society tends to still believe that thoughts are nothing more than flimsy, ephemeral consequences of neuronal activity, and have no direct ability to influence the reality we perceive or experience in our lives.

- Rupert Sheldrake saw each person as an individual Energy generator, generating either positive or negative Energy.

- The Morphogenetic Field is the sum total of all these individual Energy generations. Sheldrake's hypothesis, supported by research, is that this Field in turn affects each one of us, individually and collectively.

- If our thoughts do influence the Morphogenetic Field, then in turn we can greatly and positively change humanity's reality by choosing to engage in more positive thinking, and by how we choose to respond to our life situations.

- An 'eye for an eye' approach can only guarantee the continuation of life's discord.

- Using the Morphogenetic field concepts does provides us with a more scientific rationale as to why this 'eye for an eye' paradigm of human interaction urgently needs to be discarded.

- Unfortunately, too many humans – especially through military and political means – do still operate from this fundamental paradigm. Christian conflict within Ireland was a good illustration of this. Israel and Palestine, for example, are still operating very much from an 'eye-for-an-eye' mentality.

- The point of power for change in life does not lie in forcing specific philosophical, religious or political 'solutions' onto the masses.

- Instead, the point of power for personal and planetary change lies within ourselves, via the thoughts we choose to entertain, and which motivate our actions.

- The left brain is involved in logical, analytical thinking, where we work out mathematical equations or use our language functions via sequential processing of data. It's that part of the brain which deals with this physical reality, and is governed by time.

Chapter 3 - Thoughts Are Reality Creators

- The right brain works in a more wholistic manner, where it is able to process a whole range of data input simultaneously. It recognizes patterns, and allows us to be orientated in our space:time reality.
- The right brain deals with transcendent reality, and is the domain of our creative, artistic, intuitive thoughts or capabilities.
- Our modern Western culture is very left-brain biased, compared to many traditional Eastern cultures.
- This Western way of dealing with our reality can invalidate or discredit much of the information obtained through right-brain avenues.
- In terms of Creative Visualization, Tansley's proposal of Dimension I and II can be correlated with left and right brain function respectively.
- The Laws governing Creative Visualization are the same everywhere within our reality. However, our ability to actualize these Laws is dependent on our environment and circumstances.
- The concept 'we create our own reality' has absolutely nothing to do with blame. Once we truly understand this concept, we can see it has everything to do with self-empowerment.
- 'You are personally responsible for everything in your life... once you become aware that you are personally responsible for everything in your life' (Bruce Lipton).
- There is a big difference between 'Thought is Creative' and 'we create our reality through our thoughts'. One is a statement of absoluteness while the latter is a statement of variability, dependent on a vast range of co-factors.
- The whole aim is to become more conscious of how unconscious we've been at Creatively Visualizing our reality.
- The Laws governing Creative Visualization have nothing to do with *morality* – only whether you are or aren't yet skilled at their usage.
- The point of power for change is in this moment Now.
- This knowledge of Creative Visualization is very powerful stuff, and not everyone is ready or willing to tap into it yet. This is O.K!
- The concept of 'Planet Earth School' was introduced and explored.

REFERENCES

1. Laura, R & Ashton, J. *Hidden Hazards*, Bantam, Sydney, 1991, p.27.
2. Sheldrake, R. *The Rebirth of Nature*, Random Century, 1990, pp. 87-88; 97-98.
3. Tansley, D. *Radionics: Science or Magic?*, Saffron Walden, Essex, UK, 1982, ch.4.
4. Stone & Winkelman, *Embracing Ourselves*, New World Library, San Rafael, USA, 1989.
5. Tansley, D. *Radionics: Science or Magic?*, Saffron Walden, Essex, UK, 1982, ch. 4.
6. Ibid.
7. Lipton, B. Dr. *Nexus Magazine*, Feb/March. 2006.13.(2).33.
8. Harrison, J. Dr., *Love Your Disease*, Angus & Robertson. Sydney. 1984.
9. Newton, M. *Journey of Souls*, Llewellyn. 1994.

CHAPTER 4

MEANING OF LIFE

The ultimate measure of a man is not where he stands in moments of comfort and convenience, but where he stands at times of challenge and controversy.

Martin Luther King Jr.

You're suspended in a warm ocean of fluid; comfortable; at peace. Suddenly you notice that something has changed, and you are no longer floating. It seems the warm fluid, so long taken for granted has somehow drained away, and now you feel instead the rub and squeeze of walls closing in on you. Then waves of pressure begin to build, till it seems you might be crushed to pulp. This frightening situation continues for hours, with its painful pressure, and a myriad of other unfamiliar sensations.

Reality seems to have become quite chaotic, and you feel like you are no longer in control of your environment, particularly as this dreadful pressure starts to force your body to squeeze through what seems like the most ridiculously narrow tunnel. Then after much discomfort and even pain, suddenly you're blinded by bright lights. There's a few more waves of this awful squeezing, and next you find yourself experiencing many totally alien feelings. A breath-stopping sense of coldness never felt before; rough hands pulling at you, and before you know it, you're hanging upside down... and slap!

Welcome to Planet Earth!

So you did finally make it to this plane of reality. Now what do you do here? And how? What is this plane all about? So many questions.

Well, you have made it to planet Earth, but there seems to be no clear 'user's-guide' as to how to proceed. Yet, time goes by, and you do find yourself exposed to definitive sets of rules and regulations – usually courtesy of parents, governments, cultural traditions as well as religion, the latter inevitably defined by your birth circumstances. Or you find as you grow older, that there are a plethora of different ideas and concepts being presented as to what this experience is all about, and how you *must* proceed. It's strange, though, how often there is so much contradiction and confusion between these different sources of information.

Life meaning - usually born into – not self-explored
One thing really needs to be made clear in this part of the discussion. For numerous people, the particular religious paradigm they find themselves born into may well give them exactly all the meaningfulness and support they'll ever need in their earthly Journey. On the other hand, the reality is that for many westernized people, religion no longer provides a true sense of meaningfulness to their life. For them, what religion offers is not enough, or doesn't adequately answer those deep and gnawing questions which nevertheless keep arising from within, despite being adamantly told what 'The Truth' is. In such cases, their meaning of life is often something that has to be pro-actively searched for, rather than being delivered via a specific religious or culturally determined 'plate'. For a lot of people, where the meaning of life *is* presented to them on a plate, this may only provide an inevitably unquestioned, and therefore relatively shallow answer - almost a façade - behind which they live on a daily basis.

One important question that needs asking therefore is… 'why do people believe their particular perspective on life'? Is it only because that's what their parents used to believe – and their parents before them? Or that's what their religion or society has forcefully told them *is* the answer to life and its dilemmas? And if this way of believing was good enough for their forebears, why not for them too? Yet in such cases, this 'knowingness' as to what life is all about, comes from without, and is not necessarily vindicated by their own internal explorations or experiences. A personal experience inevitably provides a much deeper and more genuine sense of knowingness about something.

Living via a 'second-hand Truth' may also be quite an important basis to a lot of dysfunction within someone's life – especially when the person has an opportunity to look a bit deeper into their psyche. Again, a sense of meaning, *imposed from outside,* doesn't automatically negate the option that this can be more than enough to empower many people's lives. However, for others, such an external imposition of what constitutes meaning, far too often won't gel with what they have already experienced from *within*, and thus creates conflict.

We need a map if we are to start the journey

It's all very well to know that our thoughts can have an effect on our reality. But perhaps we need a more definitive layout of what life on Earth is all about, before we can make the most of this experience here. Certainly, mainstream Christianity seems to come from the perspective that we get just the one chance on Earth. One life, one death, and then an eternity in either heaven or hell, depending on how well we did in that one earthly life Journey.

However, that perspective seems to be inherently unfair. On the one hand, someone may be born into say a royal family; a wealthy family; a family living in a Western setting, in a modern era where Life is a relative 'picnic'. Compare this to someone born in Africa as an AIDS-infected child - a life where the mother dies shortly after birth; where the father is long dead, and living relatives may see such a child as nothing but an extra burden for them to deal with; just another mouth to feed when they are already starving and struggling to survive themselves. Obviously one can conjure up numerous such examples, where life is either relatively easy or one of abject poverty, suffering, and a constant challenge to even stay alive. Life seems to be so inherently unfair for billions of people on this planet at any one time.

Answers to such dramatic life differences, as given by many religions, don't seem to come close to providing any really satisfactory solutions. Indeed, those same religions' only sense of redress to this dilemma is to state that those suffering now end up with greater rewards in the life hereafter. Perhaps. But this seems a limited and unsatisfactory answer to those suffering right *now*. Such explanations also place people in a disempowered position where they inherently have no influence on what sort of life situation they may find themselves in. They just have to put up, and shut up till it's over. The only point of power is that they at least do have the choice of how they might *respond* to their life situation – but more on that aspect later.

Maybe reincarnation makes more sense of it all

Another way to deal with this fundamental earthly dilemma of suffering is to take a more Eastern approach, invoking the concept of re-incarnation. Here too, we don't necessarily end up with a simple answer, since we find ourselves still dealing with many interpretations of this concept. Nevertheless, the perspective that life is at least not a once-off scenario already brings in a greater sense of justice to the equation, even though it may not soften the challenges that so many people do seem to have to endure in a particular life.

However, one can say that in the long run of endless numbers of incarnations, at least you get to experience a more equitable share of the broad range of human conditions. From pauper to king; from thief to saint; from murderer to a doctor committed to saving life and alleviating suffering. In these endless variations, good and bad times may eventually, hopefully, somehow balance themselves out. Such lives may still be inherently challenging, but the overall human experience – when perceived from this alternate perspective - becomes much fairer to each person living any one particular life on this planet.

So the concept of reincarnation seems to provide for a bit more balance to the human condition, compared to the Christian 'one-off' experience - but tough if you happen to be that AIDS infected orphan! Then again, how do you ultimately prove one of these perspectives of life over the other? Christianity and other religions like Islam, Hinduism or Buddhism, will swing their Holy Book high into the air, and point to it as the final vindication that they are 'right'; that they hold the final 'Truth' on this and many other matters. But as previously explored, ultimately anyone standing *outside* such an organized religion will realize that this is not proof. It's nothing more than the offering of a *belief*, supported by *faith*. And if that serves a person, then well and good.

But what if such explanations do not serve you? If indeed they actually make it much harder to see any justice or reason to this human experience? If this is the case, then the freedom to have alternate explanations should not just be allowed, but become mandatory. Everyone has an inherent right, and need to a system of thought or philosophy which maximally empowers them to deal with life on planet Earth. Once again, that Mantra which will so often present itself in this book becomes invoked... 'it's not so much whether something is *true* or not; but rather, is it *useful*'?

'Planet Earth School'

So along those lines, let's fantasize a bit more, and see where it leads us. What if reincarnation is indeed true? Actually, there have been numerous researchers such as Michael Newton, Dr. Raymond Moody, Thomas Shroder, Denise Linn, Roy Stemman to quote but a few, who have provided at least some very thought provoking information that reincarnation does occur. In fact, it has been documented that even Christianity accepted reincarnation as a fundamental aspect to its world-view, but this belief was erased from its theology at the Council of Trent, which started sitting in December of the year 1545. That makes it over 1500 years where reincarnation *had* been accepted. Within the Christian tradition, obviously this hadn't been a fly-by-night concept!

Nevertheless, assuming this concept called reincarnation is real, how then could it provide a useful platform from which to feel more empowered in one's life? What if this reality here *is* about enrolling into a sort of 'Planet Earth School'? What if each incarnation was another opportunity to enter a particular 'curriculum' so as to become increasingly skilled at a range of Consciousness 'subjects'? What if we actually *choose* all the parameters of a particular life, such as which historical period we incarnate in; our sex; our sexuality; our ethnicity; our health issues; who our parents would be; our children; our friends; our 'enemies'?

Underlying all these assumptions comes another even more primary assumption - that we, as humans, are in fact not so much our physical bodies, as first and foremost an Energy Being... who *then* incarnates into a physical vehicle. What if our primary function or purpose of existence is not just to be a flesh and blood human being on Earth? What if we are **permanently** and **fundamentally** an Energy Being – albeit finding ourselves in a very *temporary* physical 'vehicle'? What if, at our deepest core we are Spirit, whose primary goal is to grow and expand its Consciousness, and that one way of doing so is to be born or incarnated into a physical realm like planet Earth?

Just as we have a vast range of teaching facilities in the human sphere, such as schools, Tech colleges, Universities, apprenticeships and more, each providing a very specific way of learning, so too with the needs of our Spirit Beings. Perhaps they also have a vast range of different agendas as to what they want to learn and experience, each agenda needing a very specific style of 'teaching facility'. In that sense, Earth provides one particular type of learning environment, and thus opportunity.

We really do have the focus wrong

As humans, understandably we focus almost entirely on the physicality of our existence - our very physical body in very physical, earthly surroundings. Although many religions will validate that we as physical humans do have an Energetic or Spiritual side to us - our soul - the emphasis still seems to be more on a physical body *containing* this soul or Spirit-like aspect to it. However, what if we have the emphasis wrong? What if we are *primarily* Energy or Spirit, with a *primary* point of reference, or 'Home', which is not of Earth, but of other Energy or dimensional Realms? In other words, who we *fundamentally* are is not of this earthly realm.

In fact, what if - at our deepest core - *we are therefore not really human*?

What if this Spirit, whose primary, fundamental 'Home' is definitely not of this Earth, then chooses to only *temporarily* clothe itself within a physical, fleshly, human body? Try to keep playing with and shifting this focus till something shifts inside you; till you 'get it' on a deep, almost cellular basis, that who you truly are, is *not* a human being! From this more curious viewpoint, our humanness is *not* our most *fundamental* characteristic or quality. Rather, our humanness is nothing more than a temporary, ephemeral and changeable form of 'drag' we dress up in, and play out on the 'stage' of planet Earth.

When we keep shifting the focus in this way, and look at ourselves from this more atypical stance, we see that who we truly are, is Spirit; that we are *primarily* and *fundamentally* Energy – with an ability, shall we say, to morph into other forms. And we need to really understand that the human form is only *one* of them! We then also see that our Spirit mode is an eternal and constant phenomenon, and that the human form is nothing but an extraordinarily temporary incident, and a very changeable one at that.

Although many religions do talk about a Spirit aspect to who we are, it nevertheless seems that many people are still living their lives primarily from their *human* aspect. They may be giving lip-service to their Spirit aspect, but not truly *living* from that perspective. For many, their life choices and decisions are still fundamentally based on the physical, material, human aspect to their life here on Earth. If this could be reversed so that our entire life is lived and experienced from our *Spirit* aspect, with a deep, gut-wrenching 'knowingness' of the relative brevity of a physical life – how different would be those decisions and choices we'd make!

Ironically, many so-called 'primitive' people like the Mayans, Hopi Indians, Australian Aborigines and others, have traditionally lived their lives based on such spiritual concepts and values, rather than on the overwhelmingly materialistic perspective we Westerners tend to base our lives on.

Our belief that the material world is the only reality is so entrenched

This over-focus on the material aspect of our life here on Earth has been going on for so long that it seems to have also blinded us. Many westernized people, despite their religious perspectives of a spirit or soul level to their reality, do appear to focus their life upon the *body*, rather than the *soul*. This has all sorts of unfortunate outcomes. One serious consequence being that despite their stated belief there is more to life than just the physical experience, in reality most such people will fight tooth and nail not to die. They will do almost anything to prevent them leaving what is after all only a relatively temporary phenomenon on this earthly plane.

If they truly believed what religions were telling them about existence *beyond* this reality, why then this incredible resistance to going there, especially when those other 'realities' are inevitably described in glowing, alluring terms? Indeed, none of us wants to leave behind loved ones, let alone the wealth or property which may have been built up over decades of hard work. Many others also greatly enjoy the human experience – seeing it as a fascinating 'holiday' in some exotic location. But, for those who profess to be religious - and who do in fact believe what their religions are telling them - why is there so much resistance and fear to *ultimately* going there?

Despite such resistance, we need to not only understand, but accept that we, as humans, do have a due-by-date. If people really did believe they're more fundamentally Spirit, and that their primary 'Home' is not of this earthly realm, then surely there would be less reluctance to finally go there? In turn, such a poor understanding of spiritual priorities does have huge repercussions on how we then live our life on planet Earth.

Living life as Spirit or just a body – makes a huge difference

If we could make this Inner shift to understanding that perhaps we are fundamentally more Energy than body, then how we perceive earthly life, and how to prioritize such a life – as a physical being - would also deeply shift. From such a Higher perspective, what would you focus on as being truly more important in a life Journey? How might you choose to focus differently on a range of life events and situations? How would you choose to interpret this earthly reality? Surely these sort of questions would be answered in a profoundly different way.

Certain writers such as Neale Donald Walsch and others have speculated that God, as an Energy Being of the Highest form, nevertheless is constantly changing and expanding in ever new, creative ways. What if we as humans – but really as *Spirit* in that very temporary phenomenon of a human form! - are equally driven to evolve and create? Then perhaps it is this which in turn generates our desire to grow in Spirit-wisdom or Consciousness. As mentioned previously, some of the things this fundamental Spirit aspect to us may want to learn about and grow skilled at needs a particular 'schoolroom' in which to most effectively learn. Perhaps one such underlying learning is to become more skilled at being able to Love - not just another specific person, but many people and situations under many different and challenging circumstances.

Within the range of our earthly teaching facilities mentioned before – schools, Colleges, Universities, etc. - each has its specialty lessons to offer. Perhaps so too with 'Planet Earth School'. What if this 'School' is *the* one where we truly learn to Love in the deepest sense of all – under *all* circumstances? So the primary aim in 'Earth School' is not actually about just accumulating wealth or power, or any of an endless range of other possible material objectives. Rather, it's about how much we can learn to Love – *despite* such human objectives or even more importantly, *through* such goals as accumulating wealth, power, etc. Hence there is nothing inherently wrong with money, power and materiality generally. It's more the *Consciousness* with which we engage in such goals and activities which is the fundamental issue. And over and above all these matters, it's ultimately about how Loving we can remain despite the challenges of so many Life circumstances.

Schoolroom set up to maximize learning – not to be changed

However, for this plane to truly become a valid 'schoolroom' in which to learn this lesson, it would of necessity have to be structured in a certain manner. It would precisely need to challenge us in such a way as to learn how to be open to, and express Love. It's not difficult to Love when we are feeling good or things are going well. But it's an entirely different thing once life isn't so co-operative anymore. Then our response all too easily can be something like anger, fear or closed-heartedness. So to really make the most of this plane and its learning opportunities, we need to change our way of perceiving things. One such fundamental change in perception could be to choose to recognize every event and circumstance in our lives as another opportunity in which to see *beyond* suffering or other challenging situations. Such a choice would allow us to respond to whatever is happening, but more through a spirit of Love.

Maya – or Illusion

This is where the Eastern concept of 'Maya' could be useful to the discussion. A fundamental belief in the Eastern religious or philosophical traditions is to acknowledge that all of life is ultimately nothing but an illusion, *through* which we can very powerfully grow in Spirit Consciousness. Much like a CyberGame as played out on a computer screen is on one hand an illusion, yet seems very 'real' as we play it. But for this paradigm of 'life-being-an-illusion' to work and empower us, it is important we first make an Inner shift of Awareness. Once that has been achieved, then it becomes possible to see our human life as an opportunity; one through which to become more deeply focused within our Spirit, and go *beyond* the suffering.

In this way, suffering is used as a powerful force through which to learn an equally powerful lesson in how to maintain our Centeredness, and stay 'In Love', never mind how painful, tragic or cruel our life scenario might be. Oh sure! So very easy to talk and philosophize about over a nice cup of tea. Yes; totally acknowledged. This is a most challenging perspective, not only to allow into our mental Awareness, but to then actualize into our moment-by-moment life situations too.

It's also completely admitted that despite all these rationalizations in dealing with the issue of suffering, and trying to make the best of a very human experience, one is still left with many unanswered questions about this distressing phenomenon. As much as we want rational, understandable answers, we are nevertheless left with a lot of mystery. When you look at this plane of reality, and see all the suffering that is occurring, and has gone on over the millennia of human existence, it is just so utterly, overwhelmingly *huge*. If there is indeed a purpose behind it all, it would need to be incredibly worthwhile to compensate or balance out all the anguish and pain that has had to go into achieving 'it' - whatever that 'it' may be. So ultimately, we're still left searching to give meaning to suffering, when suffering so often seems utterly beyond having any sense of meaning.

Planet Earth School – learn the lesson or cop 'the stick'

It would appear therefore that in 'Earth-School', one way to try and explain suffering is to see it as a potent way through which we are presented with a 'wake-up call' as we Journey through our life. Most of us aren't even aware of the possibility that we're *in* 'Earth-School', let alone that we may have been ignoring the 'lessons' set for us.

Yet that curriculum *needs* to be attended to. If we don't voluntarily choose to do the necessary 'study assignments', then from a Higher Level of Reality, there is a back-up system - one to ensure we don't totally waste a life on Earth either. Inevitably we are given many signals – although initially subtle ones – to 'wake' us up; to attract our attention to the need to do our 'homework'. But if we remain blind or deaf to such nudging from Spirit, then increasingly the Higher Realms will have to make use of more and more powerful 'signals', till we finally 'get it'. Unfortunately, most of the time, we humans are so closed off to this need to attend to our 'Earth-School lessons', that it takes an almighty final whack around the proverbial ears to get our attention!

Learning to express joy as we learn to love

As you think about all this, it would be very understandable if you found yourself cringing and closing down a bit. Not just from the possible need to now comprehend, but also at the thought of living life from this more alternate perspective. It almost seems as if we are somehow trying to validate - and even worse - give suffering a positive value. As if it is something to actually invite into our lives – god forbid! And indeed, many religions have created this sort of slant on suffering, from the standpoint that those who suffer hugely *now*, will gain so much *later* in 'heaven'; however that is perceived.

But another way to comprehend the issue of suffering is to choose to see how it can actually be used – *right now*. Suffering is something from which much can be gained, right here in our present daily life situation. Yet it all depends on the perspective you choose to predominantly focus on, and allow into your Consciousness, *from* which to then make certain choices in your day-to-day life circumstances.

In fact, let's play with all these ideas, and expand them out a bit further. A major aspect of Love is surely joy. The reality is that to truly learn how to live our lives through Love, we then also do need to learn how to choose to live our life through joy. In other words – and this is really crucial to take on-board! - it doesn't necessarily follow that to be able to learn our earthly 'lessons', we therefore also automatically have to open up to suffering.

If we allow ourselves to view life through the above 'lens', then it would seem that the primary lesson from absolutely anything life may throw at us is inevitably about how to open up more to Love. This is where we do have choice. When we find ourselves in a situation of suffering, we do at least have the potential of choosing to remain as Conscious as possible. In this way, we should also be more able to pick up on what the 'learning' is within the suffering. And if, by remaining more Awake we also remain more self-motivated to get on with the 'lesson', so too the need for life to clobber us around the ears is minimized.

Hence, learning within Earth-School really doesn't automatically have to be via suffering. We can truly also learn through joy, as long as we remain open and alert to the fact that:-

- we are indeed in 'Earth-School'
- there is a curriculum we have signed up for [1]
- such curriculums definitely do need to be attended to.

So the more pro-active we are in being aware that there are 'lessons' to be done, so too the less Life - or the Higher Realms - will need to come along and whack us into action or Awareness.

Hence looking at life here on planet Earth from these alternate perspectives does provide at least the potential for a totally different way of starting to live our life. The very essence of what it means to be alive on this plane may therefore not be quite what we normally take it to be. Rather, it may have more to do with simply learning how to be the Highest expression of Love possible in any moment, and in every possible situation. We may also find that any judgment of how we manage in this life Journey will be based more on how much we were able to maintain this Awareness. In other words, to what extent were we able to live each moment as much as possible, in and through Love, *despite* whatever else we did, or had happen to us.

A human life = training ground for learning how to Love

So this plane of reality could be perceived as purely and simply a training ground for learning how to experience all the multi-faceted aspects to Love. It's a realm in which we can learn to generate Love as well as learn how to express it – not only to others – but also to ourselves under *every* conceivable circumstance; even when this involves situations such as torture chambers; concentration camps; loss of a child due to accident or health issue; or so many other of life's nightmares. Now there's a huge challenge! Something we'll continue to explore later on.

Remember, it's not so much about whether we actually *achieve* this potentiality. It has more to do with whether we choose to at least *aim* for such a goal. Setting the intention, and backing it up with our best efforts - that's all that's ultimately required of us. Whether we in fact attain such a lofty goal is essentially beside the point.

Ways to learn to Love

One way in which we all can start to do this is to choose not to solely focus on the negative side of everything in life so much; the suffering. Rather, we need to understand that all the so-called negativity and awful events occurring all around us are primarily nothing else but a 'play performed on Earth-stage'. The challenge is to keep coming from Love – *despit*e whatever is happening. People do exist who have been through the most dreadful situations of suffering and torture, be that at the hands of the Nazis, Pol Pot or a vast range of other destructive and evil dictators or regimes. Yet, a few of these people who endured such awful life situations, either chose - or finally came to a Space in their later life - where they were able to see beyond the human drama of the suffering and torture they underwent. Instead, they focused more on the opportunity which those horrible life circumstances provided them - circumstances *through* which they were able to remain in a true Love mode, never mind how awful their suffering had been.

This occurred en-masse in post-Apartheid South Africa via the 'Truth and Reconciliation Commission' headed by Archbishop Desmond Tutu, starting in March 1996. Obviously, such unconditional forgiving in the face of all the suffering that happened in Apartheid South Africa is not easy to do, and most humans – myself included – would find this really challenging. Yet it is all about perspective and choice. How do we *choose* to see the situation, and how do we *choose* to respond to it? As victim – and validly so? Or to go beyond being the victim to our life events, thus allowing for a deep and profound Inner Healing and Consciousness Growth to occur?

Now, let's take the discussion a bit further again, and continue the 'fantasy trip'. Remember too, it's not actually about whether all this is definitely, absolutely True or not. Instead, the objective is to see if there is some way in which we can build a platform from which we can acknowledge the suffering within our human existence, yet explain or manage this 'reality' in the most empowering manner possible. And remember, explanations such as this are not going to suit everyone, so it is totally O.K. if this doesn't initially sit well or may never sit well with you. For some, these 'explanations' may just be too outrageous to accept as a possibility. But for now, how about we continue 'playing' with these 'fantasy ideas' and see where it takes us? Hopefully, by the end of the book you might be surprised!

So, one aspect of life we might have to come to grips with is the possibility that the nature of the 'schoolroom' is basically 'hard-wired' into the very fabric of this reality. It is actually beyond fundamental change. In fact, it needs to be so. If you intend to learn certain 'lessons', then it would also make sense that the 'schoolroom' provides certain parameters, allowing a specific style of 'learning' to occur. If you want to learn to fly, you need to have a flying machine, not a boat or a train or something else; and similarly with this life and reality here.

No point in primarily changing externals; better to focus on internals

If this is indeed the way the system is set up here on planet Earth, then trying to change our fundamental human reality by *only* making the changes 'out there', becomes a totally hopeless and inappropriate task. What may need to occur is for us to simply accept that this is how the system or 'classroom' needs to be. What we're then required to do is to use the 'classroom' in the most productive way possible.

Perhaps our primary option is to focus on how we can most change *ourselves* during this earthly, human experience. The aim therefore, is not about how much we were able to change our *outer* reality before we morph back into our essential Spirit Reality. Instead, it has far more to do with how much we were able to alter our *Inner* reality. To what extent were we able to use the events and circumstances which are so essentially 'human' to this earthly experience, as the catalyst to such Inner change?

Humans change more on the technological and informational levels

It's not about discounting that there have been many people who have done amazing things, which have allowed for deep change to occur to a vast range of external situations – be that in religion, science, medicine or society. But when we look at human history, fundamentally; on the deepest core level of our humanity, nothing seems to actually change, despite superficial appearances.

Hate, ego, power, greed, manipulation, corruption, war, etc. continue to occur within us as humans, although the historical, technological and geographical 'stages' on which these qualities have been played out have changed a lot over the millennia of human existence. For instance, in the West we may no longer have the sanctioned human slavery we once had.

And it is true that from a technological and knowledge perspective, much has changed over the years and centuries. We can fly to the moon, the outer edges of the solar system, and beyond. In fact so much technological growth and change is occurring nowadays, that people can barely keep up with it all.

But for all this heightened level of supposed modern sophistication, are we any more humane towards each other - or ourselves? It would appear that although the 'stage' upon which life is 'played' may be different from era to era, the 'drama' being enacted is but a variation on a theme. Still, the same ol' passions – anger, lust, fear, hatred, jealousy, spite, betrayal... all too frequently degenerating into this incessant need to fight each other. And war remains the most horrific phenomenon that we as humans engage in, during which the most heinous things are suddenly 'legitimately' done in the name of 'god' or country!

Technology 'doth not a better human maketh'

The problem is that we have confused technological advancement with fundamental, Inner human soul advancement. Yes, our science and medicine, and its repercussions on human life have changed beyond all recognition –

especially in the last 100 years. Yes, we now have planetary organizations like the United Nations, NATO, WHO and so many others, all with a major aim of curbing negative human behavior. Unfortunately, the reality is that so much still remains lip-service to the concept of 'human rights', and all too frequently is over-ridden by political rather than true human needs. One role such organizations do try to undertake is mopping up the mess after we humans have yet again lost the plot, and done things to each other which are unspeakable in their barbarity and horror.

Through such organizations, we are certainly able to respond to humanitarian disasters – like the huge tsunamis of December '04 – with amazing power, skill, compassion, co-operation and sophistication. It is ironic that by the same token, we are also capable of remaining callous or closed towards catastrophic life events occurring elsewhere; for example, the many human tragedies equally unfolding in various areas of Africa, Burma or Palestine. Why is there not a similarly potent and compassionate outpouring of help for these circumstances as was seen with the tsunamis of '04?

Why *can* we response so magnificently in one arena of human catastrophe, yet remain seemingly heartless to others of equal suffering? Is it that some are just more 'politically correct' to deal with, and others not? It's not as if the money wasn't there to begin with. Just look at the billions we were recently willing to spend in saving our economic necks, after the late '08 economic meltdown!

Peter Gomes, in 'The Scandalous Gospel of Jesus',[2] puts it succinctly when he states that there have never been more Bibles in the hands of more people, than there are today. Nevertheless, this fact has not automatically brought humanity closer to a deeper understanding of spiritual matters, let alone *living* from a more spiritual basis.

Indeed, there seems to be more war, skirmishes, killings and other atrocities occurring now, on indeed a *planetary* level, than ever before, and ironically these are far too often stirred up by various religions, and their intolerances of each other. These conflicts are also occurring despite our so-called greater sophistication in understanding the concept that all humans have certain inalienable rights.

It is therefore relatively easy to draw the conclusion that religion – let alone politics or cultural 'advancements' - has not facilitated any *fundamental* changes to our dysfunctional human nature over the millennia of our existence.

Religion especially, has certainly not been the overall solution to our human condition here on planet Earth. In fact, it has too often been a major instigator in magnifying those human qualities which are so capable of causing grief and anguish to ourselves.

Our role is not to change the fundamentals of 'Planet Earth School'

Hence, in trying to deal with the reality of all the suffering that is occurring on this earthly plane, it may serve us better to shift our belief systems or focus, from externally orientated problem solving, to looking at what we, as humans, need to change within ourselves. This is the more important, deep and fundamental change which needs to occur. It's not about putting our primary focus on changing this outer, earthly plane – be that via religious or political philosophies. Those approaches have never provided any truly *lasting* solution within the known history of humanity anyway.

If the concept of 'Planet Earth School' is correct, then this plane of reality is not able or meant to be *fundamentally* changed. It has been pre-programmed this way, precisely because this is the nature of this particular 'classroom'. Only by being as it is, can it thereby provide the right environment for the particular 'curriculum' offered on 'Planet Earth School'. If this is so, then those basic aspects about its nature are unlikely to change in any fundamental way – never mind how hard we try. It would be like changing the most basic nature of a University or school, and still expecting it to be able to serve its primary educational functions through the altered format.

However, using this metaphor of Earth as a 'school', it nevertheless needs to be acknowledged that within our more human sphere of teaching and learning, there has been at least some evolution in the way teaching occurs nowadays, compared to centuries ago. Time has allowed for much more sophisticated techniques to develop, with enhanced learning outcomes. So too with the 'planet Earth School' concept. Hopefully it is possible, through a lot of focused and externalized effort, for humanity to make some alterations to how that 'School' is set up or operates.

Nevertheless, *fundamentally*, 'planet Earth School' may have certain limits to its changeability, and hence the suggestion in this discussion that we become less fixated on altering the externals of our reality, *as our primary and sole focus*.

We may achieve much better and far greater strides in 'learning', by instead focusing our attention on first making *internal*, more Spirit-orientated change.

On one level, it's as if this plane of reality is in fact a sort of hell – at least for many humans experiencing life here. And that is unlikely to fundamentally change. What can be done is to help better empower *people* as they struggle within this 'hell'. So perhaps the focus should be to help *people* make change *within* themselves first – as well as *then* focusing on changing this outer, earthly plane of reality.

The paradox is of course, that the more we humans can truly make genuine and lasting *Inner* change, so too it *will* become possible for the external 'hell' to start to alter as well – for the better. But for such a fundamental and *enduring* external change to occur within our human realm, we humans also need to *fundamentally* transform ourselves on *Inner* levels, in a *permanent* fashion, subsequently extending into future generations.

Need to change the 'game plan'

However, the fact that it seems only *Inner* change will have any lasting or meaningful effect, does not then mean that we allow dictators to run wild; allow industry to continue to destroy the environment or allow religious bigotry to reign free. *It's crucial to understand that what is being discussed here is not a simple either/or situation.* Both the Inner, as well as the outer, earthly aspects to life need to be addressed. It's just that for so long, we humans seem to have muddled our priorities. Perhaps it is high time to re-assess what needs to become our main focus.

The way we have traditionally made such a choice is by focusing primarily – if not solely – on changing the 'outer'. Nevertheless, we still need to work as hard, and with as much focus as ever to make the needed outer changes, always understanding however, that our *primary* or sole agenda should not actually be about creating these *outer* changes. Rather, it is about working on those *outer* aspects, with the intention of creating *Inner* change first. Ironically, this tack will have far more chance of then facilitating true and lasting change to be reflected in our outer reality. We will return to this point when we discuss deeper aspects to the Creative Visualization process in future chapters.

Changing paradigms can be challenging

Accepting that nothing really changes fundamentally in our human condition may seem like a hopeless stance to take. But actually, this is not necessarily so, particularly if we can accept that the basic aim isn't essentially about trying to change our outer reality as the *sole* agenda within our existence. In fact, remaining focused only on making change *externally* is inevitably doomed to failure, repeated disappointment and disillusionment; certainly in the long-run.

Sure, it may take several decades to show this failure, as happened with communism, and so many other social systems which were imposed on entire cultures in the name of solving our fundamental human dilemma. It would appear from history repeating itself ad nauseum that this is not the way to go. Expecting outer change to somehow magically solve our human tendency to dysfunction obviously hasn't worked. Perhaps it is time we accept that it *can't* work!

Are any of these ideas really true or valid? Well, the only thing that needs to be focused on is that here you are in whatever life situation you find yourself. Next, let's assume that it is somehow your Spirit Being or Higher Self who has orchestrated your life for a reason; inevitably to do with something you chose to learn – pre-incarnationally - to provide you with the opportunity to further grow in Consciousness. Then the strange thing is that the most productive way of solving life's dilemmas would in fact not be to fight them; to ignore them or just wish them to go away; but rather to just BE with them. So, let's explore this concept of 'just Being' a bit deeper; a concept, which on the surface, seems to promise more a sense of stultification than progression within our lives.

'Being' with the 'problem' rather than wrestling with it

A strange thing happens when you make the effort, and take the time to do this Inner re-focus of 'Being' with a problem, rather than automatically trying to wrestle it into submission or resolution. Just sitting for a while with whatever situation you feel stuck in, without necessarily struggling with it, often starts to shift it to a more comfortable level. But the more you fight or try to avoid it, the harder it all seems to become. This is simply because the objective of your Spirit Being or Higher Self is not necessarily and primarily about 'fixing' whatever the *outer* 'problem' appears to be. Rather, the objective was to see how we would *respond* to the situation. From a Love perspective or from a non-Love perspective, with the latter generating all those emotions already talked about, such as grief, anger, disappointment, jealousy, rage, hatred and so much more.

It's true that it may seem very easy to simply write about all this stuff! In my own Journey, there are many times when life throws me into situations where I fight and struggle and avoid or procrastinate... whatever. So no, I haven't got it all together either, and I'm still very much on a learning curve – along with everyone else. But what it does initially require for that Inner shift to occur is to come to a point of some sort of recognition and *acceptance* of how things are - *right now*. Even though we may not *like* it one little bit. However, once *that* shift has occurred, suddenly it seems to become more possible for things to start to fall into place. Subsequently, whatever the external 'problem' may be, it frequently seems to 'resolve' itself so much more easily.

Choosing to see what can be learned from a life situation

An interesting exercise therefore, would be to look at any particular painful or difficult life situations you may presently find yourself in... but from this alternative perspective. Let's assume your Higher Self knows exactly what the Inner or Consciousness 'learning' needs to be, and that the present 'suffering' is instead a perfect 'opportunity' through which to achieve this learning objective. Initially, this angle definitely requires a huge dose of faith! But then again, this is a quality which we can all tap into, and enhance with persistent practise, along with a deep Inner trust that there is some greater level of Benevolence at work here on planet Earth.

For instance, you may be having some problems at work. Your boss may be particularly 'challenging' – or let's just call them plain nasty; a boss who is forever giving you hell. Now it could be that there are things you need to change in your work; your attitude... or whatever. However, it could also be that you are in fact doing your job correctly on every level, but that your situation has more to do with some deeper and possibly unconscious aspects playing themselves out. Perhaps, due to the way you were brought up, or things you experienced in your childhood, you may have been left with a tendency to expect people in authority to give you a hard time; endless variations and scenarios are possible. But in this example, it's interesting that this boss – as so many other bosses in the past – is doing just that. Again!

One way to deal with it could be to change jobs. Also... again! But strangely, every time you do, within no time at all you find yourself battling with the same sort of boss-orientated problems as before, no matter how good it may have looked initially, and as hopeful as you were that the pattern would finally change. Your boss is now a totally different person, in a different company, perhaps even in a different city – but the same issues are still occurring. Has changing the job - your *external* reality - truly changed the underlying situation? Or may it be better to just sit with the pain for a while, and figure out what *you* may need to change *within* yourself?

It's not about blame - it is about empowerment !

Remember too, this is *absolutely not about now **blaming** yourself.* It *is* about trying to empower yourself to once and for all break this repetitive cycle; a cycle which has been going on in your life so often now; and frankly... you're no doubt simply 'over it'! You may have repeatedly tried the former approach of just changing jobs, and hence bosses, with no real lasting success. Perhaps it's time to do it a different way, using a totally different focus and approach.

Why not look at your situation at the moment as a sort of temporary 'Life Assignment', but one which needs to be completed, or 'lived out' within the context of your present job situation? This goes far beyond 'bosses' of course. Any repetitive situation you find in your life – be that bosses, relationships or other challenges – could now qualify for a radically different approach to solving the problem. After all, the way you've been trying to do it hasn't really worked out, so why not try something else?

It seems all too often that if you try to avoid the 'lesson' - even if you're not sure exactly what the 'lesson' is all about – then life's response is to come along with a bigger 'stick' to poke or nudge you to where you need to go. Observation of life tends to suggest that it is better to initially just accept whatever situation you find yourself in; to accept at least for now - however long that 'now' needs to be.

Try to understand and see it from as High a Consciousness perspective as possible, and try to figure out what it is you need to learn. This may involve some deep, meaningful and very truthful conversations with specific, trusted and Loving friends - people in your life who are not afraid to tell you certain 'home truths', compassionately and without going into 'blame mode'. But then, you also need to listen to what they have to say. So often, when we finally are being told such 'home-truths', we may also have a tendency to block them, by trying to 'explain' or rationalize those behaviors of ours being reflected back to us.

Make a decision to say nothing; don't even attempt to vindicate yourself. Just listen to what they are telling you, whether you agree with it or not. Let it in; take it away with you; have a good think about what they've told you, and only then respond... if you even need to at this later point.

Or it may involve seeing a Counselor for a while, to try and understand your pattern from a more Conscious perspective. This no doubt will be challenging and possibly painful. It could involve finally acknowledging and accepting the less-than-functional ways you might be using to interact with others; what you say; what you do. But all this could also allow you to liberate yourself from life-long patterns which are precisely the cause of so much of your pain. At least give this concept a go before jumping right in and changing jobs – for the umpteenth time. Going into 'action'; changing jobs for example, may be a valid response. But only *after* you've sat with the problem for a while, and tried to understand the deeper layers to it.

Choosing to respond to life, rather than just react

Realize, that a good place to start in such situations is to really focus on where you are at. What is it that you don't like, and how can you try to come to grips with it all? How can you find a Space of Inner Calm *despite* the challenging situations you might find yourself in? One reason we dread suffering so much, with its attendant chaos and change, is because we fear not being in control of our life process. Later, this book will be exploring ways to give you back a greater sense of control. But for now, it is important to realize that we always retain a measure of control by how we *respond* to our life process, rather than via our more unconscious 'knee-jerk' *reactions*.

One powerful way to help us deal with this is to assume or play the 'game' of reincarnation. This 'game' presupposes that we have in fact pre-incarnationally orchestrated a Journey with all sorts of events from which to grow in Consciousness. So, do we simply stay stuck with endlessly fighting our problem situations, ignoring them or just wishing they would go away? That would be a bit like signing up for a course at College, and then spending every moment of attendance, fighting and avoiding the lessons being presented!

Perhaps your present life situation was set up *precisely* to test how you would either react or respond to these life scenarios. From ego self or Higher Spirit Self? In other words, how much is your response from fear, and how much from

Love? Here we need to remain focused on that fundamental understanding that we are primarily *Spirit* – temporarily incarnated within the physical.

Making the change internally – and give it time

To continue with the job example, perhaps give yourself a goal of say three to six months, where you really focus on getting into 'The Flow' of whatever is challenging you at work, but responding to it from a Higher level. Try to *respond* – i.e. a Conscious 'reaction' - to each confronting situation that occurs. Do so from a Love aspect, which is also more congruent with coming from a Higher Self Space, rather than *reacting* – i.e. an *un*conscious 'outcome'. Reacting is inevitably fueled by the more primary emotion of fear, and in turn, this primary emotion spawns a plethora of negative states such as jealousy, hatred, irritability, anger, bitterness, judgment, suspicion, malice, power-play, and so on.

The problem is that taking action via fear predictably generates further fear-based reactions from your 'opponent'. Just try the above approach for a while - as an experiment - and see where it takes you. But firstly acknowledge that the 'problem' being experienced *externally* may indeed be originating from some emotional wounding or destructive pattern acting out from *within* you – albeit unconsciously. How about temporarily accepting the situation as it is, rather than remaining closed to or battling it via your usual techniques, inescapably driven by your own range of more base emotions, as listed above?

Keep in mind that what is definitely *not* being suggested or insinuated here is that this now makes 'them' right and you 'wrong'. Using the above approaches doesn't suddenly vindicate what your boss may be doing to you; or your work mates; or your partner; or your children; or your.....

This way of dealing with your day-to-day problems also allows for life to change from an endless string of 'problems' and 'obstacles', into a series of adventures, possibilities and *opportunities*. It's about giving yourself a chance to see if you can generate a feeling of being at Peace, precisely where you are within your life, by focusing on making *internal* change first. What we normally do is to think that... 'if only I was......., or could......... *then* I'd be happy'. Altering the way we look at and approach our life situations, makes it incumbent upon us to work more on finding happiness within ourselves – never mind where we are at right now in our life. By the same token, we also need to keep reminding ourselves that things can change, and we're not doomed to be in this job forever, or whatever the life-situation may be.

Anyway, these are just some opening thoughts on how we could change our life sufferings by first making an *Inner* shift in Consciousness. More detailed techniques will be explored as the book continues.

Spirit in 'Planet Earth School

Recapping, then, it seems that one possible way of looking at life on planet Earth is to see us *fundamentally, primarily*, as Spirits; not just as humans. We need to go far beyond most religions' almost begrudging acknowledgement of some sort of Spirit aspect to us as humans. This shift in emphasis is crucial if we want to make any sense of the discussion here.

Let's assume then, that it's our primary Self, as Spirit, which decides to incarnate into this realm so as to be able to enroll in an infinite number of scenarios. Each chosen life Journey contains the essential components necessary to learn the 'subjects' we'd like to 'enroll' in while on 'planet Earth school.' But this means we not only need the right curriculum, but also precisely the right 'schoolroom' in which to learn these desired 'lessons'.

So let's continue this present little fantasy trip a bit further. What if we all got together – as a group of Energy or Spirit Beings, within the Energy or Spirit Realms - and discussed the various 'topics' we'd like to 'study' within 'planet Earth School'. As this discussion evolves, we realize that there are many points of overlap within the group, where the circumstances one Spirit wants to explore and learn about, could in fact be beautifully provided by the earthly role another Spirit Being wants to engage in.

After much discussion and planning, it may be that we find ourselves, as Spirit Beings, having designated and chosen the various 'roles' we wish to 'play' on Earth Stage or Earth School. One Spirit may have chosen a 'curriculum' of experiencing what it would be like to be born a Caucasian male, in a strict Christian family with many other siblings; a family run by a dominating, inflexible and racially bigoted father who had very fixed ideas about the 'wrongs' of inter-racial marriages.

This was a father who – from his own wounding and lessons to be learnt - was incapable of showing any sense of openness to his son, who had fallen in love with an Islamic, Somalian woman, and was intent on marrying her. The son was also in the process of converting to Islam; another factor which drew his father's wrath.

This situation created immense strife within the family, setting up father against son and mother; brother against sister. The pressure on this particular son to stay true to his family's religion, let alone to dump his bride-to-be was overwhelming.

Planning the earthly 'drama'

However, let's take this fantasy trip a bit further again, because we're heading towards an important conclusion. After this discussion, you might come to an understanding which could greatly empower the way you choose to perceive or manage your life very differently in the future.

Let's assume this sort of 'incarnation game' is a possibility. If this is so, then the Spirit wanting to 'play' the role of this Caucasian, Christian male, growing up in this strictly religious, prejudiced family, with such a father, etc. etc... *would also need someone in the Spirit realm to 'play' the 'role' of that rather challenging father!*

And indeed it turns out there was one of Its 'Spirit friends' who had a whole list of things they wished to learn too. About not being so inflexible; about learning to broaden their horizons on religious and racial matters; on being able to accept that each person has the right to their own life – even if this doesn't match up with a parent's expectations; and much more. A perfect match!

So after further discussion and planning within the Spirit Realms, it is then arranged that one Spirit will 'play' the child; one the father; one the mother; others the various brothers and sisters, and one the Somalian woman. Each has their overlapping agendas, which can provide them with amazing opportunities to grow in skill, wisdom, and ultimately Consciousness. A particular historical era is chosen within which to play out these earthly roles. The right type of physical 'vehicles', or bodies are chosen for the 'trip'. A basic Journey plan is organized, and once all is set we each in turn incarnate into our respective earthly 'suits' or 'vehicles'. All in just the right sequence to be able to become the father, the mother, the son, the Somalian woman, and so on.

What is there to learn – rather than blame

The whole point of this discussion is not so much whether this is all true or not. The question is yet again... 'could it be a *useful* concept, within the uncertainties and inconsistencies of this human life'? Could such ideas provide

Chapter 4 - Meaning of Life

a way through which we could choose to see our earthly situations in a more empowering manner'?

For instance, let's look at the above example of that male Caucasian. Later in his life, after he went ahead and converted to Islam, as well as marrying the Somalian woman, he suffered a lot of emotional wounding from having been disowned by his family. How could he, now as an adult, choose to see his situation differently? What alternative perspective on his life could provide a construct which allows him to break free from still having to blame his father for so much of the pain in his life?

Instead, he could *choose* to see his family and personal life situation, especially in regard to his father, as circumstances filled with immense opportunities; a situation where much suffering may indeed have occurred... but much was also learnt. However, the most powerful shift of all occurs if he can also see his father more from his *Spirit* aspect, rather than focusing just on the *human* role that Spirit had agreed to 'play out' - pre-incarnationally. And something magical happens when this son does make this Inner, perceptual shift!

Rather than continuing to judge his father as that cranky, bigoted, difficult-to-live with old man, he can now *choose* to see his father from the Spirit aspect - a Spirit 'friend' from the Higher Realms who Loved the 'son' Spirit so much that It was willing to play out this most challenging, seemingly negative human role. In other words, that Spirit was willing to play out the 'father' role, purely out of Love for Its Spirit friend from the Higher Realms, who is concurrently choosing to incarnate as the 'son'. So the 'father' Spirit was willing to be seen – within the earthly realms - as this rather negative human being, yet had the primary objective of providing the ideal human life opportunities for the 'son' Spirit, to learn *Its* 'planet Earth School' lessons!

How's that for a mind-twister! You might have to read that above paragraph a few times, but can you see how this alternate perspective totally changes how the 'son' may now be able to interact and deal with his 'father'? Simply by *choosing* to see a human situation from the *Spirit* perspective in this way, also allows for a profound revision of how that human scenario is subsequently understood and responded to. It makes it so much easier to now come from a Space of Love, rather than the previous sense of anger and abandonment.

If one wants to learn independence, self esteem, learning to trust one's own perspectives on life, rather than just accepting what any particular religion or other authority specifies is the only way to live one's life, then the above family situation would indeed provide the perfect 'schoolroom' within which to do so. And that father who seems on the surface to be such a challenging and difficult person to get on with, is in fact nothing else but one of our 'Spirit friends' from the Higher Realms - one who was kind, considerate and Loving enough to offer to 'play' this harsh 'role', *precisely* so that a range of 'lessons' could be learned by the Spirit 'playing' the 'Caucasian, Christian son' role.

There has been a tendency in recent counseling techniques, especially the more New Agey ones, to try and figure out why we may seem to be so dysfunctional in our lives. Who did what to whom, and therefore who is to blame ultimately for how we may now be so 'scarred' or 'damaged'? It's one valid way of trying to create a sense of order or understanding in a life which may otherwise seem confusing, and not going as well as one may wish.

But coming from this perspective also far too often sets up a situation of the 'blame game', where the problem is then made to lie primarily *outside* of us; with our mother, our father, our religion, our schooling, our culture, that priest... and endlessly on. As well as endlessly disempowering, because from this perspective, the problem is seen as being *that* father, *that* mother, *that* molesting teacher or priest. It all happened; it can't be denied. And there is no attempt being made here to belittle the horror of some of these events or the very real trauma they definitely created in a person's life. It's not about *condoning* what may have happened. But how does one *now* go about Healing these past circumstances in a more *empowering* way?

Shifting our focus can also shift the 'problem'

However, if we look at our present life scenarios through the lens of the above 'fantasy' discussion, then perhaps we do have a far greater role to play in how our lives unfold than we're generally willing to admit. In fact, who we are as humans, and who we interact with – both positively and negatively – in any particular life, has all been carefully staged. These choices were made precisely so as to maximize our ability to really learn certain lessons.

If this is correct, then suddenly, those people in our lives formerly seen as the *source* of our 'problems', can now be *chosen* to be viewed from a much more compassionate and empowering perspective. This is not necessarily an easy perspective, but definitely a point of view which sees those challenging role players – be that the father, the mother, the teacher, the priest... whoever – to actually be those Spirit friends. Friends who so loved us that they were willing to play out what often seems like a rather nasty role here on planet Earth.

Let's hammer it home one more time. In other words, *we are all fundamentally Spirit Beings – not humans!* Our human phase is nothing but a very ephemeral and brief interlude in the overall existence of us as Spirit Beings. Really try to take this on-board. Making this almost primordial, deep, elemental Inner shift as to who we *truly* are, also allows for gigantic and incredibly empowering ways in which to then deal with our earthly experiences here.

Forgiving is not the same as condoning

So many people seem to have truly horrible things happen to them, leaving them deeply wounded on emotional levels, and in turn stultifying their present lives. They may have done much therapy to try to get beyond their pain; to resolve their life dilemmas so they can live from a space of greater peace, fulfillment and happiness. Yet, all too often the wounds remain open and festering.

Yes, this chapter may have been nothing but a rather far-out flight of fantasy. But if we *can* somehow use the above concepts, this could in turn allow for a different perspective on our present pain and emotional wounds; one through which it becomes perhaps easier to forgive the past. Surely this makes 'playing' such 'games' worth it?

However, for some people, there may still be a semantic problem blocking their ability to forgive. *We need to understand that forgiveness is not about condoning!*

What may have been done to you, or life situations which came your way, may indeed seem beyond forgiveness. But not letting go of this pain or anger only allows it to continue to 'burn'... precisely perpetuating the pain. It was once said that anger or resentment is like a burning hot coal, which we pick up to throw at another. Trouble is... the one picking up that burning 'coal' is the first to get burnt.

So to forgive is to finally let go of that burning 'coal', which has been actually burning deeply into *us*. Over and above the original pain inflicted by whatever circumstances we may still be so angry or hurt by!

Forgiveness is ultimately about a Healing of *self*. The concept that forgiveness is being done for another, is actually the wrong way around. Forgiveness is very important because it allows *us* to become Whole and Healed again. When there is something in our lives; some person, some event that we cannot forgive, it becomes like a hole in a bucket through which our Life force – and our joy ultimately – leaks out.

Forgiveness is about blocking that hole, and thus keeping our joy and Life-Force within our own container. So, forgiving is in one way a selfish thing to do; but a good 'selfish' thing. It has the 'side-effect' if you like, of also releasing the other person or painful situation. But primarily forgiveness is about Healing and Wholing ourselves.

Nevertheless, let it be said again... when you forgive someone or something that occurred in your life, *that does not in any way condone what happened*. Yet, so often we get these two things terribly mixed up, and feel we can't forgive because it would somehow validate or condone the awful things which happened to us. For some people, such forgiveness can make it almost seem as if *they* were the 'wrong-doer', rather than having had the wrong done to them!

Playing our incarnational roles on 'Earth stage'

So in summary, let's look at it via the analogy of going to see a Shakespearean play in a theatre. During the play itself, the actors on a stage may end up saying and doing the most horrible or shocking things to each other. Nevertheless, as a member of the audience, and despite the authenticity with which the actors are performing, there is another aspect of you which does retain an Awareness that this is in the end only a 'play' - as convincing as the play may be, and as much as we may have become utterly seduced into it.

However, what if we correlate this analogy to what is actually happening here on planet Earth, via our incarnational lives? Pre-incarnationally, we may have chosen our roles; then we 'dive' down into and play out our 'roles', which might be from axe-murderer to saint. And in that interaction, we as players on this stage of life do say and do things to each other, which may indeed be shocking and horrible.

But just as with the Shakespearian play, once off stage, none of the actors feels any need to apologize or make-up to their fellow actors. Backstage, everyone involved in the play knows that it was all a play, and that never mind what was said or done, none of it was obviously meant in a real-life sense. Each actor was only performing their part of the play with skill and impeccability. It is simply understood that it was all nothing but 'play-acting'!

Forgiveness is not necessarily easy – even with this new perspective

And so too as we engage in this human Journey of life. We should try – along with those others who are Conscious enough – to play our 'games' impeccably. But we also need to remain Aware enough so as not to totally fall for the ultimate Illusion – or Maya – of it all. We need to retain enough Awareness and understanding that if *they* say or do something hurtful, then it is more an issue which *we* need to resolve. Normally, we tend to solely point the finger at *them* as being the 'source of our problem', a conclusion which may seem on the surface to be a real and valid one.

We need to remember that within this world-view, they are just playing the 'game' superbly – albeit unconsciously. And we, having explored the above concepts, hopefully are now able to come from a more Aware status, and should not take life events so personally. Instead, we could choose to accept that any event which happens is an opportunity to find out something about ourselves, thus growing a bit further in Consciousness, but more on that later.

Once we can allow ourselves to see through the 'drag' of the other players, it becomes easier to relax, let go and forgive, especially if we can really 'get it', that in fact we specifically *asked* their Spirit aspect – pre-incarnationally - to play these roles! This is not to say that such forgiveness, from our *human* perspective, is going to be easy to achieve – even once we have shifted our focus and perceptions along the above lines. The unspeakable horrors perpetrated by the Nazis – or any other oppressive faction or dictatorial regime – would appear at first glance to be impossible to forgive. Yet, enough people do exist who have been able to do so. A classic example is Nelson Mandela, but some Jewish survivors of the concentration camps, as well as many other examples, do exist.

Breaking through the illusion – the Maya – allows us to shift in the 'game'

Expect too, that when one 'player' in the Game of Life sees through the Illusion of it all, they can then move their Consciousness up to a Higher level. From that Higher perspective, they can decide they don't want to continue playing the 'game' between themselves and another 'actor' anymore - at least not from the so-called 'normal', human and therefore *unconscious* levels. However, unless the person they are interacting with has a simultaneous and similar insightful Consciousness shift, expect them to possibly react quite strongly, and 'negatively'. In a sense, it's almost as if you've decided you no longer want to 'dance' with them, and end up leaving them standing – by themselves – on the 'dance floor'. They will more likely than not try like crazy to manipulate you back into the 'dance'.

You might like to discuss your present problem with them from these new points of view. But be aware that not many will be able to understand what you're going on about! In fact, it could make the situation even worse or they'll just think you've gone stark, raving mad. Understand that possibility. And if this is the most likely response, then don't even share such information with them. However, at such a point in *your* Journey, it becomes vital for you to retain that Higher Awareness, and act appropriately from it.

Remain strong enough to now *not* buy into the other's attempt to get you back onto that 'dance floor', continuing what on one level may well be a pretty awful, messy 'dance'. Retain your Centre; maintain your point of power, and simply *choose* not to 'play' in the way you were doing before. Having a deeper understanding of the dynamics of it all, perhaps your best response may be to walk away from the situation. What the other does with your action is their business, and should not influence *your* decision. In fact, within the act of you now 'walking out' of the 'game', may lie a karmic, or pre-incarnationally chosen lesson for *them* to learn from. However, from your deeper level of Awareness, it should now also be easier to remain in a Space of compassion towards them – even if you leave them to 'dance' alone on the 'dance floor' of planet Earth.

But isn't all this just a fantasy trip?

So, once again, if playing a 'fantasy game' can also bring forth a deep Inner shift, which in turn allows at least for the possibility to also shift a long-standing emotional wound into a more Healing phase, then surely such 'game-playing' is valid? Remember the fundamental mantra of this book… 'it's not so much about whether something is True or not. The only question we need to ask ourselves is… is it *useful'?* And if it is useful, then why not 'play' with the concept – whatever it may be - to allow that Inner Healing and greater sense of self empowerment?

Or would you rather retain the so-called 'normal, politically correct and accepted' views of what this life is all about, meanwhile also remaining more the victim to your life situations? The latter can indeed serve us in some ways – usually in dysfunctional ways. But such approaches certainly don't allow us to tap into that power to move forward more productively with our lives. The choice is ultimately ours!

Life is not the same once you open Pandora's box

For many, no doubt this discussion has not been a particularly easy Journey. It's also important to realize that even if you do find it reasonable, and it all hangs together in some weird way, once you start to open this Pandora's Box, things will never be quite the same again. As you change on these Inner levels; as your perspectives modify; many previous ways of dealing with your life situations all start to transform as well, be that in your job, your relationships, your friendships, and so much more.

Unfortunately, once we start this Inner Journey of Soul Growth, we do find that certain things on the outer plane don't seem to quite work as they used to. Or we find that what we used to be really turned on by, now simply no longer has any attraction or 'pull' for us. It's as if we've outgrown the capacity to play certain 'games', much like a child who is no longer interested in the toys they once so happily played with.

These various transition phases you may start to find yourself in can also be rather disturbing, unsettling and confusing. This is especially so if you can't yet clearly see or understand exactly what is actually taking place *within* you - and which is therefore also reflected in your *external* reality.

Stepping stones on the journey

The problem is that in the initial phase of this Journey of Awakening, you'll more likely continue for some time yet to see your various life 'situations' through the old, long-habituated perceptions. You'll no doubt continue to try and solve your problems using the only ways you are really familiar with; the way 'you've always done it'. But increasingly, this will have to change, as you leave your former patterns behind you. When we haven't quite let go of our old patterns yet, plus the next arena we are traveling into is also still very new and unknown, this can make for a potentially bumpy ride.

It's like we have had to jump from one 'stepping-stone' of life towards the next, and to top it off, without actually being able to clearly see what and where the next 'stepping-stone' is. It's not unreasonable to expect this to possibly result in angst, uncertainty, and having to go on blind faith that the Universe or your Higher Self sort of knows what It is doing!

As well as having to make this gigantic leap, the other level to it is that you're now actually in mid-flight with perhaps little sense of what is up or down. You're no longer on the old 'stepping-stone', and you also haven't actually landed on the new one yet. This can be uncomfortable and unsettling.

Fuzzy structure - very uncomfortable

Due to the nature of life here on this plane, we are inevitably steeped in 'structure', be that certain ways of thinking, being, working, behaving, etc. Hence, when we are in 'mid-flight', we are left with what may often be perceived as an abyss of 'unstructured-ness'. Few, if any of the usual things we organized our lives around are now present, applicable or even workable anymore. And this can be very unsettling for creatures like us, who are dependent on structure to give us a sense of value, purpose, safety, and so much more.

When we eventually do land on the next 'stepping-stone', the 'structure' there will inevitably be different to some degree, and will take time to adjust to. Nevertheless, we'll also feel safer and more comfortable, simply because we finally have some sense of 'ground under our feet' again. Since we exist in a time zone of reality, this initial period after 'landing' onto that new 'stepping-stone' can however also be one where time feels strangely 'heavy' and 'sluggish'. All these changes in our life seem to create a sense of time distortion, in the way we experience each day if not each moment.

Who am I really? Where am I going? What do I do now? What is this Journey ultimately all about? I thought I had it sort-of figured out! Why don't the old mental tricks seem to work anymore? So many questions. Time may hang heavy within us, and altogether it can indeed be rather uncomfortable being incarnate during these transition zones.

Different 'lens' – different perspectives

There is another phenomenon which can also happen. As you seem to hurtle from one reality to another, this can cause a sense of disconnectedness; almost a sense of 'what's wrong with me'. The 'game' of life just doesn't seem to 'play' out as it used to. The other 'players' in your reality may now also look at you rather differently, surprised you don't quite seem to play the 'game' as before. You may find yourself wanting to do things differently. People around you will start to see *you* as different.

Things which were previously important to you, no longer are. Doing things the 'old way' may now seem quite odd, especially as you currently have such a different Awareness of certain aspects to life. The problem is that they, as yet, may not see what you are able to see at present, so a sense of disconnectedness can occur; a sense of misalignment between the two parties concerned. Keep in mind that metaphor we used earlier of the two travelers on that path as they were climbing the Mountain, but separated by 20 kilometers.

Trust that Higher Powers are looking out for you

By the same token, we simply need to learn to trust the Universe/God/Higher Self, would not abandon us once these Inner changes have occurred, since those changes can be a bit unsettling as we now try to work, live and play in the 'usual' way. We need to trust that Spirit has in fact set up a lot of new options for us. However, be warned that Spirit may be presenting such new and different options in a way that we are not used to; in ways that requires us to be alert to seeing things in a different manner.

In other words, even though other opportunities and solutions are definitely being put in front of us, they won't be 'packaged' as they were previously. So it's true that it can be easy enough to overlook the solutions and opportunities Spirit *is* offering, but which we end up missing. This is because we are inevitably still looking for the answer to come in its 'usual' or 'normal' format.

At this stage you may need to look at your work and other life situations differently, or be open to a vast range of opportunities coming from rather unexpected or unusual angles. Such opportunities may present themselves within a field of endeavor you might 'normally' never have seen as viable. Yet now - due to your Inner changes – this field is actually the ideal scenario for you; at least it appears so once you can look at it through your 'new vision' or perspective. This is a phase of the Journey where you need to in a sense step back from it all; try to re-focus on your life in a different way. You need to start using your mind and perceptions *beyond* how you have done in the past; in a much broader way. Learn to trust your intuition, and listen to those quiet and subtle 'hunches' as they pop into your mind… but which the left brain is so prone to dismiss out of hand. Such little 'packets of knowingness' are usually your Higher Self presenting you with another morsel of the 'map' ahead.

Knowledge is power

One way to deal with the various phenomenon we've discussed in this chapter is to firstly recognize what is actually happening. Knowledge is power, which has the ability to lessen our suffering. The discomfort or pain may be the same, but through knowledge, our ability to deal or respond to such stimuli is altered. Hence such understandings do in turn alter the degree of suffering. Next, these sort of life situations are also an opportunity to perhaps focus on honing our skills at BEING in the Moment. In that regard, Eckhart Tolle's book 'The Power of Now' is very insightful. [3] Practising this focusing in the NOW, also helps ground us from the whirlwind of thoughts such transition times may create in our mind.

We need to follow through on at least some of these thoughts, as they may be related to 'stuff' that truly does need to be looked at, sorted out and then integrated. But at other times, this whirlwind of mental activity is actually counter-productive. That's when focusing in the Moment can be great for grounding, and helping us find our Center again. Meditation is one powerful process through which to start achieving this, and will be explored in greater depth in chapter 9. Because such life transition experiences can also leave us feeling empty, dissatisfied, uneasy, etc, another technique which can help shift the focus here is to do the 'Gratitude Meditation' – which will also be explored in more detail in later chapters.

For the impatient ones amongst you, the process requires a letting go of your usual 'time-schedule' on how you want things to manifest. You may have to simply learn to flow with the Higher Forces which guide these transitional life phases. Trust that whatever needs to be learnt; to be done; to be changed, will become apparent as time goes by. Oh boy, can this be a difficult one!

Focus now on the individual step in the journey – not the goal

During such phases, our job is perhaps to learn to 'smell the roses' again along the road of life; to learn to re-focus on just BEING, as life prepares the next phase of our Journey. Such a change in emphasis may indeed be quite unsettling and challenging, particularly when compared to the way we had been living on

Chapter 4 - Meaning of Life

that conveyor belt, trying to fit 48 hours into each day. More than ever, this is the case if you're a mum, trying to fulfill all those many roles – parent, housekeeper, cook, cleaner, partner, professional….. Compared to that previous existence, it may seem like you are indeed standing still; going nowhere.

It's a bit like having to wait for hours at a 'bus-stop', impatient to simply get on with the Journey… 'and why the heck hasn't that darn 'bus' arrived yet'? You might be feeling quite resentful as you sit there waiting for it to arrive. Yet, when you take a few moments to let your Awareness roam around the vicinity of that 'bus-stop', you also realize that there are a lot of wonderful things to explore and observe… right there! And they are things you would normally not have noticed as you rushed around in your usual mad fashion.

To make an omelet you need to crack eggs

So although these transitions can be rather uncomfortable and unsettling, nevertheless they also present the opportunity - if we choose it - to learn a huge amount, as we go through them. If the fundamental agenda of this life experience is indeed one of growing in Awareness, then such transitions are absolutely essential if we wish to progress in that agenda. For meaningful change to occur, it becomes essential to 'shake things up' or loosen the existing 'structure' we might in fact be trapped in to some degree. This sense of being trapped within our lives tends to happen over time, as we almost become fossilized in our day-to-day routines. Hence there is a real need for us to somehow be shaken out of our inertia, before we can maximize the potential for further Growth to occur during the next phase of our Journey.

If this process didn't occur, we would be so 'solidified' from the previous life phase; so inflexible, that nothing new could actually enter our Being. It simply is the Nature of things here on this earthly plane that the longer we spend on each 'stepping-stone', the more we accumulate and incorporate structure into ourselves. And the more structured and solidified we become, so too the more traumatic the process may be of finally breaking out. Some people may become encapsulated in their structure to such an extent that they are in fact unable to break out at all, preferring the illusion of safety and comfort such structure can give. But maintaining this illusion does come at a price, because that structure actually becomes a jail in which we can become spiritually stunted and asphyxiated.

It takes time to make a butterfly

The metaphor of the chrysalis and butterfly is perhaps apt here. Each period we spend on a 'stepping-stone' is really a period of time in which - like the caterpillar - we feed and nourish ourselves on the opportunities *that* particular phase of life offers. Then there comes a time in such a cycle, where we very naturally start to create a structural chrysalis. This is an utterly normal process, completely consistent with how things occur on this solid and dense plane of earthly reality. That structure is valid, because it does allow a process of metamorphosis to safely occur at this point of the Journey, tucked away in that 'chrysalis'. In this phase, we transmute all we've 'eaten' and through such 'digestion', we change into a different state i.e. the butterfly.

But then there also comes a time when this butterfly needs to emerge from the comfort and security of that chrysalis, and out into the open. This can be perceived as a time of rawness and vulnerability as the 'womb' of safety is being shattered, and suddenly we become exposed to another reality. Even worse, now we also find ourselves in this unfamiliar form of a butterfly, which we're not at all used to, after having been the 'caterpillar' for so long. It might even be perceived as a destructive period, since to get out, we actually need to destroy at least part of the chrysalis - our long-standing 'home'.

Then along comes the next shock to the system - now we're also expected to fly, when we've only ever crawled before. All very disturbing, and yet all part of a very natural process. Then, after a while of engaging in the un-structured and possibly disorientating process of flying, a point comes where we do settle on the next 'branch of Life', or 'stepping-stone'. Here we lay our 'eggs' - to re-start the entire cycle all over again.

Yet, the challenge for us, once we do land on this next 'stepping-stone' of life, is not to forget the teachings this process did expose us to. The nature of life is such that we inevitably become comfortable in our new structure, and are happy just to get back into 'caterpillar' mode and feed. It takes focus and Awareness to remain open to the learning of the previous cycle, and to incorporate them into the present one.

What does seem to happen though is that as we progress in our level of Awareness, we also do start to better understand and recognize these cycles as we go through them. *Knowing* what we are going through, also allows us to progress through the various phases of each cycle with less alarm and distress.

With such Awareness, we can feel more Centered despite the apparent chaos around us, simply because we now better understand the process.

It becomes easier as the Journey continues

Hopefully therefore, we become less resistant to these changes or seeming 'traumas' as our life Journey continues. We might even get to a point in that Consciousness Journey, where we may come to enjoy some of the characteristics of such transitions - normally called 'suffering'. Flying as a butterfly; being in a temporary state of unstructuredness might even be quite an adventure, as long as we can change our perception of such events. But to create and maintain such changes in perception does put the onus on us to:

- understand the nature of what's happening;
- allow ourselves to accept that this is all part of a natural and normal cycle within the Journey of life;
- let go of how we wish it to be - based on how it was before;
- instead, simply flow with this process, by being as present in the Moment as possible, and also allow a sense of excitement and adventure to replace the experience of sadness, suffering or loss we may initially have felt.

To a great extent, this is what is meant when we keep hearing about how to BE in our lives, rather than always 'doing' our lives.

Planet Earth School – learning via health issues

The concepts discussed in this chapter can also be used most productively for those dealing with both physical and mental health issues. We need to consider the possibility that some health issues are chosen and set up before we incarnate, precisely to act as the 'curriculum' through which we, as Spirit, wish to grow. Hence the primary aim is not so much to then get rid of symptoms, as allowing them to cause some Inner Shift. Through such Shifting, we are better able to tune into to what the 'learning' is – brought to our attention *via* the symptoms. Or such Shifting can allow us to learn to come to a Space of peace and acceptance of our health or life situation. In other words, certain health issues or 'sufferings' may not be open to curing i.e. 'getting *rid*' of the symptoms or situation.

Other health issues however, are precisely about the lessons which can be learned by having a *cure* ensue. Either way, it's all about how much we can learn from such situations. Do we respond by coming from a deep Space of Love – or fear; the opposite of Love? And if we remain stuck in fear, this can only lead to an array of painful emotions such as anxiety, anger, depression, sadness, guilt, failure....

Healing – sometimes this could be like skipping the lesson

There can also be a problem with having 'miraculous healings' occur. Although one particular set of symptoms may have been magically cured, this doesn't change the reality that we are all 'students' of 'planet Earth School', each one of us here with our own curriculum and learning assignments. Usually in 'Earth-school', we tend to only 'get' the necessary 'learning', by life coming along and whacking us around the head. In other words, suffering of some sort.

In the case of health issues, this comes in the form of various symptoms. Now, a miraculous Healing could get rid of *that* particular 'life-whack' or 'symptoms'. But ultimately Healing isn't about allowing us to be able to then automatically by-pass all our 'learning assignments', or quantum leap several grades, and suddenly find ourselves transported from say 2nd grade junior to final year PhD at University. It simply isn't how the system works.

Having a 'miraculous' Healing occur is absolutely valid and possible, but it also asks of us to still find out what the 'lesson' was that needed to be learned. Time can come into the issue here, in that the body was deteriorating so rapidly, that there was literally not enough incarnational time left in which to find out or learn our lessons. Hence a magical Healing or cure was necessary to provide this further window of time in which to earnestly continue learning.

A Healing or cure may also come into our life after much work and Inner exploration, thereby providing us precisely with the deep understandings needed to be learned via that health issue. The expanded Awareness such a situation provided, may then be exactly what was necessary for the next phase of our Journey. It became the required apprenticeship for the work yet to be done on the next 'stepping-stone' of life. For instance, someone's cancer cure, due to an enormous amount of Inner and outer work they had to do, also provided them with exactly the knowledge – or apprenticeship - necessary to subsequently help others with cancer.

Chapter 4 - Meaning of Life

This is something medicine still needs to learn

Ironically, this is where orthodox medicine can actually be counter-productive, if its *sole* focus is on eliminating symptoms or disease. In one way, this focus is absolutely valid! But rarely – if ever – is there any Consciousness around what that ill-health issue may constitute on Metaphysical levels. This aspect to ill-health is either ignored or simply not understood. But the flow-on from this stance is that people in turn are not encouraged to explore their 'suffering' in a more meaningful way, and discover why it may have occurred in the first place. It's a bit like driving your car and unexpectedly one of the lights on the dash-board indicates engine trouble. But you're running late for something, and you have no desire to stop the car and investigate what the trouble may be. Too time-consuming and too messy... and after all, you're in such a hurry!

So you decide to simply break that irritating light on the dash-board and continue driving, thinking that such an action actually eliminates the problem. But several kilometers further along the highway, suddenly there is a loud bang; clouds of billowing, black smoke, and the car grinds to a halt.

The light had indicated you were out of oil. Yet you ignored that signal, hoping the fundamental problem would go away by the much easier action of breaking that inconvenient light on the dash-board. Unfortunately, that didn't work, and now you will really be wasting time as you wait for the repair truck to come along. Yet previously, a few minutes of your time spent in putting some fresh oil into the engine, would have prevented this entire episode.

So too with medicine. All too often, the primary focus is solely on getting rid of symptoms - 'lights on the dash-board'. Nothing wrong with that, but it would also be wise to explore the situation just a bit further to see what else needs to be done, particularly on Metaphysical levels, and especially if the symptoms you're dealing with are of a more serious nature. But at present, this is definitely not a strong point within orthodox medicine, which is why people can so often go into a merry-go-round of symptoms. You fix one lot, but don't seek out the deeper level to it all, and life will just come along with another 'stick' with which to whack you.

So whatever our life 'problem' – especially if in the health arena – it remains necessary to be as pro-active as possible. Choose to perceive your 'suffering' via the Higher Levels of Awareness discussed in this chapter. Keep working on understanding what the 'lesson' is. Then, by being Awake or Conscious enough – as well as motivated enough – pitch in and do the required 'study'.

Exercise
- List 3 beliefs you hold now, and which originated from your family
- Look at the most painful situation in your life at the moment, and see if you can find the 'Consciousness Lesson' it might also be presenting to you.

Summary of thoughts thus far
- Life presents us with a bewildering array of rules and regulations as to how we *must* live our lives – usually courtesy of religion & culture.
- Many of these recommendations conflict with each other, only adding to the confusion of life.
- We either accept and live by what we've been born into or we break out of the mold, and forge a personally validated perspective on life.
- There is Christianity's view that you get just one shot at life... and then it's heaven or hell, compared to the concept of re-incarnation, where you have almost endless chances to 'get it right' in life.
- We, as humans, are in fact not so much our physical bodies, as first and foremost an Energy Being, capable of morphing into other forms. In the case of us humans, this Energy Being incarnates into a physical vehicle called a body.
- What if this reality here *is* about enrolling into a sort of 'Planet Earth School'?
- What if each incarnation was another opportunity to enter a particular 'curriculum' so as to become increasingly skilled at a range of Consciousness 'subjects'?
- What if we actually *choose* all the parameters of a particular life, such as which historical period we incarnate in; our sex, our sexuality, our ethnicity, our health issues, who would be our parents, our children, our friends, our 'enemies'?
- What if 'Planet Earth School' is *the* 'Educational Facility' where we truly learn to Love; in the deepest sense of all, and under *all* circumstances?
- Life on planet Earth may therefore be a training ground for learning how to Love *unconditionally*.

- Suffering can be used as a powerful force through which to learn an equally powerful lesson in keeping our Centre, and staying 'In a Love State' – despite our circumstances.
- Nevertheless, learning on 'Earth-School' doesn't automatically have to be via suffering. We can learn through joy too, as long as we remain more Consciously Aware about our various 'sufferings' as being 'learning opportunities'.
- We need to understand that this 'Schoolroom' has been set up to maximize learning – not to change its essential characteristics.
- If the fundamental characteristics of 'Planet Earth School' are indeed hard-wired and not meant to be changed, trying to change our fundamental human reality by making the changes 'out there', becomes a rather hopeless and inappropriate task.
- We need to make the changes *inside* us first.
- When we look at human history, nothing seems to actually change on the deepest core level of our humanity, despite superficial appearances. Hate, ego, power, greed, manipulation, corruption, war, etc. continue to occur within us as humans, never mind which political, religious or ideological system we've instigated as the 'solution' to our human woes.
- We have confused technological advancement with fundamental, Inner human soul advancement.
- Looking at ourselves primarily as Spirit *in* a body, versus a body *containing* a spirit, leads to very different ways of dealing with life's problems – especially on the level of making *Inner* change first if we truly desire meaningful change *externally*.
- Life is not primarily about 'fixing' whatever the *outer* 'problem' appears to be. Rather, the objective was to see how we would *respond* to the situation. From a Love perspective or from a non-Love perspective, i.e. fear and all its ramifications.
- Rather than blaming or feeling negative towards those who seem to be giving us the greatest trouble in our lives, see them as our 'Spirit-friends' who loved us enough to volunteer to play these challenging roles here on the stage of planet Earth.
- Shifting our focus in this way can also shift the 'problem'.

- Forgiveness is *not* about condoning. Forgiveness is ultimately about a Healing of *self*.
- Life is not the same once you open this Metaphysical Pandora's box of ideas.
- Making these quantum shifts in Awareness can be quite disorientating and difficult, but it is important to realize this is a natural aspect to the process of Consciousness Growth.

REFERENCES

1. Newton, Michael. *Destiny of Souls – new case studies of life between lives,* Llewellyn. USA, 2005.
2. Gomes, Peter. *The Scandalous Gospel of Jesus,* HarperOne. NY, 2007.
3. Tolle, Eckhart. *The Power of Now – a guide to spiritual enlightenment,* Hodder Headline Group, Australia/NZ, 2000.

CHAPTER 5

HOW DOES RELIGION FIT INTO ALL THIS?

If God didn't exist, it would be necessary to invent Him.

Voltaire.

Blinkers as part of the human condition

Before we can allow empowering changes to occur in our lives, perhaps we do need to take a searching look at certain beliefs we hold about ourselves and others, and especially at those perspectives and ideologies which are so deeply engrained in our consciousness that they may no longer be 'visible'. Such fundamental, psychological 'blinkers' appear to be an inherent aspect of our human condition here on planet Earth. Since these sort of 'blind spots' seem to come with the territory, it is important to be able to acknowledge that this is how our reality seems to operate here.

The point is not so much that we have blinkers, but rather that we need to work at discovering, exposing and becoming fully aware of them. Once aware, then can we start to make different choices, thus allowing for change to occur.

Why are we so fearful of difference?

On sociological levels, we recognize that we all like different foods, clothes, entertainment, art.... Indeed, our Western consumerist cultures would implode if we didn't foster such differences. This push to constantly differentiate product, and other aspects in our lives is fundamentally accepted, and seen as a good thing. Yet when it comes to differences in our beliefs, we humans do a very strange thing. Suddenly we insist we must all believe in the same Higher Being and Holy Book. And then, depending on who we are talking to, naturally, *their* brand of 'God', and *their* particular brand of Holy Book is touted as *The* one to accept and live one's life by. Why do we humans make this sudden illogical leap when it comes to our beliefs? We really do need to think about it!

It's not about 'religion-bashing'

One point needs to be made crystal clear here. Although certain confronting things will be said about religion in this chapter, please understand that the aim is definitely not to indulge in 'religion-bashing'. For many people, religion remains a very empowering institution and construct through which to live their lives. Most religions have also achieved amazingly positive feats along the way. They have been the source and inspiration to much of the greatest art ever produced by humanity. Most religions have cared for the homeless, the ill, the dispossessed and the troubled. Much good has indeed been done by so many religions. This is completely acknowledged and accepted.

However, existing in duality as we do, it's inevitable that religion will also have its dark side, and *that* particular aspect to most religions has unfortunately also been the source of much suffering and pain for humanity. This too needs to be acknowledged and accepted before we can move forward in as positive and empowered manner as possible. Witness this phenomenon in the recent ugly back-lash by ultra-conservative USA Christian groups against Ophrah Winfrey's YouTube discussion groups, which explored a range of New Age or Spiritual topics. She's had to endure vitriolic hate-mail – even being labeled the Anti-Christ! - simply because she had chosen to air a broader view on what this human life is all about from a Spiritual perspective.

That's why it is important to try and understand what drives such negative responses to another's point of view, particularly when this comes from people who proclaim a loving God. So please, do keep these statements in mind as you read this chapter.

The aim is not to destroy or replace religion. The aim is to be able to see it as clearly as possible for what it is, and thus give people the ability to make other choices – if appropriate. Or let people continue working within their present, chosen system, but to do so with new insights on how they can nevertheless still empower their human Journey in many ways, perhaps not formally condoned by most religions. Unfortunately, the bottom-line is that despite all the good religion has done it has also been a fundamental source of so much of humanity's woes. Until we can look that fact in the face and deal with it, there probably will be no hope for humanity to ever live in peace and harmony.

Human diversity – trying to squeeze a square peg into a round hole

But getting back to the point made earlier in this chapter, the reality is that humanity is incredibly diverse. So if we start from that observation, it's a big jump, and a big ask to expect all that diversity to somehow then fit into just one, single, confining belief and dogma. Is that really the best way to do it?

Within any one religion, the reality is that many splinter groups do exist, be that in the Christian, Jewish, Muslim, Buddhist or other traditions. This process of splintering is precisely a consequence of people all having their own particular slant on life – and therefore their specific interpretation of any individual Holy Book. Peter Gomes makes it clear again and again in his writings, that interpretation of the Bible inevitably is done according to the predilections and *already* established persuasions of the people reading that Bible. Hence, the sense of disjointedness one finds in the Christian realm – as in other religions too.

So anyone with a particular perspective on life will also have their own unique and personal view of what is 'The Truth'. If you are a Liberal, you will read and understand the Bible in one way, and quite differently if you are a Labor supporter. The interpretation of the Bible by a white person in the era of slavery would be far different from any interpretation by a black person. The way the Bible would have been interpreted in the 1600's would obviously be quite different from how it is interpreted today in the 21st century.

Too often, we tend to forget or overlook this plain and simple fact. Even if we only look at the Christian Holy Book or Bible, the reality is that its interpretation is *already* different, one Christian faction from the other, according to each group's perspectives and biases! This is happening despite these various Christian factions trying to standardize such interpretation, allowing only one official version. Indeed, Google 'Bible' and it is overwhelming to see how many different versions of this supposedly standard 'Holy Book' do exist. Wouldn't it be better to simply acknowledge that since such diversity of interpretation is happening anyway, let's therefore just make it *formally* acceptable, instead of one faction coercing everyone else to focus on and accept *their* view of the Bible?

Rather than forcing conformity, why not apply a Caveat such as... 'you may think and believe what you will, *as long as it doesn't interfere with the freedoms or rights of another human on mental, emotional, physical, spiritual or other levels*.'

Perhaps turn this concept into some questions... you can believe absolutely anything you want; you can believe any Holy Book you want, as long as you put it through these next few queries:-

1. Does this interpretation, even though it may divert from the classical or 'normal' interpretation of the Holy Text, empower you in positive, healthy ways?
2. Does it give you hope or inspire you to good things, such as living a more productive, healthy and happy life – for yourself and for others?
3. Does or could your interpretation of this Text in any way drive or cause you to impinge on the freedoms or rights of other people?

If the answer to the first two questions is 'yes' and the third question is 'no', then each individual human being should surely have the absolute right to interpret any religious or Holy Text according to their own unique human background. Such interpretations will inevitably be ruled by their historical era, personal age, ethnicity, traditional religious backgrounds and Spiritual maturity. These factors aren't – and can't – be the same for everyone on this planet. So why then this obsession with having just one, single 'standardized' religion? Perhaps the incentive is an honest one of wanting to minimize dissent, believing that by forcing uniformity and conformity, less chaos will be created. Perhaps it is nothing more than a political power-play, as happens in so many other arenas of life.

Nevertheless, this obstinate need to homogenize ourselves within the religious arena of life does need to be questioned, especially when we stop to think how we are also willing to kill, maim, torture, persecute, and commit all sorts of other atrocities against anyone daring to be different from some religions, declared to be the one and only True one. By its followers of course! There's another thing which is particularly distressing – certainly to any *outsider* looking *in*. This is the fact that just about all these belief systems have

Chapter 5 - How Does Religion Fit Into All This?

inherent in their teachings, the need to honor and Love each other; forgive and be tolerant of each other. How strange and ironic.

Certain religious systems go even further, actually forbidding the killing of other humans. One such Law says it most succinctly... 'thou shalt not kill'. Simple, clear, unambiguous. It doesn't have a string of codicils or by-laws which say, 'yes but in such and such a situation you *can* kill'. Although the religion in question here has done a lot of good in the world, it has nevertheless also caused so much dreadful suffering – especially in the past. And all in the name of *their* particular brand of God.

What exactly is it within our humanity which so profoundly overtakes us when it comes to religion? What sort of spiritual 'disease' is this... which, by the way, can be extraordinarily 'infectious'?

Inconsistencies and absurdities within religions

As touched on above, these attitudes can only end in one obvious, although bewildering conclusion. If you allow yourself to stand *outside* all this – as an observer – then something aberrant immediately smacks you right between the eyes. Almost all religions state that *their* world view is the only correct and true one. And in each case, such a dogmatic approach is then 'validated' by a particular Holy Book. The problem is that there are many of these Holy Books around which are supposed to be absolutely infallible. So the very simple yet unavoidable question is... 'which one then is the *truly* correct one?'

Once again, within these religions there are many splinter groups all pointing the finger and declaring each other the 'lost ones'. This is particularly strange when you look at the fact that three of the five major religions – Christianity, Judaism and Islam – all have at their source the one prophet... Abraham. Historically, the Old Testament Abraham is indeed the father to all three of these religions, yet so much of humanity's woes, down through the ages, can be directly related back to the strife between these three faiths.

Whose interpretation of religion is correct?

Ultimately, the only thing that can be done is to realize everybody should have the right to interpret the Bible or their particular Holy Book according to the needs of their own unique spiritual Journey. And accept their personal responsibility for it too!

Allowing ourselves such a shift in philosophical perception, also creates a wonderful Space - one within which we could permit each person's interpretation to be an *enrichment* towards the overall understanding and experience of Consciousness and Spirituality. Surely this a better option, compared to having people constantly fighting as to who is right; who has 'The Truth' and who is being manipulated by the devil?

If we could more freely and openly share our interpretations amongst ourselves, rather than fight about them, we might just end up possibly enriching each other! Indeed, *we* may be the ones who need to open up towards another's perspectives and perceptions - and evolve more in *our* level of Spirituality. But the main intention is to use such interpretations as a point of *enrichment* rather than of *conflict*. It's about seeing alternate interpretations as just different; not right or wrong.

Unfortunately, far too often the typical religious way of dealing with 'Holy Book' interpretation has lead to nothing else but bloodshed, war, turmoil, torture, and all sorts of other abominable actions. Look at the Middle East; look at Ireland, and at all the other far too many examples going back in history, all the way to Christ and beyond.

Is God playing games with us?

Perhaps we need to look at the possibility that it is actually God who is therefore the source of all this confusion. After all, within our traditional understanding, people are usually a Christian, a Jew, a Muslim, a Buddhist or whatever – simply by dint of birth. If it is indeed true that God has made *all* of humanity – not just the Christians or Jews or Muslims or Buddhists, etc, - does this then possibly mean God is playing some evil game with us all? Setting one off against the other? However, in turn does this make sense of a supposedly 'Loving God'? Or does it mean that God – (although this begs the question ….'which God'? - Christian? Muslim? Jewish?!) – was responsible for solely creating the 'correct' humans?

But if this is so, does it mean that there is some other Force who has therefore created all the 'wrong' people? Surely though, that would contradict the very essence of what a God is supposed to be; something that is by Its very nature apparently the Ultimate, the Be-all and End-all. Or do we have a situation of several equally powerful Gods, at loggerheads, each creating their own 'brand' of religiously 'correct' people - a bit like the ancient Greek and Roman concepts of gods?

Such deep inconsistencies and almost absurdities become a major reason why it is so important to ask pertinent and searching questions. Questions about so many things otherwise taken for granted; swallowed hook, line and sinker... 'because that is just how it is'. 'That's what *our* religion teaches us'. 'That's why we need faith'. Yes, little wonder that, because any rational thinking and questioning soon creates such terrible inconsistencies in so much of what religions would force us to believe... just on Faith alone'!

Dogmatism and rigidity within religions

The problem actually is not religions or philosophies per se. Rather, it's the *dogmatism* which too frequently accompanies such ideas, concepts or beliefs which then leads to all the trouble. Ultimately, it's all a matter of belief – not absolute Truth. So as an outsider, how does one resolve this fundamental dilemma? They can't *all* be the True religion, nor can *all* the Holy Books be '*The True*' one; it's such a contradiction in terms!

Yet, this dilemma is a fundamental reality within most religions. The problem starts when people become completely embedded in their own particular brand of world-view. They become so blinkered that they seem unable to understand, let alone acknowledge how ludicrous it all is for them to emphatically believe that they are the 'chosen ones', yet see everyone else as the heretic or infidel.

For such people to then stubbornly refuse to perceive beyond their own worldview is actually not necessarily a sign of loyalty to their particular brand of religion. It is more a deep statement of an ego-centric blindness, arrogance, prejudice and the inability to stand in the shoes of another. Surely something is fundamentally wrong here? Especially when none of these individual religions can in the end prove, beyond a shadow of doubt, that *their* Holy Book or *their* world-view is the correct one. It is based on pure belief - which is ultimately beyond proving.

You cannot prove a belief, based on a belief that your own brand of Holy Book is THE one and only True one!

Philosophically, this is something which is inherently and fundamentally impossible. You can only *choose* to believe or not to believe it. The problem with belief is that it can so easily blind us to much of our generally shared reality, as well as making us act irrationally towards each other.

Yet so many religions behave as if proving a belief is an obviously feasible thing to do. Using some Text – never mind how Holy it is *perceived* to be – cannot and does not constitute proof. This should be obvious when there are at least five major religions, all declaring – to the point of being willing to kill and mutilate each other - that only *their* religious belief is the true one. And of course, based on *their* Holy book.

Again, certainly as a bystander observing all these mental machinations, such conclusions are obviously ludicrous. They can't all be right. Wouldn't it be much better for everyone concerned, if they could go *beyond* having to be right for *all* and rather see themselves as right for *themselves*? It should not be so much a matter of who is 'right' and who is 'wrong'; instead the issue should perhaps be one of… 'what suits *you* best'? What belief or perspective on life would maximally empower *you* to get on with *your* life in as loving and functional way as possible?

Christianity vs Buddhism – follow the rules vs follow your own experiences

It is interesting to look at a significant difference between Christianity and Buddhism. In many branches of Christianity you have this attempt at upholding standardized protocols, belief systems, ways of behaving and thinking. This is imposed from the outside according to the interpretation of a select few, and is required in order to become a member of that system. To remain a viable member, you just have to take on board such an entire 'package', and relinquish any sense of your own capacity to think or experience.

This is rather interesting, because a lot of these religions also have an inherent 'theme', that the Creator or God gave humanity Free Will, which could be defined as our ability to *choose* what we focus on, and therefore become aware of. Supposedly, our capacity to think and reason, using our Free Will is the one thing truly distinguishing us from the animals. Yet, when it comes to religious thinking, we are under duress to relegate this capacity to a select few, and *they* will then conveniently do the interpretation for us! Now if it is really true that our ability to think and reason is such a distinguishing point between us and animals, and if it is true that God has given us Free Will… why stifle such an amazing capability? Especially when it comes to choosing a Path which really suits that individual!

After all, as mentioned earlier, most of the time people just happen to be a Christian, Buddhist, Muslim or Jew for no other reason but a fluke of birth. Mostly, the question simply isn't asked... what if that same soul had been born into a different religious family background? Would that then automatically make that person an infidel, a pagan, a heretic? Someone therefore worthy of persecuting or killing? Or someone who will now automatically go to hell?

It needs to be pointed out again, that if God is indeed the creator of *all* humanity, then we have a real dilemma here. Does that mean God Itself is then the origin for this so-called 'evil' of some people not being born into the correct and True Faith? Doesn't seem quite rational either!

It is interesting to note however, that generally speaking, within Buddhism there is a greater allowance for the individual to discover their own spiritual path, via their personal experiences and understandings.

Inherent right to choose our own path

Everyone should automatically have a right to their own *choice* of world-view which maximally empowers that individual to deal with the very real challenges, sufferings and inconsistencies of life. *It's when dogmatism rules, that the heart often closes.* And when this happens, it precisely sets the stage for all the conflict we so frequently see in our reality. So much of that conflict could be instantly solved, if those involved could stand back a bit from their own world-view as 'The Ultimate Truth'. This just might allow them to get enough perspective to realize there is no need to enforce or ram their version of reality down everyone else's gullet.

Why the need to convert?

Why this incessant need to convert all and sundry? For many people caught in this scenario, they no doubt genuinely – although naively – believe themselves to hold that sole 'Truth'. But what if, on psychological levels, this relentless and deep need to then convert everyone else to the same view is perhaps more driven from a deep, fundamental and unconscious fear that *perhaps they aren't right*? In other words, wouldn't it feel so much safer or comfortable if everyone else *does* believe the same? Because then the possibility of being wrong oneself is neatly avoided.

No more need to explore, expand or grow in Consciousness and wisdom. After all, 'The Final Life Explanation' – 'The Solution' – has been achieved.

Need for a different way to perceive our religions

Perhaps we desperately need another way of allowing ourselves to be guided when it comes to philosophical or religious perspectives on life. Perhaps there is a need to ask ourselves that question already raised in this discussion i.e.... 'the issue is not whether something is the ultimate 'Truth' or not; the only question we should ask ourselves is... 'is it *useful*'? Does it empower us in our Journey as humans, on this very challenging plane of reality? Does it allow us to give each other the space to live that reality in our own individual way? Surely there is validity to whatever serves to help *that* individual deal more effectively with *their* own path in life, without then also impinging on the paths of others?

Biased responses to selected human situations

For now, let's take one last look at human biases – inevitably fueled by religious and political perspectives. We presently have the situation in our Western world where certain sects of Indian men wear their turbans; Indian women wear their saris; some Jewish men wear their skullcap or Kippah, while other more conservative Jews wear their lengthy black robes and top hats, long hair and curly pig-tails for side-burns... yet basically no-one bats an eyelid. Such rather stark differences to 'normal' Western garb seem to be successfully absorbed into people's overall view of cultural differences. Indeed, many might even remark on how colorful and elegant the Indian saris are, for instance.

Yet, let an Islamic woman now walk past these same people, wearing her hijab, and suddenly a very odd thing occurs. In too many cases, it's as if someone flicked a switch, creating a sense of bias, fear, judgment and strong, negative sentiments about *this* particular type of dress needing to be banned. Such bias as occurred in the latter years of the Howard era, even activated calls for Islamic people to realize that they are now in Australia, and should therefore integrate and adhere to Aussie ways of life. Yet, the Indian men and women, and the various Jewish sects are turned a blind eye to!

So what is going on here? If we truly and rationally mean what we say about the Islamic women and their headdress, then we need to be equitable, and apply such restrictions to *all* other nationalities or religions too. But we don't – *and rightly so*. Hence what we are dealing with here is an example of how cultural bias, fueled by even more deep-set religious bias, causes us to be most unfair in the way we allow only certain ethnic groups to express their individuality.

This is a dangerous thing for any culture to do. We must never forget the lessons humanity should have learned from the Nazi era. There the culturally targeted groups were the Jews, Gypsies, handicapped and homosexuals – and we all know what eventually happened to them in Germany. Yet we need to realize that the Nazis are not the only historical example of such cultural bias leading to culturally sanctioned atrocities. The Hutsi and the Tutsi in Africa are another example, as were the Serbs and the Croats in Europe. Similarly with the Turkish slaughter of Armenians or the many atrocities committed by the Taliban. A more recent example is the attempt at ethnic cleansing in Kenya, where the Kikuyus were slaughtered.

Hence, we need to start to learn to not just tolerate each other's differences, but as human cultures, to luxuriate in, revel in and enjoy the many colorful differences in our humanness. Instead, far too often we are so very afraid of each other's differences – particularly when it comes to beliefs.

But the question should be… 'does such a fear ultimately serve us as a human family'? 'Does it allow us to live together on an increasingly crowded planet, in harmony and tolerance of each other'? If the answer is perhaps a resounding NO!... then why is it that we so vehemently persist in trying to maintain that fear of each others' differences?

Religious 'boxes' – exploring beyond the boundaries

Religions often force people to live in 'boxes', beset by boundaries, rules and dogmas. This usually stifles or prevents any real, dynamic exploration and growth. But surely this fundamental and deep need for growth and exploration is an inherent and essential aspect to the human condition? It's a tendency and capacity we all have, yet which too many religions force people to deny and repress. Although it is true that you're allowed to explore within the boundaries, dare to go *beyond* such boundaries, and suddenly you run the real risk of turning into a heretic.

However, there is one very important thing which people caught up in this religious/conceptual framework do need to do. They need to be given - or more importantly, give themselves - the right to ask questions that get them to go beyond these boundaries. Then again, an effective way religions throttle such exploration is to invoke the issue of Faith, in the sense that if you are questioning something about your religion, it indicates that you don't have any - or enough Faith. This is a huge sin according to such organizations. It's also an ultimately brutal form of psychologically oppression.

In asking such paradigm-changing questions, inevitably a powerful resistance occurs from within some organized religions. It's exactly at this point that the seeker needs to ask the most important questions of all... who says I can't make further queries? Based on what authority? And most importantly... *for what reason?* Inevitably these are issues of power and control, rather than truth or faith. The Bible, as with most other Holy Books is usually one of the ultimate 'sticks' with which to beat others into submissive acceptance of what those in power have determined to be 'The Truth'.

But those in power of any one religion will of course answer that it is forbidden by the dogmas and rules of the religion to go your own way, and that such prohibitions are inevitably derived and validated via their Holy Books. However, as already touched on several times now, how does one ultimately prove the veracity and authenticity of such Holy Books?

They're THE Truth because *they* say so? Isn't this just a bit contradictory?

And if it is indeed true, as alluded to earlier, that this innate human tendency for diversity has already played itself out in the human arena of religion anyway – verified precisely by the huge number of splinter groups within any one religion – why not just accept this human reality and make it official? Humans are a diverse lot, depending on their time in history; their cultural background; whether male or female; even what stage in life they are at. Their teens? Their 30's or in their final slide towards 'check-out time'?

The fact is that diverse interpretations of each Holy Book have already happened. *It has only been given the veneer of acceptability in each case, by making such dissent from the official interpretations into a new 'religion'!* For example, from Catholicism to Protestantism to Puritanism to Anglicanism and so many more, and then these splinter groups battle with each other via words, the sword or nowadays, with bombs. Just bring to mind Ireland.

Why not simply allow – not just any one group – but *all* individuals to have the inherent human right to their own particular interpretation of any particular Holy Book, as long as this is what they want, and as long as it serves them in constructive and Loving ways? However, there is one major Caveat –

as discussed earlier. It would certainly save a lot of conflict and killing if *no-one* was the inherent holder of 'The Truth'.

The problem is that as long as people continue to 'play' within the 'box' – endlessly re-arranging the 'furniture' according to certain rules and guidelines – no truly fundamental change can ever occur. Surely life is on many levels an evolutionary Journey, where change and growth is the foundation and source of such life?

Bonsai concept in relation to religion

Perhaps the metaphor of a bonsai tree in a confined 'box' or pot is appropriate here. Yes, the tree is indeed able to remain alive, but it nevertheless becomes inevitably twisted and gnarled within its confinement. There may be beauty in that bonsai form of the tree, although on another level it can also be argued that this tree has never been given the chance of achieving the full potential of what it is *genetically* capable of. So too with a soul, all cramped up within the confines of the 'box' of a strict religious or philosophical paradigm.

As cleverly and as beautifully as it may arrange itself in that 'box', via all sorts of ingenious philosophical convolutions, that person is *never* going to express their full potential of what they could be - as a soul free to explore itself. Not if they rigidly and faithfully adhere to the inevitable rigorous rules and regulations of most religions. Obviously, an oak tree in a small bonsai pot just doesn't have the grandeur of an oak tree in the middle of a meadow. Here it can stretch out to its fullest height and potential; its leaves maximally soaking up the energy of the sun.

Then again, there is another option. Some people do choose to remain within a particular religious framework. Although they have also given *themselves* permission to pick and choose which aspects of that religion's dogmas and articles of Faith they then choose to accept for themselves, in *their* particular Journey. They choose to remain in the 'bonsai pot', but have also chosen a much larger 'pot'! This allows them the comfort of living within a structured, philosophical paradigm, but also allowing for a sense of expansion or growth within themselves.

Religion – 'baby in the womb' metaphor

Admittedly, there is a 'right time' during which it is best for a person to remain within the confines of the 'box'. But then there also comes a point in the soul's Journey, where one needs to step *out* of the 'box'. This is a process very similar to a baby in the womb. For those initial nine months, it is absolutely crucial and correct for that baby to remain *inside* the protective and nurturing environment of the womb. However, if the baby refuses to leave the womb, although there is some lee-way in the timing, there will come a point where the child will actually become stifled, and die.

There comes a point in time, where the baby needs to leave that comfortable, secure environment and become born, a process inevitably associated with much effort, pain and blood. So too it can be for us – Metaphysically – when we leave the 'womb' of religion, and finally have to make it alone. A point is reached where we do need to be cut off from our 'umbilical cord' of automatic nourishment and sustenance, security and stability. It is the nature of life! Not only in the development of the *body* but also in that of the *soul*.

'Doing our own thing' surely will only cause chaos

Now on one level, the fear is that if we allow everyone to believe what they like, this will then create a total free-for-all situation with everyone wanting to do exactly what they wish. *Ironically, that's exactly what is going on anyhow*! But this freedom of choice of which religious or philosophical package one wishes to choose and live out, is predicated heavily on that very simple, basic and important Caveat, expounded upon earlier in this chapter. Namely... 'you may believe whatever you like, and you may follow your own soul's guidance, but the fundamental rule is... as long as such beliefs and consequent actions don't injure or interfere with another; mentally, emotionally, physically or spiritually'. In other words, you cannot force your will on others; you cannot foist your belief on others; you cannot use your own choice as a means of creating harm to others – just because they choose to think and believe differently to you.

In that sense, such an approach of allowing a greater freedom of choice increasingly resonates with Buddhism. The focus becomes more one of what your *experience* guides you to accept as a reasonable way of navigating through your life, rather than what *dogma* you *have* to steep yourself in – and then unquestioningly follow. What is your personal and individual experience and observation of life telling you? What sort of deductions, conclusions and concepts most fit *your* very individual perspective as well as most empower *you* to cope with this Journey called life? Again, there needs to be the very solid understanding that in no way is any such personal choice allowed to impinge on the wellbeing or inherent freedoms of other human beings.

So in using all these points above as a guiding light, you are not going to get chaos. In fact you are going to get *less* chaos because you're not going to have every religion trying to force each other to *their* brand of 'The Truth'. It is precisely this shift in perspective that provides the fundamental difference between Spirituality and religion.

As Barry Goss has argued, Spirituality has to do with our *personal* experience in how we relate to God/Source - or however we conceive of this Ultimate Being. In comparison, religion provides a specific, structured and often dogmatic format *through* which one is then allowed to relate to God, thus making it a far more vicarious experience.

Religions – need for some fundamental changes

Some may say that the approach being touted above, of allowing each person the freedom to have their own personalized experience and interpretation of God is utterly naive. But is it any *less* naive to believe that a system which has demonstrably not worked for several thousand years, and continues to generate death, torture and general mayhem is somehow magically going to completely reverse itself, and suddenly produce a totally different result? Instead of stubbornly persisting in using the 'old formula', surely it is high time that we as a human species try a different way? We have already been following the rules of uniformity and conformity for far too long. We have been trying to get an homogenized sort of situation where everyone is the same religion; believes the same thing; lives their life in exactly the same religious way, ad infinitum.

And look where it has taken the human family... into endless wars, hatred and *separation*. It has only caused enormous division amongst humanity. Perhaps we could give these other ideas a go, where each person is allowed to believe what they find most empowering, liberating or inspiring – albeit with the previously stated Caveat. We may find instead a much higher sense of tolerance and care. Dare it be said – such an approach may even encourage a genuine Loving amongst people, simply because that *competitiveness* has been taken out of the equation. That sense of 'I'm right... and by god, you're wrong'!

Nevertheless, it also needs to be realized that even if this alternate approach were to be taken on board by the majority of religions, it would still take several decades for any meaningful change to pervade the general community, especially in areas where conflict has raged for generations. For example, in the Middle East, where many Jews and Muslims – and their respective splinter groups - are still at each other's throats. Or in Pakistan and India, where Hinduism and Islam can't see eye-to-eye. Or Croatia and Serbia, where bitterness between various Christian and Muslim sects still festers.

These various cultures have had their hatred of each other so deeply engrained into them that it has almost gone into their genes. It may therefore take several generations to be 'bred' out of them. Hopefully, though, each new generation will become increasingly more open to playing with such innovative ideas, which are instead based on mutual respect and compassion towards each other.

But is this Caveat nothing but a useless New Age idea?

As far as the Caveat we've discussed before is concerned, some people may feel this idea to be totally naive, in regard to how far it could realistically transform humanity's attitude towards each other. However, the point is precisely not about converting every last human being *directly* to this concept. What *is* the point is to allow as many people who are *already* amenable to this idea, to do so. It's when enough people have actually taken this idea on-board, and start to live it out, that Sheldrake's 'hundredth monkey' effect will activate, thereby affecting and changing the Morphogenetic Field – a concept we've already touched on, and will explore more fully elsewhere. This Field in turn will automatically start to unconsciously influence those who are still stuck in the old paradigm, so that they too, slowly but surely get drawn into the new way of thinking. Ironically, when that point is reached, they no longer see the issue as something way-out and unworkable, but rather as the obvious way to be thinking and living.

Hark back to the sudden and dramatic change in the recent governmental and community perception about Global Warming. First, there were those people, dismissed by the general community as nothing but crack-pots, who were endlessly going on about this purported dangerous phenomenon. For almost two decades they were ignored, yet during that time they were nevertheless slowly convincing an increasing number of others to their perspective, until a 'tipping-point' was reached, and suddenly the entire community was able to see clearly what previously only a few had seen.

Relating this back to the Caveat concept, it's therefore important to first make such new ideas available to those who are most amenable to it, thereby creating a groundswell of similar 'thinking-Energy'. This in turn feeds back Energetically, via the Morphogenetic Field, to all of humanity, influencing them unconsciously and subtly to a point where a 'ripeness' occurs in those locked in their old paradigm, and they too find themselves transmuted in their thinking. This may take time, but the process has to be started by someone at some point.

Forced to the edge before finally making change

Sometimes people become more open to these concepts when they seem to have reached the end of the road with the usual, conventional systems which were supposed to cure our problems. When the 'normal' system fails us... what then? Do we just give up or do we search deeper? Even if such searching leads us into territory previously seen as fringe, New Age, quackery... and possibly dangerous?

This Journey into confusion, pain and bewilderment, which is such a part of the human experience, can also become a force through which to re-assess fundamental beliefs we have about ourselves and life, beliefs which actually have not been serving us all that well anyway. Hopefully, the more we can allow other perspectives to enter our awareness, the more we increase the chances of Healing ourselves.

Different ways of looking at our human Journey

Hopefully, this book will start to provide a way of going beyond such differences, allowing you to perceive your life here on planet Earth through alternate 'lenses'. Perhaps this book will allow you to explore new ways of enhancing your own life, to take on board new concepts which empower you to make positive and constructive changes. But perhaps it is time most of all, to stop trying to change everyone *around* us, and rather to start changing *ourselves* first. Let us become true role-models of Loving, caring people, who honor the inherent rights of all others to live their lives according to their own beliefs.

If people become such inspirations to others, then the need for proselytizing disappears. Others will be so drawn by our way of life that they will then actively seek us out to discover what it is that can create such a dynamic, productive and Loving way of life. And we should never forget that there are many roads to the same destination. Who are we ultimately, to decide - let alone foist - our particular route on others? Let diversity reign, rather than some homogenized and deathly sameness.

Indeed, we may not want to be part of another's 'otherness'. That's perfectly O.K! But surely – just as *we* want to experience and live *our* world-view – why should we then so vehemently deny others theirs? If you are already a Jew, a Christian, a Muslim, a Buddhist or whatever, and you feel empowered and happy with your particular Path, it does not mean you now have to *become* those others' differences. Stay with what serves you; you don't need to convert or change to something else. But by the same token, do allow others their choice through which to live their life in a style that empowers and suits them most too.

Exercise
- List three 'blinkers' which affect the way you see your reality
- Describe three things in your reality, on a philosophical level, which really confront you or make you feel uncomfortable

Summary of thoughts thus far.
- Humans are inherently steeped in many biased views of themselves and life.
- This can be seen as the basis to so much of our human strife.
- Unfortunately, religions are responsible for much of this bias.
- As much as religions are the source of a lot of good, their 'shadow side' can be dark and dangerous.
- We need to acknowledge this 'dark side' of religion if we desire fundamental, Healing changes to occur within our cultures and societies.
- Humanity, by its very nature is the essence of diversity – yet most religions demand a stifling uniformity when it comes to religious beliefs.

Chapter 5 - How Does Religion Fit Into All This?

- You cannot *prove* a belief, based *on* a belief that your own brand of Holy Book is *the* one and only *true* one.
- It's when dogmatism rules that the heart invariably closes.
- Faith can be a great source of comfort to an individual – or become a brutal form of psychological oppression when abused in a dogmatic manner.
- True freedom of choice in what and how we believe, and giving everyone else the same freedom, won't generate greater world chaos; in fact the opposite is far more likely.
- A fundamental Caveat humanity might like to take on-board is... 'you may think and believe what you will, *as long as it doesn't interfere with the freedoms or rights of any other human on mental, emotional, physical, spiritual or other levels'.*
- Diverse interpretations of each Holy Book have already happened. They have only been given the veneer of acceptability in each case, by making such dissent from the official interpretation into a new 'religion'.
- Spirituality has to do with our *personal* experience in how we relate to God/Source - or however we conceive of this Ultimate Being. In comparison, religion provides a specific, structured and often dogmatic format *through* which one is then allowed to relate to God, thus making it a far more vicarious experience.
- Perhaps it is time most of all to stop trying to change everyone *around* us, and rather to start changing *ourselves* first.
- We should never forget that there are many roads to the same destination. Who are we ultimately, to decide - let alone foist - our particular route on another?
- We may not want to be part of another's 'otherness', which is perfectly O.K. But surely – just as *we* want to experience and live *our* world-view – why should we then so vehemently deny others theirs?

Lifenotes - A user's guide to making sense of life on planet Earth

CHAPTER 6

SUFFERING ISSUES

There is nothing either good or bad, but thinking makes it so

Shakespeare, Hamlet.

No two ways about it: suffering is a major issue for the majority of humans experiencing life here on planet Earth. Many attempts have been made by religion and philosophy to try and explain it, just as we've already tried to make some sense out of suffering via our explorations in the previous chapters. Yet, all too often, it remains very difficult to even begin to understand what could possibly outweigh the amount of suffering humanity has gone through, thereby somehow validating or counter-balancing such a phenomenon.

This is especially so when one considers the wail of cumulative agony emitted from the planet as a result of the misery accrued over the eons of time that humanity has existed: the tortures, the wars, the lies and deceit; the murders, the manipulation of power and ego to strip people of basic human rights. And then there is the suffering created by planet Earth itself via earthquakes, volcanic eruptions, tsunamis, drought, floods, devastating fires, and so much more. So let's explore this ubiquitous human phenomenon in an even deeper fashion than we have done thus far.

Suffering – can the good things in life ever balance it out?

For those wrestling with the enormity of human suffering, to even suggest there might be some redeeming value to this phenomenon seems to make a mockery of a God who is supposedly the epitome of Love, Justice and Compassion.

One possible response is to be mad as hell at God for allowing such a colossal fiasco to occur within Creation. But then the question is whether this attitude will ultimately serve us? Will it actually make suffering go away? Or will such seemingly valid anger at God then only leave us with a sense of frustration, rage, confusion, betrayal and powerlessness, in turn potentially drawing us into an implosion of mind and soul? So how else can we deal with this very real phenomenon of suffering, in as productive and empowering way as possible?

Seeing suffering more as an issue of mystery

In regard to dealing with suffering, perhaps we can boil it down to three primary issues. Firstly, we have to accept that suffering is an integral component of the human condition. That's the 'no-brainer', and certainly is the easy part to it! Secondly, what do you do with the suffering? Do you try to understand it? Figure it out till you can come to some sort of rational conclusion?

But after a lifetime of trying to understand it – via the left brain – the only conclusion about suffering seems to be that it inherently doesn't make much sense at all. Sure, we can learn from it; we can see why some people may be suffering, based on their actions. But ultimately these explanations don't seem to be good enough either, when compared to the intensity and horror of so much of the suffering that humans are exposed to.

In the end, and after a lot of heartache in trying to really understand suffering, it therefore seems that one potent conclusion is that *you can't really understand it*. Ultimately, when logic fails so miserably in trying to get a handle on it, all you can do is to finally live with the *mystery* of suffering.

Despite not being able to perhaps understand suffering in a logical, rational way, how does one then deal with it on a day-to-day basis, in as positive, constructive a manner as possible? And this is where we'll explore some of Eckhart Tolle's concepts about suffering, thus providing a useful platform from which to achieve at least an empowering response to this all too human phenomenon.

'Life is perfect' - cruel to say to someone in suffering

So many Eastern religions, gurus, teachers, as well as New Age pundits have declared 'everything is perfect just the way it is'. Full stop. And then the mind goes into complete disarray and disbelief as we think of the list of atrocities we humans have perpetrated against each other over the millennia. Such declarations can only suggest some horrific misunderstanding as to what a God of Love is all about.

If we use various religious or New Age paradigms which acknowledge a 'perfect heaven', this does provide the possibility of believing that somewhere – out there – a plane of reality does exist, far removed from this one, where all is perfect. But various spokespeople for the New Age go even further, declaring that ultimately reality here on Earth is nothing but an Illusion; all is therefore well; all is perfect. Tell that to a mother who has just lost her child to leukemia! Such allegations by many in the New Age that 'all is perfect' bring up some sensitive and important issues which can't be glossed over, and will be explored in greater depth towards the end of chapter 10.

Yes, theoretically, philosophically, on some Higher Dimension, this assertion that life is all an Illusion may actually be true. But does it serve the average person to declare this so assuredly, and even vehemently? All you have to do, they say, is to see it from a Higher perspective. Indeed! Yet how many people are truly able to experience life on *this* plane of reality, from *that* Higher level? It's possible, but only after much work has been done on our Spiritual Self.

So the worst thing a guide or teacher can say to someone who can't yet 'hear' or comprehend this fact, is that 'everything is perfect'. All that such an attitude will accomplish is a lot of negative response, utter disbelief, anger, and inevitably a closing down around the entire topic.

All these arguments about how it is 'all perfect'... from one level, may indeed ultimately be true. But it hardly empowers someone being gassed, beaten to death or tortured in some prison. Those people have to deal with the reality as it is *right now* in their lives. It hurts; it feels utterly real. This is no illusion to the one undergoing the suffering! Such Metaphysical, but ultimately ephemeral discussions about 'everything in life is perfect', are all very nice in the drawing rooms of the philosophers amongst us.

'Everything is perfect' more on a Higher Level – which we can operate from

Perhaps there is a more empowering way to look at our human experience, where this human 'reality' and its suffering are indeed acknowledged and honored, but where practical techniques are also provided, through which to better help people deal with this earthly situation. Surely it would be more productive to teach people how to tap into a much Higher Level of Reality, a Dimension of thinking and doing, *from* which almost miraculous change can be manifested into our human experience.

To begin this process, we first need to acknowledge and let people know that there is a Perfect Dimension of Reality that we – as humans *in* incarnation – *do* have access to. It's by accessing this Dimension that we can then minimize or negate our sufferings, here, on Earth. As well, via this Dimension, we can learn to transform the human experience into so much more than if we just remain locked into the belief – and thus the experience – that this human 'reality' is all we have access to.

So on one level, Perfection does absolutely exist. But it is in another Dimension of Reality - a Dimension of Reality which is definitely and fundamentally interwoven with our human dimension here. Now everyone has heard of 'Heaven', and would assume this is what is being discussed here. By the same token, Heaven is normally seen as 'somewhere' you *go* to; it's not supposed to be a place you can somehow *use* while on Earth. So to all extents and purposes, the average human would find this concept of heaven less than useful.

This perspective of Heaven also side-tracks them from an Awareness of an incredibly powerful Plane of Reality – of Perfection – which they *can* actually learn to tap into, while still incarnate on planet Earth. This slant on a 'Plane of Perfection' is generally not well understood in our human understanding of how things operate. All an average person *is* generally aware of is their daily, human dimensional experience of reality, as dictated by their five senses.

The skill in this Journey of expanding our Consciousness is to initially become aware that this Other Dimension of Perfection does exist; to realize it can definitely be tapped into. But we also need to understand it takes a certain amount of skill and work to become proficient at 'Being' in these two Dimensions simultaneously – the Earth plane and the Plane of Perfection. As our skill improves however, so do the benefits of working simultaneously from both Dimensions start to manifest into our daily *human* life experience - to the point of potentially creating more of a 'heaven on earth'.

Chapter 6 - Suffering Issues

Pain Body – a powerful metaphor through which to handle suffering

Let's first explore a rather novel approach to understanding suffering. There are many paradigms through which to explore this ubiquitous phenomenon, but for now let's just choose one of these many approaches, using the work of Eckhart Tolle, an author who has done very interesting work on the topic. In his book 'The Power of Now', [1] Tolle explores the issue of suffering through the model of something he calls the 'Pain Body'. Keep in mind that this is just a metaphor, meant only to get a handle on exactly what pain and suffering are, and how to then best manage them. Ultimately, therefore, it is not important whether 'Pain Bodies' actually exist or not. Again, the only thing to focus on for now is whether such concepts can ultimately allow us to better deal with suffering, rather than being overwhelmed and crushed by it.

Yet, when one follows Tolle's ideas, he does seem to provide a compelling platform from which to manage this human phenomenon in a more empowering way. His perception is that the Pain Body is an Energetic phenomenon, created as the cumulative end result of every painful experience human beings have ever had in their lives - from birth to death. He also speculates that there is not just a *personal* aspect to this Pain Body, but that it also exists in an overall *species* format.

In that sense, this notion resonates with Rupert Sheldrake's hypothesis of the Morphogenetic Field – already touched on in earlier chapters, and to be explored in greater detail when we look at the concept of Creative Visualization in chapters 10 to 13. But for now, just bring back to mind that this Morphogenetic Field can be seen as an Energetic accumulation of every iota of *knowledge* ever learned by all forms of consciousness, be that human, animal, insect or whatever. We can see that both Sheldrake and Tolle made use of the concept of an Energy field to explain either pain or knowledge-growth.

As we continue to explore the Pain Body concept, it seems that a process occurs whereby the accumulation of pain, over time, creates this form of Energy Field, whose primary characteristics are negativity and dysfunctionality. This Field also has the capacity to take over a human, via the mind, with resultant strong, negative effects on the body. It exists in two formats - dormant or active - and any little stimulus, either from our environment or our minds can set it off.

This Pain Body, according to Tolle's model, almost has a consciousness or sense of its own existence, and thus has a deeply driven need to survive. However, it can only overtake or possess a human who is unconscious to its existence, as well as its power. Our *un*consciousness then is like an open door, allowing this energy to enter. And once it has, it does so via our minds; which means through our thinking. What sustains it is pain - plain and simple.

So it needs to induce in us an awakening to painful situations. One way to do this is to activate suffering in response to past, present or future events and memories - real or imagined - from which it then 'feeds'. Once the Pain Body has become activated in a human, it can so easily cause a person to descend into a nasty spiral of suffering, with its own negative momentum to sustain its existence. This process is possible because of the way human nature operates - especially *unconscious* human nature.

Pain Body - always feels so justified

A major problem with the Pain Body is that when it arises, it will just about always feel so incredibly valid and real, never mind what seems to be instigating the emotion. We inevitably experience this undeniable sense within us that not only do we have a right to, but also almost a duty to react to whatever is causing the pain. Someone says or does something hurtful, untrue or unfair to you, and it seems utterly right to then pull them up on it or get justifiably angry.

Many other events can happen which equally evoke a sense of suffering, such as our car being stolen; our house burning down; losing our job; our partner leaving us - endlessly on. But that is precisely one of the most seductive aspects of the Pain Body. Once the Pain Body has taken over, and is well and truly activated, it is almost as if it then forces us to activate or seek out more pain - with its consequent additional spiral of suffering. Precisely what this Pain Body wants, because the more pain, the greater its 'feed'.

Two things allow this Pain Body to survive - unconsciousness of its existence, and the deep fear of facing our pain head-on, the latter being something we humans automatically shy away from. Interestingly, in some ways, this description of the Pain Body can be seen to correlate to the religious concept of the devil. However, the general way religion would have you deal with the devil is by fighting and resisting it. When it comes to the Pain Body, this is definitely not the approach to take. Fighting it or even trying to avoid it by an endless number of strategies which involve a sense of 'doing', only 'feeds' it more.

In regard to fighting or resisting the Pain Body, it needs to be understood that this entity is huge beyond comprehension. Therefore trying to deal with it by *doing* something with it is a bit like trying to empty all the oceans of this planet, from one little spot on one of its shores, using nothing but a tiny thimble. This is a total no-win situation, which can only lead to a complete failure to drain that 'ocean', and utter exhaustion if you nonetheless try to do so. The other factor needing to be understood is that although we are only scooping a thimble-full of 'water' out of that 'ocean' each time, this amount of 'water' is nevertheless still constantly feeding that Pain Body - not depleting it.

Another correlation could be made between the Pain Body, and what some in the New Age circles call 'Entities'. These are described as negative energy beings or spirits, capable of attaching themselves to humans, causing much chaos and suffering in the process. Coming therefore from a more religious stance, one could, as noted above, equate the Pain Body with the concept of the devil, while if one were more inclined towards New Age ideas, then a link could be seen to exist between the Pain Body and Entities. It is interesting to note that from a Buddhist perspective, suffering is seen as a consequence of our *attachment* to the many desires which so constantly flood our mind.

However, for now let's continue along the lines of just using the Pain Body metaphor, as per Eckhart Tolle. Via this approach, Tolle does however also alert us to a most important fact. Ultimately, this Pain Body is ironically nothing but an ephemeral illusion, which can be made to simply melt away, like snow on a hot surface.

Pain Body – like a boat on a rough ocean

To make more sense out of this last statement, let's use another analogy for the Pain Body. Tolle describes the Pain Body *experience* as nothing more than the waves on the *surface* of a very deep ocean. His perception is that the Pain Body itself is like the 'wind', which creates the waves. However, this 'wind' has less and less effect on the water, the deeper we dive into the Ocean.

By remaining *with* the Pain Body; by trying to somehow fight our suffering or pain, we are like a boat *on* the surface of that deep ocean. Simply trying to battle the waves - small or tsunami-like – only results in being bashed about in that little boat of ours. Even capsizing... and sometimes drowning too.

The latter would correlate with the experience of those so overwhelmed by their battle with the Pain Body that they die from the struggle itself - through suicide for instance. Perhaps for those people, this choice is seen as the only means of ending what had become an unbearable and overwhelming level of suffering. And yet, all we need to do is realize we are not just a 'boat', but in fact a 'submarine'. It seems the best 'attack' or solution to battling the raging storm on the ocean surface, is to dive into its calm depths instead.

So it is precisely the power of our Awareness, consolidated by certain choices, which can dispense with what otherwise seems such an overwhelming and evil force. As noted earlier, it's by going into what the New Age calls the 'Witness State', from which to *observe* this energy rather than *wrestle* with it that then provides a point of power - a position from which to negate what can otherwise be seen as a most destructive force, operating in disguise in so many people's lives. By becoming the Witness to it, we also allow for a sense of separation. Instead of the Pain Body taking over and us *becoming* its energy - us actually morphing into *being* the Pain Body itself – creating this sense of separation from it thereby pulls the plug on its power over us. And the most potent way to allow ourselves to become completely centered in the Witness State is to be *fully* in the Moment. This is another of Eckhart Tolle's concepts, which he discusses in depth in his book, 'The Power of Now'.[1]

Ego is that part of our being which runs the show unsupervised

But first we need to explore the concept of the ego and Higher Self a bit more. This 'vehicle' we 'inhabit' as humans, which within the earthly realm is designated a body, seems to function on three, over-lapping levels. Within its design, one level is that of a basic, inherent 'operational system'; the 'set-up software' if you like - which is capable of keeping the 'machinery' ticking over. This level has an automatic, inner knowingness of what to do. The more conscious 'I' aspect of a human; that part of your awareness reading this book, doesn't ever have to be involved in its efficient operation. Using the analogy of a business company, this 'operational system' of the human apparatus, often called the 'subconscious', can in a sense be likened to the basic computers in any office of such a company. These are all hard-wired with their respective programs, running on automatic, and simply doing their job - efficiently, effectively and silently in the background.

Then there is that part of the human which needs to only keep the 'company office' working efficiently - the office manager if you like. This is called the 'ego'. Finally, there is another, much more Conscious component to who we are as humans, which could be likened to the Boss of the company – or in New Age parlance... the Higher Self. Beyond the Higher Self is what can be termed the Oversoul, then the Ultrasoul and then, many more 'layers' further, lies what we perceive of as God. But more about the Oversoul and Ultrasoul in chapter 7 when we'll discuss the incarnational Journey in greater detail.

In our typical human 'vehicle', these various roles should all intermesh and work together smoothly. However, the busy-body ego is rather prone to grandiosity, often believing it has to run the *entire* show. It's often found sticking its nose into areas which simply aren't its responsibility, such as checking every program within the office computers; doing its own day-to-day running of the office, as well as thinking it needs to run the entire company too!

To get a much more efficient and stress-free 'office', plus have the 'company' generally perform much better, it's important the ego learns to keep its meddling nose out of areas of responsibility it was never meant to handle. Ego self in a sense, provides the 'secretarial service' to functioning efficiently on this earthly dimension of reality. Higher Self provides the general overview of the human endeavor; it holds the 'blue-print' to the entire human Journey here on Earth.

In turn, and from this greater perspective, the Higher Self is that aspect of our overall humanness most capable of providing smaller, individual 'projects' which the ego can work on. There can however be a problem, in that as the ego then tries to work on these 'smaller' projects, it inevitably can't fully grasp the grander perspective of what the entire project may be about, as perceived by the Higher Self. But the 'office manager' - the ego - needs to learn to accept and trust that the 'boss' knows what It's doing. The ego needs to stop worrying that it often can't see the significance of each and every smaller job it is asked to focus on.

All the ego-self needs to therefore do in this human Journey is to organize and deal with the day-to-day events. Getting you up in the morning; getting you showered; having you make breakfast; getting to work on time; catching the right bus or train. Its great skill - and value - is in running these basic aspects to your daily life here on planet Earth. Within that context, the ego is a vital component to our ability to function efficiently on this plane of reality.

This New Age idea that the ego is somehow inherently bad, and needs to be permanently eradicated from our humanity, surely comes from a most confused and distorted way of looking at the overall human being? It comes from an inability to see the vital role the ego does perform in enabling us to live safely and effectively on this planet. Ego is therefore something we as Conscious humans need to learn to *transcend* – not get *rid* of.

Ego – Tolle's definition

Eckhart Tolle has further insights into what constitutes the ego. To start with, his view is that the Inner Consciousness Journey we make as incarnate Beings is ultimately about learning to live our reality here through Higher Self, rather than through ego. This is an important and fundamental platform of his worldview. Next, Tolle talks about how, as we grow up, we form a mental image of who we are, based on our personal and cultural conditioning. He calls this phantom-self the ego. It consists of mind-activity, and can only be kept going through constant thinking. Ego is that ceaseless little voice in our brain, chattering away non-stop – at times driving us nuts! So ego is more like a false self, created by 'us' as we unconsciously identify with the mind.

The human condition - run by this ego or lesser self - seems to be an experience of endless needs, wants and desires for an infinite number of 'things', be that money, friends, power, partners, sex, houses, jobs, etc. However, if we look for the *underlying* thread that motivates all this plethora of needs, then it would appear that what we're really after is a State of *Being* - a State where we feel more complete, joyful, fulfilled, and so on. Yet, the ego's primary agenda seems to be focused more on achieving this *State,* via the manifestation of endless lists of outer '*objects*'.

However, if we perceive this Journey here on planet Earth through the lens of Higher Consciousness - the Higher Self; then a fundamental shift in focus and emphasis is required. By taking even a brief look at our lives, it soon becomes obvious that we rarely feel fulfilled – certainly in the long-term – by external objects or experiences. Yes, as we finally obtain that new house, new car, new job, win some money... there is indeed a definite increase in our happiness. But inevitably it doesn't take long for the glamour to wear off; just another in an endless list of fulfilled desires which again didn't quite make the grade after all. So off we go chasing the next dream.

Instead of focusing on obtaining our sense of Inner fulfillment through outer objects or experiences, we need to first learn to differentiate between manifesting that *Inner* State, versus obtaining endless amounts of *outer* objects as the 'source' of our contentment. The former aim of manifesting that Inner State needs to be seen as the primary and most fundamental objective of our Consciousness Journey here. If this is indeed so, then we need to make the appropriate changes within our Being, allowing for this deep and fundamental Shift to occur - *from* which we can then manifest the outer. This concept is also going to be most important when we explore the mechanisms of Co-creativity in future chapters.

Nothing lost and everything gained

One advantage of such a different conceptual approach to life is that even if this outer manifestation doesn't occur, we're not left empty-handed, as it were. There is no need to then feel betrayed by life, simply because we will already have achieved that *Inner* State, via that Inner shift in Awareness. If we look more closely at why we so desperately want to fulfill our desires, it's that Inner State we're really after all the time anyway; ultimately that was the end goal. However, we're normally not able to see that fact clearly enough, due to the way we traditionally focus on fulfillment being *only* possible via external 'things' or events. This is indeed the big Illusion we humans are so trapped in.

An important conclusion therefore arises from this discussion. What we need to realize is that it's just as possible to *choose* to 'do' something within our head-space, which will then allow this *Inner* State of joy to occur. Not easy necessarily, but definitely possible. In this way, we don't automatically need that *outer* event, person or whatever, to be the sole, 'magical' trigger for achieving such an Inner State.

It's therefore about understanding, on deep, fundamental levels of *experiential* Knowingness, that this entire human Journey is ultimately about learning to achieve these *Inner* States. These need to be triggered by *Inner Shifts of Awareness* within us. In the end, this objective provides so much more than all this endeavoring to achieve or force happiness into our experience, via the *outer* 'reality' of Maya.

Ego as the flight attendant

Another metaphor for ego is that of a flight attendant on an airplane. Flight attendants have a very important, valid and vital function to play in the overall smooth management of a flight: organizing the passengers; supervising seat allocation; ensuring people on the flight know the safely rules; are adequately fed – (decreasingly so nowadays!) – as well as other general aspects of creating an efficient, safe and pleasant flight. This is a role for which flight attendants are specifically trained, and which they are well able to carry out.

On that same airplane there are also the pilots, who have a fundamentally different role to play; metaphorically equating more with the Higher Self. Yes, they too are concerned about the safety of the passengers, and that they have a pleasant trip, but their primary role is to actually fly the plane. Their job is not to directly look after all the passengers. Both the pilots and the flight attendants are highly trained, capable people, each with their specific field of expertise. Nevertheless, if these two groups of highly trained experts suddenly decided to swap roles, all hell would break loose.

So too with the ego and the Higher Self. Both have their respective roles to play, and both are good at what they are 'trained' or meant to do. The problem starts when the ego decides, in some delusional way, that it can now actually fly the 'plane', instead of simply managing its human cargo. Not only is the flight itself suddenly in grave danger, but it would end in disaster sooner rather than later. It's when the flight attendants think they can also fly the plane that the passengers really need to ensure their seat-belts are fastened!

Ego in overwhelm

It's little wonder the human ego can often get itself all frazzled and twisted up in knots, if it persists in believing it is responsible for jobs it was never meant to handle. This causes nothing but a sense of being overwhelmed, feeling inadequate, worried and insecure. Just as the office manager needs to learn when to hand over to the boss, so too the ego needs to learn when to hand over to the Higher Self.

Point of awareness can be very mobile

Every experience we have as humans which is not aligned with these fundamental aspects of our Spirit Self becomes less than Spirit's inherent qualities - in other words, suffering. Let's expand upon this. We have two fundamental ways through which to experience any particular human event – either through ego self or through Higher Self. Ego self is ultimately locked into, and therefore blind to the Maya, or illusion, of human existence. This blindness to what is truly important or more fundamental to life, becomes a major source driving human suffering. So the solution to suffering is to give *more* credence to the Spirit Aspect of who we are - in other words, to the Higher Self Mode, rather than to the *human* aspect of who we so compellingly seem to be.

The challenge in this Journey is to have an understanding of what is the *true* Level of Reality, something which we as humans, spellbound by our experience of life, are so disconnected from. First, we need to realize such a Higher Level of Reality is of equal - indeed Higher - importance to how powerful and fulfilling our human experience *could* be. Then we need to train ourselves in giving *this* Higher Level of Reality more value and credence than what our eyes, ears and human senses convince us about our earthly reality.

But this is the illusion! This is where we get so lost... and so disempowered. As already discussed, we are first and foremost Spirit. It's about truly 'getting it' that we are *Spirit* incarnated into the *physical*. We are *not* primarily a physical being who happens to have a spirit aspect to us. Being able to differentiate and really 'get' this subtle yet crucial point, underpins the entire discussion here.

This belief in our separateness - body from Spirit; one person from another - is so very core to our existence as humans, that we basically never question it. We can't even seem to conceive that there is a question to be asked. But until we *do* question this seemingly unassailable 'truth' of our different levels of separateness, we are unfortunately doomed to remain within the powerful grasp of the Pain Body - endlessly forced to remain on the treadmill of suffering.

Living in a dualistic way

It's almost a matter of living within a dual perspective. On one level we acknowledge the 'reality' of our very human, incarnational experiences here on planet Earth, along with all its attendant 'challenges' such as disease, disappointments, accidents, and the usually string of human sufferings. It is indeed crucial to acknowledge the reality of such situations, and it is nonsense to tell a human, in incarnation, that this is not real - as we've already mentioned some New Age authorities are prone to do. On the other hand, we also need to recognize where our point of power does lie, in order to understand that there is a much more Fundamental and exceptionally Real Level of Reality which we can tap into. By doing so, we can help to overcome, or at least mitigate our 'sufferings' within the human experience.

Bi-location capacity of human awareness

It's as if our primary human sense of awareness can actually bi-locate itself quite easily. It has the inherent capacity to therefore reside in either the ego awareness mode or move to the Higher Self Awareness state. Problem is that most of the time, we as humans have our awareness well and truly locked down in the ego mode. But from this vantage point, the 'view' of any particular life situation is also so much more limited. However, with practise, we can enhance the necessary skill whereby our inherent human awareness can consciously choose to relocate its point of view - from ego mode of operation to Higher Self mode. In New Age parlance, this is called the Witness State, because it is from this perspective that our Awareness has a greater capacity to observe or Witness what is going on in our lives.

Another way of describing the difference between ego self and Higher Self is to see the former as that part of us; our awareness, which is 'asleep' to any Higher or more Spiritual perspectives on life. In contrast, the Higher Self is very much Aware of, or shall we say, 'Awake' to Its Spirit aspect, thereby giving the Higher Self Its broader and more in-depth understanding of life situations. So the human journey is about the ego self increasingly *awakening* to its need for a Higher perspective on its reality here on Earth.

Hot air balloon concept – getting to Higher Self

What really prevents us from moving up to this level of Higher Self is the emotional 'baggage' the ego so inevitably gets caught up in. It's a bit like a hot-air balloon, whose sole function is to rise higher and higher. Let's assume it's all pumped up with hot air - but still well and truly grounded due to its heavy load of ballast. In a similar way, our 'ballast' keeps us in ego mode, and thus unable to rise to Higher Self Mode. And the 'ballast' itself consists of all the strong investment and attachment we have to our beliefs, as well as the inevitable emotional baggage which is such an inherent aspect of our humanness. Yet, the irony is that we don't actually have to do all that much to allow this shift to occur - automatically and with great ease. Perhaps it's not so much about always *changing* or *processing* things, as much as just 'letting go of our stuff'.

Therapy – seeing the patterns and simply side-stepping them

In our Western, counseling-orientated culture, there is a widely held belief that unless we can figure out *where* our dysfunction or suffering comes from, we won't be able to get rid of it. Now, counseling is an extraordinarily powerful and valid way of dealing with so many of the issues we humans find ourselves confronted with. But sometimes we just can't figure it out. Ultimately then, it may be so much more empowering to just *Be* with what's happening, rather than to *understand* what's happening - especially if we have already gone down the path of trying to comprehend the problem or suffering, via a range of other techniques or approaches.

Sometimes, never mind how long we live; how many Consciousness Courses we do; how much counseling we engage in, etc. etc. – in the end it's perhaps more about *recognizing our patterns*. And for that, such 'work' - the courses; workshops; counseling - can indeed be most useful. Totally acknowledged. Eventually however, it may have more to do with becoming really skilled at not *engaging* with the patterns, once seen. Rather, we can just Witness them. 'Ah, there's fear again'. 'Oh my, there's anger again'. No judgments; just observe and name the patterns as they arise.

So we'll probably go to our graves still dealing with a long list of dysfunctional behaviors and patterns experienced on a daily basis. But hopefully, what will have been achieved in our life Journey is a vastly enhanced skill at not having to automatically buy into these dysfunctional patterns. Additionally, we may be able to increase our skill and ability to *choose* to allow our experience of such life scenarios to be more from Higher Self versus ego self.

Just look for the ballast - and dump it

The point is to increasingly train our Witness State to be able to see what our 'ballast' is... *and then dump it over-board*. As the ballast is decreased, the 'balloon' starts to rise. It's actually so easy and guaranteed! It's in that moment of 'seeing'; of understanding what holds us back, that we then also re-gain our power to make the necessary Inner shift. And as we release, our point of Awareness or Consciousness automatically rises to the Higher Self locus. It's a bit like climbing up onto the roof of your home to get a better view of some commotion that seems to be occurring down the road, but which is not visible from where you are presently standing at ground level.

But for now, summarizing the 'mechanics' of how the human organism runs itself on planet Earth, we can differentiate the various 'management' roles into three primary 'departments' - the subconscious, the ego and the Higher Self. Classical psychiatrists and psychologists would have a fit with this analysis of the human being, but for the moment it serves the purpose, and is employed more as a usable construct than as an absolute 'truth'.

About deserving to enter Higher Self

One huge stumbling block that may occur for quite a number of people is a belief that they are not yet 'good enough' to be allowed to go to this Higher Level of Being. That truly is something to get over. It is not an issue of whether you have *earned* the right to go there. It is more a matter of... have you *learnt the skill*. Inherent to such skill is the ability to let go of the lower consciousness, ego-mode 'stuff' which holds you there, and prevents you from floating to the Higher Level of Reality.

The only procedure you therefore need to be capable of, in moving from one level to the other, is simply the recognition that it is not necessarily about 'fixing' anything on the lower ego level. This recognition and subsequent skill is the 'ticket' which allows you into the Higher Level. Actually, all this 'stuff' in our lives, which we feel we need to 'fix' or process, has more to do with us understanding that it is life providing us with the opportunities *through* which to become skilled at recognizing the difference between ego and Higher Self Mode.

Once the 'stuff' has alerted you to the fact that you are in ego mode, then you can make a *choice* to move into this alternate Higher Level of Awareness. So it's not necessarily and automatically always about *fixing* things; it is about *letting go*. Let go of all that 'ballast' in the 'balloon'. It's as easy as that. If it truly was an issue of 'deserving' to go to the Higher Level; if indeed we needed to somehow earn 'brownie points' before we qualified to go to the Higher Level, we'd be on this lower ego level for a long time!

In that sense, the exercise of giving thanks, the 'Gratitude Meditation' discussed in detail in chapter 12, can be seen as a very easy means of training ourselves to release from the lower ego level. But for now, realize that the

'Gratitude Meditation' works, simply because from this lower, ego level we always tend to feel incomplete; not good enough; that there is something wrong. Yet, if we are constantly thankful, we are in a sense manifesting or validating more of the qualities we would experience if living from the Higher Level. So the 'Gratitude Meditation' or technique is an easy daily exercise through which to try and live more from the Higher Level. Just doing this process already moves you into Higher Self Mode, and you start to feel more at peace and complete.

Doing versus Being

Ego, as it operates within the human, also has an inherent need to attach itself to something, so as to be able to give it a sense of realness; of truly existing. One way it can derive such a sense of existence or reality is by identification with the mind and our thoughts. But these are precisely the aspects to our humanness which are usually in such disarray - if not frankly dysfunctional.

But there is a way around this issue. We need to take on board the point that going into Witness State allows us to disconnect from all this emotional 'gunk', inherently such a part of being in ego mode. Another important factor to understand is that in ego mode, we humans are truly not living up to our name, and are instead always *doing* things. In Higher Self mode however, we come much closer to who we truly are as human *beings,* because it is only by *Being* - rather than *doing* - that we can get to the Witness State.

3-D metaphor

You might remember those 3-dimensional patterns which became a bit of a fad at one stage. When standing in front of them, and viewing them from a flat, 2-dimensional perspective, all you see is a lot of strange patterns and mishmashed colors. But if you then re-focus in a *different* way - often by actually going into a sort of 'soft-focus', or focusing *off* or *beyond* the pattern, then suddenly you experience a full-on 3-D image. Yet, a few seconds ago it was nothing more than a 2-D mish-mash. But simply by delicately changing your focus, now it stands out like a hologram.

That 3-D image was there all the time. However, you only *saw* it once you shifted your *Inner* focus! It's not as if you moved closer or further from the image. You only *focused* differently - still from the same spot you stood at before.

Both 'realities' were actually visible to your perception via your eyes - even though you were only *seeing* one of them. Simply by some minute adjustment of your eye mechanism, you suddenly do see that there are in fact two 'realities' available to your sense of vision. It was all there *together*; at the same time. But which one you saw depended on how you were focusing your eyes.

Similarly, the shift from ego mode to Higher Self mode is - on one level - as easy as going from the 2-D to the 3-D version of all those colorful squiggles. Initially it may have seemed difficult to go from the 2-D to the 3-D image, but once you had achieved it a few times it actually became relatively easy to do on demand. Practise is the answer, in the same way as using our daily situations of suffering provides an endless array of opportunities to yet again master this Inner shift from ego to Higher Self.

Fighting the Pain Body = being in ego mode

In this learning and skilling process, you need to keep remembering one thing. If you end up fighting the Pain Body - the most automatic and 'natural' initial reaction to pain and suffering - it means you inevitably are doing so from an ego mode of human operation. If you wish to effectively deal with this force or energy, then it is paramount you learn how to move your primary focus from ego to Higher Self mode of human operation. From *doing* mode to *Being* mode; from somehow grappling with the suffering to just observing it.

In the former you actually end up becoming the Pain Body, by trying to *do* something about it. In the latter, you in fact separate from the Pain Body, by just *Being*. Simply Witnessing the Pain Body effectively disconnects its ability to 'feed' off you. This approach does provide a tactic to our many human dilemmas and problems which at first seems completely counter-intuitive, ineffective, if not plain dangerous. Yet it undoubtedly *is* a powerful and effective way of dealing with the Pain Body.

Becoming Witness to our suffering creates an extra advantage beyond just disconnecting the Pain Body, and therefore changing the experience of that suffering. Interestingly enough, suffering can therefore become an opportunity to gain increased skill at moving between these two dimensions of our human reality. In turn, this also becomes a powerful way through which we can gain greater skill at accessing and living from a more Spiritual level of our humanity. Slowly but surely, we can learn to operate more from 'pilot' rather than 'flight attendant' mode.

Chapter 6 - Suffering Issues

But in our 'normal' human existence, our instinctual and most spontaneous response to any such 'attack' from an external enemy, threat, or 'the devil' - or from something like a Pain Body - is to jump into *doing* mode... and *attack back*. The majority of religions would vindicate such a method as being the most 'spiritually correct' approach. In contrast, the idea of just sitting there and observing such a threat; facing one's demons, seems utterly counter-intuitive and idiotic.

Yet, the former approach is so often what religion certainly advocates its followers do, when confronted with 'temptations' from 'the devil'. The only advice given is to fight it - as hard and actively as you can. Now if this approach works for you: great! Then don't make any change to such life tactics. But you might also find that other approaches could actually be more powerful and effective. At least it's worth a try.

Resistance to suffering won't necessarily dissolve it

Following on along the vein of 'fighting our pain and suffering' – there is one game the mind sometimes may play out. It may actually believe - unconsciously - that its resistance to a life situation of suffering, if fought against strongly enough, will in the end somehow dissolve the undesired situation. From this perspective, our ego-based thinking may go something along the following lines. Ego's belief is that endlessly and bravely fighting our pain could be perceived as a possible way of trying to in a sense blackmail the source of our suffering into relenting and going away. Hopefully such an approach will make it feel that 'we have suffered enough for now', and thus give us respite from our suffering.

In other words... 'if I can only become 'unhappy enough' or 'suffer enough', surely the source of my pain - be that God, human or whatever - will finally feel some sort of pity for me and would capitulate, allowing a resolution to occur'. It's an irrational belief, and the problem is that this negative - and ultimately very unrealistic - way of trying to solve the problem only *adds* to the problem. It definitely comes from, and strengthens the ego, slams the door on the Higher Self as a solution, and certainly maintains a prodigious feeding of the Pain Body. Exactly what the Pain Body wants.

However, totally accepting and working with what is in this Moment Now, may actually serve us much more in getting out of a state of suffering. Choose instead to deal with it by working *with* it - not *against* it, as ego would.

Indeed, surrender to it; although this can be a most frightening thing to even contemplate doing, let alone attempt.

At first people are horrified when it's recommended they let go and enter right into the pain. Their fear is that since the pain is already virtually unbearable, if they stopped trying to resist it, and gave in to it altogether, then the overwhelm of such pain would almost lead to annihilation or madness. Yet the irony is that it is precisely the opposite of what is expected and feared. Our resistance to the pain or suffering; our 'staying brave' and fighting it, paradoxically only feeds it to a greater extent.

When we fully release into such deep pain, something utterly unexpected can occur which is almost miraculous. The pain is still there, but its nature changes. Somehow it becomes less constrictive or suffocating. It's as if a sense of spaciousness occurs within which that pain can be contained more comfortably. In turn, this allows for quite an unexpected situation to enter... a deep sense of Peace, there *beneath* the pain.

If these ideas seem to be too challenging, then this is very much a situation where you might consider initially engaging in such strategies under the competent supervision of a trained counselor.

Surrender as a means of dealing with suffering

When we are asked to surrender, the first thought that might strike us is that we're being asked to 'give up'; that this is an act of weakness or failure. However, surrender needs to be understood as a purely *Inner* phenomena; an Inner shift in how you perceive what is happening to you on an *outer* level. The crucial point to take on board is that surrender doesn't mean you can't take action on an outer level in an attempt to change the situation. There are so many human experiences which are very real, and needing a response. The washing machine has broken down; the car has run out of petrol; the cupboard is empty of food; the house is burning down. Each of these situations can definitely activate the Pain Body, causing you to experience suffering – annoyance, frustration, anger, despair, fear.

For most of us, the automatic and immediate response to such situations is inevitably from ego mode. This is after all where we mostly live from. This ego mode gives a direct and easy window through which the Pain Body becomes activated, causing us to go into some form of 'suffering'. However, it would be so much more productive to choose to firstly go to Witness State instead,

Chapter 6 - Suffering Issues

rather than immediately flying off the handle that you are 10 km away from town and have run out of petrol - for instance, and as we'll expand upon below.

When some form of suffering strikes us, first move your Awareness to the Higher Self perspective; name the pain while also just observing it. Once you feel you've got yourself anchored in this Higher Space, *then* from that perspective of being in Witness mode you initiate an action to rectify the 'problem'. Such a stance automatically means you're not so emotionally caught up in your suffering. Hence, any actions you initiate are now also hopefully free from anger, frustration or whatever.

Let's assume the car has run out of petrol. There are several options available to you. Either you use your mobile, and see if you can organize for a taxi or friend to pick you up, or hope for a hitch-hike into town. Or you are just going to have to walk! Those are your options in this example. Now, you can engage in any one of these options, while legitimately fuming, cursing and swearing. All very valid under the circumstances, but do understand that none of those emotional responses are going to get you out of your predicament *any faster or more efficiently*.

In fact, it is going to be just so much more painful to 'solve the problem'. You definitely have your problem - out of gas on the highway - but if you react to the problem by staying in ego mode, with the consequent instigation of the Pain Body... now you have two problems. Out of gas plus a monster of an emotional storm to deal with too, as you fume, fret and curse.

Or you can choose to go to Higher Ground by invoking the Witness State. Here, you are still very much stuck on the highway, 10 km out of town, with no petrol in the tank. Exactly the same problem. However, by choosing to go to Witness State also allows you to get *beyond* all the emotional rage and frustration, where you are only likely to kick the car tires - and in the process probably end up with a broken toe as well.

Pain – staying in eye of storm

By becoming increasingly skilled at quickly moving your awareness from ego to Higher Self mode also allows you to get a much greater clarity around some of the issues associated with being human, and 'touristing on planet Earth'. Being in Higher Self mode of Awareness is a bit like the concept of remaining in the eye of the cyclone. Here everything is calm - yet from here you can also Witness the fury of the storm, without being flung around *in* it.

Otherwise, the attempt to *do* something with the storm is like jumping right into the storm itself. Not only do you have absolutely no effect on changing the storm, but by jumping right into it, you lose this Centeredness, as well as diminishing your sense of objectivity. Inevitably you end up further hurt and bruised by all the buffeting as you tumble along *inside* the storm itself. The reality is that life is one continuous storm - at times perhaps only a gentle breeze, but nowadays more often than not turning into a brutal, raging cyclone with great potential for damage and suffering.

But you *do* have a choice within this reality of life. Storms there will always be - of minor or major ferocity. But the point of Power, and the choice you do have is - in that moment of understanding the Storm is upon you - again! – to either step into the eye of the Storm, or to continue being tossed around in the Storm itself. But because we are such *doing* creatures, it seems downright unrealistic that by simply remaining in the eye of the storm; just *Being*, could somehow be a more effective response.

The power of 'Being' in Higher Self mode

So, using the concept of the Pain Body, and that of the Witness State, does give us a very handy, powerful and productive technique with which to *respond* more Consciously to whatever inconvenient or difficult situation presents itself in your life. It's not that this way of responding is automatically easy. Again, the choice is simple - you either do or don't go to Witness State to deal with your 'problem'. But easy... hell no! It absolutely does require a lot more focus, determination, maturity, and ultimately a Higher Level of skill at being Conscious.

Initially you may only realize hours after the event, that there had indeed been another option open to you from which you could have dealt with your 'problem'. If you had, you could also have converted that 'problem' into an opportunity to actually skill yourself at this change in Consciousness approach to life situations. As with all skills, the more you do it, the easier it becomes, until finally it even becomes automatic.

Hence over time, you'll find that you'll move from initially becoming 'Aware' that you had another way of dealing with the pain, *hours* after the event, to *soon* after the event, to *during* the event, to *just before* the event. Eventually, you'll find yourself responding automatically to your pain and suffering, *way before* it has any chance to take a hold of your emotional being.

The Pain Body is sneaky

The Pain Body is a most sneaky entity though, and knows many ways of getting its 'feed' from you. It has lots of tricks up its sleeve with which to fool you - yet again! – thereby allowing the Pain Body to become activated. It certainly doesn't need to rely on external events to trigger its 'feed'. One way the Pain Body can do so is by activating our typically vivid human imaginations into a negative spiral. This can set off waves of fear, anxiety, panic or whatever, as we contemplate in 3-D and technicolor, what it would be like if... 'our partner left us'. 'What if we were fired'? 'What if the Stock Market collapses and our shares lose their value'? Endlessly!

Yet, all this suffering is created solely by a capricious imagination, allowed to run riot. Sure, these things *could* happen - but very often they haven't as yet, and probably never will. This doesn't mean that worry or anxiety are inappropriate. Many situations can occur in your life where such an emotional response is entirely valid, as long as these emotions are entertained for just long enough to alert you to the reality that there is something in your life needing attention; just long enough to allow you to *choose* to respond by using Higher Self mode, rather than ego mode... from which to deal with the issue.

In this sense, anxiety, worry or other seemingly 'negative' emotions can be used to activate you into responding in far more positive and productive ways. However, so often our worries are unproductive, generating nothing but negative emotions; activating the Pain Body; providing it with a huge 'feed', and taking us right out of the moment. In turn, this makes us totally oblivious to perhaps the most beautiful things or events happening all around us - *right now.*

Surrender as an effective tool

As touched on earlier, surrender usually carries rather negative connotations, such as weakness or a giving up. Yet, there can also be immense power in the act of surrender. It can be a way of allowing yourself to re-connect with Higher Self, and in doing so allows you to then operate from Its Energy Level versus ego-energy level. So when your car finally splutters to a grinding halt, miles out of town, as discussed in that example above, you can certainly feel most vindicated for going right into a full-on ego mode reaction.

You're already running late; you've promised to pick up not just your own kids, but also those of your neighbor. And now here you are in a situation which means the kids will all be waiting god knows how long; dinner will end up very late... and you've got a 10 km hike ahead of you before you get anywhere near sorting out this mess!

From one perspective, you have every right to be angry, cursing your husband or wife for not having warned you the tank was already low. Indeed, cursing yourself for not having automatically checked the fuel level before you left home! But never mind how much 'right' you have to your emotional reaction to all this, the most important question to ask is... 'will it actually serve to sort it out any faster'? 'Will such an activated Pain Body response make it any easier'?

Or do you surrender to the situation - on one level - acknowledging what is happening; make a choice as to how to best solve the problem, and then go about doing so? This cuts out the reaction and resistance modes of 'doing'. *Surrender therefore doesn't necessarily mean doing nothing.* All it means is that any 'doing' comes from a far more Conscious dimension, making it non-reactive, and therefore so much easier to get through. It becomes a true *response* compared to just a *reaction*.

In other words, our *response* to the problem facing us is transformed, thus making it easier to deal with. Such a choice for surrender - as understood in the above sense - becomes a choice of empowerment; not weakness or giving up. Once we surrender, at least we then stop creating further negativity and suffering around the situation we're in. The struggle against it stops, and this cessation of resistance and struggle stops the pain and suffering cycle, thus also most effectively disconnecting the Pain Body.

Being with pain doesn't mean automatically getting rid of it

There is another subtle trap that often comes with these sorts of concepts through which to deal with our human suffering. It's the belief that if you could only stay in Witness State, then somehow, magically, this would also guarantee you'll be able to 'get rid' of the pain. It's still coming from a subtle form of *doing* something to the pain in order to eliminate it, although it represents a step up from the 'normal' way we humans jump in with one of our techniques, and then try to wrestle the pain or suffering into submission.

The whole point of this exercise of choosing to move to Higher Self - in the examples presented, and catalyzed by our pain - is ironically not in fact to get *rid* of pain or suffering, once and for all. Rather, it's about *transforming* the *experience* of that pain or suffering - as well as increasingly skilling ourselves to simply BE. It's precisely by coming from such a different state of Being, which then allows us to also more effectively and efficiently deal with our human 'problems'.

Hence, it can serve us more pragmatically to simply acknowledge that as humans, we run according to a 'factory pre-set'. We do, however have a choice and ability to *change* this 'pre-setting', which is to move our focus of Awareness from ego – 'factory pre-set' - to Higher Self setting. This allows us a broader, deeper and more efficient way of dealing with this human conundrum of suffering.

There is another important advantage to learning this skill of *how* we deal with our suffering. In other words, learning to move with increasing ease from ego mode of 'doing' to Higher Self mode of 'Being' is in fact a fundamental aspect of this process the New Age so often talks about – Enlightenment. But more on that later.

Pain Body is an inherent, inescapable fact of human existence

So the 'Pain Body' will always be part of our human experience. Our power, and our challenge as humans is to increasingly learn to shift our automatic tendency to operate from ego mode, to being in Higher Self mode instead. The beauty is that we can conveniently use our range of daily experiences from which to instigate a choice to deal with them from this totally different plane of reality.

Let's use the analogy of a Recording Studio. Here we have one room in which the performers are playing, and then there is a separate room in which the recording staff resides. Despite the separation of these two rooms, there is a complete capacity for both groups to interact together via audio-links.

However, the staff in the Recording Studio can certainly control how much of the music - or just noise! - created by the musicians is allowed into their room. They can see the musicians; they can observe that they are very involved in making their music, but those in the actual Recording Booth have total control over how much of the sound is allowed in to be experienced - or suffered.

We can therefore either remain in the Performing Booth, completely inundated by the sound/noise or we can remove ourselves from there and relocate into the Recording Booth. Here, although we can see the performance occurring, we are also in control of how much of that sound is actually allowed to be experienced. This shift is akin to having ourselves, via our 'normal' ego mode of living, inundated and totally overwhelmed by the sheer volume of pain hitting the human 'vehicle'. Or we can choose to move to Witness State, from which the pain 'volume' can be decreased - or *altered*. We are still human; we are still vulnerable to the 'Pain Body'. But with this approach to our humanness, at least we can turn down the 'volume' of pain 'static' being broadcast from the personal - or communal 'Pain Body Field'. In this way there is therefore less ability for that suffering energy to resonate within our 'instrument' or body-mind.

The choice is actually very simple – but not necessarily easy

All of this discussion, and the many life examples where such situations would be applicable, all boil down to a ridiculously *simple* issue. You either choose to play with the Pain Body - and all the repercussion of such a choice - or you choose to disconnect. Couldn't be *simpler*. But it is also true that this is not necessarily an *easy* thing to do. Nevertheless, do remember the Pain Body cannot exist, let alone take you over, when you are in the Witness State; when you are coming from an Awareness of what the Pain body is and how it operates. This is your point of power over *it*. Judging, analyzing, fighting it are all ego mode operations within the human being. And it is precisely in ego mode that the Pain Body has the greatest access to possessing or overwhelming you.

Where am I?

Sometimes the question is raised about how you can distinguish whether you are in ego mode or Higher Self/Witness mode. It is actually very simple. If you find yourself deeply caught up in any of a range of negative emotions, such as anger, shame, fear, guilt and so many more, then you are undoubtedly in ego mode. If instead you are feeling centered, even joyful or at least relatively peaceful under any particularly challenging circumstances, it is most likely you have managed to get yourself out of ego mode, and into Higher Self mode. Or you're on some pretty powerful tranquilizers!

From the Higher Level though, you are more able to simply Witness the drama, rather than *being* the drama.

What to do when the Pain Body kicks in

As soon as the Pain Body kicks in - and remember the Pain Body is capable of making us do a lot of pretty nasty and dysfunctional things - the most important thing to do is to focus on the feeling inside us, and keep clear of the mind. The mind, unfortunately, loves to fabricate a story-line to our feelings, and it's when we then buy into that story-line that we thereby also tend to lose our point of power - our ability to step aside from the Pain Body, thus disconnecting from it.

For instance, you've just had an argument with your partner. You're still so absorbed in the various things which were said that you become careless in pouring your tea, spilling it all over the table. Instead of simply accepting that some tea has been spilled - which can easily be mopped up - you now immediately jump into blaming your partner for the spillage; it's their fault your hands are so jittery. What's really happening is that your mind is jumping in to create a negative story-line to your present situation, rather than simply accepting there is a bit of moisture on your table.

No big deal really, but the way your mind is playing this out, certainly allows for an even greater response from your Pain Body! The suffering you are experiencing from this tea spillage is inevitably due to your ego-based resistance to 'what is' in your life – just a bit of tea on your table instead of in your cup. Certainly no catastrophe in the overall scheme of things.

The best thing to do is to simply accept that the Pain Body has - yet again - become activated into your experience. Over time however, and by practicing your ability to be in Witness State, you'll find you definitely develop more skill at becoming aware of its presence, earlier and earlier.

Emotional distress check-list

There may be some value in summarizing the discussion thus far and to give a protocol for dealing with our pain.

- See the pattern, feel the emotion, and let it go rather than trying to wrestle with or somehow process it.
- Remember, by wrestling with it, you are actually adding Energy to precisely what you're trying to get rid of.
- Label it, i.e. anger, sadness, fear, jealousy, hatred, frustration - without judging it.

- Where does it come from? Did the car break down? Did your partner just say something nasty to you? Try to put a context to it.
- Become the Witness to it; *Be* present with it rather than trying to automatically *do* something with it. This provides a natural sense of separation from what's ailing you. It puts you in the 'eye of the storm' from which it will be easier to deal with 'the storm'.
- Just for now, accept it - don't resist or fight it.
- Then, from the Higher Self Mode of Being - rather than ego-mode - check if there is anything more substantial you can do, e.g. phone to have the car towed; respond appropriately to your partner, rather than flying into a fit of rage, and saying things which would only worsen the situation.
- It might also be quite appropriate to take certain Bach flowers, herbs, medications, phone a friend, do EFT, (see appendix III), etc.
- If your feel such remedies would help, then yes, definitely take these more mundane measures. If not, then don't worry about such material approaches to your situation, and just choose to stay in Higher Self Mode as much as you can, while dealing with the 'problem'.

Ego likes the drama of suffering – needs the investment

It must also be understood that the ego loves drama, and therefore finds it easy to be drawn and seduced into pain and suffering. There is almost a sort of addictive 'energy hit' that our ego can achieve from doing so... 'aah, I've had *such* a terrible day'! 'Ooh, my arthritis is soooooo painful'! 'Oh boy, the kids have been totally out of control, and my husband is not here to help'. At least it gets us pity - and perhaps pity is better than nothing, even if it is really Love we're after.

If this is the way we are stuck in our suffering, then there may also be a part of our mind which feels that it would be easier and more convenient to simply remain blind to our patterns. The momentum driving this approach let alone the incentive for our tendency to stay with the suffering and problems in our lives, will be quite strong. Plus we may tend to feel - unconsciously more often than not - that the pay-off we get from the suffering is somehow still worth it.

To be able to clearly see our patterns, an Inner shift needs to occur first. Perhaps this is where some form of counseling or therapy would be most effective and useful. This in turn can lead to a certain 'ripeness' and readiness to give up the suffering approach to dealing with life's challenges. Only then do we perhaps stop and actually look at how we are buying into our suffering... again. At that point, simply acknowledge it, and make a different choice.

Another important thing to do is only focus on dealing with just *this* one specific episode occurring *right now*. It's not about getting caught up in how many more similar moments of temptation may exist, all lined up for us over the coming years, nor focusing on past situations where we did lose our focus and gave in, thus 'failing'. Neither strategy is empowering; in fact, precisely the opposite. So just remain Centered, in Witness State, from which it is more possible to deal with each event as it happens... at that point in time. Don't automatically extrapolate forward or backwards to better or worse times.

Becoming more who you really are

Every time you can see yourself going into one of your patterns, you are becoming Aware of another part of your ego-self - which is *not* your Real Self. So each time you see *through* the ego illusions, you are connecting more with who you really are - the Higher Self. This is what Eckhart Tolle believes to be one of the most important choices we can ever tap into during a human life experience or dilemma. Hence, whatever pattern you see - be that anger, shame, hatred, fear, and however 'un-spiritual' these emotions may seem, it's actually totally O.K.

All these aspects to your humanity completely belong to ego - not Higher Self; your *real* or *essential* Self. It's all about re-awakening to that Higher Self of yours; the *true* Self. It's about increasingly disassociating from the illusionary ego self that as a human we have become so bonded to, and through that connection, made it into our primary reality, generating in turn so much of our human experience of pain and suffering. But we need to become increasingly grounded in an experiential Knowingness that what we've always accepted as 'real' and 'normal', is indeed the Illusion. At least from one point of view. Hence, via moment by moment experiencing our Witness Awareness, we start to relocate our primary focus of who we are, more and more into our Real Self - the Higher Self.

Choosing joy as a means through which to learn

And each time we are able to relocate our primary focus, we are automatically choosing to learn from joy - rather than suffering. But it does require us to come from this Higher Plane of Reality and thus a Higher Level of Awareness. In this way, each and every situation of 'suffering' in our life can be chosen to be transmuted into an *opportunity*, one through which to increasingly skill ourselves at more readily, easily and effectively giving ourselves access to experiencing life from our Higher Self mode. In turn, making such choices will translate into a much more joyful way of living our life, as well as a more efficient way of dealing with life's inevitably complex scenarios.

The alternative to trying to live increasingly from Higher Self Mode is just to continue doing it the way we have done it for sooooooooo long now. However, thereby we also remain more the victim to life's circumstances, and our own ego's reaction to them. Again; it's our choice. But this is a choice we need to remember to invoke each and every day, until it becomes an automatic way of living our life. A rare number of people are blessed with this shift happening in one quantum leap of Enlightenment. For most of us however, this Journey of re-location from ego self to Higher Self, and beyond, occurs step by step - and involves time and much effort.

We are ultimately all One

The concept of the Higher Self also propagates some other useful outcomes. A major problem we humans experience here on planet Earth - especially if we are steeped in our secular cultures - is the seeming inability to truly comprehend that everything is ultimately all One. We appear to be such discrete 'units'. It's true that most religions, and certainly the New Age, all preach that we are fundamentally and ultimately just One. Yet a quick look around this plane of reality here on planet Earth, and it's obvious that we have definitely not understood this ubiquitous teaching, let alone lived it.

Other than with conjoined twins, each human being appears to be so obviously separate, and at least biologically independent of each other. This is one of the most fundamental 'blinkers' we humans are prone to, as mentioned in chapters 2, 3 and 5. Yet, it is precisely this deeply entrenched view of ourselves which also provides the basis for so much of our human dysfunction, and our ability to do such evil things to each other. To say that stealing from, hurting or killing another is the same as doing it to yourself seems initially quite ludicrous and irrational. From the perpetrator or observer's point of view, the harm is obviously being done to *another,* not *yourself.* However, once it can be recognized that on the deepest levels possible, we are actually all One, then a whole different set of conclusions - and responses - need to occur when interacting with each other as humans.

The waves and the ocean are all one

An analogy here may help give greater clarity. Eckhart Tolle again uses the metaphor of the ocean, and its seemingly separate waves. Yet the reality is that despite the *appearance* of each wave being so separate, nonetheless, the *substance* of each wave is the same. And in turn, each wave - as water - is inherently connected to the ocean - as water. The solution to the 'wave's' dilemma of feeling and seeming so separate is to move its awareness from just being the water *in that wave,* to being part of such a gigantically larger ocean of water. It's a situation where the ocean very definitely and inherently connects each separate wave into One Whole.

Do we therefore continue to identify as the wave... or as the Ocean? Both are composed of water - but in a different manifested format. Continue to identify as the wave, and our experience of that can be quite ruffled if not chaotic. Identify with the Ocean, and we immediately connect with a Vastness, Depth and Quietness not usually found on the surface.

In this discussion on suffering, the above are all rather limited and basic metaphors. Hopefully, they do however provide enough of a stepping-stone to allow for different perspectives to be seen more clearly within your Mind... and somehow resonate within your Soul. The problem is that our identification as separate 'waves' is utterly and fundamentally hard-wired into our human perception of life on planet Earth. To then be told we are - on the Deepest level possible - actually all One, with the crucial ramifications emanating from this statement, is usually dismissed by too many people. Simply too hard to deal with!

Yet, this statement is fundamentally very real. The wave, although it does exist in its own sort of 'separateness', is nevertheless only an aspect of the wider Ocean. On one level, many people would accept this metaphor, and its relation to life as self evident, and therefore superfluous to the discussion. 'Yes, we already know all this stuff about "Oneness", and we've also heard this Ocean/wave analogy so often before' - boring!

But the point is... *do we in fact **live** this ever so 'obvious' fact in our day-to-day lives?* Or do we just give it lip-service? The problem is that as humans, we choose to hold steadfast to the fundamental notion that we are all discrete, separate beings. There is obviously a 'me' and a 'you'; an 'us' and a 'them'.

There is another interesting and not very functional consequence of seeing ourselves as separate entities. Such a perception inevitably drives us to then commandeer as much as we can of those things we feel we lack, before the 'other' grabs it, and leaves us empty-handed, be that money, power, property, land, natural reserves or whatever. Another consequence associated with our sense of separateness is that inherent feeling which humans are so prone to, i.e. the frequent experience of aloneness, lack and emptiness.

Believing in our separateness also makes it that much easier to play off one seemingly individual person, nation or religion against the other, and to do the most horrific things to these 'others'. After all, they are so clearly unassociated and different from 'us'. Yet, once we allow that deep, Inner shift to occur, where we realize we are in fact all one 'Ocean', how could we then possibly do harm to 'the other', when the 'other' is in fact a fundamental aspect of ourselves?

When it comes to looking at our human experience of pain and suffering, such concepts do create quite a different platform from which to perceive them. Moreover, they allow us to start looking for different ways in which to then deal with this most fundamental of human phenomena. So much of the unnecessary pain and suffering within humanity is precisely made possible because we conveniently ignore our Oneness, thus making it so much easier to do a whole range of painful, dreadful things to 'another'. However, it becomes - at least initially on an intellectual level - so much harder to do these things, when you have fundamentally 'got it', and every cell in your body *knows* that you and the 'other' are indeed One. In other words, what you are perpetrating on that 'other' can ever only end up being done directly to yourself.

Life is for happiness – Dalai Lama version

'No pain; no gain' is a rather fundament and powerful belief system within our human existence here on planet Earth. And indeed pain and suffering can be a most effective way to prod or motivate us into making change. Or pain can cause us to just implode into a sense of powerlessness, seeing it as an inevitable and un-negotiable aspect of the human existence. Such an attitude can result in us never really trying to do anything about pain, other than to simply endure it, believing perhaps, that somehow there will be great rewards for all this present suffering in a future heaven.

Yet, according to the Dalai Lama, the pursuit of happiness is a valid and fundamental human drive we all seem to be hard-wired with as well. At first, this approach to life strikes many 'spiritually orientated' people as a rather superficial assessment of an earthly existence. But interestingly, the Dalai Lama may not automatically mean happiness as defined by a 'normal' level of consciousness within the human condition. If this were so, then the Dalai Lama's definition of the pursuit of happiness would be more likely based on how much money we had in the bank; how good our job was; did I have the perfect partner; did I live in the right neighborhood; had I gone to the right school... endlessly on.

Perhaps what the Dalai Lama is referring to when he says 'happiness', has more to do with the consequence of living our lives *through* an experiential sense of Connection with Source; through our Higher Self, rather than just through materiality. Perhaps the primary aim of life is to Consciously learn the skill of Connecting to Source - which Is Love. The reality is that within the human condition, we have but two choices of how we experience our moment by moment existence i.e. through joy or through suffering. When connected with Source, the consequence is to experience our reality through the lens of Love. But when experienced through disconnection from Source, this results in quite a different outcome. Here we would be experiencing our lives through the plethora of emotions emanating from such a disconnection i.e. fear, abandonment, sadness, depression, anger, hatred, aloneness, etc.

There comes a point where we must choose to learn through joy

From a certain level of awareness, this idea that we can only grow via suffering is indeed a valid option. It is a choice we can and do make. But if we are truly interested in increasing the level of Consciousness from which to live our lives as humans, then a point will be reached in that Journey where the option to only respond or learn by suffering has to be left behind. Instead, we actually have to Consciously choose to learn through joy, and not through suffering. Ultimately, we need to fully grasp how suffering is simply a less productive way of learning.

It's also important to make quite clear that learning through joy or suffering has nothing to do with it being either a 'good' or 'bad' choice. It's not a matter of morality. It's simply that *up to* a certain level of consciousness, suffering can indeed be a most effective, as well as productive way of growing in Awareness. But then *beyond* a certain level of Consciousness, it no longer remains a productive way of growing through the use of life's more painful events. Learning to ride our bikes with safety wheels attached is absolutely fine. It's useful, and has nothing to do with such a practice being 'good' or 'bad'. However, there does come a point in riding our bikes where those safety wheels will actually hamper our agility and maneuverability, and are best taken off.

Ultimately, learning through suffering is not just less efficient, but also less appropriate for a Spiritually evolving person. So we eventually have to give that up, and learn Consciousness through other means which are not involved with suffering, but rather through joy. Or another way of putting it is to learn through Love rather than through fear, because ultimately, those are the only two choices through which anything can be done or experienced: a Love portal or a fear portal.

Love gives rise to joy. Fear gives rise to just about the entire range of all the other not so productive emotions. The option of learning through suffering is definitely coming through a fear portal. This choice repeatedly takes us *out* of the Love mode of being – which even religions will acknowledge is the most fundamental Nature of God. Thus not being able to allow joy into our life is on some level akin to not being able to let God into our life either. When we get to the Co-creation chapters, it becomes obvious that joy is also that 'juice' which fuels the Co-creative process.

So in this Journey of human Consciousness, a point of choice is reached where the 'normal' way of accomplishing that objective, through suffering alone, is also understood to be a rather limited way. Never mind how much this is validated, condoned and even heavily promoted by far too many religions. Instead, a realization starts to dawn upon us how such Consciousness Growth can actually be achieved so much more easily and productively through joy. However, learning through joy in turn does entail coming from a much Higher Level of Awareness or Consciousness.

The irony is that ultimately the Energy of joy, as the Essence of Source, is really all around us. As my dear, recently deceased aunt would say… 'we are a bit like fish in water, searching *for* water'.

Resistance to stopping the suffering

In this Journey towards greater joy in our lives, initially, we may still be living more from a space of negativity, depression, heaviness, sadness, and a plethora of other painful emotions. Such energies, which many people experience on a 24/7 level, will have an amazing amount of force and impetus behind them. This may seemingly make it impossible to do anything else but continue in the same, familiar, albeit painful life-direction, driven by the powerful energetic momentum we seem so caught up in.

As much as we might like to change it, there may nevertheless also be another level to this maintenance of momentum. Strange as it sounds initially, we may have become 'sort-of-comfortable' with the pain and distress in our lives. Suffering has become such a familiar and thus almost 'normal' aspect to our daily life that oddly enough, there could be quite a resistance to giving up the 'devil we know' rather than swap it for the desired State of more joy. After all, this is something which is still an unknown quantity as well as seemingly unattainable anyway.

However, there will come a time in our Journey where the balance starts to tip towards being *truly* 'over it', as far as our constant state of un-joyfulness is concerned, however that may be manifesting - by emotions such as depression, loneliness, sadness or fear. At this point in our life, it becomes actually more feasible to use that increased motivational energy of 'I've had a gut-full of this suffering', to then power our Journey along a different trajectory.

One thing does need to be made crystal clear here. In the initial stages of our Journey towards trying to live our lives via a Higher sense of joy, we may for example, still be heavily depressed, and definitely needing anti-depressants - medical or natural. Or we may be suffering a particularly painful health issue, requiring frequent or constant analgesia. Starting on this more Conscious way of living our lives, does *not* then mean we suddenly throw all medications or therapies in the bin, somehow hoping that this joy will magically come knocking on our door. Far from it! If serious depression, pain, illness or other situations are a major aspect to our daily life, it is vital to understand that any tools, such as anti-depressants, counseling therapy, analgesia or other medications, are still absolutely valid as we start off on this new tangent to our Journey.

We do exist on a time plane of reality, and it will take time for this process to unfold. In the early days of this process, there may still be a most viable and valid reason to keep taking such medications, regardless of the health issue being treated – be that mental, emotional or physical. It can be guaranteed that as you progress in this Journey, a point will come where, from the depths of your being, you will *know* that it is now O.K. to start weaning off them. Nevertheless, it is *critical* to only do so under the correct naturopathic or medical supervision!

We need to understand that it is very unlikely that as humans we can suddenly make a quantum leap from feeling down, in despair or unhappy, to the other extreme of feeling total joy. Usually such a transition is done step at a time. Initially, all that we might be able to do is to just find enough strength to smile at someone rather than scowl at them; make a point of dropping some coins in the next beggar's bowl; provide a tip for the meal you've just had. Just do something – even seemingly small – which has a bit more of an up-beat Energy to it. Also do the Gratitude Meditation – (see chapter 12.) All such endeavors will – over time – start to pay off, and slowly but surely move us up that continuum towards more joy manifesting in our lives.

See it metaphorically as a situation where we are like a 'fuse-wire', and that each day, as part of our daily life experience, we are carrying a certain amount of 'current'. Joy is a particularly potent 'current' indeed. If we were to suddenly make that quantum leap from our present level of energy to that associated with total joy, we would probably only end up blowing our 'fuse-wire'.

Yet, by slowly increasing the 'current' we expose ourselves to, and thus allowing to flow through our 'circuits', so too are we allowing time for such 'circuits' to become strengthened. In the fullness of time, when we then do come to a stage where joy is a much bigger daily component of our life experience, we also hopefully have a 'circuitry' system capable of carrying that 'current' without any discomforts or dangers.

Need for daily, incremental but cumulative effort

But what is necessary is a deep and determined *choice* to make this change in how we look at, and respond to our daily life events, never mind how chaotic or problematic things still seem from the 'normal', earthly way of perceiving them. We also need to keep re-affirming on a daily basis that this is the option we choose to make; particularly during the initial period of time when it seems like nothing is happening and we just don't feel any increased joy in our lives. Initially, change will be very slow, and it then becomes all too easy to say… 'it's not working' - and conveniently give up. This is precisely what one aspect of our being - particularly the Pain Body - wishes us to do. The reality is that as we start out on this Journey, it may all seem so false and unreal, and that this sort of process just couldn't possibly work.

However, this is the window period where to begin with, one has to 'fake it till you start to make it'. At first you might only get the slightest glimpse of an Energy shift; fleeting micro-seconds where the clouds lift just that teensy bit. And then they come crashing down again. Maintain your effort, because there is still so much momentum in the old ways of doing. But such glimpses - despite being still incredibly far off from what you truly desire - are nevertheless absolute vindication that you *can* change the sort of Energy you run through your 'circuitry'.

And yes, it will take a lot more effort, commitment and focus. Just as it did each time you fell of that bike when you were learning to ride it as a kid, and where you simply had to pick yourself up, dust yourself off and... *get back on that bike.* Use whatever tools you can think of to keep the Awareness going, to stay with your new life choice. Paste reminder notes all over the place - in the car; on the mirror; by the stove; on your computer; on your pillow - wherever.

Keep reminding yourself that perhaps in this human Journey, *this* is now the point at which you need to make that choice to let go of all those dysfunctional beliefs you're still holding onto. Especially the pernicious belief that Consciousness Growth can only be achieved via much suffering. Actually, this is one of the biggest con-jobs ever perpetrated on humanity, and unfortunately, many religions have been major players in its propagation and maintenance.

So it's not about getting *rid* of the Pain Body. It *is* about increasing our skill at observing it, and using this increased 'State of Being' to drive us into growing Enlightenment. What we need to remember is that for most of us, Enlightenment is a step-by-step; day-by-day process, rather than a once off 'wham' event, after which we can rest on our laurels.

Oh please... it's all just too much to deal with!

My goodness, all this 'stuff' about devils, entities and now the Pain Body - oh pleeeaase! What are we doing in this chapter?! But again let's invoke the mantra of this book... 'it doesn't matter whether this is all real or not. Rather, ask yourself whether it is useful'?

All that we are really trying to do here is to firstly acknowledge that suffering occurs. That's the easy part! O.K, so now what? What precisely is suffering? Can we permanently get rid of it? How do we deal with it? Can we somehow even use suffering as a means to a powerful, empowering and useful end? And it would appear that we can. Some ideas have already been touched on above. Much more will be explored in further chapters of this book.

Eckhart Tolle's concept of the Pain Body, and how we can really only 'fight' it by *observing* it, and then only successfully so by being fully in the Moment are powerful concepts. We'll also find these concepts to be fundamental and essential in becoming skilled at Creative Visualization, about which much discussion will ensue in later chapters. So, not only are these ideas hopefully one particularly valuable way of looking at, and thus helping us to deal with suffering, but they are also already laying the foundation to being able to successfully do Creative Visualization.

Exercise
- List five life situations which really trigger your Pain Body.
- List at least five things you can do when pain hits – make an emotional distress check-list

Summary of thoughts thus far.
- Suffering, seen from the average human perspective, is an insane, cruel, often horrific situation or phenomenon occurring to far too many people, often with no rhyme or reason.
- Whichever way we philosophically squirm and wrestle with the issue of suffering, ultimately it remains a mystery. Perhaps the best we can do, when logic fails so miserably in trying to get a handle on suffering, is to learn to use it to grow in Consciousness, via a range of techniques.
- Some Eastern religions, gurus, teachers, as well as some New Age pundits, have declared 'everything is perfect just the way it is'. Such statements can be nothing short of cruel and misguided when used inappropriately.

Chapter 6 - Suffering Issues

- On one level, Perfection does absolutely exist. But it is in another Dimension of Reality which we can access *from* our earthly realm, while still alive and incarnate.
- Such access is achieved by learning to move our point of Awareness from ego to Higher Self mode.
- Another technique, based on such a shift of Awareness is called Creative Visualization.
- It does take a certain amount of skill and work to become proficient at 'Being' in these two Dimensions simultaneously – the Earth plane, and this Plane of Perfection, *through* which we can powerfully change our reality here on Earth.
- Eckhart Tolle's concept of 'The Pain Body' is described as an Energetic phenomenon, created as an accumulation of every painful experience human beings have ever had in their lives.
- This Pain Body also has the capacity to take over a human, via the mind, with resultant strong, negative effects on the body. It exists in two formats - dormant or active, and any little stimulus either from our environment or our minds can set it off.
- Two things allow this Pain Body to survive - unconsciousness about its existence, and the deep fear of facing our pain head-on.
- In New Age parlance the 'Witness State' is where our human awareness can consciously choose to relocate its point of view - from ego mode of operation to Higher Self mode.
- Counseling can be very powerful and useful, but doesn't always automatically resolve our psychological 'stuff'. Sometimes we may have to focus more on seeing our dysfunctional patterns... and then learning to become skilled at disengaging from them by going into Witness State.
- Tolle calls ego our phantom-self, which consists of mind-activity, or 'mind-chatter', and can only be kept going through constant thinking. It's that ceaseless little voice in our brain, babbling away non-stop.
- Ego self, in a sense, provides the 'secretarial service' to functioning efficiently on this earthly dimension of reality.
- Higher Self provides the general overview of the human endeavor; it holds the 'blue-print' to the entire human Journey here on Earth.

- Another ego metaphor is to see it as a flight attendant on an airplane, rather than the pilot, who can be compared to being the Higher Self.
- All the ego-self needs to therefore do in this human Journey is to organize and deal with the day-to-day events.
- In ego mode, we're always *doing*. Going into Higher Self mode is about *Being*.
- When something bad happens, going into Higher Self mode is definitely *not* incompatible with appropriate action, but now it becomes a Centered, more calculated and constructive action, rather than the actions we would elicit via ego mode.
- Suffering is intimately related to the degree with which we solely identify with our ego self. It's by learning to live our lives more via the Higher Self aspect as humans that we can most powerfully break out of this suffering cycle or our identification with the Pain Body.
- Going into Higher Self as a way of dealing with our pain or suffering, doesn't automatically get rid of that pain. Rather, it transforms the *experience* of that suffering into something less painful.
- Being in Higher Self mode is associated with deep feelings of Centeredness, calmness and joy. Here, you're witnessing the drama, rather than *being* it.
- How do you know when you're in ego mode? ….when you're in any of a vast range of negative emotions, such as anger, guilt, fear, shame, etc.
- Ego is something we as Conscious humans need to learn to transcend – not get rid of.
- Surrender doesn't mean doing nothing. All it means is that any 'doing' comes from a far more Conscious dimension, making it non-reactive, and therefore much easier to get through. It becomes a true *response* vs just a *reaction*.
- We also need to differentiate between pleasure and joy. The former is something which ego can lead us to, but the latter is something we can only truly experience by being connected to our Higher Self.
- We have but two choices of how we experience our moment by moment existence i.e. through joy or through suffering.

- Ultimately, learning through suffering is not just less efficient, but also less appropriate for a Spiritually evolving person.
- Another way of putting it is to learn through Love rather than through fear. Love gives rise to joy. Fear gives rise to just about the entire range of all the other not-so-productive emotions.
- Not being able to allow joy into our life is on some level akin to not being able to let God into our life either.
- For most of us, Enlightenment is a step-by-step, day-by-day process, rather than a once off 'wham' event, after which we can rest on our laurels.
- A major aim in life's Journey is to understand that so many of our desires are actually only substitutes for trying to create an *Inner* state of fulfillment.
- Believing in our separateness rather than our Oneness, makes it so much easier to do a whole range of nasty, if not horrific things to another; from cheating, lying and stealing to killing each other in a 'legitimate' war.

REFERENCES

1. Tolle, Eckhart. *The Power of Now – a guide to spiritual enlightenment*, Hodder Headline Group, Australia/NZ, 2000.

CHAPTER 7

INCARNATIONAL METAPHORS

*Whenever you find yourself on the side of the majority,
it's time to pause and reflect.*

Mark Twain

To some extent, we've already started to explore the idea of reincarnation, as well as the phenomenon of suffering, but let's now take those explorations a bit further, and see how there is also an interplay between the two. Remember, we're trying to generate a construct, a metaphor which allows us to make more sense out of our reality here on Earth.

So far, we've looked at the possibility that reincarnation does occur. Not only that, but how it can also offer a powerful platform from which to make more sense of some of the connections we may have with significant people in our lives, be they friend or foe. As well, this concept allows us to more clearly see the deeper roles we may be engaged in or have 'contracted' ourselves to play out with others.

Reincarnation – not just about past or future

One thing the New Age seems particularly caught up in is the notion that there is a sense of past and future to our incarnations, with most of the focus usually being on 'past lives'. What doesn't seem to be discussed enough is the equal possibility that all incarnations are actually occurring *simultaneously*, rather than *just* sequentially. This puts a completely different slant on the whole topic of reincarnation. It also allows for rather novel ways in which to not just view past or future lives, but to consider how we might deal with the *present* life.

Ultimately, whether incarnations occur sequentially or simultaneously really depends on your perspective, and where you choose to 'stand' as you observe this incarnational play. Here on Earth, the 'game' of life is definitely ruled by time. We experience a present - something most of us have great difficulty being truly focused and 'present' in - as well as experiencing the memories of a past. Plus there is the potential promise of a future set of experiences too. Problem is, we have tended to extrapolate that sense of time beyond our earthly plane, and into the reincarnational sphere of reality.

But that plane of reality *from* which we incarnate, ultimately originates *beyond* time. In a way, our presumptions about incarnation are similar to how we have extrapolated so many human characteristics onto our concept of 'God', almost to the point where we now seem to subconsciously believe God to be nothing more than some variation-on-a-theme super-human; albeit with vastly greater powers. Nevertheless, our perception is of a 'God' who is somehow still fundamentally 'human' – male; prone to emotional outbursts just as we humans. Big mistake!

So too with reincarnation. If we look at it from the earthly plane of reality, indeed, there would be past lives, the present one we're in, and then future lives to come. Certainly sounds feasible, rational and 'scientifically' consistent with our understanding of time here on this earthly dimension. However, Quantum Physics, and even religion will acknowledge that time may either be experienced very differently on other non-Earth dimensions, or just not exist at all as we know it here. Nowadays, science also predicts the existence of a multitude of 'times', existing in ways we can't even conceive of as yet. It's a bit like trying to explain and demonstrate a 3-D image or structure, but only having at our disposal a 2-dimensional 'tool' like a flat sheet of paper.

Nevertheless, let's assume then, that time in other Dimensions is not necessarily the same as experienced here on Earth. If this is so, and we shift our perspective *beyond* the Earth plane, placing it in the Spirit Realm instead, then quite different conclusions might be drawn - conclusions which may initially seem quite contradictory. Remember, in previous chapters we've discussed how we may *fundamentally* be more Spirit or Energy Beings than just fleshly humans. Equally, we've discussed that our primary 'Home' or origin is not of Earth, but of a Spirit or Energy realm, and that this human experience is only one of many

Chapter 7 - Incarnational Metaphors

options this Spirit Self can morph into. Is this what Christ meant when He said: 'In my Father's house are many mansions...'? [1]

What if time doesn't exist in quite the same way in these Spirit realms? It may therefore be possible - *looking from this Spirit perspective, which is the source of each individual incarnation* – that reincarnation could be seen to be possible in a *simultaneous* way... compared to the *sequential* manner we view reality *from Earth*.

Oversoul concepts

It's true that a lot of assumptions are being made in this discussion, but again, just hang in there and see where it takes you. Let's explore the Spirit hierarchy a bit more than we did in chapter 6. So far, we've looked at the concept of humans being composed of a subconscious aspect; then the ego-self – or 'office manager', followed by the Higher Self – or 'company CEO'. But it doesn't necessarily stop here. Further up the line into the Spirit hierarchy is what has been called the Oversoul, a much more Primary Energy Entity up the 'ladder' towards 'Ultimate Source'.

In this scheme, the Higher Self acts as the *interface* between ego self and Oversoul. But let's assume it's actually that particular Energy Entity or Oversoul which has the original desire to incarnate onto the Earth plane. Let's say then that our primary Spirit Self, *beyond* the Higher Self we've talked about previously, has a whole list of things It wishes to experience on planet Earth. It also has the capacity to 'extrude', as it were, an aspect of its Spirit into a specifically constructed 'container' or 'vehicle', thereby allowing it to experience the density of planet Earth.

Incarnation – need for a 'diving suit'

A very human, earthly analogy may be of value here. Let's assume you wish to explore and experience the deep ocean floor. There is no way your body could survive at the pressures existing at such depths, nor could you hold your breath for long enough to get even a fraction of the way down to that ocean floor. So if you are serious about experiencing what it would be like to be able to walk, talk and explore on the deep ocean bottom, then you would need some sort of 'vehicle'. Such a 'vehicle' would have to be capable of sustaining life under the pressures, and other life-threatening conditions otherwise found at such depths. Having these capacities would allow you to not only experience the ocean floor reality, but to also survive that experience.

So a diving suit was designed, capable of withstanding the otherwise lethal pressures found at such ocean depths. Initially though, you are on the ocean surface. This is an entirely different environment, with a much greater intensity of light, and without material density issues to deal with – air compared to the heaviness of water. You then decide to put on your diving suit, checking all the gadgets necessary for survival once down in the water. You especially check the working status of your oxygen hose and radio connections to 'base station', back on the boat, which is floating serenely on the ocean surface. Once suited up inside your diving suit, you allow yourself to slowly sink deeper and deeper into the denseness of the ocean waters, right to the very bottom.

But then you realize something. To fully understand and experience how it feels to be totally and completely part of the density of such ocean depths, you actually need to cut off entirely from the surface. Compared to the ocean floor half a mile down, the surface reality was utterly different. Let's extrapolate this fantasy story about a journey to the ocean floor, and say that something analogous to this is in fact exactly what Spirit did.

To make the experience of this 'ocean floor' truly 'believable', It decided to sever all *conscious* connections with the 'ocean surface'. You, in your diving suit, decide to cut the radio link with the surface base. As time goes by, you become so absorbed in the reality of that ocean floor, it seems you even lose memory of what it was like above.

Indeed, a sort of amnesia develops where you eventually forget that there *is* a surface reality! Analogously, could this be what happened to these aspects of Spirit which decided to 'play out' an experience within the human realm, in the material density of planet Earth? Perhaps Spirit wanted to see how far it could push itself into matter. And the ultimate extreme end of such a desire was to therefore completely disconnect us from any *conscious* memory or knowingness of 'base station' back on the 'ocean surface' - of Source Itself.

Incarnation - lost in our Cyber-game of life

It's as if we have set up, or become involved in a sort of Cyberspace 'game of life', with a well defined set of rules and 'truths' of how that 'reality' functions. Then we become so engrossed in the 'Cyber-Game' that we actually forget to check back with our more Fundamental 'Home' and Reality – beyond our bodies

Chapter 7 - Incarnational Metaphors

and human dimension. We seem to have become blind to that aspect of who we really are, on our most fundamental level.

Harking back to the diving suit metaphor, it's as if we've also begun to identify more with the diving suit, than the person *inside* that suit. It seems we've now given an inordinate credibility to this new reality we've become entranced by, way down on the ocean floor, and our 'home base' – on the ocean *surface* – has become nothing more than a misty memory.

In many ways the 'reality' here on Earth is indeed a most convincing illusion, and not one to deny, even though we seem to have become so lost in it. But there is a sad consequence to having become so engrossed in this 'Cyber-Game' on planet Earth. It's meant that we've also forgotten how we could experience this earthly life in many more constructive ways than we're doing at present. We've in fact forgotten what powerful Beings we fundamentally are. If only we could maintain an Awareness of *both* realities: the Higher Dimension from which we actually originate, which is our true Home, but which we've fallen 'asleep' to, and the Earth bound dimension in which we are 'playing' out this 'game'.

It's almost as if we need to learn to live this human experience in a dualistic way – being fully present in the human incarnation; completely honoring and validating the earthly experience. But then we also need to be truly Aware that there is so much more to who we fundamentally are, beyond what our basic senses can tell us of our experience on planet Earth. By being more Aware, or 'Awake' to both realities, we could also end up playing the 'game of life' with enhanced power and Consciousness.

In the end it's a matter of what we choose to give more credence - this reality here on earth, which does seem, and is so real on many levels - or understanding that there is a much more Fundamental and Powerful Level to who and what we are. Unfortunately, this Spirit level is usually not as amenable to our 'normal' eyes and senses, while experiencing life in the human format. By the same token, this does not mean that the human 'illusion' should therefore be ignored or denigrated; indeed, it needs to be experienced with as much gusto, skill and acceptance as we can muster.

For whatever reasons we might like to speculate, we obviously are here on planet Earth. We can but assume – and hope – that there is a purpose and value to experiencing this reality here.

We need to realize, however, that this other more Fundamental Level of Reality does exist, and is truly the Real Source of Everything. If this is so, then it offers possibilities through which to tap into this Higher Dimensional Level of Reality. Using techniques such as Creative Visualization, we can create extraordinarily powerful changes, here in our human dimension of reality.

Reincarnation – setting up the 'game'

Anyway, assuming the above gives us some sort of structure within which to better understand our experience here on Earth, let's now look in more detail at how such an incarnational life may be set up. Let's carry on from the assumption we made in an earlier chapter that the Oversoul has a desire to engage in certain learning agendas down on planet Earth. After much thinking and consultation with other similar Spirit Beings, it has arranged a very intricate and multi-dimensional 'game play'. It has decided which historical settings each particular 'learning' would most profit from, as well as whether it would be better to experience any one particular incarnational Journey as a male or female; which ethnicity; which religious persuasion, and so many other variables.

Then it 'extrudes' an aspect of Its Spirit Self into each of these 'diving suits' - or what on Earth are called 'bodies'. From an earthly perspective, each 'body' seems a very autonomous and separate entity, locked into a specific time/space frame of reference. However, from the Spirit realm perspective, each of a series of such 'bodies', although 'separated' by time and space *while on Earth*, is nevertheless very connected to the same Spirit or Oversoul. This latter Spirit Entity continues to exist in its primary 'Home', found within the Spirit or Energetic realms.

Metaphors are such powerful instruments through which to make sense of the nonsensical. Let's therefore utilize computer terminology through which to get an even better handle on all this. Imagine a really high powered, futuristic computer, capable of having several thousand 'computer games' open and active, all at the same time. As the operator at the computer console, your Spirit Self or Oversoul can open and create each individual 'game'. It sets up the story-line of events and experiences any one particular character 'incarnated' into that 'game' will then go through.

Each 'game' has the ability to unfold in its own unique way, although it is true that there are also some basic rules which govern the way these 'games' are able to be played. By the same token, there are many specifics about the 'game' and the major 'game player' – you – which are pre-chosen.

Chapter 7 - Incarnational Metaphors

O.K. Your Spirit or Oversoul has just set up one 'game', but there are many other variations on a theme It wishes to create, each with their own unique and specific set of parameters, experiences and learning opportunities. So your Oversoul continues setting up these seemingly individual 'games', each one nevertheless fundamentally connected to your Oversoul Energy, the primary orchestrator of all these 'games'. Again and again, a full story-line is created for each separate 'vehicle' or body, all with their own unique characteristics and experiences to live through within the 'story-line' depicted within their individual 'game'. Each time a 'game' is fully organized, it gets 'minimized' to the 'toolbar' – in other words, inserted/incarnated into the time realm of planet Earth school!

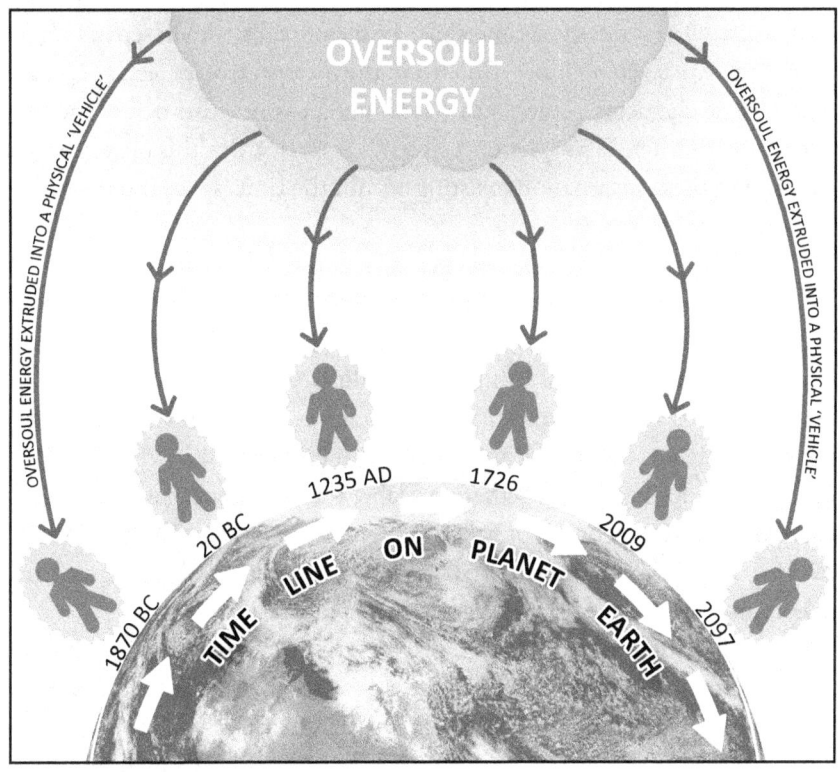

Diagram 1
Oversoul setting up the incarnational game.

This process continues for 'hours', with your Oversoul creating endless, highly individual story-lines for a vast array of human 'vehicles', i.e. incarnated Spirit in a physical body. The Oversoul determines what those 'vehicles' will experience within the 'reality' of these 'CyberSpace games', played within the 'computer' – analogously, within the physical realm of planet Earth. Finally your Oversoul looks at Its work, and sees that It has now 'created' thousands of different characters or 'lives', all in separate 'games'. But the most important point to grasp is that within this metaphor, every one of these 'characters' are now all residing *simultaneously* on the lower toolbar of the computer – within the earthly time/space realm of Earth 'reality'.

The point to really hammer home here is that *from the perspective of the Spirit Realm and the Oversoul*, each 'game' now exists *simultaneously* on the 'toolbar' – on the Earth plane. But from the human perspective on planet Earth - existing as it does in a time:space frame of reality - each separate 'game' exists in a *sequential* manner. So, from the perspective of each separately created 'game character' – each incarnated human - one exists before the other. In other words, there is a *sequentialness* to *their* reality. But this only *appears* to be so, due to these incarnations existing within the time/space frame of reality found on planet Earth.

In other words, one 'vehicle' was perhaps plunked down in the year 45 BC; the next in 544 AD; the next in 1432; the next in 1691; the next in 1739 and a second *also* in 1739 – but in a different *geographical* part of planet Earth! Remember, Earth consists of a time:*space* reality. And so on; each life therefore existing in a definite *sequential* manner – as far as *earthly* time:space reality is concerned. Hence, it all depends on which perspective you *choose* to come from, in turn determining whether you label these separate 'games' as being a *sequential* human experience or acknowledging that in fact each game is really occurring *simultaneously*. Again, the latter perspective is 'real', when seen from the 'computer operator's' - or Oversoul's stand point.

So all this focus within the New Age as to whether our incarnational lives are past or future is – on one level – a totally illusionary concept. It depends entirely on your perspective! From the Oversoul's... or the incarnated human's perspective? So yes, from one point of view, we as humans may indeed be reincarnating – and from within this time:space frame of reality, such incarnations are perceived to be in a *sequential* manner. However, to the

Oversoul, from whom each incarnation is in fact originating, all these myriad of lives are occurring *simultaneously*.

But it's actually from the standpoint of the Oversoul that these perspectives become really interesting. From *Its* perspective, It can tap into the richness of what's going on in each separate 'incarnation'... all at once. At any point, It can amalgamate what is being experienced in one separate incarnation, with what is happening in another.

To maximize the learning opportunities inherent within the process of incarnation, it therefore makes sense to send into the Earth realm as many portions of Itself as possible. These portions are scattered in as many different earthly reality settings as possible - of culture; religion; historical setting; geographical location, etc. In this way the Oversoul is capable of learning about any particular 'topic' It wishes to explore, via a huge array of different and separate experiences, all created and set in motion via individual incarnations. But the totality of that 'experiencing' is ultimately being collated, monitored, analyzed and utilized *simultaneously* – from the Oversoul's perspective.

So, from one point of view, we don't actually have past lives and future lives. From the Higher Plane of Reality; from the Spirit Realm where the Oversoul exists, it is all happening at once. When one particular 'game/incarnation' is over, all the data, knowledge and experience, accumulated from that earthly experience is simply 'up-loaded' back into the 'main-frame computer'; back into the Oversoul.

Oversouls – and now Ultra-souls??

It also needs to be understood that there is probably much more to all this. It may be that it is not simply about the Oversoul morphing into a human body on planet Earth, with the Higher Self as the interface. Just as we have hierarchies on Earth, so too the Spirit Realms seem to have such stratification. Michael Newton explores this concept in his books, three of which are 'Destiny of Souls'; 'Journey of Souls' and 'Life Between Lives'. [2] These books are highly recommended, and will allow for a deeper understanding of spiritual hierarchies, which can only be briefly explored here.

Just as a myriad of incarnated human 'vehicles' are individually set up and managed via the one Oversoul, various writers suggest that in turn the Oversoul is but one of many 'incarnations' - or extensions – of an even Higher level of Spirit. Let's call them the 'Ultra-Souls' - for want of a name. So, they can be seen as the next hierarchy up the Spirit ladder. These 'Ultra-Souls' also seem to have a Consciousness Growth agenda. Just as the Oversouls incarnate an aspect of their Spirit or Energy into human 'vehicles', so too the Ultra-Souls appear to extrude a portion of *their* Energy/Spirit Essence into separate Oversouls, each 'set up' in a broad choice of various *Spirit* Dimensions or Realms. Indeed, such Realms are way beyond what we could even conceive of from our earthly reality.

But is any of this true?

Oh boy! Is your brain spinning yet? And is all this differentiation of Spirit 'realities' into these various layers actually real? What proof is there to vindicate such statements? How does one in fact validate that this is an inherent aspect to our human situation or has any relevance to human existence?

Certainly, one major difference between us and the animals is that we can think and reason. Without doubt, this capacity instigates a curiosity, and a need to understand our experiences here on planet Earth. Within that context, it seems reasonable that we tend to want to create a theory, a concept, a paradigm. Something which can at least help make some sense out of our human experiences, and often our suffering too. Even if we don't hit on 'The Truth', such possible explanations ultimately can help us better deal with life. Surely that is all the vindication needed to allow such 'explanations' to be taken on board?

Gravity and time – we still don't know exactly what they are either

This phenomenon of accepting something because it happens to provide a useful platform to other things doesn't only occur within Metaphysical circles. It's too easily forgotten – or conveniently ignored – that such practices are just as prevalent in science and medicine. Here too, scientists and doctors often operate from theory alone in so much of what they do; theories, which in most cases have never been vindicated to be 'The Truth', or even fully understood.

Although science does acknowledge gravity and time, and can explain the *effects* of these phenomenon; knows how to utilize their respective laws; is able to describe them in mathematical equations, nevertheless there is still a level of mystery to exactly what these forces of Nature are. In regard to gravity, the question of *why* atoms attract each other is still not known. But this has never stopped any scientist from using every scrap of information and understanding they do have about this phenomenon, in turn utilizing it to harness the power of gravity in many productive ways.

So too, equal validity should be given to attempted explanations to our reality here. What are the different layers to Spirit existence? It helps to have a theory, even if it is not fully validated and provable. Such explanations do, however, like any theory, offer a structure within which it becomes easier to maneuver. Yet again, the question we should ask ourselves is not whether these different 'layers' being proposed are actually the fundamental, absolute Truth of how it really is. Perhaps all that you, the reader needs to answer is... 'does it somehow resonate for me'? 'Does it somehow give me a handle on how to deal with my reality here as a human'? If yes, play with it. If no, dump it.

God – marrying science and mystery to solve the problem

There is an aspect of mystery associated with the phenomenon of the Spirit Realms - or God for that matter. These Spirit Realms are almost beyond the capacity of our classical, scientific means of deduction, where everything is broken down into infinitely small units of left-brained data. Although science may initially baulk at the suggestion of allowing mystery into its hallowed halls of science, nevertheless, isn't a lot of Quantum Physics itself quite mysterious? How is it possible for instance, that light can be both a particle and a wave? It's not the black and white sort of answer which science expects to deal with. Yet science does allow this particular example - and many others – of a more fuzzy reality into its hallowed halls of learning!

Interesting – but not essential

Actually, as far as this book is concerned, all these extra concepts of Oversouls, Ultrasouls and others, are not really of fundamental importance. Touching on them has more to do with making a statement that this entire phenomenon of life, and Spirit, and incarnation, and Consciousness Growth, may not only be limited to what Spirit does on the 'stage' of planet Earth. It goes so much further than we might even be able to imagine. Hence, for now let's not get too caught up or side-tracked in these wider ramifications to the whole story, and leave these sort of issues as a subject for another book!

As humans, we tend to have a parochial, anthropomorphized and limited ability to grasp such colossal 'existence scenarios'. We just need to be able to at least acknowledge that the 'Game' of Consciousness Growth, as perceived within the realities of planet Earth is but the tiniest 'pixel' within the grander 'picture'. And even that amount of data is already hard to process through the relatively diminutive capacity of our human neuronal synapses!

Incarnation - consequences of simultaneous vs sequential

However, getting back to these rather challenging ideas about reincarnation, this shift in perspective as to whether reincarnation is simultaneous or sequential has hugely important repercussions on our daily lives. From the above discussion, it would then appear that the impression of sequentialness to reincarnation is actually only an artifact of this earthly reality, defined and confined by time. In turn, if it is true that from one perspective each 'you' that is incarnated is ultimately doing it in a 'once off' sense, *then it would also be wise to maximize each lifetime to the fullest.*

In other words, this life you have now - from a *simultaneous* perspective of reincarnation - is in fact the only one you will have. So you really do need to make the most of it, rather than have an attitude which says... 'well, what I can't achieve this time around, I'll catch up with in the next life'. Such an attitude is unfortunately deeply entrenched within certain Eastern cultures, which firmly believe in the sequential version of reincarnation.

Making this shift from how you might presently perceive reincarnation as a fundamentally *sequentially* occurring phenomenon does put a whole different feel on what you are doing in this life *now*. You might decide you really do need to make the most of your opportunity *now*, rather than let things slide for another occasion. Especially if the traditional view of reincarnation is that we get to experience millions of these incarnations anyway.

This sort of shift is incredibly important, precisely because what you are experiencing in this life now is such a unique opportunity to do whatever it is *you* had pre-incarnationally planned to do in this lifetime. Your unique learnings will provide great benefit, as they are subsequently added to the overall 'soup' of experiences the Oversoul has put together for the fulfillment of Its own learning agenda.

So the essence of this issue is to preferably look at reincarnation from the simultaneous, Higher Self or Oversoul's perspective. Doing so makes you realize that the 'ego-I' who is primarily experiencing this reality here and now is only actually getting a once-off chance of incarnating. Such is the case even

Chapter 7 - Incarnational Metaphors

though your Oversoul has indeed incarnated into perhaps millions of different 'vehicles' or human bodies, scattered throughout the length and breadth of Time. This raises the interesting point - which part of 'you' is it that is really incarnating? Is it in fact your ego/personality 'you' which goes from one vehicle to the next? Or is it your Higher Self/Oversoul which is the principle aspect of 'you' which is incarnating each time?

It would appear, along this line of thinking that it is not the ego 'you' which goes from one life to the other, but rather, it is that Higher Self aspect of your Oversoul, which is the one that actually does the incarnating. The ego-you is ultimately only a by-product or construct *of the human 'vehicle',* and only does it once, i.e. in this life now.

What this also means is that perhaps – if this is a valid perspective of our existence here – both Christian religions *and* the Eastern Religions/New Age have it right. Christianity comes from the angle that we have but one life - and what we do with it is most important, while the Eastern or New Age perspective is that we have almost endless lives. Yet, if we look at incarnation from this *simultaneous* perspective, we actually do in a sense only have one life too – and once again, what we do with that one life is therefore of great importance. Don't waste it!

But what about the 'reality' of my past life regression-therapy experiences?

If all this is indeed one possible way of looking at our human experience here on planet Earth, then there may also be many readers who will have a very valid question to ask. How does one then explain the experience of their own 'past lives', through techniques such as Regression or Rebirthing therapy? How does this 'fact' fit into the equation, if incarnations are viewed as being fundamentally simultaneous, rather than sequential? And yes, those experiences can still be made sense of via the previously discussed paradigm of incarnation. Within this perspective, those who have experienced past lives via these techniques have actually *by-passed* time and space. They have done so *via* the Oversoul.

Remember, the Oversoul is the source of all those many incarnational 'vehicles' on planet Earth. It's the 'main-frame' aspect of the computer analogy we used before. Each incarnation is but a side-terminal as it were, to the main-frame, but in constant communication with that main-frame, up-loading and down-loading information all the time. Hence, if we keep this computer analogy in mind, any one particular out-lying 'terminal' within this 'computer' network is then capable of going up into main-frame and then – under certain circumstances – down-loading into another 'terminal' elsewhere. In other words, one incarnated human becomes capable of accessing another incarnational vehicle, connected *via* that same Oversoul.

No doubt there are 'fire-walls' which would normally prevent such sneaking around into other 'terminals'. However, perhaps such techniques as Regression, Rebirthing or Hypnosis may be able to allow one particular 'terminal' – this incarnated you – to by-pass such 'fire-walls', and have access to what is normally off-limits or unavailable. See if the diagram below can help make more sense of these statements.

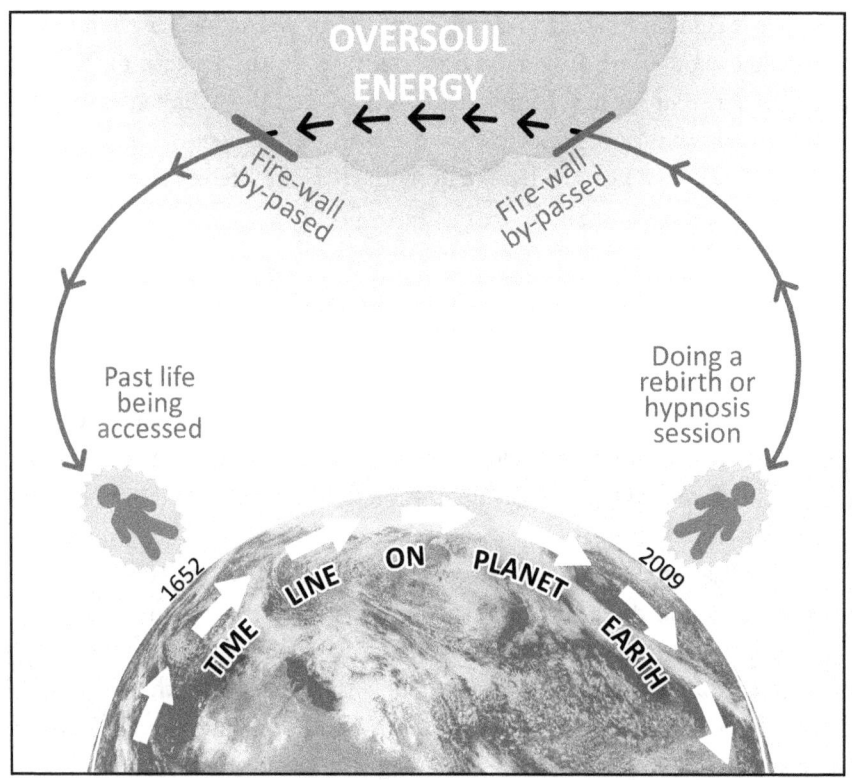

Diagram 2
How the oversoul concept can help explain past and future
life experiences obtained via rebirthing, hypnosis, etc.

If you definitely feel you have experienced a legitimate 'past life', then the above analogies may help explain – and validate – those experiences. Through such 'up-loading' and 'down-loading' within the overall 'computer *network*', it should be feasible to see how information about one life experience can be transferred to another. But the main point to take on-board is that it is all done *via* the Oversoul.

And what about Karma?

What about Karma? Isn't that seen as an integral component to the whole concept of reincarnation? In a sense, isn't Karma a factor which supposedly dictates and explains so much of the good or bad experiences dumped onto us in any one particular incarnation? One definition of Karma, according to the Penguin Modern English Dictionary is: *intentional good or evil acts which will bear fruit in this or future lives.* [3]

This normally accepted concept of Karma seems to suggest that it is a phenomenon much like a 'bank account', from which, and into which we as humans can make endless 'withdrawals' or 'deposits'. However, if we look at how humans so often get things wrong in their day-to-day life, there is going to be more chance of that 'account' being in 'debit' rather than 'credit'. This is simply because the inevitable scenario is that far more 'withdrawals' are likely to occur over all those millions of lifetimes, compared to 'deposits'. In turn, it will therefore take untold more lifetimes before there is even a smidgen of a chance of getting the 'account' 'balanced out'.

Knowing how our basic human nature works, and how it will more likely conjure up more 'withdraws' than 'deposits', it would seem we as humans are in a fairly hopeless situation as far as our capacity to pay off any karmic 'debt' is concerned. The system would appear to be very heavily biased against ever 'balancing the books'. Never mind, therefore, how many incarnations we might have access to, it would seem that with human nature in the equation, incarnation can't be other than endless. So much then, for certain New Agers who claim... 'this is going to be my last incarnation'!

On the other hand, good ol' Eckhart Tolle has a fascinating definition of Karma, which allows for an interesting and empowering slant to how this phenomenon may actually work itself out in the human sphere. His perspective is that... *Karma is equal to all past conditioning and pain which we **identify** with and **thus continue to live out**.*

This is a most fascinating way of looking at Karma, because it provides a more empowered way of dealing with this issue, in the sense that it therefore depends very much on *our* choice to *identify* with our suffering or not. The essence of this discussion is about going back to the concept of learning to increasingly live our lives from a Witness State, and also ties in with Tolle's concept of the Pain Body, and how this is another situation where we can choose to plug into suffering or not. Hence, Tolle's perspective on Karma does open a door to quite a different way of viewing – and thus managing - the effect of Karma within any one particular lifetime.

It's therefore not just about having to 'pay off' a huge Karmic debt from countless past lifetimes, via constant suffering; as if suffering is the only 'currency' with which Karma can be paid off. In other words, the 'normal' concept of Karma is that for every hurt you have done to another, so too will you need to be hurt in turn. For every theft we may have done in one lifetime, will need a theft to occur to us; for every betrayal we did to another, so too will we need to be betrayed... ad nauseum! An eye for an eye and a tooth for a tooth – so to speak.

Even if the Karmic correlations are not quite so rigid as some believe, in that a theft has to be repaid by a theft; a murder by a murder; a betrayal by a betrayal, nevertheless Karma is still seen as having to be paid off on equitable levels. If one person does something bad to another – worth say '10 Karmic units' - then the 'payment' in reciprocal Karma needing to be 'suffered' in another lifetime, would have to be of an equal 'value'.

However, Tolle's definition allows for perhaps quite a different, but equally valid 'currency' with which to 'pay' off these huge Karmic debts - *Awareness!*

Accepting Tolle's version of Karma also provides another potent reason why we shouldn't automatically buy into pain and suffering. Rather, it would serve us better to learn to remain in Witness State when it comes to Life's painful situations. From Tolle's perspective therefore, pain and suffering are very powerful instigators or drivers of Karma.

In other words, via Tolle's perspective, Karma is very much linked to the Pain Body concept, in that Karma is as minimal or endless as our sense of Awareness is developed - or not. This in turn determines our tendency to automatically tap into that suffering - or not. So if we remain *unconscious* about the Pain Body, this actually causes us to automatically morph into *becoming* that pain, *living it out*. Tapping into suffering so easily, via our *un*consciousness, then also equates with us remaining caught or locked into the seemingly endless Cycles of Karma.

Awareness as the more empowering solution to Karma?

However, the more we can bring Awareness to the human equation of life and its challenges, the more such Awareness allows us to 'pay off' our Karmic 'debt'. This involves becoming increasingly skilled at being able to move our point of Awareness out of ego, and into Higher Self mode. In other words, it's not as if we have say fifty quadrillion 'debit units' of Karma which have accrued over the millions of lifetimes, which somehow need to be 'paid off'... one at a time. Instead, using Tolle's concept, the Karmic 'account' is as quickly or easily 'paid off' - or perpetuated – as we can bring Awareness to our Moment by Moment life situation. It's by using those points of power, in those Moments of NOW, from which to then either buy into and *become* our pain – the Pain Body... or not! Dealing with our Karmic 'debt' therefore is as difficult or easy as being able to dive into and become our pain or jumping our point of Awareness into Witness mode, giving access to the Higher Self, and thus dissolving or disassociating us from any hold our Karma may have over us.

Indeed, for every action there is a reaction – this is a Law of Physics, and most applicable within the physical dimension of planet Earth. So it is true that on one level, we constantly do generate consequences – constructive or unconstructive - from each action we initiate while in the human form. But the extent to which the consequences of negative actions – Karma if you like – need to be endlessly endured is dependent on how *Aware* or 'Awake' we are as that incarnated human being. Do we overly identify with the earthly realm as the only existing reality? Or do we understand that we are fundamentally not of Earth – but of Spirit? If it is the latter, then from one perspective we will also understand that much of the human experience is only an 'Illusion' - and on that level, so too is Karma. Karma is therefore only as real as the extent to which we allow ourselves to fall for the ultimate Illusion of it.

Karma *is* extraordinarily real, *if we have no Awareness or skill to move our point of reference from the 'asleep', human ego-self mode to the 'Awake', Higher Self mode*. But, when perceived from the Higher Self mode, the exact nature and consequences of what Karma is, altogether changes. Hence, by making, or 'awakening' to this internal shift of understanding does give us – while in human form – a window of opportunity through which we can avoid becoming so engrossed, and therefore lost in the human experience. Being so lost in the human drama subsequently keeps us locked into the Karmic Cycle as well.

Becoming more skilled at shifting our point of Consciousness from ego to Higher Self Mode therefore becomes a possible way of breaking the Cycle of Karma. Not by endlessly 'paying it off', but rather by increasingly being able to enhance our sense of Awareness or Consciousness, *through* which we simply disconnect from that Cycle. As long as you 'stay in the game', you end up playing by the rules or concepts of that game. Consciously step out of that same game, and things change. Keep in mind however, that this perspective does not mean we therefore don't need to take responsibility for all our actions. For every action - or thought – there is still very much a consequence.

However, this alternate view of Karma sure does provide a more empowered standpoint in regard to the sense of hopelessness so often associated with the 'normal' view of Karmic debt, and our seeming inability to ever pay it off. Hopefully too, the above alternative slants on reincarnation as not automatically being sequential, also provide a greater sense of empowerment when dealing with your present life now.

Exercise
- Name one powerful way in which we might alternately pay off Karmic debts, other than via suffering.
- Write a few points about the concept of Oversouls, and why this is a useful idea through which to explain many difficult Life situations.

Summary of thoughts thus far.
- It's just as possible that all incarnations are actually occurring *simultaneously*, rather than *only* sequentially. This puts a completely different slant on how we might consider dealing with this *present* life.
- So far, we've looked at the concept of humans being composed of a subconscious aspect; then the ego-self – or 'office manager'; followed by the Higher Self – or 'company CEO'. But it doesn't necessarily stop here.

Chapter 7 - Incarnational Metaphors

- Further up the line into the Spirit hierarchy is what we could call the Oversoul, another 'stepping-stone' of Energy, up the 'ladder' towards 'Ultimate Source'.
- In this scheme, the Higher Self acts as the interface between ego self and Oversoul.
- The analogy of using a strong, metal diving-bell to go down to the depths of the ocean correlates powerfully with our Spirit Self using a human body as its 'vehicle' for experiencing the dense reality on planet Earth.
- As Spirits, we seem to have become lost in the 'Cybergame' of life here on Earth. This sense of disconnection from our Source has many limiting consequences to how we live our lives as humans.
- Incarnational lives can be likened to playing with a super-computer, capable of playing many games simultaneously. Each game is active at the same time, *to you the operator.*
- If reincarnation is simultaneous, then this one life we 'have' now should be made maximal use of. It should make us more present to what we have now, rather than postponing things 'to another life', or time.
- Tolle's definition of Karma is that it is equal to all past conditioning and pain which we **identify** with, **and thus continue to live out.** However, suffering need not be the only 'currency' through which Karma can be paid off.
- Tolle's definition allows for perhaps quite a different, but equally valid 'currency' with which to 'pay' off these huge Karmic debts - *Awareness!*
- Karma is as minimal or endless as our sense of Awareness is developed - or not.
- Tolle's version of Karma also provides another potent reason why we shouldn't automatically buy into pain and suffering. Rather, it would serve us better to learn to remain in Witness State when it comes to Life's painful situations.
- Becoming more skilled at shifting our point of Consciousness from ego to Higher Self Mode therefore becomes a possible way of breaking the Cycle of Karma.

REFERENCES

1. Bible. SJV. John. 14:2

2. Newton, Michael. PhD, *'Destiny of Souls – new case studies of life between lives',* Llewellyn, 2005; Newton, Michael. PhD, *'Journey of Souls',* Llewellyn, 1994; Newton, Michael. PhD, *'Life Between Lives',* Llewellyn, 2004.

3. Garmonsway, G.N; Simpson, J. *The Modern English Dictionary,* Galley Press, UK, 1965.

CHAPTER 8

BEING IN THE NOW

The world and its affairs are moving so fast that there are days when the person who says it can't be done is interrupted by the person doing it.

Unknown

The single most common problem presenting itself in my professional practise, day in, day out is that of stress. People find themselves caught on a 'treadmill' which is not just going too fast, but has in fact gone out of control, causing exhaustion and burnout. Inevitably, such a demanding state of affairs is also the basis of many of the unhappy feelings they are experiencing, as well as their health related issues.

As Westerners, we seem to have lost the capacity to be truly present in the Moment. We live so much in the past and the future that we are virtually never in the NOW. It would seem that this is a major source of the rumbling disquiet and discontent that pervades the very fabric of our existence. Why do we allow ourselves to live in this crazy way? Let's explore this issue a bit further: what it is doing to us, and how we all can take steps to slow down or step off this 'treadmill'.

It also needs to be acknowledged that this chapter draws heavily on the deep and insightful ideas of Eckhart Tolle, via his book 'The Power of Now', [1] and his various DVD's and CD's. Out of all the Metaphysical books presently available on the market, his are pivotal in any search for the meaning of life, and are highly recommended.

Technology – what a treadmill

We live in a culture addicted to numerous things, and it would appear that many of us are certainly addicted to being busy. There seems to be an unspoken, but powerful rule in our society that we are not allowed to have any down-time till... 'all our work is done'. Indeed, we often boast about how 'busy we are', as if this is some sort of wonderful character trait. But the problem is that realistically, there is no end to the amount of things needing to be done - often urgently so, and especially in work situations with a boss breathing down our necks. But there is another level to this 'treadmill' we find ourselves caught on.

It rather looks like our technology has out-stripped our ability to handle what it creates in our lives.

Instead of having more time off for leisure and rest, the reality is that many people are working longer and harder, with ever *decreasing* free time available to us, despite all the supposedly time-saving devices cramming our lives. The problem is particularly acute in the arena of communications. We now have a plethora of devices - phones and emails being probably the worst slave-drivers in this category - which demand our constant and instant attention, 24/7. Remember, there was a time - when we only had corded phones - where a phone call meant we had to take time out to sit near the darn thing if we wanted to continue the call. Now, with the magic of 'cordless', we're encouraged to multi-task while also somehow trying to connect and communicate with our caller.

Enter the mobile phone, and suddenly we don't even get a respite once out of the home, and away from the cordless. The magic of 'mobile' ensures that we can be reached anywhere, anytime. And if you are required to have one of these ultimate 'slave devices' for your work situation - guess what? You are then truly open to invasion of your time, energies and privacy 24 hours a day. And a lot of bosses have absolutely no concept of boundaries.

Let's not forget the wonders of 'txt'. Yes, it may relieve us of a more lengthy call to respond to, but txt also invades our lives 24/7... and people expect *instant* responses, as they do with the mobile. We haven't even got to the email system of never-ending communication invasion; nor faxes, all of which soak up a lot of time from our lives, especially in work situations. Again, the unspoken expectation is that you need to respond ASAP. And if you don't, a lot of people will quickly send you another message, or follow-

Chapter 8 - Being In the Now

up the initial message with a phone call... just to make sure that you did in fact get the first one. 'Yes thank you, but I happen to be brushing my teeth or using the bathroom'. This technological invasion is rather unrelenting and overwhelming. Not a sacred moment anywhere.

Techno-intrusion

People sending txt messages and emails, or connecting via the many other forms of electronic communication, frequently seem to have developed a psychological blind-spot. They invariably appear to think they're the *only* one demanding your attention, when the reality is that their communication is inevitably just one of dozens hitting you that hour or that day.

If you are feeling really needy, alone, unwanted, unloved... or just plain bored with your life, then by all means go ahead and answer every phone, or txt, or email, or fax. However, if your life is already on a really tight schedule, then only answer if it really suits *you*. Especially if you're trying to juggle a whole lot of things in a very limited period of time, and yet these sources of communication keep intruding into your daily routine. There simply is no law which says 'Thou Shalt Answer All Incoming Calls – whether it suits you or not'!

Yet many of us live as if such a law exists, and what invariably happens is that you rush off to answer that instrument in a truly Pavlovian manner, and at a time that invariably doesn't really suit you either. Result? You're now caught up in perhaps a half hour or more of often utterly unimportant conversation. This in turn makes you run late for all the other things on your agenda, which then... stresses you out. Don't do it!

Look at it from a lateral angle. Surely you wouldn't dream of barging up to someone's house, and crashing right into their life totally unannounced? More likely than not, this would occur at an inappropriate moment for them. Would you really expect them to now drop everything, and attend to you alone? Surely you wouldn't do this *in person*. Nevertheless, we seem to have absolutely no qualms – or no insight – into the equal reality that every time we phone or txt or email, we are crashing in unannounced into that other person's life – albeit *electronically*.

Out of the goodness of their heart they may try to accommodate your intrusion, but far too often at a huge and cumulative cost to themselves; again, in the form of stress. So if you wouldn't do this consciously to another, why would you allow others to do so to you? Most people are aghast when they hear these comments, thinking this to be a harsh and un-caring response to people's attempts to simply connect with you. But it's not about being uncaring. Rather, it's got everything to do with getting a firm grip on the present daily reality of our lives. We need to realize that this day after day technological intrusion has been sneaking up on us for several years now, yet, in a sense most of us are almost blind to what's actually happening, or see no socially acceptable way of dealing with it.

Bit by bit, we've tried to accommodate it all, somewhat like the frog in a bowl of cold water, put over a slow flame. The rise in water temperature is so slow and is occurring in such small increments that it has lulled that frog into almost a state of apathy and unresponsiveness. Until it is actually too late, and the poor ol' frog ends up getting cooked. This was only possible because of the frog's lack of awareness of how it was being overcome by the heat, slowly but surely. So too for us humans, and our communication-invasion. Hence, it's about creating alternative strategies in a world of techno-overwhelm, where the reality is many of us simply can't handle it all anymore.

Remember your point of power therefore; you *choose* to either answer that phone – or you don't. Why not only answer it when it works in with your schedule, and won't end up stressing you? If you only receive occasional calls or you do have the time and inclination, by all means go ahead and answer those devices. But because such forms of communication are nowadays so overwhelmingly intrusive into our space – wherever we might be - we do need to figure out some sort of system whereby we can better manage this. And we need to do so in a manner which will help decrease what is already for countless people a huge load of daily stress.

This subject is rarely mentioned in conversation. Most people somehow just haven't 'tweaked' to the fact that a huge proportion of their every day stress is currently being delivered to them via the wide range of communication devices. We're all soldiering on as bravely and as well as we can – without calling it for what it is. On this issue there seem to be very few trail-blazers ahead of the mass, so there are also no real socially acknowledged guidelines for properly dealing with, and responding to these intrusions. On one level people almost seem needy for all this communication. Yet on another level they are also being utterly overwhelmed by it. It's as if we've created yet another form of addiction within our culture, which has become a huge problem, with dire consequences to our lives.

One thing you *can* do, for instance, when you next start your conversation with another is to ask if this is actually a convenient moment for them. Don't just assume it is. Let them know that it is perfectly alright for them to say 'no, it isn't', and then organize a more appropriate time which suits both parties. Set the trend, and before you know it others will follow suit – and everyone will feel more relaxed and be better off. So it's not about being cold and callous. It's actually about survival – mentally, emotionally and physically.

Our local village has turned into a global city

Another level to why we are so stressed out is that we now live in a 'global village'. In the past, we only had to directly deal with unfortunate Mary down the street who was ill or Johnnie next door, out of work, and down with a broken leg, etc. However, at the flick of a switch, via TV; Radio, Internet, and now even the mobile with its enhanced capacities, we find ourselves having to deal with the collective pains, miseries and sufferings *of an entire planet* – in addition to what's happening within our own families and circle of friends. And then we wonder why we feel ourselves to be in emotional over-load, burn-out or simply numbed to the horrors we are connected to via all this technology? Most people definitely underestimate the effect such daily exposure to all this sorrow has on our psyches... and ultimately our physical health too.

There is no longer the time to deal with, let alone emotionally process this constant deluge of 'stuff' we are exposed to. Once upon a time, our culture dictated that there was to be at least one day a week - albeit in the name of religion - where we had a complete day off. Here, we had the ability to slow down our pace; rest; do some contemplation – via some sort of religious service - and catch up with the events of the previous week. But those days are gone, and along with it we are left with a very unhealthy situation where we no longer have the ability to 'catch up and process'. Instead, it means we have to keep piling all this 'stuff' onto what is already a huge pile in our mental 'pending tray'. And then we hope that 'one day' we'll get to it... or that it will somehow magically 'go away'!

But we don't get to process this pile of 'stuff' - and it doesn't go away either. Indeed, research has now proven that we pay a huge price for carrying around all this unprocessed material in our lives, on top of trying to keep up with the myriad of chores needing doing. 'Time-out' is as vital to our health and well-being as food, air and water. *It is not a luxury meant only for some lucky few.*

Western life – constantly not living in the moment
Something has to give in all this relentless bombardment. A big part of the problem is that although our thoughts are incessantly being generated in the NOW, most of the time we are in fact not truly *present* in that Now. Instead, we may be deep in the past or far into the future, at the same time as we are trying to deal with whatever is in our present moment.

Living our lives this way, un-focused from the moment NOW, does have repercussions on our mental, emotional and physical health. The more we are actually 'living' in the past or the future – for whatever reasons – the more we are also not present to fully deal with what is occurring right here and now for us. So whatever is occurring, certainly from an emotional processing perspective, goes into that 'pending tray' to be dealt with at some future time.

As Westerners, we tend to live so much in the past or the future that there is a disproportionate amount of our Life Force or Energy 'stuck' in that 'pending tray'. But the 'conveyor-belt' of life just keeps churning along at its furious pace. And the more the 'baggage' on that 'conveyor-belt' doesn't get processed, the more all that psychological/mental 'stuff' keeps crashing off the end, piling up in a huge stack.

It also makes it really difficult to attend to the Higher Levels of our Awareness or Consciousness; our intuition if you like. It's a bit like trying to listen to really interesting information being broadcast on the radio, but the dial is 'off-station', creating a lot of static, and making it almost impossible to hear that 'Broadcast'. The result of being so disconnected from the Now is that we also become increasingly disconnected from Higher or Deeper levels of really useful Knowledge, from which to live our lives. In turn, this disconnection from Higher Self forces us to remain stuck in ego self.

It's a bit like having one of the junior 'office managers', trying to run the entire Company – instead of leaving that up to the CEO. Like any Company, in order to have it run smoothly and efficiently, it's necessary for the organization to have a regular and clear sense of connection and direction from the Boss. Anything less will inevitably result in inefficient and counter-productive behavior occurring, with its equally inevitable decline in overall Company function.

So too with the human system. Lack of clear, concise connection to Higher Self is a major reason why humanity is so dysfunctional in many ways. With all this 'static', it's not surprising really that we as humans are so prone to mismanaging the daily running of our 'company' - our life. Such 'static' is caused by our human tendency – especially in the West – to be constantly distracted from being able to live our lives more truly within the 'Now'. Eventually, such lack of clear communication is guaranteed to distort our internal Energies, and we can even fall ill – mentally, emotionally or physically. Huge amounts of research do exist to unequivocally prove that disease or ill-health is initiated first on such subtle, Energetic levels.

Limits to how much energy distortion our physical vehicles can handle

A physical body can handle such energetic distortions for only so long, before it then starts to negatively affect our physical functions; until we reach a state of explosion or implosion. At this point, if we are lucky, we finally organize to take time out - hopefully to sit quietly and just BE. This is a State of mind from which it then becomes possible to start catching up with processing all the 'stuff' accumulated in the 'pending tray'.

There is a great need to become increasingly Aware, and thereby more able to see how we so often get drawn into ego mode 'solutions' – which usually are nothing more than further pleasure distractions. Such Awareness then gives us the opportunity to side-step the ego, and use the portal of the Now-Moment through which to directly connect to Higher Self. It also needs to be emphasized that there is nothing inherently 'wrong' – let alone 'sinful' – about ego mode distractions, be they sex, money, power or endless material 'things'. It's just that such distractions have an incredibly strong power to keep pulling us into ego mode – and then remain stuck there, entranced by all these 'things'.

For the first few days - or longer - of finally taking a holiday break, it's as if all this accumulated, chaotic Energy running amok in us is in such a spin. It makes it hard to find the first 'thread' from which to start unraveling this tightly bound mass of 'stuff'. Slowly but surely, however, and as we hopefully are simply too exhausted to even add more to this bundle, its chaotic spin slows down. We gradually start to get some perspective on so many of the things that we had previously put away for future processing. It's just that we never made time or space for such a reflective moment. And if we continue to have genuine 'down-time', we will find ourselves able to finally catch up with processing a lot of this previously postponed 'stuff'. Eventually, our bodies will be able to recoup, grow strong and more balanced again.

The problem is that for many of us - when we finally do organize to have 'time-out' for holidays - instead of truly resting and being quiet, we organize a far too ambitious list of things to do. This only adds to our inability to effectively access that 'pending tray'. So by the time we get back home again, although on some levels we've had respite from our usual daily grind, nevertheless, we haven't really processed what we needed to clear. And now it's back onto that fast-forward 'conveyor belt'; into that same style of life again. Once more we are not truly focusing much on what is actually happening in the here and Now. This can only cause us to go back into yet another negative cycle of cumulative disconnection.

So one of the things we need to learn is to first see the dynamics of how we tend to live our lives. Next, we need to realize the consequences of not processing such Energetic accumulations. It's only by understanding what those consequences are that we can then do something productive about it. The most important thing we can skill ourselves at is to learn to live more in the Now – never mind what activities we are engaged in. Meditation is one powerful way we can start to do this, and will be explored more deeply in chapter 9.

Women are especially prone to the Western 'treadmill'

This constant need to perform; be active; keep 'doing', is especially heightened for women, where our culture expects them to wear a number of 'hats'. They are often expected to be a 'mother', 'wife', 'house-keeper', 'shopper', 'cook', 'cleaner', 'child-minder', 'nurse', 'taxi-driver' for the kids and... oh yes, I forgot... somewhere in amongst all these multitude of chores, she is also expected to have a professional career of some sort! No wonder that women are inevitably the most burnt-out of all my clients.

Trying to be the 'super-woman' is guaranteed to end up with a nasty case of psychological and/or physiological burn-out. Something will eventually snap... and it ain't gonna be technology or the 'treadmill'! The large array of health issues that such women present with are testament to this sad but inevitable reality.

Mind you, men - especially in the corporate world - aren't that far behind with the experience of burnout. The utterly unrealistic hours they are forced to work, plus constantly being at the beck and call of the boss via the mobile - even after work hours or on supposed days off – exacts its toll too.

The other problem is that this over-activity of mind and body causes very clear physiological, hormonal and biochemical consequences. Firstly, it results in a huge increase in the sympathetic nervous system function - the 'fight or flight' aspect of our response to life. Here, tsunamis of stress hormones, like adrenalin and cortisol, are constantly squirted into the blood stream. This is akin to sitting in a car; gunning the engine; not in-gear; handbrake on, and going nowhere... but causing the engine to grossly over-heat as well as waste an enormous amount of 'fuel' – or Life-Force. But the reality is that no system can keep up this relentless over-activity, and expect to stay well.

Enter a myriad of symptoms such as blood pressure, headaches, migraines, PMS, arthritis, immune dysfunctions, heart attacks, strokes, cancer... and the list goes on. Yes, all these, and many more health issues are now scientifically known to be caused or aggravated by stress, especially by unrelenting stress; and above all by stress we feel we are unable to escape or have no control over, and which thereby creates a sense of endlessness or hopelessness.

Western life – never satisfied

So often in our Western Culture, we are in 'chase' mode - always chasing the next thing we believe will make us happy. Yet, the irony is that if this is how we live our experience of life, then even when we finally do get all these 'things', ironically we aren't really fully present to enjoy them anyway. We're inevitably already chasing the next dream. Dreams guaranteed by an insidious and all-pervading advertising machine, as it eats into our mind like a cancer... 'to make you happy, healthy, desirable, secure, sexy...' and so much more.

Western Culture is incredibly effective in how it manages to keep us on this consumerist 'treadmill'. It coerces us to frantically chase an endless list of 'things', supposedly promising to fill this awful void we Westerners seem to suffer from so deeply. But no matter how much more 'materiality' we obtain, it never seems to truly satisfy that emptiness... other than for a brief period. Strange, that! All too soon, we usually find that what we did actually manifest, didn't quite hit the spot either. We still feel dissatisfied and empty.

Wishing for 'now' to be different to what it is

One major way we also create dissatisfaction in our lives is by wishing our moments to be different to what they are. It's as if we get a firm idea of what it is that will give us satisfaction or happiness. And unless that precise thing or event is actually in our lives, we feel deprived and unhappy. Ironically, this is despite the fact that so often we nevertheless do have an amazing number of other things or situations already manifested in our lives. But as these don't fit into what *we* feel is the *only* thing to satisfy this present moment's 'desire-itch', then they get dismissed, over-looked or undervalued as equally possible sources of happiness and satisfaction.

It's this constant need to have one moment be *different* from how it actually is. Constantly wanting *that* special person in your life; wanting *that* job; holiday; money, etc. to exist in *this* moment – Now! And so many people truly believe, albeit unconsciously, that unless they specifically get that wish fulfilled... there's little chance they could be happy in all the *other* arenas of their life. This feeling pervades their mind, despite so much else they do have in their lives which could make them equally happy – if they *chose* to allow it to be so!

Negating life due to lack of.......

What's really happening here – besides being totally spoiled Westerners with already more material goods than we know what to do with - is *not* being present in the Moment Now. Instead we are always looking to the past or future for the culprit of our 'current' dissatisfaction. Either we *had* something which we now no longer have or we *want* something which we don't *yet* have.

There's a real need to become Aware of just how caught up we get in this endless 'desire game', thereby pulling us out of the Moment. In this way, such desires keep distracting us from the huge amount of things we inevitably already do have, but are not consciously present with, and therefore not truly experiencing.

What if we could utterly remove our desire from our consciousness

We're usually not Aware of how we block and self-sabotage our own happiness in this sort of way; how we often make our lives miserable and empty, because we haven't yet got... you name it. Endlessly! Well, here is an exercise you might like to try. Just imagine for a moment... what would your life be like if whatever it is you are so desperately craving for at present, were to be magically and totally removed from your consciousness? To the point that it leaves you with a complete lack of awareness that this could even be anything to possibly desire. Be that a special partner; a new job; a better and bigger house, car or whatever.

Hopefully, this little exercise might allow you to see that if this desire was utterly absent, then you might actually allow yourself to be more than content with what you *do* already have in your life. In fact you might end up counting your blessings, realizing just how rich and full your life really is, especially when you consider what the majority of this planet's population has to live with: for example, those in many areas of South America, the Middle-East, Asia and various other African nations. It's just that the lack of focus on what you *do* have, and the inability to be truly *present* – in each Moment – with all you have, can also have the effect of often negating the multitude of things already enriching your life.

So much of what we think; how we think and what we do, becomes secondary to our obsessive focus on what it is we *don't* have, yet desire so strongly. Usually, with that unspoken assumption that... 'once we have xyz... *then* we will be truly fulfilled and happy'. But what an illusion that ends up being. So, even if you do get it, and feel 'happy' for a while, before you know it you're back to desiring something else, creating an endless loop of desire that can eat you up alive.

Glass half empty – rather than half full

The problem with such an approach to life is that our main way of connecting to this reality occurs primarily through the 'window' of our desires. So if this desire hasn't somehow manifested, then in a metaphorical sense it's as if the 'lens' to life becomes opaque. This causes all of our life - beyond our desire – to be seen as a dim blur, with no real sense of reality or fulfillment.

Hence we tend to suffer from a chronic feeling of disconnectedness. The trouble is that we too often judge every event, and every moment in our lives against whether these other things or situations we're presently obsessed with are also experienced - concurrently. And as this is frequently not the case, so too does our life seem empty, frustrating or disappointing, to the point where for some people, it may seem unbearable, despite how much they actually *do* have in their life. If only they could but truly see how blessed they really are, by focusing on, and acknowledging all they do already have. But this can only be achieved by being fully present to our richness - in the Moment; in the Now.

Just look at Hollywood and some of its inhabitants. They are drowning in large amounts of money, material goods and fame, yet so often are utterly miserable, because they still don't have......

Blind to our own patterns

As humans, this has all too often become the sort of pattern of our lives. Worse, we are usually not even Aware of this fact, and just how crucial it is to break out of it if we want to start truly *experiencing* our lives. We need to learn how to walk, talk, and be in our lives, without always being so focused on needing an end goal. We need to learn to do such activities simply for the sake of truly being present in those moments. By being in the Moment, we can actually *experience* all those activities or situations more clearly and directly. It's all this chronic focus on 'doing', which then also results in such a sense of desperation and deprivation when our desires aren't fully met. Especially when we have fallen for that seductive expectation that such desires will absolutely be the source of our happiness.

Just BE who you are; remain focused in each Moment, without your desires constantly pulling you out of the Now. Then you'll find such focused-on-events becoming much more fulfilling, rather than being colored as satisfying or empty, according to whether or not they are accompanied by your as yet unfulfilled desires. Again, let it be clearly understood that desiring anything at all is not inherently bad. Absolutely, definitely not; it's a hard-wired aspect to being human. But, such desires do become really dysfunctional and destructive of true happiness when they so possess our souls, and so monopolize our minds that we become utterly blind to everything else *already* in our lives. This is true blindness, guaranteed to cause us much suffering.

Life so empty, worthless, because I don't have......

Let's look at an example of someone who has spent many years primarily focused on experiencing a fulfilling relationship – but hasn't achieved it. Often, what has happened instead is that this search for a magical person has also made the rest of their life seem empty and lonely. Their present tack in achieving a sense of fulfillment in life has obviously not worked. If anything, it has badly backfired. That special person never manifested; they are still alone and without a partner. Despite having lived their life to date from the perspective that they would only feel completely fulfilled *once* that special person manifested – it may be more productive and healthy to now cut loose from that hope and approach to life.

They need to recognize and admit that despite their wish and expectation, life hasn't come up with 'the goodies'. It might therefore serve them so much better to simply start living their life, right now, more from the point of just experiencing as fully as they can the numerous things and situations they *do* have access to. So many of these could equally give enormous joy and fulfillment – if they but allowed it.

As we explore this issue, we may come to realize something profound – as well as possibly disturbing. In the West, we live surrounded by great abundance, and much of the time we usually have many wonderful experiences occurring in our lives. But because of having such a rigid and narrow criteria of what a 'successful' or 'memorable' day should be like, then what can happen is that our life becomes mostly lived via *invalidation*. For instance, our life feels full and validated *only* via the presence of having 'that special partner' in our life. The sad reality is that this is how many of us do live our daily life.

What a waste of a life

Ultimately, what a wasteful way of living, because what we are in fact doing is to put just about all of our life on hold, instead of allowing it to be fulfilling. 'I'll be happy when I get…..' becomes a constant postponement as well as a negation of our lives. But when we are always looking for other things to satisfy that emptiness, this approach can also create a deep and constant sense of restlessness, and lack of fulfillment in us. In turn, this can lead to a constant, underlying urge to then move elsewhere; to do something else, driven by an often unconscious agenda of fulfilling our desire. 'Maybe I'll have more luck finding someone if I move to Perth; to Auckland; to Timbucktoo… to Cyberspace'. But each time we are also simply transplanting our primary problem – *us*.

Change of tack is what's needed – not necessarily change of location

This doesn't negate the fact that we can be incredibly proactive in manifesting any desire we may have. Indeed, a major theme to this book is precisely how to do this, via such techniques as Creative Visualization, soon to be discussed in chapters 10, 11 and 12. But remaining so locked into the *lack* of what we want, as described above, is certainly not the way to go about it. Ironically, it is of course the other way round. Letting go of that incessant need for a partner, for instance, will allow for so much more joy to flood our present Moments, with all the good things we inevitably do already possess. This can happen despite not having that one specific thing we've been obsessing over, and which we've become fooled into believing is the *only* thing which could possibly give us joy.

This present discussion is really important if we are to explore the concept of Co-creation. It's not therefore just a matter of learning how to manifest our reality.

We also need to be able to celebrate our creative manifestations.

And the most potent way of doing so is by Being fully in the Now; moment by moment. A very powerful and effective way to learn this skill is via the concept of meditation. Here, the skill is to learn to remain focused on a Mantra, but we can equally transfer this skill into being truly present in every moment of our daily lives – by *using the Moment as our Mantra*. But more on this in chapter 9.

Perhaps this discussion does somehow ring true on the fringes of your consciousness, although at the same time seems confusingly counter-intuitive or simply unattainable at this point in your life. Hang in though, because there is still much to discuss on these sort of issues in further chapters, hopefully providing a greater clarity.

Loss of boundaries aggravates the problem

When we look at how we can tend to get so busy in our lives, it's easy to understand why we might feel as if we're emotionally drowning. Always on the go; everyone wanting a piece of you; a sense that there are no boundaries left to protect you any longer. Ultimately, this constant invasion of your personal Space can result in the erosion of any sense of 'self', to the point where it seems as if 'you' have ceased to exist. Indeed, it may feel as if you exist solely to service the endless demands placed upon you, by this culture and everyone around you. Ask any mother!

There was a spiritual Teacher who once said something that is most applicable to today's stress and burnout dilemma: 'Love thy neighbor... *as thyself*!' It is truly interesting how we seem to have conveniently forgotten this latter part of the phrase. Yet we work ourselves to death trying to 'love our neighbor' - however this presents in our lives. Unfortunately, what gets ignored is the fact that we, too, have a most legitimate right to some nurturing. Not as a luxury, but indeed for survival.

The power in naming 'the problem'

To solve a problem - and this Western 'treadmill' so many of us are caught on is a *huge* and *deadly* problem - we first need to understand and acknowledge that there is a problem. Also, that it is not a matter of thinking somehow *we* are deficient for not being able to keep up - while everyone else seems to cope. Believe me, scratch the surface, and you'll find that the average person out there is only pretending at coping. We need to acknowledge and understand what this stress is doing to us; mentally, emotionally and definitely physically. We need to 'name' it. Once this is done, then it becomes easier to look at ways of solving the problem.

It might serve you well to spend a few moments to re-assess your own 'treadmills', and where you might be able to make significant reductions to your stresses. You could make a list of all the things which hassle you. Just jot them down as they come to mind. Keep adding to the list over the next few days, ensuring this list is kept handy to write down ideas as they arise. Now create three columns:-

1. totally un-negotiable stresses - usually direct family issues and situations.
2. stresses or situations which are important to handle, but nevertheless are open to change or delegation.
3. stresses caused by people and situations of minimal direct significance to your lives, and which can definitely be deleted from your reality - even if such deletion does initially cause some 'ruffled feathers'.

Setting limits

The only way to survive this constant barrage of life-demands, and subsequent stress is to set your limits. Somewhere along this deadly trajectory you need to make a decision, based on a clear understanding that this situation you find yourself in is only going to get worse in the near future, especially as ever more 'clever' devices are added to the list. These will only ramp up that 'treadmill' even further, and drive you right over the edge - which so many people are already tottering on. Start setting limits, albeit in some simple ways. Place a message on your answer-service which explains that it may take a few days for you to get back to your calls. Only answer the phone if it really works for *you*.

If you are already busy with something, there are gadgets available called answering-machines. This is one bit of technology which *can* help reduce your stress, so make maximal use of it. Rarely are the phone calls you receive associated with true life or death situations.

Don't multi-task while on the phone. Perhaps choose to only answer the phone when you have time to sit down, and truly focus on your caller. That should immediately limit how many calls you answer! And one powerful way to guarantee you will end up doing this is to go back to a *corded* phone – if you can still find one. That in turn should keep you away from the stove, ironing board, washing basket... or whatever.

Similarly with emails. Send out a general email, letting people know that from now on, it may take 'x' amount of time before you can get back to them. This takes the pressure off you to somehow respond immediately, thus reducing your stress. It's really interesting to note how some people find this approach to dealing with calls and emails shocking and inappropriate. Yet the question you should be asking yourselves is... 'How appropriate is it to drive myself into burnout; into ill-health; into a stroke or heart attack'?... just because our culture on some unspoken level demands we keep up with it all?

Don't multi-task in the car - especially by using the mobile. *It could kill you and others.* This activity - in the name of 'saving time' or simply because you are bored - is truly insane, especially if you are a mother or a father. Do you really want to orphan your children that much? Research has again and again proven how dangerous this particular form of multi-tasking can be. Besides, trying to drive and speak on the phone at the same time definitely doesn't allow you to focus 100% on your caller either – let alone the road. Plus it then also

Chapter 8 - Being In the Now

leaves you with having to emotionally deal with whatever extra stresses such calls themselves generate.

Instead, use that time in the car in a more positive way - contemplatively - for emotional processing or simply 'time-out'. If you're going to be spending a lot of time in the car, choose to use it in a non-stressful manner, rather than catching up on calls. For example, you could play some of your favorite music – which you otherwise just don't get any time to do while at home or work.

The magic two-letter word – 'No'

Start saying one magic word a lot more often in your life... 'No'. 'No, I can't see you tonight'. 'No, I can't make it to that meeting tomorrow night'. 'No, I can't pick you up after sport - catch the bus home instead'. 'No, I can't fit in another committee'. Say 'No' to picking up the phone or mobile like some automaton every time it rings. Notice how many people feel they have no choice but to answer when that piece of plastic sends out its chime. Pavlov would be proud! Say 'No' to switching on the News every night. The world won't disintegrate because you didn't watch all that misery and Spin. But the amount of emotional processing you will need to do may just be cut back a bit.

These 'No's' can all be said with compassion, yet with firmness. Schedule time out in your diary that is to be as sacrosanct as it would be if you had made an appointment with a very dear friend. If someone or some situation wants a piece of you on that day and at that time, explain that you are already committed... to yourself. This latter aspect is none of their business, and doesn't need to be explained to them.

Don't be so shocked. You wouldn't bump a commitment to see a friend, yet most people don't think twice about bumping an important commitment to themselves. How odd!

The Western 'treadmill' is not only seductive – but addictive

In reality, and to call a spade a spade, this quandary we as Westerners find ourselves in is really nothing else but a most addictive habit we have allowed ourselves to become seduced into. Western style consumerism, driven by sophisticated, powerful and saturation advertising is a very addictive phenomenon; worse, this usually occurs unconsciously. Its control over us is even more so, precisely because too few of us are willing or able to call it for what it is. Again, the first thing to do in dealing with any particular problem is to be able to name and define it.

Not that economic growth, driven by consumerism, is totally wrong or evil. Far from it. After all, it is also the driving force which has generated so much of our wealth and comforts, as well as the technologies which can provide such incredibly sophisticated solutions to our many daily life challenges. I wouldn't have been able to write this book as easily, without the use of word-processing; just one spin-off from our consumerist system. All totally acknowledged.

But it's the run-away, out-of-control consumerism, especially when disconnected from any sense of Higher Self perspective or from any sense of ethics or morality, which then creates so much collateral damage to our societies, bodies and souls. The problem is consumerism in an extreme form, to which many people have allowed themselves to become slaves, and which drives them to acquire so much *beyond* what they actually need for what is already a comfortable life. It's our largely unquestioned capitulation to Western style consumerism that may therefore need to be questioned.

After 'naming' the problem, one powerful way to deal with it is to not only have a clear and concise plan of action, but as with overcoming any addiction, to ultimately tackle it moment by moment. It becomes harder to be seduced into past and especially future materialistic desires, if we increasingly skill ourselves to be able to come more from the Now.

Accepting the moment as it is

One critical factor in truly living one's life is to be able to accept the Moment for how it is. Not for how it 'should' be or 'could' be, or how one would wish it to be, but rather coming to grips with the reality of how the Moment is. By the same token, there is absolutely nothing inherently wrong with trying to change the Moment, especially when it becomes clear that there is a better way of being in a Moment. And indeed, we will be looking at very powerful techniques, such as Creative Visualization, through which to do so.

But if the Moment is not changeable, you only have two options. You either live with that Moment and make the most of it, remaining as present in it as possible, while also extracting as much value and joy out of it as you can. Or you rebel against it, and go off into fantasy lands as to how it could be or should be. But the latter approach inevitably makes things worse, as already discussed in chapter 6, where we looked at running out of petrol on the way to collecting the kids from school.

Sometimes we just need to surrender to what is

There are going to be those circumstances in life, where it doesn't really matter what we might like to have in our reality... it just isn't going to happen that way! And then we do have to come to a point of simply surrendering to such situations and accepting them. In these circumstances, we need to realize that our power is not in *changing* it - but rather, in *accepting* it. On such issues, we need to strike a realistic balance, something which the New Age seems to have forgotten or over-looked in its apparent over-focus on us being such complete masters of our own destiny.

Aside from this latter New Age belief, it would appear that far too much of our discontent in the West is because we somehow feel as if life owes us our reality exactly as we wish it to be. This is especially so when we have used various New Age techniques, and worked really hard to change an un-wanted reality. That's all well and good; such techniques have immense value, and we should definitely consider going down that road initially. But we also need to remain open to the possibility that there are life situations which may not be fundamentally amenable to change, even when using our Creative Visualization powers in as skillful a manner as possible.

This is where some of the discussion on pre-incarnational 'planning' by the Oversoul, discussed in chapter 7, comes into the picture. Where our Creative Visualization attempts don't seem to be paying off, despite doing it the correct way, then the more Conscious thing to do for now is to accept the situation as it is. Try instead to find Peace and a sense of contentment - *despite* how our reality is.

Point of power is in the Now

The point of power is always in the Now – where you *can* make a *choice* about how you respond to your situation – even if you can't make a *change* to it. That choice, although it is simple, is not necessarily easy. Yet the consequences of making the appropriate internal shifts are huge. In that moment of becoming Aware, we then also need to have the discipline, tenacity, and drive to make the choice to disconnect from that negative cycle, and just be present in the Moment.

It's always about choice. This is the realm within our lives where the concept of Free Will does have validity. Ultimately, even though we may not be able to have a free choice about *changing* the actual structure or experiences of certain events in our lives, what we can always change is our *interpretation* of that event. This remains the case, never mind how much we may not want to acknowledge or play with this concept as a solution to our dilemma.

It's an internal mental process that we *can* always do, never mind how difficult the situation. This is a point of power which can never be taken away from us. That is a simple fact; it's about a simple choice. It is however, far from an *easy* process, until, as with any skill, we have done it sufficient times, whereupon it then becomes an *automatic* process.

Each moment is a new moment & point of power to start again

So many of the points raised in this discussion here are very clearly and concisely presented in Eckhart Tolle's book 'The Power of Now'. [1] He also explores another interesting aspect of trying to really live in the Moment, which needs to be clearly understood, or else it can turn into a subtle form of self-sabotage. It's about that feeling of paralysis due to past failures. There may have been many times in the past when you did try hard to be in the Moment. Yet, despite such effort, you didn't truly succeed in being there constructively, using that Moment from the Highest level of Awareness possible. So this can create a sense of... 'what's the use, I'll more likely than not fail to utilize future Moments as well'. ...'It's all too hard; it's all too overwhelming'.

Yet, this is all 'mind-play' - and ultimately rather effective too – keeping you out of *this* Moment with its new window of opportunity. You should also realize that just because you may have stuffed up *this* Moment, doesn't mean you should therefore waste the next. The incredible blessing and generosity of this human life is *precisely* that we have yet another Moment... for as long as we are incarnate. Don't allow past moments to incapacitate or paralyze your choices in the present moment. Simply choose to learn from those past moments, *through* which to enhance and empower your ability to choose in *this* moment, Now. Each moment of life is another chance to choose to shift our Awareness out of ego-driven perspectives, and instead choose to live *this* Moment from a Higher, more 'Awake', Source-Connected perspective. Coming from such a Higher Connection is inevitably associated with being connected with Love Itself, which in turn can only result in more of a potential State of joy.

So the generosity of life, with its many Moments made available to us, should also be something which encourages us to continue with this Journey. This is a voyage where we can allow our life to be flooded with joy - *through* this window of the Moment. Each Moment is a new opportunity to do it differently, and hopefully more constructively. But life being what it is you can be guaranteed that it will take many Moments to learn this skill, just as it did to learn to ride your first bike. Nothing 'wrong' with this; it just comes with the human 'package'.

Awareness of 'growth opportunities' – not blame

Another deeply engrained facet to our humanity is this tendency to go into guilt or blaming cycles, either of ourselves or others. Such a tendency can also spill over into the arena of learning how to 'Be' more in the Now, thereby acting to dampen rather than encourage us on this Path. Once we recognize ourselves caught in a particular life pattern, we can learn to be Aware of how often we then also condemn or blame ourselves for being in this dysfunctional position. Too often we make ourselves wrong, rather than realizing that this moment of recognizing ourselves being dysfunctional *is in fact a moment of success*. Success in having seen through the web of Illusion we were caught up in.

And that moment of recognition is also the point of potential freedom from Illusion, if we then choose – in that Moment – to disconnect ourselves from our pattern. Hence we need to shift the focus onto the fact that we did at least have a moment of escape from the Illusion - that we had a moment of being able to *see* ourselves in a negative pattern. This is a real breakthrough, because mostly we remained 'asleep' to our patterns; a phenomenon that seems fundamental to being human. Having a moment of 'waking up', and *seeing* ourselves caught in the Illusion is a step towards becoming more trans-human; connecting more to our Higher Self mode of Being.

This is an attitudinal shift much promoted by Eckhart Tolle, which allows us to therefore own whatever pattern arises, without the constant resistance or mind chatter of guilt and blame *about* having the patterns. It's rather about allowing our Witness to simply see the pattern. And in that seeing, also allow an acknowledgement – without blame or guilt – through which to then disconnect our Energy from the pattern, even if only for a moment. But with further practise, these moments grow more frequent, more powerful and more consecutive, until we are living far more from our Witness focus, compared to our ego focus. That's why catching ourselves out in those moments where we are indeed lost in ego mode – or Illusion - *are in reality all moments of success.*

Life needs a purpose

Let's explore one more aspect to this whole issue of using the Power of Now to alter our lives for the better. For a disquieting number of people, there is the issue of feeling a distinct lack of purpose within their lives. They seem to have little idea of what it is they are alive for. Maybe it's about simply looking at various options available to you – right now. Then, from this list, make a decision to go ahead and get involved in *something*; anything. Just get started! However, also look at the concept of simply living each Moment – in whatever you are doing – from the perspective of choosing to do so from Love versus Fear.

Such an approach immediately gives us a definite purpose to our lives, which is to train ourselves to focus on the skill of living in the Moment. Next, choose to do so from a Loving, and therefore automatically more meaningful perspective. The other alternative is to keep 'living' from a perspective of feeling lost, hopeless, empty and inundated by the meaninglessness of our daily life. This is an awful Space to find oneself in, making life itself a very challenging process.

Perhaps one way to start dealing with this issue is to look at where you are *right now*, in the sense that in this life Journey, the fundamental reality is that we only have this Moment now. And within that Moment we truly have but two choices. We live that Moment from a Space of Love... to ourselves; to our friends; with that client in front of us now; with that pesky neighbor hanging over the back fence – again; with the check-out girl at the supermarket, who seems so bored and disconnected from life. Or we live that moment of our lives from a negative perspective, inevitably driven by fear, but manifesting as boredom, anxiety, discontent, anger, frustration, irritability, sadness, etc.

It seems that we truly only have those two fundamental choices, **whether we are living lives full of meaning or haven't got a clue where we are going.** *That* choice, in *both* scenarios, is exactly the same!

Chapter 8 - Being In the Now

I've observed, from sharing this point with many clients, that they found it so subtle as to be almost invisible. You may therefore need to read the above paragraph a few times to really grasp the deep significance of this perceptual shift, and how it can truly transform your entire life.

In this world of ours, it's almost as if we postpone any meaningful living, until... 'I've found my true destiny'; or... 'now I know what I've always wanted to do with my life'. But in the meantime, we allow those precious *Moments* of life to simply slip away. Not really *living* them because... 'so far I haven't found what I really want to do with my life'. 'I haven't yet found my life purpose'. How often don't we hear that one nowadays.

Nevertheless, another way you could *choose* to live your life is to become much more fully present to *this Moment now* - to focus on just this one basic criteria from which to experience your daily life, regardless of what you might be engaged in for that day.

And then, *choose to live it from the perspective of Love rather than fear.*

The latter - with all its many manifestations of feeling dissatisfaction, frustration, anxiety, shame, sadness, hopelessness, guilt, anger - only makes you feel empty and often useless. But if the former perspective is invoked, where we choose to live each Moment from Love rather than fear, then the Journey suddenly becomes so much more manageable - and purposeful! Simply because *all* you have to do is to act out, and live *this* Moment in front of you right now - through Love, rather than fear. That's it! Simple – although again, not necessarily easy.

Have you found your destiny in life yet? Do you know the meaning of life? What it is all about? Yes, all important questions to try and answer, but questions which can also become so Esoteric, putting us into endless, sometimes unanswerable loops. These are loops which can also ironically make us *avoid* or postpone our life and living – till we supposedly find 'that answer'.

Final thoughts

Hopefully this discussion has stirred up enough resonance within you to generate a very focused and Aware look at your own life, and make the appropriate changes to cut back on that 'treadmill'. A relatively brief investment of time now, to see where you *can* make changes will pay off handsomely in health and quality of life. Technology isn't going to go away. Our cultural mindset around 'keeping up' isn't going to change in the near future. Our over-focus on materiality being the answer to our human woes is unlikely to change much either. Although, within the economic meltdown of late 2008, also lies a potential for a major shift in such overly materialistic myopia. One can but hope!

However, using concepts like those in the above discussion does now leave it up to you to more fully understand what you are caught up in, and the negative repercussions our modern lifestyle is having on our wellbeing. It also leaves it up to you to re-claim your power to slow down your participation in this rat-race. Make the years ahead less driven years, where *you* are more in control of time, technology and the Western consumerist perspective on life, rather than have these factors drive you. But the most important point in this entire chapter's discussion is to understand how simply becoming more Aware also allows for at least starting to live more in the Now, in turn providing a powerful and effective way of truly *experiencing* our lives.

Exercise

- Name three technological items that have a powerful intrusive affect in your life.
- Name one important way in which you might be negating the experience of wonderful things happening in this Moment Now.

Summary of thoughts thus far.

- It looks more like our technology has out-stripped our ability to handle what it creates in our lives.
- Most people haven't 'tweaked' to the fact that a huge proportion of their daily stress is being delivered via the wide range of communication devices we have become slaves to.
- Another level to why we are so stressed out is that we now live in a 'global village', in turn having to deal with a planet-worth of suffering and distress.

- 'Time-out' is as vital to our health and well-being as food, air and water. It is not a luxury meant only for some lucky few.
- There's nothing inherently wrong with being in ego mode, but it's when the ego self distracts us a disproportionate and inappropriate amount of the time that trouble can be expected.
- Our Western, furious paced culture has turned us into - not human 'beings' - but human 'doings'.
- One major way we also create so much dissatisfaction in our lives is by always wishing our moments to be different to what they are.
- It can be all too easy to see our entire life only through the lens of what it is we feel we are *lacking*. Then it should come as no surprise that our life may also feel empty, neglected or without purpose.
- Far too often, the problem is not the lack of something in our lives, but rather the limitation we put on what we'll define as an acceptable, valid or worthwhile experience.
- Start saying one magic word a lot more often in your life, i.e. 'No'.
- Sometimes things happen in our lives which just won't or can't be changed. We need to realize that in such cases, our power is not in necessarily changing it - but rather, in accepting it.
- The point of power is always in the Now – where you can make a *choice* – even if you can't make a *change*.
- Being caught in the Illusion of life is fundamental to being human. Having a Moment of seeing ourselves caught in the Illusion is a step towards becoming more trans-human; connecting to our Higher Self mode of Being.
- Each Moment we become Witness to a dysfunctional pattern within us is a Moment of success – not failure, because now we can choose to make another choice.
- Even if we still haven't 'found our *purpose* in life', we have but two choices as to how we respond to any one *Moment* in that life – through Love – or through actions driven by a lack of Love or compassion.
- Having found our 'life purpose' or not, that choice is always the same, but the consequences of which choice we make are enormous.

REFERENCES

1. Tolle, Eckhart. *The Power of Now – a guide to spiritual enlightenment*, Hodder, Sydney, 2000.

CHAPTER 9

MEDITATION AS A POWERFUL TOOL

All those who have achieved great things have been great dreamers.

Orison Swett Marden

So what exactly is meditation? There are a multitude of layers and purposes to meditation, depending on what you want to do with it. This practice can be used from one end of the spectrum simply as a powerful stress management technique, right to the other extreme, where it becomes a Pathway towards Enlightenment. But somewhere in the middle, meditation can also become a very useful tool to get us to an *experiential* understanding of what it feels like to be in that 'Inner Space'. This is something we have touched on so often now in this book – in other words, the Higher Self; the 'eye of the storm'.

The most powerful platform from which to do your Creative Visualization is when you get into that particularly Centered, Spacious Dimension within your mind. Meditation, therefore, can be a very useful way in which to get you ready for becoming an effective Co-creator. With practise, and as your skill is enhanced, it becomes increasingly quick and easy to find that Space, whenever you want to go there to do your Creative Visualization. But there's another angle to why it's so important to be able to find this Inner Space of Centeredness. In our day-to-day life, becoming skilled at readily moving from our ego self space to this Higher Self Space can be a most productive and robust way in which to manage those challenges life inevitably throws at us.

Indeed, the ultimate aim of meditation, according to the Indian sage Patanjali is the destruction of 'primal ignorance' (ego-mode consciousness), and learning to establish your point of Awareness more within the 'essential nature of the Self' (the Higher Self Mode of Consciousness). In other words, meditation provides a relatively easy way to release yourself from living your life primarily via ego mode, thereby allowing a more direct access to your Spiritual Self. Ego mode of living is that space in which the world around us seems cruel, heartless, unfair - a place where you have to fight for everything, and where anything might be taken away from you.

To survive in such a cold, heartless world, ego convinces us that we need to do whatever it takes to get our share, or to hang on to what we are lucky enough to already have. Yet, deep within us lies a Space from which we can live our lives in such a different way – the Higher Self Mode. And meditation provides a direct portal to this Realm. Once we operate from there the rules change, and certainly our ability to *influence* our reality... truly becomes a reality! Using the increased level of Consciousness found in this Space, you will have a far superior way through which to influence and Co-create your life.

When we find ourselves in a stressful situation or one of suffering, then a much more productive and comfortable choice is to *respond* to that circumstance from the Higher Self Mode. Think back to that example in chapter 6, of the mum whose car runs out of petrol while driving to pick up the kids. React to this situation via ego mode, and all hell will indeed be experienced. But taking a deep breath, and *choosing* to find that Higher Self – that 'eye of the storm' Space within us – from which to respond, will take much of the sting out of whatever suffering we are experiencing. Besides, using this latter approach in such circumstances tends to resolve them so much more easily.

Each time you can make that positive, constructive choice, and use this approach towards your daily challenges, so too does it allow you to skill yourself, step at a time, towards Enlightenment. That sounds like an awfully big promise, but this Journey towards Enlightenment is inevitably a step by step process. It is of course possible that Enlightenment happens to you like a bolt of lightning out of the sky, as it has for some people over the ages. But frankly it is highly unlikely, and you're not advised to 'hold your breath'!

Enlightenment process – what is it exactly?

When we speak of Enlightenment, what exactly is meant by this amorphous term? Far too often you will hear of such and such a person being 'Enlightened'. You'll especially hear this within the New Age community, with all its

Chapter 9 - Meditation as a Powerful Tool

workshop leaders, authors, authorities and Gurus as candidates for this much vaunted state. This is not to suggest that many of these people aren't Highly Conscious Beings, who have already done an enormous amount of Inner work, and traveled a long distance along the Path *towards* Enlightenment. Indeed they have. But that is not necessarily the same as *being* fully Enlightened.

By the same token, let it be clearly understood, that I have definitely not had an Enlightenment Experience myself! Hence, the best that I can do is to extrapolate and interpret from the available recorded data on other people's personal experiences in this arena. Having said that, it appears from their explanations and descriptions that some are equating, and mistaking, this Illumined State more with what it feels like to be in Higher Self Mode of Living.

Certainly, being able to easily and repeatedly access this Level of human Reality, the Higher Self State, is itself a huge step along the road towards that ultimate human Consciousness goal of full Enlightenment. Living from the Higher Self perspective does give us at least a small and tempting taste of what is still to come. However, it seems that someone who is experiencing a full-on Enlightenment incident is in a situation where all the veils and barriers between the ego-self and the *Oversoul* – not just the Higher Self - have been dissolved on a Conscious, Experiential level.

And for that moment – or period of time which apparently can last hours, to days to months - the channels of communication between ego self and Oversoul Energy are torn wide open. This leaves one open to the raw, full-on Energy of your true Spirit Self; not just your Higher Self, which is only an intermediary between ego and Spirit Self/Oversoul. This is seemingly an extraordinarily powerful event, and certainly potent enough to just about fry the 'circuitry' of the ego, as well as blast it right out of its normal groove. The latter's experience of life is so altered that it becomes very difficult to ever again see the human phenomenon in the same way. It is an opening, and a connecting to the life-changing Energy of the Oversoul, which appears to absolutely, radically and forever alter one's perspective on life.

By the same token, neither does it mean that life on planet Earth suddenly turns into an ongoing party. Far from it. Within the New Age fraternity, it is too often implied that once 'Enlightened', there is no more need for further Consciousness work to be done. It's as if you now have your… 'freedom-ticket to jump off the 'reincarnational merry-go-round'. Such assertions do more disservice to the many who then believe that this quantum experience will set them up for life, with no further need for challenges or suffering. Wrong! Life continues – Enlightened or not. Jack Kornfield's book 'After the Ecstasy – the Laundry',[1] is really worth reading here, and sheds a lot of light on this common misunderstanding.

Daily life chugs along: you still need to eat, sleep, cook, clean, shop and do all the myriad of other things involved with being in an 'incarnational vehicle', a body. But the *way* in which all such mundane activities are able to be carried out, is utterly and forever transformed. It's like being permanently in the 'eye of the storm', where it actually doesn't matter anymore how chaotic life itself may be. One's ability to respond to any life situation is from such a different, and more Centered anchorage, that the experience of life itself seems definitely and utterly changed in many positive ways. It appears our ability to deal with daily life events is from a far less painful as well as a much more empowered stance.

However, having a deep expectation that all of life's problems will be instantly solved when this Enlightenment 'thunder-bolt' strikes; when you have won the 20 million dollar 'Spiritual Lotto', is itself a big trap. What often happens to many people obsessed with this quest is that every day Enlightenment hasn't yet happened, becomes a day where everything is seen and experienced as 'less than'. Our desire and expectation can thus create a deep sense of lack, which may sneak into our minds, and unintentionally become our central focus. We look at life as if it has deprived us, when in fact, we might discover our lives to be more than abundant and full – even if not yet Enlightened.

It's like a form of Spiritual greed, and can become a powerfully *diminishing* force in one's life. There is a definite similarity between this latter situation, and what we explored in the previous chapter, where we so often use the lack of materiality, and our focus on that 'lack', to undermine our Moment to Moment living. It's awful to think how much energy and focus can be wasted if we are coming from these expectations.

In regard to experiencing full Enlightenment, it would be much better to be more pragmatic; acknowledge that yes, a quantum breakthrough may occur – but the question is when. And as life is itself a time-limited experience, it may be wiser to just accept that the nature of the Journey is more realistically seen as one of a step-by-step process. Better to simply 'get on with it', and if for some lucky reason you *are* going to have a quantum Enlightenment experience, well then nothing is lost in the meantime, and you're still ahead.

Chapter 9 - Meditation as a Powerful Tool

Perhaps that's all Enlightenment is actually about. Not to become the most perfect person on Earth, nor to achieve a certain, almost unattainable degree of holiness. Rather, to simply try - in whatever way we can - to increase the Love on this plane, and therefore the Light. En-Light-enment – bringing the Light of Spirit directly into the human condition and experience. Yes, this can happen as a huge 'Spiritual whammy', but to be practical, it's more likely to happen step-at-a-time for the greatest majority of us.

Yet, if enough people are able to achieve this step-at-a-time process, it can't help but make both us, and our human reality here on Earth a much more positive and illuminating experience. Perhaps it is too easy, and too idealistic to strive for *perfection,* when what would serve us better is to simply strive for *excellence* – with whatever situation we're in, and with whatever resources we are capable of tapping into.

Meditation – what is it exactly

Meditation is primarily a discipline in which a person focuses their mind on a word, thought, object or their breath. The aim is to concentrate the busy mind exclusively on any one of these focalizing points, thereby quieting it. This process allows the person to then travel inwardly to a Space of much deeper Calm than usually found in our external environment. In turn, this has powerful effects on our biochemistry and physiology, causing positive internal changes on mental, emotional and physical levels.

Besides the constructive health benefits on all these levels, meditation can also lead to altered states of Consciousness, and ultimately to supposed Enlightenment. Such a final goal would take enormous and continued effort for the greatest majority of people. But certainly, along this route towards Enlightenment, many other worthwhile Spiritual – as well as material - benefits would be achieved by the continued, daily use of this powerful practice.

Learning to be in the Witness State

Another great benefit of meditation is learning the skill of 'watching the mind' – or entering that Witness State we've mentioned several times now. This is a mental Space where an aspect of your Awareness becomes increasingly skilled at observing the content of your mind. As you first start the practice, this usually appears to be nothing more than an unbelievable amount of 'mental chatter'. So much so, that for many people it is enough to put them right off meditation. They find it virtually impossible to achieve that experience of supposed Calm and Centeredness so many proponents talk about. However, this internal 'mind chatter' is really the result of many years of accumulated, unprocessed mental 'stuff'.

We are bombarded and overwhelmed each day by billions of stimuli, many of which also cause subsequent mental stimulation, in turn producing floods of random and chaotic thoughts. We find each second of our life crammed with things to do, especially with our predilection to multi-task as much as possible. So many experiences happen to us, which we never have the time – or never *allow* ourselves the time – to fully process. The mind is flitting from one thought to another; torn from one area of concern to another. No wonder we feel so restless, and just can't seem to find a sense of peace in our life. Inevitably the result is internal confusion, mental chaos, physiological and biochemical mayhem, all more likely to drive us into breakdown and disease.

I've got better things to do than sit and cogitate

This is where the average Westerner finds themselves in a quandary. In those 24/7 conveyor-belt life-styles, we can barely get through our daily agenda as it is, without now also being expected to somehow simply sit there and contemplate. 'Such a waste of time' would be the inevitable response. Yet such 'contemplation' is a process which is extraordinarily vital, not only to our mental health but our physical wellbeing too.

All religions use some sort of meditation

Let's explore this issue a bit more. In the 'olden days' – pre-New Age - the word meditation would not have been used much, but most people would certainly have understood exactly what the word 'contemplation' meant. Every religion, from Christianity to Hinduism to Buddhism to Islam to Judaism - and not just the New Age – has its own format of meditation. This is important to realize, because too many people think that meditation is some sort of weird 'cult thing', associated more with the New Age than with religion. Not so! In many religions, this sense of meditation, of entering a calm, centered Internal Space, is often achieved by the use of repetitive prayer; by doing endless rounds of the rosary; one prayer for each bead.

Chapter 9 - Meditation as a Powerful Tool

The Catholic version of a rosary is a string of beads containing five sets of ten small beads each. In the Hindu and Buddhist rosary, there are 108 beads, while the Muslim rosary has 99 beads. Even though each style of Rosary may come in different colors, sizes and designs, their primary purpose is the same. Each time, the aim is to pray in a repetitive manner, often allowing the person to drift into an altered state of reality.

How to do a meditation

There are countless different ways of meditating. Essentially, you need to find yourself a quiet, comfortable place where you are guaranteed not to be intruded upon, either by people, phones or pets – and especially children! Ideally, find yourself a chair in which it is easy to sit comfortably, and yet keep your back straight and upright. This would be better than a 'bean-bag', where the strong temptation is towards leaning right back... and subsequently falling asleep. Lying horizontal on a bed will virtually guarantee this to occur. Next, ensure you sit with your feet flat on the ground and legs un-crossed; hands in lap.

Close your eyes, withdraw your attention inwards, and start using your focalizing object – be that a word or sound – often called a Mantra. Observing your breath as it goes in and out of your nostrils is another focalizing possibility, as is visualization; or a riddle - what is sometimes called a 'koan'. Another technique, taught by Vipassana Meditation, is to systematically and repetitively focus attention on various parts of your body.

Most people have the idea that meditation can only be done in a hip-fracturing, knee-cracking, ankle-aching, generally tortuous traditional 'lotus posture'. If you are a regular at Yoga, such 'lotus' postures would present little challenge to your spine and joints. If you are a classic Westerner, such postures are sheer hell, and certainly not essential to the successful practise of meditation. In fact, this unfamiliar posture with its inevitable discomfort would only distract you from your meditation, thereby sabotaging it.

It's best to choose a time of day that will be easiest to maintain as your specific, daily meditation slot. One word of advice – try and make it in the morning – preferably one of the first things you do after waking up or showering. Otherwise, what invariably happens is that the daily 'conveyor-belt' kicks in at its usual 200 km per hour, and before you know it, everything else has come in between you and that meditation... and now another day is over. The other reason why doing it at night is perhaps not such a good idea is because too often that's when we are also most tired from the day's running around, and more likely to simply fall asleep as we meditate. Yes, you'll get some rest out of it – but that's about all.

Create a personal 'meditation niche'

The next thing to consider in getting your meditation routine set up is to preferably do it in the same spot. Find somewhere in the house which you can definitely claim as 'your meditation space'. This way, there can be no excuse for not doing the practice due to someone else using the space for their own needs. There is also the belief that over time, you actually generate a sort of Energy 'field' in that spot, which in itself can help facilitate your meditations to a deeper and deeper Inner Space.

So, choosing the same time of day, and same physical location each time, in itself seems to augment the meditative process. Some people also find it useful to light a candle, burn incense, or do some other little ritual which over time almost acts like a 'Pavlovian signal', allowing you to enter into meditation much quicker and more readily.

But I just don't have the time to meditate

As already mentioned, many people never get meditation off the ground 'because... I simply don't have the time for this'. Well, here is a little trick you might like to play on yourself. Do you have 5 minutes in your day to go to the bathroom in the morning? Do you have 5 minutes in your day to brush your teeth? Do your hair? Or any one of a number of other things you *do* find yourself time for? O.K. So, now start with just 5 minutes of meditation per day!

Most people's rather incredulous response is that surely this is an utter waste of time; what could you possibly achieve in 5 minutes of meditation? Admittedly, not much. But what you *will* have achieved is at least *starting* the process! And you will be surprised how after a while, you will find an extra 5 minutes to now let it go for 10 minutes.

Before you know it, you will get so hooked into meditating, you'll find you actually *want* to stay in the process for the 20-30 minutes it has slid into. And magically, somehow, it now also does in fact fit into your day. But you had to get the process started with those initial 5 minutes. Just give this approach a

Chapter 9 - Meditation as a Powerful Tool

try. Particularly if – like so many others – you feel you 'simply don't have the time for meditation'.

Which mantra do I use?

As already mentioned, there are many ways of doing a meditation, but using a Mantra, a special word, is one favored by the majority. To at least start you off, here are a few classic Mantra 'words' in common use:-

- One you're sure to have heard of is 'OM'. Say it silently in your mind, on the in-breath and again on the out-breath, so that you are slotting it into your breath cycle.
- Another one is 'OM NA*MAH* SHIVAYA'. The first two 'words' are pronounced much as you read them, but with 'NAMAH', most of the emphasis is on the 'MAH'. The last one is more along the lines of...'SCHE – VAI – YA'.
- Another two Mantras are 'HAM SAH' - spoken much like 'HUM SAH' and the other is 'SO HAM' – or 'SO – HUM'.
- YAHWEH is another Mantra some people use.

The first and the last three Mantras are especially good to tie in with your breath. For instance, 'HAM' (HUM) on the in-breath and 'SAH' on the out-breath. So too with 'SO HAM' and YAHWEH (one of the Jewish words for God). However, when using the 'OM NAMAH SHIVAYA', it is less readily tied in with your breath. Just allow any of these Mantras to settle into whatever pattern feels comfortable and rhythmic for you. Experiment with a number of ways of silently saying the Mantra within your mind, and settle on the way which feels most natural for you.

Also realize that this may change over time. Sometimes one particular Mantra feels absolutely appropriate to do, yet another time you may feel drawn to a different one. You definitely won't be hit by a bolt of lightning for changing Mantras! Allow your intuition to guide you here. There are many more Mantras besides these few, so this is something you might like to explore further, once you've really gotten into the swing of it. TM (Transcendental Meditation) will provide you with a very specific Mantra, selected for you according to certain criteria. However, they usually charge an arm and a leg too!

Back and forth; back and forth... it's O.K!

As you first start meditation, your sessions may seem nothing more than a chaotic flip-flopping from using your 'focalizing object' – usually a word or Mantra – to wandering off into 'mental chatter'. At this point, simply notice – Witness – that you are in 'chatter'; don't judge yourself; don't get irritated that you have wandered off the Mantra - yet again! Just choose to go back to the Mantra. This back and forth may happen many, many times in a session, and most people initially believe such sessions to be a total failure and waste of time. Absolutely not so! Such sessions are *precisely* successful, because as many times as you may have lost your focus on the Mantra, nevertheless, you did become 'Witness' to that situation, thereby making the choice to go *back* to the Mantra.

This is nothing more than training your mind to become increasingly able to 'see' where it is focused. And then from such Awareness, to Consciously choose to make a change – back to Mantra in this case. A similar situation would be learning to ride a bike. As you first started to learn this skill, you will inevitably have fallen off many times, but the only solution was to dust yourself off, and jump back on. Otherwise you would never have learned the skill of remaining balanced on this weird, metal contraption called 'a bike'.

However, as you continue to remain focused on the Mantra, or whatever you decide to use, you will – with time and practise – find yourself ever more quickly falling into a comfortable state of Inner Calm. This process of meditation eventually acts as an anchor to hold you powerfully in the moment – that NOW-Space which Eckhart Tolle speaks so much about; that 'eye of the storm' we've discussed previously.

As your skill at finding this Space of Inner Calm increases, you'll find yourself experiencing either this lovely sense of being at Peace or you may discover the most amazing thoughts, memories, visions or insights suddenly popping into your Consciousness. Just allow it all to happen... *and go right back to the Mantra*! Whatever you do, don't then go and 'play' with, explore or process it. You can always write down and delve into the various insights later, once out of meditation.

How ego might try to sabotage your meditation

One important thing to be aware of in regard to meditation is that as you enter into this process, the mind will come up with the most amazing array of things

Chapter 9 - Meditation as a Powerful Tool

you suddenly need to do. As soon as you sit down to meditate, notice how the ego will constantly try to upset this process by reminding you of things that just *have* to be done – right now! Suddenly needing the bathroom – again; you forgot to hang out the washing; you still need to feed the cat.

Or out of the blue, you'll feel hungry, and want to fix yourself a snack; or feel thirsty ...or itchy all over; or achy; suddenly overwhelmed with tiredness; you're feeling too hot; too cold... endless excuses to 'get up from meditation and quickly fix the problem'.

The bottom line is that the ego just doesn't want to hand over to Higher Self – which is ultimately what you are doing in meditation. Be prepared that the sneaky ego will try every trick it knows to get you to give up on doing that meditation.

But this is where you just need to learn to step back from that rushing around; that crazy internal mental chatter which has suddenly revved up by 200%. Don't even attempt to *do* anything with it. Just watch it. In fact, make this the very first step of your meditation, where you're simply 'watching the mind'; the ego doing its thing. Remember the concept of the Pain body we discussed in chapter 6? Keep in mind therefore, that engaging the Pain Body was exactly what it wanted you to do, and was exactly how we then 'fed' it to ever more prodigious levels. One way to help in this process of disconnection is to name the demon... and then let it go.

In other words, name what it is you are thinking or feeling – that's impatience; that's thirst; that's body discomfort; that's 'important' – I *must* do this first and *then* I'll get back to meditation. Sure! But don't even think of buying into all this 'stuff', which will seem so urgent and real, but whose only agenda is to get you away from that meditation. Just keep stepping back from it all; name it and let it go; name it and let it go. Essentially that is the core of meditation – watching where the mind is at. What games is it playing to distract you? Basically, the busy mind will do almost anything to get you to postpone your session till... 'tomorrow'. But off course we know that 'tomorrow never comes'.

This aspect to meditation; this often intense restlessness and sense of distraction is the consequence of all that 'stuff' that's been happening in our lives. It's all that 'stuff' which we just didn't have the time or energy to sit and properly focus on, thereby allowing ourselves to process it. So now, we have a 'pressure-cooker' full of unprocessed 'stuff', and it will absolutely come spewing forth as soon as you finally sit down somewhere quiet, and try to go inwards.

Attempting to battle all this 'gunk'; trying to process it here and now while also trying to meditate is the complete opposite of what meditation is all about.

However, in our life, we – as the ego, and as discussed in previous chapters - are incredibly programmed to knee-jerk into trying to 'do' something as the ultimate answer to our problems. But this is not necessarily going to work, and there are many important times when the best way to deal with issues is to just observe them. In other words, just go up to Higher Self mode, and become the 'Witness' to what's going on. Just *Be* with it rather than trying to *do* something with it. Contrary to our inner fears, just *Being* with the energy of fidgetiness, anxiety, fear, frustration, anger, or whatever, won't overwhelm, engulf or destroy us. Instead, *not doing* anything with it will over time actually bleed it empty of its 'energy', and it will subside like a sinking ship into the more Deep, Fundamental Ocean of Awareness we have mentioned before.

In contrast, latching on to whatever arises in meditation, and trying to somehow struggle with it only guarantees failure in this process. Any 'doing' response from the mind will feed it, until it then *does* ironically overwhelm us – and we give up. And guess who's won?

SCORE: ego - 1: Higher Self - 0 !

So when we enter into meditation, be warned that there is a lot of momentum behind us always trying to *do* something within our minds. To sit there, and watch our 'stuff' seems counter-intuitive and just plain wrong. Yet, what *will* work is to simply sit there, watching this dross rise to the surface of our minds. Name it if you wish... but definitely then let it go – like steam vaporizing into thin air. Just let them be. Observe them and return to the Mantra. Observe them and return to the Mantra. Over and over again. As time goes by, and you continue this process, you'll find that your ability to become increasingly skillful at picking up where your mind is at, then also allows you to so much more quickly re-focus on the Mantra.

We need to realize that we live in a time dimension, and sometimes it just takes time to let our revved up systems slowly but surely wind down. Unless we're very skilled, it's hard to dissipate all that revved up momentum in a few moments. Meditation can become a powerful way to speed up the rate at which we become increasingly skilled at slowing down our internal pace. Ironic twist!

Meditation – resistance to connection with Source

Another facet to our often rather surprising resistance to doing meditation is the existence of what is almost a primordial fear of making Connection with Source. And the more absorbed we are in our classic Western lifestyle, with its endless distractions, the more disconnected we inevitably seem to be from Source. Keep in mind though, that this feeling of disconnection which appears so real on an *experiential* level is really only an illusion. As discussed in earlier chapters, the Spirit that we truly are on the most fundamental level of our existence can never be disconnected from its Spirit Source. Nevertheless, due to our sense of disconnection, the ego – strangely enough - often goes to extraordinary lengths to *prevent* a re-connection to Source.

It also stems back to a pretty fundamental phenomena within a lot of Western cultures – the fear to give, and especially to *receive* Love, even from another human. Hence no wonder there is an even greater difficulty for some people, in facing the prospect of letting the Strength and Depth of Source/God-Love flow into and through us. So we need to be prepared for the fact that the more we are into the mode of being constantly busy, and occupied with zillions of demands and needs, the more resistance we *may* experience as we try to connect to Source.

The aim in meditation, in our ever so busy life schedules, is dual. Firstly, meditation itself can help settle down a bad case of 'Western culture jitters' – feelings of stress, anxiety, panic – of being strung-out. However, in this regard, it's a bit like the cat chasing its own tail. So many people are perpetually in 'the jitters', and desperately need that portal which meditation provides, through which we can connect to that deep Inner Well of Peace. But to effectively reach that meditational Space in itself requires some degree of focus and centering. Initially, that may be quite a challenging thing to achieve. Nevertheless, meditation would still be the starting point, even though in such cases it may take a longer time to find yourself able to settle into the process. However, just keep at it, and your persistence will eventually pay off.

Meditation can seem quite chaotic at first; this is normal!

It's important to keep in mind that to begin with, meditation can be a bit like a pressure-cooker releasing its pent-up steam, creating much noise as the steam is vented. Eventually, this settles down. As your experience with meditation grows, you will find yourself increasingly in a much Calmer and more Centered Space which will feel absolutely delicious. Nevertheless, be prepared to expect that as you first start to practise this powerful process, it may initially seem as if all hell breaks loose. If you don't realize that this is exactly what could happen, it would be easy to feel that your meditation is 'failing' when it is precisely working!

Far too many people have not realized how in this early period of using a meditation technique, such results are actually 'normal'. Yet, this is also the period during which many people feel they basically aren't suited to meditation, and give up, feeling this practice simply 'isn't for them'. This would be a terrible loss indeed of an opportunity to use a technique which can truly help transform their life. Let alone amazingly empower their Creative Visualization efforts.

So, even if you never achieve full Enlightenment via your regular use of meditation – which will be the reality for most people who practise it! – nevertheless, many other benefits can be obtained by regularly doing this powerful exercise.

Many ways of doing meditation

Certain meditations can also be done while walking or doing other repetitive tasks. Visualization meditations would include practices such as Qi Gong, where the practitioner focuses on the flow of Energy within the body, or *to* another body. Even Yoga can be undertaken as a form of meditation.

Whichever way you choose to do meditation, the end result is to create a period of time where your Awareness is able to withdraw from the normal hustle and bustle of daily life. It allows your mind to catch up on its emotional and mental processing, as well as providing an opportunity for your body to get some high quality, deep rest. In that sense, meditation is a way of allowing us to re-connect with a much deeper aspect of our Being than we could possibly achieve while in daily activity mode. It's a process which sadly has been just about lost in our hectic schedules – and with huge repercussions for our wellbeing on mental, emotional, physical and spiritual levels.

It's when we experience glimpses of that deep, Inner Calm that we get a sense of what it is like to be truly alive on many more levels than just the superficial, conscious mind. Ultimately, it can be argued that so much of our unhappiness; our sense of emptiness; of dissatisfaction; of disconnectedness so classic of Western life is fundamentally due to this lack of regularly Connecting to our Inner Self – the Higher Self. Let alone our God-Source. We allow ourselves to be constantly distracted by our chronic need to always be busy, and its associated mental preoccupations.

Ironically, it's precisely that Higher Level of Self, *from* which Creative Visualization can also be done most successfully. However, as Westerners, most of us seldom make it to that Higher Level of Awareness – hectically busy 48 hours a day, and inundated as we are with loads of material 'goodies' to play with. Or working ourselves to death... to pay for them all! It's about re-directing our life experience from that constant, daily state of change we tend to live in, to an Inner *Changeless* State that does exist, but needs to be specifically sought out.

Krishnamurti had an interesting slant on meditation, believing that the act of meditating was based too much on the 'urge to achieve', which he said implied struggle and conflict to get to the final goal. In that sense he saw meditation still involved with too much activity. His approach was associated with just focusing, moment by moment, on exactly what you were doing in the pursuit of your daily activities. In other words, practising a sense of 'mindfulness' as we go about our daily activities.

It's about becoming the 'observer' of your every action: how you eat; the way you walk; what you are saying; the vast range of unconstructive emotions we humans are so prone too, such as jealousy, rage, despair, anger, sadness. Just watch it all – anywhere and everywhere. *That* to Krishnamurti was true meditation, although for most of us that may also be a bit too demanding; certainly when you first start this practice.

Minds in constant bombardment & over-stimulation

Stress is one of the major issues we deal with as Westerners, day in day out, causing our 'fright, flight and fight' response to be constantly 'on'. This in turn causes cascades of neurotransmitters and stress hormones to flood the body, over-stimulating the sympathetic nervous system. Our blood pressure can rise; we can become anxious, panicky, irritable and even aggressive. Anyone who has had an episode of 'road rage' – or had to withstand the brunt of it – will know how negative and damaging such an experience can be to your psyche, and your body.

The more the stress response is turned on in us, the less we have the ability to become peaceful and quiet. Eventually, we seem to get trapped in a chronic stress state. It's almost like the accelerator getting stuck in our car, excessively revving the engine, and making it very difficult to control the vehicle. So too with us, and the end result can be mental and physical burnout – as well as a large array of ill-health issues.

The reality is that we are all inundated and bombarded by so much stimulation – via TV, radio, txt, computers, emails, mobiles, advertising, etc - that our brains simply don't get the same sort of 'time out' breaks we used to have in days gone by. This has already been explored in depth in chapter 8. However, it means that our brains are constantly running at a million miles an hour, till we either go bonkers or simply flop down in an exhausted heap.

What we first need to do is recognize that we can get lost in these out-of-control cycles. Technology has indeed outstripped our ability to deal with it all. One result is to simply tune out and go numb. But that also has negative consequences on Consciousness levels. In such a situation, we can become callous to the suffering around us, to the point of totally ignoring what's staring us in the face. This is something which seems to occur too often within the 'caring professions', where people like doctors and nurses may finally become quite cold and heartless in the way they interact with their patients. It's also classically found in our response to what we may see on the News, where the most horrific things are occurring to people, right in front of our eyes. Yet our only response is to 'tut-tut'... while we carry on peeling the veggies or drinking a nice cuppa tea.

Closing the heart is a poor way to deal with stress

Closing our heart is certainly one way of managing the stress in our reality, but also comes at a huge cost to our ability to have compassion. On the other side of the coin, you find those in the 'caring profession' who have their heart too wide open. This is equally associated with a huge 'price tag', as they nearly always go into deep burn-out. An alternative approach to suffering is to do a very delicate tight-rope act. Here the heart is kept open, and compassion is available for those needing it, but the people dispensing such compassion and caring must also learn how to care for themselves.

The old injunction from J.C. is worth repeating here... 'Love thy neighbor... *as thyself*'! And meditation can be a most powerful way of allowing such people to re-nourish their own souls.

Those who tend to 'over-care' are a bit like a person hearing desperate screams for help from someone who has unfortunately fallen into a deep hole.

However, instead of throwing a rope down to them or fetching a ladder, they decide instead to jump into the hole with the victim – in the name of consoling them. But now there are two stuck in a hole! Better to stay in the 'eye of the storm', *from* which to reach in and grab at anyone who is being flung around *in* the storm. Jumping into the storm itself to save another just doesn't serve anyone. Again, meditation is a most powerful and effective way of remaining grounded and Centered – despite all the apparent chaos that may be whizzing around you. And in today's culture, with various 'melt-downs' occurring virtually all the time, this is a skill which will be much needed, just in order for us to survive, not to mention remaining functional enough to help others.

Multiple benefits of meditation

Studies have verified that a wide range of physiological changes do occur while meditating. EEG's have shown the electrical activity of the brain to settle down into alpha patterns, which are more consistent with relaxation, allowing the *body* to gain a state of profound rest. At the same time, the *mind* will go to a much more 'restful alertness' state. An Indian Yogi, Maharishi Mahesh, who did much work in the West, introduced the concept of Transcendental Meditation or TM. He also instigated a lot of research which found that many fascinating events occurred within the body of a person doing this form of meditation. For instance, it was found that there was a striking drop in the metabolic rate, accompanied by a huge decrease in oxygen consumption, as well as decreased heart and respiratory rate.

The sympathetic nervous system is that branch of our neurological system which becomes activated under stress. When it is switched on, its counterpart, the parasympathetic system – which causes calm and quiet in the system – is switched off. Only one or the other can be dominant. During these studies on meditation, it was shown that the parasympathetic nervous system became active, causing the entire body and mind to come to a much more restful and relaxed space.

During stress, one chemical which increases in our blood is lactic acid. This is the same acid which causes cramp in athletes after too much exercise. What fascinated researchers was the finding that not only was this yard-stick of stress reduced during meditation, but it seemed to come about because of an improved blood flow around the body. This too would have many benefits to the body as a whole, not just by increasing the rate at which waste substances were being cleared, but also by increasing the level of nutrients and oxygen to the tissues generally.

All these changes would help enhance body function and repair. What also became obvious from these studies was the fact that such changes were actually so much larger than those achieved via sleep. Hence, meditation not only allowed one to become far more relaxed, but allowed a much higher level of body repair than sleep itself.

The Australian psychiatrist Ainslie Meares did a lot of work with the use of meditation in enhancing cancer regression, some of which was written up in a 1976 edition of the Medical Journal of Australia. Now vindicated by further research, it is understood that such cancer regression can be achieved via increased immune function which regular meditation stimulates. Another researcher, Dr. James Austin, investigated the use of Zen Meditation, proving - via the use of MRI - that this practice even allowed for re-wiring of the brain.

Similarly, it's been confirmed that meditation creates improved cardiovascular and respiratory health, as well as improved pain control. Any condition related to stress can be positively affected, such as chronic insomnia, PMS, irritable bowel syndrome, arthritis, drug addiction, depression, infertility, fibromyalgia, asthma, emphysema, chronic airway obstructive disease, psoriasis, high blood pressure, angina, elevated cholesterol, anxiety and panic attacks. A pretty impressive range of health issues – and these are only the ones vindicated by studies!

Even life expectancy has been shown to increase in those who meditate on a regular basis. Using standard measures of aging, it was found that those who had regularly done Transcendental Meditation for longer than five years measured an average of twelve years younger than their chronological age. Not surprising really, because research has actually shown that such people are producing much higher levels of the 'youth hormone', DHEA. Hence, never mind what your health status or what the label of your disease may be, it would definitely be worth your while to give meditation a go.

Meditation therefore, is not just a 'feel-good' therapy; it also provides significant benefits within a range of health issues, even in conditions as serious as cancer. Most people usually start meditating for its relaxation effects or the ability for them to better handle a wide range of health issues. However, as time goes by, they often find themselves increasingly opening to the more Spiritual aspects of this process, which seem to almost drift in laterally. Whatever your initial reason for starting this amazing process, nothing but good invariably comes from it, and like runners with their 'endorphin rush', so too the sheer pleasure of doing meditation is usually more than enough to keep us at it.

The only contra-indication to doing meditation is in those who have a diagnosis of serious mental disorders, epilepsy or previous psychotic episodes. In such cases, meditation should ever only be engaged in with their therapist's approval and under their supervision.

Some final thoughts

This chapter is certainly not meant to provide you with a total overview of meditation. Hopefully, what it has done is to whet your appetite enough to now take it further. Every bookstore will have a vast range of books on this subject. Just put the word 'meditation' into a Google search, and you will have more stuff to read than hours in a day. However, above are at least some of the basics about this powerful process, as well as several suggestions on how to start making this a regular part of your life.

Exercise

- Discuss one definition or perception of Enlightenment
- What is meant by the 'Witness State'?

Summary of thoughts thus far.

- Meditation can be used from one end of the spectrum, as a powerful stress management technique, right to the other extreme where it becomes a Pathway towards Enlightenment.

- Meditation is primarily a discipline in which a person focuses their mind on a word, thought, object or their breath. The aim is to concentrate, and thus quiet the busy mind by exclusively focusing on any one of these centering points.

- The most powerful platform from which to do your Co-creation is when you get into that particularly Centered, Spacious Dimension within your mind so typical of the meditative state.

- Meditation provides a relatively easy way to release yourself from an ego mode of operating in your life, to a more direct way of accessing your Higher Self.

- Having already done an enormous amount of Inner work, and travelled a long distance along the Path *towards* Enlightenment is not necessarily the same as *being* fully Enlightened – as some New Age 'gurus' are perceived to be.

- From some people's description of 'Enlightenment', it appears they may be confusing this Illumined State more with what it feels like to be in Higher Self Mode of living – a totally different experience.

- However, it seems that someone who is experiencing a full-on Enlightenment incident is in a situation where all the veils and barriers between the ego-self and the *Oversoul* – not just the Higher Self – have been dissolved on a Conscious, Experiential level.

- After Enlightenment, the mundane aspects of life continue. However, the *way* in which these are experienced and lived out is irrevocably changed.

- What can happen for too many people obsessed with this quest for Enlightenment is that for every day in which Enlightenment hasn't yet happened, becomes another day where everything is seen and experienced as 'less than'.

- Perhaps it is too easy, yet unrealistic, to strive for *perfection*, when what would serve us better is to simply strive for *excellence*.

- Witness State is a mental Space where an aspect of your Awareness becomes increasingly skilled at observing the content of your mind.

- As you first start meditation, your sessions may seem nothing more than a chaotic flip-flopping from using your 'focalizing object' – usually a word or Mantra – to wandering off into 'mental chatter'.

- Such 'flip-flopping' is no problem, as long as you are Aware of it, because every time you lose the focus, coming back to the Mantra proves you were at least in Witness State.

- This back-and-forth process is nothing more than training your mind to become increasingly able to 'see' where it is focused.

- As you first sit down to meditate, you may find yourself inundated with numerous things that just have to be done... *right now!* This is the ego's way of not wanting to hand over to the Higher Self – which is ultimately what you do in meditation.

- Jus *Be* with all these mental machinations, rather than trying to *do* something with them.
- Studies have verified that a wide range of physiological and mental changes do occur while meditating. EEG's have shown the electrical activity of the brain to settle down into alpha patterns, which are more consistent with relaxation.
- Meditation not only allows one to become far more relaxed, but allows a much higher level of body repair than sleep itself.
- Meditation therefore, is not just a 'feel-good' therapy; it also provides significant benefits within a wide range of health issues, even in conditions as serious as cancer.

REFERENCES
1. Kornfield, Jack. *After the Ecstasy – the laundry,* Rider, UK, 2000.

Lifenotes - A user's guide to making sense of life on planet Earth

CHAPTER 10

CO-CREATIVITY – WHAT IS IT?

Miracles do not happen in contradiction to Nature, but in contradiction to what we know about Nature.

St. Augustine

A lot of time has been spent thus far in trying to get a clearer concept of our human make-up, divided into its ego and Higher Self, and how it is possible to move our point of Awareness between the two. This has hopefully laid enough of a foundation from which to now explore some of the techniques behind Co-creativity. Such concepts are indeed fundamental to being successful in this endeavor of at least *influencing*, if not 'creating your own reality'. But first let's clarify why sometimes the words Creative Visualization are used in this book, and then at another point the words Co-creativity. Is there in fact any difference?

From one perspective, they both describe the same phenomenon. However, the word 'Co-creativity' does add a very important additional understanding to this process. Namely, that we are only **Co**-creators – not *The* Creator. Nor does it suggest we even attempt to somehow become, or play at being this Ultimate Energy, Being or Source.

*Keep in mind that God **is** Creativity; we are only able to **tap into** Creativity.*

This is a major point of distinction, which definitely needs to be brought to our attention. Far too much of the New Age philosophy has tended to imply – if not even declare - that we *are* God. All we need to do is just wake up to this reality, they say. Yes, we are indeed powerful beings, and we can be amazingly creative, but only *through* Infinite Creativity. One appropriate comment here would be to point out that the above over-inflated view of ourselves is precisely the sort of thing the human ego would love to believe. Remember, in chapter 6, it was mentioned that the ego has a tendency to grandiosity? This propensity is often the basis to so much of our human dysfunction, and in the case of Co-creation could lead us into serious trouble.

It's like someone working for the Queen of England who starts to believe they *are* the Queen, simply because they are in such close and constant proximity to that personage. It's about a loss of sensible boundaries to who is who. So too with the ego. If it starts to believe it is God, and able to do so much more than it was ever designed for, then this will only cause a huge distortion in ego functioning – indeed, gross *mal*function. The effect would be a bit like running far too strong a 'current' through the 'wiring circuits' of the ego, causing the 'fuses' to blow.

Two understandings of creation – religious and New Age

It also needs to be clearly understood just how much religion has tended to be a major obstacle to the use and honing of this natural, inherent skill of Co-creativity. Most religions come from a space that it is only God who can Create, and for any human to even think they can is seen as utterly blasphemous. However, what usually hasn't been clarified enough are the different levels of creativity.

Put yourself in the shoes of a loving parent who has created a beautiful play-pen for their young child. It's an enclosed space with definite boundaries, but provided with a huge array of toys and wonderful building blocks. Inside that play-pen, their child is able to play to their heart's content, *creating* an endless variety of things with its Leggo building blocks and toys. But the child certainly didn't create the play-pen. That was created by the parents. Perhaps so too with humans here within the 'play-pen' of planet Earth. We definitely had nothing to do with the formation or creation of Earth, let alone the solar system, galaxy or wider afield.

It's true that it depends on your belief, but let's just for the sake of argument assume that the 'play-pen' of Earth, and its unimaginably vast Cosmic surroundings were in fact Created by some Higher Force – whatever you might wish to call this. Nevertheless, *within the sphere of Earth*, we definitely do have creative abilities to play with the vast range of 'toys' and opportunities we as humans are exposed to. On both levels – the Creation of the entire physical

Chapter 10 - Co-creativity - What Is It?

Universe, and the creative capacities of humans on Earth - we are indeed dealing with creativity. But surely no-one would argue the fact that one is quite different to the other, although both are equally valid and real... *within their own sphere of activity?*

Another interesting thought is that as a parent, wouldn't you be quite peeved if your child decided to curl up in a corner, turning a blind eye to all the toys and games you had so lovingly collected and put there for their enjoyment? Actually, for their education too, because as a parent you knew that there was so much more to the toys than just being able to play with them. It also had to do with learning a whole range of skills, precisely *by* playing with such toys. These were specially designed to act as a prelude to the huge amount of learning your child will be challenged with as it strives for yet higher levels of skill during the years ahead.

Yet what would you feel if your child stubbornly refused to play, believing that to be creative within that play-pen was somehow an evil, sinful or otherwise bad thing to do? What a waste of a play-pen! Well, perhaps that analogy is not so far off the mark when it comes to us in *our* 'play-pen' of 'planet Earth School' – as already discussed in previous chapters. Yet, realistically, that turning away from exploring and honing our own inherent human capacities is exactly what's happening far too frequently within our reality - and is enthusiastically endorsed by so many religions.

Co-creativity & God issues

Religions are ultimately the most important reason why so much of humanity has been inculcated into believing it is somehow bad to want certain things, especially those of the material kind, with money singled out as top of the list. This in turn can often result in deep feelings of resistance to engaging in Co-creation. Not only aren't we supposed to desire material things, but from a religious perspective, even thinking we might be able to manifest them ourselves is seen as challenging the most fundamental role of God Itself. Yet, it's not that materiality is the problem... as much as our potential for becoming so addicted to it. If our primary focus is only on the material aspect to life, then that is trouble with a capital T. But in and of itself materiality is not intrinsically bad; just how we use or abuse it.

Over the millennia, religion has been able to shape our fundamental thinking around this issue of creativity, and has successfully fashioned huge internal blockages to the creative capacities of humans. Such abilities are nevertheless an inherent aspect to our humanity, and do need to be explored, enhanced and further skilled. By the same token, the whole focus of Co-creativity is not just about manifesting endless amounts of material goods or situations. Rather, it is an invitation to learn how to *re-connect* more Consciously *to* this Higher Source; not *become* It.

Many people, coming from a religious background live with the deep fear that to even think of becoming a Co-creator may send down a swift and nasty bolt of lightning. As much as our *conscious* mind might reject such a fear, nevertheless, there are deeper aspects to our systems of beliefs which one could argue *do* still remain stuck in this notion. This in turn does create a powerful way of sabotaging or blocking any attempts at Co-Creativity, simply because it would go directly against these more deeply held ideas, almost subconsciously hard-wired into our system from childhood on.

The power of belief

Here, the most powerful answer to this dilemma is to quote from the Christian Bible... where Jesus actually taught this process over 2,000 years ago. Yes, you read that correctly! Off course, he didn't call it 'Co-creativity'. But when you look at what he is reputed to have said, it is most fascinating to realize that fundamentally he was in fact teaching his followers how to use the mind in order to manifest desires into their reality. Let's take a look:- [1]

Therefore I say unto you, what things so-ever ye desire, when ye pray, believe that ye shall receive them and ye shall have them. [1]

Although this is stated in rather archaic, biblical language, the essence of this extraordinary statement clearly outlines the process of Co-creation. In other words, make up your mind what it is you desire – *'what things so-ever ye desire'*; visualize it – *'when ye pray'*; do so with a feeling as if you already have it – *'believe that ye shall receive them'* - and you will succeed – *'ye shall have them'*. This statement by Christ truly is a potent encapsulation of the entire Co-creative process!

Interestingly, Jesus also taught that:-

'Verily, verily, I say unto you, He that believeth on me, the works that I shall do, shall he do also, **and greater [works] than these shall he do**...*'* [2] (emphasis added)

Chapter 10 - Co-creativity - What Is It?

Now if that isn't an encouragement for all humans to go ahead and work on these sort of skills, what is? Here we have a clear situation where J.C. is actually telling his audience that they too will be able to do the sort of 'miracles' he is capable of; in fact even more so. How interesting!

So yes, it would seem that even one of the great Masters Himself urged us to try and at least play with this inherent skill. Equally, buying into this whole issue of whether you have been good enough; whether you deserve your deepest desires to manifest or not, is ultimately nothing else but a glib abdication of the inherent talents and skills we do have as humans.

For many who come from a religious background, they have been told that you can definitely pray to your God for what it is you want. But the implication or frank declaration is that such prayers are really only answered if on some level you stand favorably in the sight of God. Have you been good enough to deserve the answer to your prayer? Such an attitude, unfortunately also automatically introduces a dynamic of doubt into any attempt to do Co-creation via prayer. After all, the usual, underlying assumption behind prayer is that it is a process that can *possibly* work. It just depends on how worthy you are and how good – or bad – a day God is having. So nothing's guaranteed. The problem is that doubt is one of the most powerful saboteur energies we can engage in during any Co-creative process.

If this process is to work, we have to come from a very fundamental level of *knowing* that the Laws of Co-creation work, whether we are 'worthy' or not. But feel 'unworthy', thus introducing doubt as to your ability to attain the final manifestation, and hey presto... you've just pushed the 'delete' button on any particular Co-creative project. So this sense of 'knowingness' which is such an essential component to successful Co-creation, needs to exist beyond any impression of not being good enough. Feeling undeserving, unworthy or any other such negative inner 'self-talk', can only contaminate or frankly sabotage your ability to Co-create. Remember, Christ said... '***believe*** *that ye shall receive them and ye shall have them*'. His only stipulation was to *believe;* not that you had to be *worthy* or *good* enough before receiving.

Once again, this Journey of working with Co-creativity invites us to work on ourselves, this time focusing on an inherent sense of self-worth. If we have low self-esteem, and feel ourselves to be unworthy, then we will obviously also feel we don't deserve what it is we desire - even if this is only occurring on some subtle inner level. In a sense it's a choice of viewing ourselves via the traditional

Christian concept of 'original sin' versus the opposite, more Buddhist view that we all have deep inside us an inherently good 'Buddha Nature'.

For many readers of a religious persuasion, these previous few paragraphs will probably be most confronting. Absolutely admitted. But this is precisely one of those points along this Journey of Co-creation, where – for now - you might just want to leave this contentious point 'on hold'. Continue reading a bit more – even if skeptical or doubtful. What you will probably find is that after a while, having been introduced to a few more 'pixels' to this whole 'picture', what initially seemed preposterous or really difficult to accept, will actually hang together when seen within a broader framework.

God, seen through human eyes is often perceived more human than 'God'

We seem to live with this mental construct that there is this God sitting 'up there' somewhere, who has nothing better to do all day than hang around judging whether what you desire or want to Co-create has merit or not. It's as if we have this rather strange perception of God, who seems very prone to having 'bad-hair' days. Almost as if God could get into a bit of a mood, and decide that today is going to be a 'pester-Peter' day. Today, God is going to ensure that absolutely anything I might wish to Co-create will be blocked. However, if I am very lucky, God may be having a 'good-hair' day instead, and decide to be very generous to me. So much so that It is willing to grant me something that normally I might feel I'm just not worthy of.

This sort of concept of God is destructive, restrictive and needs to be deleted from our minds. Co-creation works *beyond* whether you are in fact worthy or not of manifesting your desires. However, if you *feel* unworthy or have other doubts about your ability or right to do Co-creation, then that will absolutely guarantee to sabotage this capacity – *from within yourself.* So it is about allowing ourselves to utilize the capabilities of this Higher level, and to do so with gusto, adventure and joy, rather than from that lower level, ego-energy sense of cautiously looking around; feeling we don't somehow belong here or can only do Co-creation by sneaking behind God's back.

Chapter 10 - Co-creativity - What Is It?

Co-creation – just follow the recipe
In other words, it's a bit like viewing planet Earth as the schoolroom, where we have come to learn to 'bake a cake'. And to 'bake a cake', there are some very simple rules that you need to follow. If you follow those rules, you end up with a 'cake'. Actually, it's as straightforward as that. However, if you want to feel guilty or unworthy about being able to 'bake a good cake', then that will just hinder the process – nothing more; nothing less. We really do need to come to a point where we can take on-board something very important. Namely, not only is it a *duty* as humans, to work with these inherent capabilities, but it's also our fundamental *right* to do so. This is the reality, despite the fact that religion too often has a contrary view, and has frequently brainwashed humanity to ignore or malign this very great gift we've been given. Otherwise, as far as our existence here on the planet is concerned, we surely wouldn't be much more than the animals.

Biblical parallels
There's a rather interesting parable in the Bible [3] - Matthew 25:15-30 - where a master called his servants, and gave them each a different amount of 'talents' (money.) He then left them for quite some years, and when he returned, asked each what they had done with their gift. All but one had invested the 'talents' given, and made capital gains on their investment. For this they were greatly commended.

However, there was one man who had been too afraid to use the talents he had been given, and had buried them in the ground. So, on return of his master, all he could give back was the exact same amount of talents originally given. No investment had been made, and in that sense his gift had been utterly wasted. At this, the master became angry, and severely reprimanded his servant for having done nothing with the gift he had been given.

In a sense, this parable is very applicable to those still coming from a religious background, and afraid to use their inherent human 'talents' of Co-creation. These talents represent an ability which each and every human being *is* already tapping into anyway – inevitably unconsciously - but which we all need to learn to do more skillfully, and with more Consciousness. In other words, there is a real need to 'invest' in this Co-creative skill, so that we can indeed create more from what we have been given.

Co-creation is beyond deserving or not

The issue is not whether we *deserve* to get something in our life; it's simply about whether we have *learnt* the proper skill to manifest something into our lives. The whole Creativity issue needs to be seen as a two-way process. In other words, it can be seen as a Co-operative venture between a Higher Power - however that is perceived - plus our own input and talents. Again, let's invoke the analogy of you as a parent, teaching your child to bake a cake. Would you, as a parent, feel more inspired and proud of your child taking up the challenge, by trying to do as well as possible at learning this new skill? Or would you rather see your child play dumb; act incompetently; whine that 'it's all too hard', and generally sabotage this learning opportunity in as many ways as it can?

Now replace the word 'parent' with the word 'God'... and re-read that sentence! Do you really feel God wants us to fail; act incompetent; sabotage ourselves through false feelings of ineptitude, unworthiness, guilt, etc, and generally side-step our inherent capacities to **Co**-create? It's altogether too strange how we can see the validity of this human parent:child metaphor, yet our minds simply seize up on us when we try to deal with or apply the God:us aspect to our reality here.

Co-creation - begging for our desire to manifest

Even if you were to come from a religious perspective, where you pray to your God or Guru for your desire to come true, there is an interesting twist to this situation you need to be aware of. If you come from a space of begging for your wish to be fulfilled, by the Grace or whim of your God or Guru, this may not be effective. Understand that when you plead for something, you are automatically coming from a space where there is an inherent aspect of uncertainty about getting your desire fulfilled. Otherwise you wouldn't be pleading!

Consequently, this in a sense distorts a most important and fundamental aspect to the Co-creation 'recipe', which is to be coming from a space where your feeling is precisely one of *already having* what you desire, and therefore having gratitude is an automatic and realistic response. This fundamental point will be explored in great depth as we go along. But for now, be Aware that the former space of pleading is equivalent to uncertainty; the latter to certainty. The first is more likely to sabotage; the other more likely to allow manifestation to occur.

Chapter 10 - Co-creativity - What Is It?

This is a subtle but most important distinction to make. If you don't 'get' this point, it could become the basis to persistent failure in the Co-creativity arena.

Obviously, if you are praying to your God or Guru for something, it means that you don't have what it is you are praying for. Understood. But it needs to also be understood that praying *can* be most effective as a means to Co-create. As long as you can keep a focus going in your mind that what it is you desire has already been granted. Go back to that biblical injunction by Jesus we touched on earlier in this chapter, where he clearly says:- *'believe that ye shall receive them and ye **shall** have them'.*

He doesn't say *'hope* ye shall receive...' In other words, you need to be coming from a space of *fulfillment* and certainty, rather than *lack of*, when you send out your prayer. This makes all the difference, because coming from that 'lack of' space generates a state of doubt within your feelings, which in turn means you are trying to Co-create from doubt, not certainty. Hence the 'generative' or Co-creative Energy you are engaging in, and sending out into the Matrix/Field/Source is one of negativity, which in turn manifests precisely what you are focusing on – negativity and doubt. No surprise then if your desire doesn't materialize the way you really wanted it to. This point can't be hammered home enough, because it seems to be a concept which many people seem resistant to or find hard to fully grasp.

Therefore, within the concepts of Co-creative skills, you can indeed use a secondary agent such as a Guru or other Higher Being. But *only* do so if on one level you are absolutely convinced that this 'agent' *will definitely* give you what you desire, despite whether you feel worthy of it or not. That's why this worthiness issue is of such importance. Let's ram this point home one final time, especially for those of you with a religious background, for whom this is so much more likely to be a real sticking point. Remember, in that quote of J.C., he states:- *'believe that ye shall receive them and ye shall have them'.* He doesn't mention anything about getting it or not getting it, dependent on whether the Heavens see you as worthy or not. All that is requires is that you *'believe'!*

So this is where Faith comes into it, thereby creating an Inner sense of absolute assurance of success. This will in turn generate that feeling of already *having* what it is you desire, thus energizing your sub-conscious into Co-creative mode. Shortly, some of these subtleties will be explored more fully.

Need to be willing to break through cultural boundaries
To tap into, and utilize these Co-creative abilities, does mean we need to be willing to go into areas strongly regarded by most religions as utterly dangerous and 'foreign territory'. In fact, such spheres of activity are declared by many religions to be an absolute 'no-go' zone. There is just no way around it, though. The more we are willing to think and act beyond the 'normal' realms of 'reality', the more effective we also will be at this powerful and inherent talent.

But one thing we do need to keep in mind is that every single human being will get to this point in their own good time, and when they are mentally, emotionally – and especially spiritually – ready to go there. It would be foolhardy, as well as unfair, for those already able to play with this talent, to then force others to do so too. Becoming skilled and confident at Co-creativity is a major life-Initiation stage if you like, in the human Journey towards Higher and Higher levels of Consciousness. Although people can be *encouraged* to explore this capacity, they should never be *forced* to do so.

So what exactly is Co-creativity?
This word has been bandied around a lot thus far, but what exactly does it mean? O.K, for those of you who absolutely need definitions... 'Co-creation is a technique whereby we are capable of manifesting into our very physical reality, those things we first dreamt of, or desired within our much more ephemeral mental ruminations'. It is further based on a fundamental axiom that 'Thought is Creative', and indeed we have already explored the power of thought earlier in this book. Such a concept is easy enough to understand in relation to many circumstances where we wish to create something; for example, a house. You can visualize it clearly in your mind. You can even dream how it would feel being in your new home, walking around; going into the yard; upstairs to the bedrooms, built exactly as you would like them. Windows there; cupboards here; ensuite in that corner.

So this level to manifesting doesn't really stretch the mind. You simply get the idea of what you want, order in the appropriate material you'll need to build that house or get in the right builders to do it for you. Quite clear, obvious, and no particular problems thus far. It's something we do all the time, be that for obtaining a house or other material things. The situation changes a bit though, if we still insist that 'Thought is Creative' in such circumstances as manifesting

Chapter 10 - Co-creativity - What Is It?

that perfect partner or that perfect job. Especially when we have specified that it needs to be that 'ideal' one, with a long list of explicit characteristics attached to our request. To then still say that 'Thought is Creative', does start to stretch things a bit more in regard to how plausible this might be.

After all, how could you possibly create or manifest some of the more detailed and specific things you're desiring – just out of thin air? Unlike the house example, we can't really gather bits and pieces of a human body, putting them together into the form of our ideal partner. Similarly with that ideal job, especially if we wish to include all the specifics we have listed around *that* wish. Never mind how clearly you can visualize that partner or job, to the most minute detail, how could you possibly draw them out of thin air… just by thinking about it? Seems ridiculous and impossible. Yet, such manifesting – or Co-creating – is absolutely possible, but it does require knowledge, and as with most other things in life, skill. And as with any skill, some people will do it easily, and for others it will be much more challenging and seemingly impossible.

Co-creation and the Matrix concept

The hardest part for beginners is when we look at our reality, and it is just so obvious that what it is we desire is *not* there in our lives. In many ways it seems far too fantastic to expect our desire to somehow magically pop into our reality, simply because we have done some rather bizarre processes in our minds. And even if we did do all these Co-creation techniques, the reality staring us in the face is that our desire hasn't suddenly and immediately appeared in front of us, with a clap of thunder and a puff of smoke - like some genie popping out of its bottle.

After we have done the processes, it's precisely this lack of instant appearance of our desire which causes all the mental problems, never mind how correctly you know you have done the procedure. It's this *obvious* absence of our desire which then makes it so difficult to create that internal feeling of *'already having what it is we desire'* – an essential feeling that needs to be generated if the Co-creative process is to work. One level of our consciousness or awareness is so prone to continue locking into that 'lack of' aspect to our reality. Unfortunately, doing so thereby also gives it more 'power' than the reality that we desire to manifest… 'but, damn it, which hasn't manifested yet'! Initially this point about having to pretend your desire has already manifested does come across as some sort of gibberish, never mind how clearly one tries to explain it.

Either you need to read some of these sentences several times to really 'get it' more fully, or you will find that as you read further, slowly but surely this concept will start to gel. Not so much in your mind, as in the very cells of your body. It ends up going beyond just a 'neuronal knowing' somewhere in your brain cells alone. These mind twisters need time to get used to, as well as needing to be repeated many times, with a variety of slightly different slants. Nevertheless, despite the apparent repetitiveness, this approach to what is otherwise a rather challenging sticking point in Co-creation will hopefully allow these unusual and often counter-intuitive concepts to eventually sink in.

A way to get beyond such mental stumbling blocks is to look at the situation in the following manner. First we need to understand that within the Matrix lies the slumbering possibility of absolutely anything and everything that can be imagined. To be able to imagine something is to cause that something to become an instant reality - *within the Matrix*; the Matrix being the 'Cosmic soup' from which *anything* can be made manifest. It is the Source of everything conceivable.

But the main trick here is to really 'get it', that absolutely *anything* you or anyone else could possibly desire, is *already* existent within that Matrix soup, *albeit in an Energetic or sort of 'shadow' format.* That's just the inherent nature of the Matrix, never mind how irrational this may sound. The 'magic button', as it were - to manifest what is initially un-manifest, and thus at this point still only a *potentiality* - is whether we can generate that absolute, deep level of Inner *knowingness* that the above discussed phenomenon is real and does occur. We need to project our focus deep into the 'Matrix-soup', while in our mind's eye 'seeing' – and *knowing* – that what it is we desire is *already* present in that Infinite 'soup' of possibilities. It's not as if it still needs to be manufactured or created in some way. It does already, fully exist! But, it's via that Inner focus, empowered by that sense of deep *knowingness,* which can then precisely and easily 'choose' the *Energetic* form – already existing on that Matrix level - to manifest into *physical* form.

Let's try and make this a bit easier to grasp by using a computer analogy. Think of a situation where you have access to a computer keyboard, from which you as a writer, can create absolutely any literature you wish. The possibilities of what words, and in which order you set them, is infinite, only hampered by

Chapter 10 - Co-creativity - What Is It?

your imagination and intention to tap the appropriate keys. So it is too with the Matrix, needing only our clear, focused imagination and intention through which to manifest a specific desire.

This may all sound simply 'too weird'. But nowadays, Quantum Physics vindicates that this Matrix can be viewed as an infinite source of absolutely anything you could imagine. This is scientific fact. Whether it is called 'The Field', 'The Matrix', 'The Ether', 'God', 'The Akashic Records'... or 'Dimension II', as proposed by Tansley, the bottom-line is the same. There is a Plane of Reality; a most Fundamental level to *all* Reality, which is in and of itself Pure Potential – of absolutely everything. So to be successful at Co-creation, it helps enormously if you are willing to accept that this is now a fundamental, scientific reality.

So what *we* need to do is to learn how to tap into this Field or Matrix. Then, by using our imagination and emotion, we can generate a feeling through which to draw those potential, or 'shadow' Realities, into our physical dimension of reality. But it is that inevitable period of time between knowing what it is we wish to manifest, and the manifestation of the 'hard-copy' into this reality, which presents the most challenging psychological hurdle for us to overcome. At least until you become more skilled at this Co-creation process, by having chalked up some successes. Each success makes it easier to be more confident the next time.

For every action there is a reaction

There is a law in Physics which states that for 'every action there is a reaction'. Let's re-phrase it slightly differently and say: 'for every *output* there needs to be an *input*'. Or putting it differently again, with a slight twist to it, 'nothing comes for nothing'. Everything that you want to achieve in life does require some sort of input. Now, in the Co-creativity level of our reality, our input is Energetic. So our 'currency' in the Co-creation sphere has to do with learning how to work with Energy, rather than with materiality.

Let's start with the example of saving for a holiday. If you want to go on holiday in twelve months time, and you can only save $50 per week, then at the end of the year you're going to have $2,600. This amount will buy you a holiday, but it's going to be a holiday within certain constraints. That amount of savings is not going to finance a round-the-world trip for six months, staying in all the most luxurious hotels at each destination.

Building up 'attractor credits'

Step one, therefore, in the Co-creative process is to simply image our desire. We then go to the next step which is to 'save' up enough 'attractor credits' till we have sufficient 'attractor energy' – or 'currency' – with which to 'buy' or draw our desire from the Matrix into our reality. Like anything else in this human existence, we need to 'buy' what we desire, but in the case of Co-creation, the currency is Energetic – not dollars. It's as if every desire has a 'price', and like everything else in our daily, physical lives, we have to spend some time working and saving to be able to 'afford' it. Be that to put bread on the table; pay the electricity bill; the rent or any of so many other daily life costs. Each of these utilities needs to be financed; each has a price, and it is not till we have saved up enough dollars that we can then take possession of whatever it is we are trying to buy.

As with any project in normal Earth life, once we have established what it is we would like to purchase or produce, we need to set up a budget. So too in any Co-creative project. In a sense we need to open a new 'Account' – from which we can then 'finance' our desire, whatever that may be. But at the moment it has no 'Creativity Credits' in it - yet.

These seemingly mundane aspects to life are equally applicable to the Co-creativity scenario. Many out there who advocate Co-creation are often a bit too flippant when they say you can create your own reality. 'Just follow the rules, and you too can have whatever it is you desire'. Fundamentally that is definitely true. However, like the holiday example, it might be more realistic to understand that as we start out on this Journey of Co-creativity, it involves a huge learning curve. It's a Journey of small steps being taken one at a time, just like saving our $50, one week at a time.

Initially, when we start on this Co-creativity Journey, we may not actually be able to 'finance' very much. In other words, when we start in this field of Co-creative endeavor, we also need to be realistic. It's not about down-grading or underestimating ourselves. Nor is it about having to sink into low self-esteem, because we aren't yet fully *skilled* at this process. It's far more about becoming rational and realistic about what your skill-level in Co-creativity can actually 'finance'. At least at this point in time.

Chapter 10 - Co-creativity - What Is It?

Need for realism when doing Co-creation

And so an unfortunate thing happens in a lot of Co-creation situations. People read books; go to workshops; see a program, many of which give them the implication - if not the frank declaration - that straight away they can basically 'order' absolutely anything they want... and expect it to manifest into their life tomorrow! Of course, they can wish for anything they want. But the problem is whether they have acquired enough skill with which to manifest it. Are they able to generate enough 'resonance credits'?

The fact is that this is the requisite 'currency' through which to 'finance' the necessary level of 'coherence' or resonance with what it is they desire. In other words, it's only via such 'coherence', that desires can be made to manifest from the Infinite soup of the Matrix, into this physical, material reality. Shortly, we'll look more deeply into the issue of coherence, or resonance, and explain it further.

So, on this Journey of Co-creativity, we first have to understand that the Laws governing this phenomenon do work every time. But in Co-creating *specific* projects, they only work every time, *to the limit or to the range of our skill to use this technique.* We therefore need to be realistic enough to say that if we are just starting to 'ride our bike'; if we have only now started 'saving for our holiday', then we can also only successfully do Co-creatively within the limits of our skill or our 'savings'.

'Everything is perfect' has more to do with the Laws working perfectly

In chapter 6 we looked at how some 'Teachers' and Gurus will talk about how everything is perfect within this earthly experience, never mind how utterly horrific it may appear from our usual human perspective. These statements may seem outrageous to most people who hear such comments. Well, let's see if we can add a few twists to this perception, thereby making such statements more realistic, and possibly more palatable. What we first need to do is really 'get it', that there are Laws governing Co-creation just like there are Laws governing Gravity.

In regard to Gravity, this is a black and white Law. It has no personal agenda and is incapable of reasoning, through which it can somehow decide to have an effect on some people but not on others. Similarly with Co-creation. The Laws ruling Co-creation are a cold, calculating, precise, *scientific* phenomenon. In that sense, they are indeed 'perfect'. They always work, in all cases and situations - at least within this physical universe of ours. They operate in a very specific way, and whether you work them constructively or destructively; consciously or unconsciously, you always get a result.

So when various New Age or Eastern Gurus say that 'all is perfect', one can put a lateral slant on this. Instead of accepting such statements on face value, we need to extrapolate the interpretation of these statements away from *this* reality of ours, and instead direct our attention more towards the *Laws* governing this reality. So then perfection lies with the Laws of Co-creation itself, and how they *work* rather than how they are *worked* - by us. Any 'imperfection' therefore has more to do with how we choose to use, or misuse these Laws.

In other words, how skilled are we at utilizing the 'recipe' to create the 'product'? And that's where the imperfection comes in. Even if we don't know how to use the 'recipe' properly, the Laws governing this recipe - Co-creation - work perfectly every time. If we muck up the 'recipe', then we also get a mucked up result. However, that 'mucked up' result is nevertheless a 'perfect' manifestation as produced by the *poor* usage of the 'recipe', or the Laws governing this process of Co-creativity.

So in that sense, the manifestation is a 'perfect' end product of a perfect process. But where imperfection comes into it, is in the degree to which we, as Co-creators, are capable of using that perfect Law in a perfect manner. So with this more lateral interpretation, we can make a huge quantum leap. Otherwise, this Esoteric concept that 'everything is perfect', remains a very problematic issue.

Hence, if we perceive imperfection in our environment, then that imperfection is more a judgment of the *input*, by us, rather than the *output*, as manifested through the Matrix and the process of Co-creation. For some, this may all be too esoteric a point to take seriously or wrap their brain around! However, if nothing else, it may give them an alternative framework through which to deal more constructively with the obvious reality of imperfection and suffering within our earthly existence. Simply because it now also offers at least a potential way in which to try to overcome the imperfections we face in our lives on a daily basis.

By understanding that the 'outer' is but a reflection of how well or Consciously we are using Co-creation on an 'Inner' level, does offer hope for change – *via Co-creation*. This puts the power back in our court somewhat, rather than feeling overwhelmed and disempowered by the constant deluge of

Chapter 10 - Co-creativity - What Is It?

life's daily 'imperfections'. Some might now even be able to go as far as calling such 'imperfections'... 'learning opportunities'.

The laws aren't the problem – it's more the operator

The problem is that for so long, humanity just hasn't had an inkling that these Laws existed, let alone an Awareness of how they work. It's just that most of us aren't even Consciously Aware there is such a process as Co-creation, let alone how to utilize it – skillfully or un-skillfully. From one point of view, maybe it's less to do with blaming the 'Heavens' – or whoever or whatever – for all the awfulness which exist in our reality. Maybe we need to step back and re-think our previously discussed stance. We need to realize that much of what we perceive *outside* of us is only a reflection of what is *inside* us, usually Co-created *unconsciously*.

Where the imperfection comes in has more to do with *our* level of skill in *working* these Laws of Co-creation. Hence the focus should become one of investigating how they operate, as well as start to practise using them with increased regularity and Awareness. Only by doing so can we become more skilled in their utilization. Aside from that, our skill also needs to come through a 'lens' of Love. Once we can do this, we should indeed see an enormous, positive transformation in our external day to day reality. But more on that later.

For now, it is important just to make this lateral shift in our understanding around these all too frequent New Age statements declaring 'everything to be perfect'. The problem is that the 'normal' way we tend to understand such statements, only causes most people to shut down, and in that sense only serve to back-fire onto those propagating such statements.

Having so-called authorities on the subject constantly repeating the Mantra of 'everything is perfect in this reality', only causes further anger, frustration, confusion and doubt about a lot of other Metaphysical issues. Bottom-line - it does not empower. Such statements can't stand alone. They demand a much deeper and clearer explanation. What could be said is that from an Ultimate level of Reality; if we could perhaps see it through the 'eyes' of God; the 'Highest' pinnacle of the 'Mountain', then everything may indeed be 'perfect'. We'll explore this very important concept a lot more in-depth shortly. But in the meantime, for us mortals, what we are witness to does tend to show there's obviously a lot of imperfection on Earth, and in our lives.

However, what we can do is to use those imperfect situations as fuel towards becoming more 'perfect' in our lives – or at least more Consciously Aware. We could also choose to use them as feed-back that tells us to what extent we are or aren't yet skilled at using the Laws governing 'Thought is Creative', through the process of Co-creation. From one perspective, 'input = output'; for every action there is a reaction; for every thought there is a manifestation. This is the Law of Creativity. And that Law works all the time – perfectly.

Explaining Co-creation of atrocities

In as far as Co-creation is concerned, there is however one huge problem which is invariably brought up in discussion. If it is indeed true that we Co-create our reality, then how does one explain the horror of either an individual or a whole group undergoing a combined ordeal of some sort, such as the Jews in Nazi Germany? Or those who were slaughtered by Pol Pot; the genocide of the Hutsi and the Tutsi in Africa? How does one explain the absolute, undeniable hell such individuals went through, from the Co-creative perspective? Equally, we need to somehow deal with the issue of babies and children who are born dreadfully deformed or who develop cancer, and many other awful diseases so early in their life. How did they get to 'create their reality'?

In earlier chapters, where we explored the ubiquitous phenomenon of suffering, we already started to look at the how and why of certain horrific forms of affliction. This is a very prickly and difficult situation to explain. Whether there is any explanation at all, which can somehow make these atrocious situations 'O.K', is already stretching it for many. Perhaps the best we can do is to acknowledge the inherent dismay and revulsion we feel at what humanity can do, one against the other, or what simply seems to 'happen' to some humans.

Having acknowledged that this is an all too frequent human situation, which beggars rational understanding, nevertheless still requires us to attempt to find some sort of answer – even if it isn't... 'The Truth' - which may at least give us a handle on making sense out of what is otherwise an intolerable situation. This is especially so for parents who have had to deal with awful things happening to their children.

Chapter 10 - Co-creativity - What Is It?

Does it all boil down to Good versus Evil?

Let's now delve even deeper into this phenomenon of suffering, and especially how it may tie in with a concept such as Co-creation. Earlier in this book, and this chapter, we've already explored the idea of how we can use our suffering as a growth opportunity. Similarly, a major theme has been about understanding the need to become increasingly skilled at responding to life's situations more from the Higher Self perspective, rather than from ego's take on things. Life is all about duality, and normally we automatically tend to view our reality as a war between the forces of Good and evil - and that much of our suffering would be fomented by the evil forces. Certainly, this is what most religions would teach.

However, just as we've looked at shifting our perspective from ego to Higher Self, when living our lives, so too can we learn to shift our perception that perhaps there is only one operative Force in our reality – that of Good, a single, unified Force, which *within the human dimension of reality* nevertheless manifest in a *dualistic* manner – either as 'pleasant' or 'unpleasant' experiences. Yet, the primary shift we can choose to take on board is to accept that never mind *how* this One Force plays Itself out in any one moment of our lives, Its *one* and *only* intention is to offer us an opportunity to grow and change; to increase our level of Consciousness. Gregg Braden explores this concept in some of his lectures.

Therefore, if we primarily accept that in fact there is but one fundamental Force operative in this reality, and that it is essentially aimed at providing opportunities for growth, then the whole picture shifts. If so-called 'bad' things subsequently happen within our lives, we need to realize that on one level, this perception of 'bad' is perhaps nothing else but a pre-conceived or distorted judgment of that situation, rather than an absolute statement of fact. Inevitably, if only we could but *choose* to view the situation via the more discerning 'eyes' of the Higher Self, such 'bad' event or situation could equally be seen or judged as opportunities for growth in Consciousness. The choice is to see this as a *challenging* situation, rather than just viewing it as a *'bad'* situation. With the latter choice, we unfortunately tend to also allow ourselves to become more the victim of it.

There is no doubt at all that such a shift in thinking does require a much broader and deeper perspective on this reality, from which to then judge our life events. Either way we choose to view life's realities – be that as a constant struggle between the Forces of 'good' versus 'evil', or that this reality is run primarily through just One, fundamentally Good Force - it will result in us still being challenged by whatever situation confronts us in any one moment. However, the problems of life become more overwhelming when we *allow* ourselves to remain stuck in a more restrictive view, resulting in seeing it solely as 'bad', rather than stepping back, and allowing a far more discerning perspective to emerge. With such an enhanced viewpoint, we can indeed acknowledge the 'suffering' we might be going through, but also choose to look for, and identify what it is we could *learn* from that situation.

Are we humans really caught in a battle between two powerful Forces?

For all this to work, we need a primary shift to occur in our thinking. We either view this earthly realm as a war between two fundamental forces – Good and evil – with each out to either 'get' us or help us. Or we could *choose* to view our reality as infused by just One Primary Force; one of Good, although the situations that It may then present in our reality are nonetheless 'challenging'.

Ultimately, it's again a matter of asking ourselves which perspective of life on Earth could provide us with the most constructive way of not just viewing, but also dealing with our human existence. This plane of reality is either about endless suffering, where we as humans are being constantly and horrendously torn asunder by the Good and Bad Forces running the show here. Or it is a plane of reality where there is no Higher Force – good or bad. From this perspective, it's all a matter of random events with no meaningful purpose other than some sort of evolutionary process which was instigated by god knows who, and is heading towards god knows where!

Another point of view however, is that it's about just One Force of Good being in command, with the sole intention of helping us grow in Consciousness – even if on the surface, so many life situations do appear to be primarily about suffering, and therefore judged as 'bad'. To make more sense out of these perspectives, it would help if we could re-introduce the idea – as developed earlier in this book - that Earth is a 'school of learning'.

If we can make that primary shift *inside* us, of seeing *everything* that occurs in our lives as fundamentally a gift or opportunity from just One Primarily Good Force, then this can also allow for our experience of life to change deeply. Such an Inner perceptual shift allows us to feel more empowered by choosing

Chapter 10 - Co-creativity - What Is It?

to search out the 'lesson' or 'Consciousness growth opportunity' within the 'suffering', rather than just remain a victimized grain of sand between the two millstones of Good and evil.

Even if this model as to the source of suffering seems to perhaps hold for light to moderate levels of suffering, admittedly it becomes a lot harder to accept when we are confronted by the more extreme forms of suffering: the genocides, the hideous murders, the concentration camps, the many terrible wars we humans wage against each other. Yet the model can be seen as valid, as long as we also allow ourselves to see things from a much higher than normal perspective.

Extreme suffering requires an extremely High Perspective

Extreme suffering requires a tremendously Higher 'pinnacle' from which to view that suffering. We can hark back to chapter 2, where we used that metaphor of gaining very different perspectives as we climbed the high Mountain. For these extreme forms of suffering to fit into this above model of only One Source of Good being operative within the human dimension, we also need to be standing on the very 'peak' of that 'Mountain'! From that Highest of possible 'views', we can hopefully gain an expansive enough perspective to encompass the idea that even the most horrendous forms of suffering are still only 'opportunities' provided by just One, Supreme and Good Force, rather than from a secondary and more 'demonic' source.

Equally, it helps if we can choose to perceive this earthly reality as a 'School of Learning'. Some curriculums – and their 'exams' - are of a 'PhD standard', while other curriculums – and their 'exams' - are more of a secondary if not primary school level. It would seem that most people incarnating onto this plane of learning, choose the easier curriculums! But that shouldn't exclude the option for those *Spirits* who wish to do so, to equally go for the much more challenging 'PhD courses' offered on planet Earth. After all, within our earthly realm, most humans like a relatively comfortable, safe and predictable life, but this doesn't negate the fact that there are also some people who do like to put themselves through rather extreme 'challenges', and gain much satisfaction from testing themselves under such circumstances.

Why not choose to look for the 'learning opportunity'?

So, why not give this other perspective a go first? Ask yourself what possible *gift* lies within the 'suffering', choosing to view this situation as fundamentally intended solely for our good; not for us to just suffer through. You can always go back to the standing view of your reality being one of suffering due to 'bad' forces tempting or taunting you, if you find this alternate concept just doesn't work out after a while!

The bottom line is that we all have beliefs as to how our reality here on Earth works. But each choice of belief comes with automatic consequences as to how we then *experience* those same lives. So then we could equally validly ask ourselves which perspective will actually allow for the least suffering in dealing with life, thus providing the greatest opportunity for growth. Whether our reality here is one of 'heaven' or 'hell' is therefore primarily tied in with our perspective or belief of whether this reality is ruled by two Forces - of 'Good' or 'bad' – or by just One Force of Good.

Due to the nature of this physical reality we inhabit, with its inherent qualities of duality, this same Good Force may then also manifest Itself in a dualistic manner of either 'heavenly' or hellish' *perceived* experiences. But these are experiences presented with only one agenda – that of allowing us the opportunity to grow in Consciousness. And whether we experience a 'heaven' or a 'hell' is really ultimately dependent on how we *choose* to view our 'situation' here. One through which to grow... or to suffer. Hopefully, these alternate views of 'perfection' versus 'imperfection', do provide you with an additional handle through which to manage what life so often throws at you.

Getting back to the Oversoul

Remember, this present discussion is not about providing *The* Answer; only about attempting to provide some *possible* ideas to play with in helping to take the sting out of the many awful situations which humans endure far too often. Another way to attempt to explain some of these unpleasant human realities is to hark back to the issues we discussed in chapter 6, regarding the Oversoul. Here we looked at how this Spirit Entity had set up an agenda of what it wants to learn down on planet Earth.

Within the framework of that concept, it would seem this Energy Entity or Spirit has in fact already made the 'free will' choice of going through such a

Chapter 10 - Co-creativity - What Is It?

seemingly horrific experience, because of what It could potentially learn from that. Or, more challengingly, *what It could teach another*. This latter scenario would especially apply for situations of deformed or seriously ill children, and what sort of 'learning opportunity' they may be providing for their parents or the entire family.

'But why on Earth would anyone in their right minds ever decide to put themselves through something like that'?! - you might scream back. And rightly so - on one level. But from another level, this may not be as weird or sick as it seems at first.

It can be educational, and even mind-blowing to have the chance to actually talk to someone who has survived a range of life-horrors, or has had to deal with a deformed, damaged or ill baby. In the latter example, although on one level most such parents have indeed been terribly scarred, some do claim to have also grown enormously in their level of compassion - or Consciousness; which some would argue is what it's all about anyway, here on planet 'Earth School'. To the average human, incarnated on planet Earth, it seems ridiculous to even suggest someone would choose to go through something as awful as that... 'just to learn some Compassion or to increase their Consciousness'?

Indeed, for many of us here on this planet, already struggling to get through yet another challenging day, such an idea seems preposterous. However, perhaps from the Oversoul's perspective, it is a valid choice. Remember, we are not talking about vindicating or validating so many of the dreadful things that do happen to people while in the human form. We're just trying to get some sort of perspective, which at a pinch, may help make at least a little bit more sense out of something which otherwise appears to be making no sense whatsoever, or is just plain horrific.

Love born out of suffering

It is also interesting to note how many parents of deformed, disabled or very ill children say that those same children do give them enormous joy, and how such children have totally changed the entire family dynamic to something so much more Loving and positive. Perhaps it's the intensity of their situation which equally has opened these parents' and families' hearts to such a deep level.

This obviously doesn't happen to such parents in every instance, but it does happen often enough to take note of, and ponder upon. It's definitely not to say that such positive, Loving responses by some parents were easy for them. Inevitably, their Journey with such children was extraordinarily challenging, and often quite heart-breaking. But overall, the joy and Love which was unleashed in these peoples' lives far outweighed the difficulty and pain.

Thoughts are like magnets

In trying to explain the suffering found in peoples' lives, in some cases there may be yet another valid layer to this phenomenon. Firstly, we need to stress again... the thoughts we continually focus on and therefore 'invest' in, are what we're more likely than not to also manifest into our reality. This is especially so with those more unconscious, background thoughts which so many of us play with on a daily basis. Yet most of the time, we also seem to have little direct recognition of what we are in fact doing.

So, if we are constantly focused on watching every horror movie we can lay our hands on; watching every murder mystery presented on TV; if we insist on playing endless video games filled with unbelievable violence and horror; if we indulge in that all too human phenomenon of just having to see all the gore on the road after a dreadful car smash; if we just *have* to see those planes crashing into the twin towers on 9/11, now for the 50th time; if we constantly need our daily 'fix' to really hook into the awful things presented each night on the News... then this just may come at a price! It could be that if our attention is so powerfully drawn to these more destructive and negative aspects of the human situation, then in turn we might also find a semblance of such horrors being drawn into our daily life experience.

What we focus on is what we more likely than not will get

At the risk of becoming boring, it is so important to remember... 'what you focus on is what you get'. Fortunately or unfortunately, this is how the Law of Co-creation works. Just like the Law of Gravity. These Laws are non-discriminatory. Step off your 10th floor balcony... and you end up as strawberry jam down on the pavement. Gravity doesn't suddenly decide to act differently because you happened to be sleep-walking when you stepped off that balcony. Similarly with the Laws governing Co-creation.

Various life examples may resonate with you here. For instance, you are having some problems with your boss, and you 'just know' they are going to fire

Chapter 10 - Co-creativity - What Is It?

you. And they do! You left home without your umbrella and you 'just know' you'll get caught in a major downpour – and you do. You're about to go on a long, carefully planned trip, but you 'just know' there are going to be major delays or your flight gets cancelled – and it happens. Just because we don't *mean* for such situations to really occur, doesn't suggest the Matrix knows *not* to manifest your anxieties and fears. Unfortunately, this process of Co-creation will work, whether we know it or not; whether we are skilled enough or not, and equally – whether we want it or not.

If we happen to focus on something very strongly, with a deep sense of knowingness that it will happen – or *fear* it will happen – the system will simply churn out what we have 'desired', be it from a negative or positive angle. Even awful things we really don't want in our lives. This is 'tough' knowledge, but is a point we need to take on board if we're truly serious about making positive changes to our lives. Once again, it highlights the crucial importance of getting to understand exactly what thoughts and images you are playing with in your mind, especially when they are also fueled by strong feelings. Get a clear understanding of what you are in fact 'investing in' when it comes to your thoughts!

So many people tend to think that their thoughts are these ephemeral things which have no real substance. After all, they are 'just in the mind, aren't they'? In turn, most of us think a whole array of thoughts, without really being truly Conscious of how these are connected to the many realities manifesting in our daily life. Sadly, most people haven't understood how much of their thought-focus may not be so healthy for them.

This is why it is so importance to learn the skill of becoming more the 'Witness' to our minds; noticing where our thoughts are prone to 'play'. Think again of meditation, as discussed in the previous chapter. Once you are better skilled at Witnessing your mind, then you might like to make some Conscious *choices*. For instance, do you now continue to do what you may have been doing for the last 20 – 30 – 40 – 50 – 60 years - or do you make new choices, understanding more clearly the power of your thoughts, and the repercussions of remaining unconscious of what you are constantly entertaining in your mind? It's once again a simple choice, although not automatically easy. But a choice you can nevertheless make, and become increasingly skilled at making with persistence, focus, and over time.

Ultimately, these are only attempts at explanations
Now, these 'explanations' may not seem to answer the predicament of a lot of people or situations you know about. Accepted. Yet our perspective of this entire human process – at this stage of evolutionary level of Awareness or Consciousness – is nevertheless still limited. There are areas that we simply don't understand, or can only see vaguely. There are indeed many aspects to the human situation which we can't fully explain in any logical or rational manner, especially through the lens of Co-creation. Perhaps the best we can do is to put such life situations into as acceptable a hypothesis as we can invent. Hopefully, such hypotheses give – to our *left*, rational, logic-seeking brain, that is – at least some sense of sanity in what is already often a truly insane world.

So much in science and medicine is based on theories too
We need to keep in mind that a lot of our daily life experience and activities – especially in the sciences and medicine – are based not so much on fact... but on theory. Yet, such *theoretical* constructs do at least provide us with a basis through which we can make life more functional and even productive. Maybe, therefore, we also need to take this approach in regard to the more Metaphysical issues we've been discussing, where we are trying to explain the inexplicable horrors of life. At least one choice we *do* have before us is to accept such human scenarios through these type of constructs or theories too.

We can accept that they are not automatically or necessarily 'the truth', but may be giving us some foundation from which to manage our suffering or challenges more productively. Perhaps this is still a better option than feeling utterly destroyed by these life circumstances. We seem to have no problem whatsoever in taking this approach within the arena of science, basing a whole range of our actions on theories – not truths. Why then, should there be any less reason to use various theories as attempts at understanding the inexplicable within our more daily lives?

Perhaps as much as we'd like to de-mystify such abhorrent life scenarios, the best we can do is to acknowledge and accept that there is an inherent level of mystery to certain aspects of Life. From our perspective here on Earth, perhaps certain Life circumstances just aren't meant to be fully understood – as much as one part of us may scream out for an answer.

Chapter 10 - Co-creativity - What Is It?

Some comfort around 'thought is creative'

However, 'Abraham', in the Esther Hicks workshop DVD's and books [4,5] – (we'll explore just exactly who 'Abraham' is in a short while) - does provide a comforting perspective on this whole issue of our 'thoughts being creative'. Indeed, every thought is creative, and every thought we produce generates an Energetic aspect or duplicate of it within the Matrix. However – and this is the comforting part! - it does *not* mean that every thought will then automatically manifest. We are constantly creating Energetic 'blueprints' as it were, of every thought. Actually, this is really what Rupert Sheldrake's 'Morphogenetic Field' concept is all about. But it is only when we create an *ongoing pattern of focusing* on that same Energetic thought, fueled by strong emotions such as fear – but preferably Love! - that we then start to add 'substance' to it, thus making it more able to manifest.

It also puts us on notice that we need to equally become aware of what sort of things we hook into in our daily lives. As mentioned earlier, do we watch the News every night with bated breath? Do we love being scared by horror movies? What emotions are we constantly playing with? Anger? Jealousy? Being endlessly critical of everything?

Fueled by the violence and horrors we so easily access via TV and movies, what sort of inner 'mind-movies' of negativity are we prone to regularly play out in our minds? What form of negative 'mind talk' do we have with ourselves? You get the idea. Yet, why is it then that we seem so bewildered when our lives are filled with drama; with pain; with so much negativity showering down on us?

Fundamental change can occur, once we're Aware of the thoughts we play with

To change such a situation, we need to start by investigating where our minds, emotions and imaginings are at – moment by moment. Such an investigation is important, even though what we seem to be focusing on appears entirely 'normal' to us, simply because this is what we, as well as so many around us, have been doing for so long. But just because you and everyone else has been doing it forever, doesn't make it 'normal', let alone healthy.

The fact is that all of us, in our daily life routine are definitely in Energetic resonance or congruity with a lot of negative thought patterns we have been sending into the Matrix – even though unconsciously. But such *unconsciousness* doesn't detract from the reality that this nevertheless results in a form of 'Creativity Credits' investment going on. At least consider the possibility that we may indeed be attracting so much negative stuff to manifest into our life, because of the thought patterns we return to again and again.

One simple way to help negate this is to firstly start training yourself in mental Awareness. Become the Observer – or Witness - of your mind content, and from that point of Conscious observation, you have an opportunity for change. This is precisely what meditation is all about. Then, as you notice your mind playing with un-wanted thoughts, acknowledge that you are doing this without automatically going into judgment or criticism, and use the 'Delete Button' technique, soon to be discussed in chapter 12.

As has been mentioned before, don't now necessarily go into battle against such thought patterns. Simply observe that you are in one of your patterns, and re-direct your attention elsewhere. Don't put any further Energy into such patterns by now trying to process them or by *doing* something with them. That would be a typical ego-mode response. The Higher Self Mode of dealing with it would be to just 'Be' with that pattern for a second, and then move on.

The less we feed and identify with these thought patterns, the less resonance we can establish with them too. Keep in mind that each time you can be Aware of your patterns, and shift into a Higher Self Mode of response, has also been another wonderful opportunity. One in which to become increasingly skilled at not just being in Witness State, but also in Consciously accessing those Higher Levels of your Being.

The power of thought on water

Another powerful technique is to do the 'Gratitude Meditation', based on the good things you have in your life. Activating gratitude also activates a level of vibration which is automatically not consistent or coherent with such negative thoughts. Therefore, focusing on gratitude for the good things in your life is a very effective diverter, as well as negating the manifestation of negative thoughts into one's reality. We'll explore the 'Gratitude Meditation' more fully in chapter 12, but meanwhile it is interesting to note Masaru Emoto's [6] research, which has pioneered the effect of thought and emotions on the formation of crystal shapes within water.

Emoto's work shows a clear correlation between thoughts and their effects on the physical world. He presents many extraordinary and powerful photos

Chapter 10 - Co-creativity - What Is It?

of how water crystals are consistently affected and changed by such emotions as gratitude compared to anger or other negative feelings. The crucial point to take home from his research is that we, as physical bodies, are made up of about 70% water, and if thoughts can affect water *outside* the body, there is no reason to suspect it wouldn't also affect water *inside* our bodies.

Once again, as we consider all the above ideas, we find that the ball therefore does lie in our court. Knowing more about how mind and matter do interact does give us at least the *choice* of whether we continue as before – or not. And that point of power does lie with us continually – in each and every moment. You haven't permanently 'blown it' simply because you made less-than-constructive choices in so many previous moments. Each new moment is a gift from life to make another choice; hopefully this time, a more constructive one.

Bad things created, small steps at a time

However, there is yet another layer to this whole saga of how or why we would allow suffering to be Co-created and manifested into our lives. One could rightly be certified insane to suggest you or anyone else truly wants awful things to happen in their reality. However, it's not quite that simple. Even as adults, if we are diagnosed with a truly serious and life-threatening illness, the first overwhelming response is inevitably going to be something along the lines of… 'How the hell did I get here?' 'Why would I want to manifest something so terrible into my life?' But such indignant questions are based really on an almost unspoken assumption that we somehow got into this most unfortunate position in one huge, quantum leap.

The reality is that we usually got to where we are by a lengthy series of many, many tiny, seemingly insignificant and innocent steps. The end result we find ourselves in may have more to do with an escalating pattern over the years, during which we allowed increasing amounts of negative thoughts to sneak into our consciousness, compared to positive thoughts.

Initially, this may have been set off by something painful or traumatic which happened to us – even way in the past. But such events may also have somehow 'soured' us, almost making us feel vindicated in feeling a bit negative, resentful or guilty. Such events however, may have started a trend where we increasingly focused our attention more on what we have been lacking, or how we were hurt in some way, rather than on the many good things we do have in our lives. Yet such 'lack-focus' inevitably sets up a negative vibe in our reality

- from which further negativity can then also manifest Co-creatively; albeit unconsciously and undesired.

And so, slowly but surely, like the proverbial frog being gradually boiled to death in an increasingly hot pot of water, we got 'cooked'! Hence it's really important to understand that it wasn't necessarily any *one* particular *momentous* thought which caused us to topple over into our present difficult dilemma. Instead, it had more to do with an almost infinite series of tiny thoughts, one stacked on top of the other, which then finally led to our present position.

The Journey happens step at a time

By the same token, we shouldn't necessarily expect to then undo our cancer or whatever in one quantum leap either. Yes, this is indeed theoretically possible, but to be more realistic, it's entirely dependent on our overall skill at Co-creation. And the reality is that for most of us, we are yet babes in the woods when it comes to skill levels in the 'School' of Co-creation. So it may be far more productive to understand that we now may equally need to take many small steps in getting ourselves out of where we presently find ourselves; with our cancer, multiple sclerosis, AIDS, relationship breakdown, loss of job... or whatever the source of suffering may be. This style of approach is more likely to be successful than going into the Co-creative process expecting one giant quantum leap to easily and quickly take us out of our dilemma.

Again, it has to be stressed that miracles *do* happen; so don't discount that possibility either. But more likely our Journey will be made up of many little improvements, and becoming Aware of how we allow certain thought patterns to be entertained in our mind becomes a crucial skill for us to achieve. What thoughts do we constantly focus on and play with, and thus empower through the often *unconscious* Co-creative process? Perhaps then, we shouldn't be all that surprised to find ourselves in this now very much unwanted position.

Co-creation concepts do offer hope

But there is hope! There is a way of looking at our life situations that can hopefully give us a greater sense of empowerment. The 'normal' explanations range from God having a 'bad hair day'; or we are terrible sinners and this is our 'just' reward; or it's all simply a matter of 'bad luck'. However, we could also acknowledge that we *are* Co-creators to our reality, albeit that this particular

Chapter 10 - Co-creativity - What Is It?

painful scenario we may now be in was not exactly *consciously* planned or intended.

This is indeed a very challenging perspective to take on board; no arguments about that. Yet if we are honest with ourselves, we may be able to see how we arrived at this point. Not to then *blame* ourselves, but rather to *understand*, and then *empower* ourselves by subsequently using the various Co-creative skills more *Consciously*, and therefore also more constructively.

Unfortunately, people so easily and quickly jump into the 'blame-game', either judging themselves or judging others who seem to be in a pickle. But what truly has to be taken on-board is that such life situations have absolutely nothing to do with *morality*. Getting cancer or any other awful illness, or having an endless array of other nasty things occur in our lives is not an issue of then making us into 'bad' people. Indeed, it is true that we may have made unconscious, and therefore *unconstructive* choices, whose cumulative consequences we are now dealing with. But that is just an inherent aspect to this human reality and life.

Perhaps we don't always need to understand everything

Most people are simply muddling along as best they can, with the limited knowledge and information they have been given or had access to. The situation *does* change however, if we remain stubborn in the face of now having learnt more as to what may have been instrumental in bringing us to this point in our lives, and yet refuse to change a pattern which has obviously not been serving us.

Even here we need to be very careful about judgment. It brings up an earlier point that there are some things about life which are just too complex to understand or figure out. All we can do under such circumstances is to ultimately give over that urgent need to know it all, and initially just *BE* with what is happening, rather than try to *understand* what is happening. So the prayer or affirmation we might like to use goes more along the lines of... 'give me the strength to *Be* in this Life, rather than to understand absolutely everything *about* this Life'.

Going into blame or judgment is incredibly disempowered. And if the explanation is that God caused us to have this dreadful situation, then there would appear to be nothing we can do but plead with God to change it. Within that context, no guarantees there either! However, we can also choose another perspective – as challenging as this may initially be. If we have indeed had a role to play in Co-creating where we are now at, then such an acceptance can at least offer a potential way out of our mess.

Nor are there guarantees here either, but at least within this paradigm, it does put the 'ball in our court'; it does give us back a certain sense of self empowerment via Co-creation; it can provide for a 'project plan', which does in turn give a semblance of hope for *us* to be able to alter our predicament. What can definitely be said is that many people have been able to achieve such success by Consciously and diligently focusing on using the Co-creation processes. Not everyone is automatically successful every time, but many people feel drawn to this way of perceiving their predicament, rather than imploding into victim-hood, and feeling there is nothing much to be done.

Ultimately, how long it takes us to get out of our disease or unwanted situation is related to a wide range of issues. It can depend on how long it takes us to re-direct our minds into more positive thinking and aspirations, as well as how often we allow our minds to slip back into old patterns of negative thinking. The latter is especially easy to do, when faced with serious illness or other drastic life situations.

A final point here is to strongly impress upon you that what is absolutely, definitely *not* being suggested here is to rely only on these sort of Metaphysical approaches to our healing. Use whatever you need to use – be that medical or natural - or a combination thereof. There is that old saying again... 'tether your horse... and trust in God'. Indeed! Do whatever it takes to ensure your survival or reversal of the present dilemma. Use any of a range of 'normal', earthly-plane, physical interventions. Then also dive right into the Metaphysical approach as outlined in more detail in the next few chapters, and use these approaches as a *complementary* aspect of your overall strategy.

But learning these skills takes time – and practise

Trouble enters if we get the wrong impression as to how much we as humans can suddenly achieve via all these concepts. For instance, the fact is that a young child is not really able to fly a Jumbo Jet. All they are able to do at this stage in their overall human development is to sit on a little tricycle – with stabilizer wheels, no less. However, this doesn't then make their level of skill, at this childhood stage of their life, bad or negative in any sense. Instead, it's just a realistic acceptance that at this point in their Journey this is all they can skillfully manage. Yet, when they become a full adult, having grown in maturity,

Chapter 10 - Co-creativity - What Is It?

skill and wisdom - and with a lot of effort! – they may end up flying the Space Shuttle. But that takes time, and a lot of input to get to such a stage of skill.

In a sense, the New Age has misled a lot of people. The implication has been that by doing just one course or reading one book, they can now instantly manifest all sorts of things into their lives. This is indeed *potentially* true. But it's also true they may not yet have enough skill with this concept to manifest quickly and easily at this point in their Journey. So of course, if they initially start off trying to Co-create really big and ambitious projects, there's a good chance they'll also 'fail'. But, this can have the unfortunately consequence that they now also debunk the *process*, rather than accepting their *limitation* – at this stage – in being able to do this process effectively. It's not that the process of Co-creativity is flawed. It has more to do with them not yet being very skilled at following the 'recipe', or that they simply haven't accrued enough 'currency' – the internal capacity for resonance – with which to draw their desire into this material reality.

Quite a few unusual words and concepts have been introduced thus far, which may have left some people a bit puzzled. What we'll now do over the next few chapters is explore these much more thoroughly so that they make sense, and can maximally empower you in this Journey.

Exercise
- What is a fundamental and crucial difference between the concept of Creative Visualization and Co-creation?
- Explain what is meant by the Matrix, and what its function is within Co-creation.

> ### Summary of thoughts thus far
> - Co-creation is a technique whereby we are capable of manifesting into our physical reality those things we first dreamt of or desired within our minds. It is further based on a fundamental axiom that 'Thought is Creative'.
> - There is a need to draw away from the New Age proposition that we **are** God. Hence the use of the word **Co**-creation, rather than Creative Visualization.

- They both describe the same phenomenon; however, the word 'Co-creativity' adds a very important additional understanding to this process, namely, that we are only **Co**-creators – not **The** Creator.
- Keep in mind that God **is** Creativity; we are only able to **tap into** Creativity.
- Religions inevitably are quite opposed to seeing humans as 'creators'. However, Co-creativity is more a process of relative creativity capabilities, which we nevertheless do have a right to. Hark back to the 'child in the play-pen' metaphor.
- Materiality is not so much the problem, as our potential for becoming addicted to it.
- Co-creativity is not just about manifesting endless amounts of material goods or situations. Rather, it is an invitation to learn how to *re-Connect* more Consciously to this Higher Source; not *become* It.
- What is so often conveniently ignored is the fact that Jesus Christ actually taught the essence of Co-creativity – although obviously it wasn't called that in the bible!
- For those who are religious, and feel they can't use Co-creation, they need to remember Christ's words... *Verily, verily, I say unto you, He that believeth on me, the works that I shall do, shall he do also, and greater [works] than these shall he do...* [2]
- Doubt is one of the most powerful saboteur energies we can engage in during any Co-creative process.
- Co-creativity represent an ability which each and every human being *is* already tapping into anyway – usually unconsciously - but which we all need to learn to do more skillfully and with more *Consciousness*.
- The issue is not whether we *deserve* to manifest something into our life via Co-creation; it's simply whether we have *learnt* the proper skill to manifest it.
- When you plead for something, you are coming from a space where there is an inherent aspect of uncertainty about getting your desire fulfilled. Otherwise you wouldn't be pleading.
- Praying *can* be most effective as a means to Co-create, as long as you can keep a focus going in your mind that what it is you desire has already been granted – as per J.C's injunction.

Chapter 10 - Co-creativity - What Is It?

- To be effective at Co-creativity, we need to go beyond 'doing', and enter a Space of 'Being'.

- We need to learn how to *Be*, Energetically, what it is we wish to *become*, experientially, in our lives.

- Thus, for Co-creativity to work, we need to learn how to generate a feeling of...'already having what it is we desire'.

- We need to understand that within the Matrix lays the slumbering possibility of absolutely anything and everything that can be imagined. To be able to imagine something is to cause that something to become an instant reality - *within the Matrix*.

- Co-creativity depends on the maxim of...'for every *output* there needs to be an *input*'. In the Co-creativity level of our reality, our input is Energetic, and our 'currency' in this sphere has to do with learning how to work with Energy, rather than with materiality.

- Co-creation draws upon an 'Ultimate-Source-of-Everything-Possibly-Conceivable', and whether it is called 'The Field', 'The Matrix', 'The Ether', 'God', 'The Akashic Records'... or 'Dimension II' - the bottom-line is the same.

- Many people are unfortunately misled that just reading certain books; doing creative visualization workshops; seeing a program or DVD on this subject will allow them automatically and immediately to 'order' anything they want; and expect it to manifest into their life tomorrow!

- We need to understand that the Laws governing this phenomenon work every time. But they work to produce what we desire, limited only by our level of skill in *using this technique*.

- We need to realize that much of what we perceive *outside* of us is only a reflection of what is *inside* us, usually Co-created *unconsciously*.

- The thoughts we continually focus on, and therefore 'invest' in, are what we more likely than not will also manifest into our reality.

- When we find ourselves in a bad situation, we need to understand that we usually got there via a lengthy series of many, many, tiny, seemingly insignificant and innocent steps.

- Just as it inevitably took many small steps to get us into trouble, so too – even with the use of Co-creation – it may take many small steps to now get us out of that trouble.

REFERENCES

1. Bible, King James Version, Mark 11:24
2. Ibid, John 14:12.
3. Bible, King James Version, Matthew 25:15-30
4. Hicks, Esther & Jerry. *Ask and it is Given – learning to manifest your desires*, Hay House Inc, 2004.
5. Hicks, Esther & Jerry, Videocasettes:- *The Art of Allowing, The Science of Deliberate Creation*. See Hay House Australia - www.hayhouse.com.au
6. Emoto, Masaru. *The Hidden Messages in Water*, Beyond Words Publishing Inc, Oregon, USA, 2001.

CHAPTER 11

CO-CREATIVITY – FURTHER EXPLORATIONS

Your outer circumstances are but reflections of your inner thoughts.

Various authors

But what exactly is visualization?

Coherence? Matrix? 'Resonance Credits'? What on earth is all this about? Hang in there; we'll increasingly clarify all this as we go along! But first let's clear up some issues around the very act of visualizing. One thing many people worry about is their capacity to even visualize – or they're unclear as to what that exactly entails. Well, here is a very simple exercise which will clarify this uncertainty once and for all.

In a moment, I'll ask you to close your eyes and think of your bedroom. See – in your mind's eye – where your bed is; see what color the bedspread is; what sort of floor covering you have; is it carpet? If so, what pattern is in that carpet? If the floor covering is made of tiles, describe them. Where is the window, and what do the curtains look like? What type of lampshade do you have hanging from your lamp? Is there an alarm-clock by the bedside, and can you see the buttons on it?

If you have just done this – and no-one seems to fail this exercise! – *then you are able to visualize.* It's as simple as that. It's true that everyone's visualization will be different. Some people are more visual, while others are either more auditory or kinesthetic – touchy-feely. So they will each 'visualize' their bedroom – or whatever – in their unique manner. But this is all you have to do. So that's one worry you can now cross off your list – because everyone can visualize.

Even blind people can visualize once they have had their surroundings described to them. Therefore, when you are actually doing a Co-creation exercise, all you need to do is to 'see' what it is you desire, in the same way, and to the same extent as you *were* able to visualize all that detail in your bedroom.

Humans obsessed with making change - externally

The next thing we need to explore a bit further is this fundamental belief we humans have that change to our reality and lives can only be brought about by changing things on the *outside*. We've already broached this topic in an earlier chapter, but now let's take this exploration to much deeper levels.

We remain obsessed with changing everyone and everything else around us, because almost automatically we believe them to be the *source* of our problems. It is *that* religion; it is *that* political party; it is *that* philosophy. *They* are the cause of our problems. It certainly isn't *us*. Witness what much of the Western World, and especially the USA did post 9/11.

But trying to change such outer aspects of our reality, in an attempt to change the fundamental nature of our misery or problems is misguided and ultimately useless. Just look around you to see the validity of that one. Certainly, the situation we've found ourselves in with Iraq a few years ago clearly highlights the futility of that approach.

The message here is not that we shouldn't change whatever evil we see being done in our outer reality. However, *only* focusing on changing the *outer* reality is ultimately not going to fundamentally change anything - certainly not in the long term. It only takes a quick look at history as far back as we can go, to see this is how we as humans have operated. We inevitably tend to only focus on changing the 'outer', which in turn inevitably ends up being nothing more than window dressing.

It's interesting to again bring in J.C. here, when he said...'*Thou hypocrite, first cast out the beam out of thine own eye; and then shalt thou see clearly to cast out the mote in thy brother's eye*'. [1]

Indeed: do absolutely everything you can to make positive and Healing change within the external reality of the human experience. But understand this will inevitably fail unless you have also more fundamentally and concurrently dealt with what may first need to be changed *within you*. This is nothing new. Indeed, it's nothing more than a most fundamental teaching of Christianity, and yet it gets to be so neglected or down-played when it comes to dealing with our modern, external world challenges.

Making outer change before making inner change hasn't really worked.

What's actually happened is that somewhere along the line we've lost sight of ourselves as powerful beings who first and foremost create their reality - *from the inside*. The fact that after all this time, we still have the amount of chaos here on this plane of reality, should surely alert us to the truth that this outer focus, or way of dealing with problems is just not working. Indeed, it's highly unlikely to ever truly work, until we are willing to look *inside* for the solutions.

It is our *Inner* reality, which so desperately and initially needs changing, way before we start making changes on the *outside*. Until we are able to focus on this aspect of life's endless chaos, nothing will truly change in any fundamental and lasting way. To date we are like a person who comes into the bathroom to find the tub overflowing. Yet all we've done is to grab a mop and start mopping... without first turning off the tap, plus pulling the plug. Neglecting such common-sense and basic actions will certainly guarantee we'll be moppin' for a loooooooong time!

Co-creation – what is it we are really wanting?

This is another concept we've touched on in a previous chapter, but let's explore it too in greater depth. The human condition seems to be an experience of endless needs and desires for an infinite number of 'things', be that money, friends, power, partners, houses, jobs, etc. Yet if we look for the *underlying* thread that motivates this plethora of needs, then it would appear what we're really after is a *State of Being* - one where we feel more complete, joyful or fulfilled, deep within ourselves. The problem is that the journey of the ego is to endlessly try to achieve this *State* through the manifestation of a bottomless list of outer *'objects'* on which we so resolutely project our desires.

Many people aren't even Aware that there is this differentiation. They just *know* that getting that job or partner or house or money is *the* thing which will give them that sense of satisfaction and fulfillment they have been looking for. They simply can't conceive of obtaining that Inner sense of fulfillment, joyfulness and gratification without having access to their externally desired object. They sincerely believe the desired state of fulfillment and happiness can only be switched on in them *through* these external objects or situations.

The reality, however, is that to experience such states of joy or bliss on any fundamentally real level is ultimately only achievable *within* us. An outer event, person or situation does indeed *trigger* off that Inner experience of joy. But we then make the huge mistake of projecting onto that outer situation the belief that it is the *source* of and fundamental reason for our Inner experience. Yet that experience is in essence an Inner one. The fact that an outer event or person can trigger this in us, should put us on notice as to what it is we need to primarily focus on in our seeking.

Yet, the reality is that any such outer event can ever only trigger what is already within us - but which thus far has remained only a potential State of Being. The most important thing to realize is that we are capable of experiencing such Inner states of joy. It's just that we also choose - on unconscious levels - to be very picky or specific about what it is on the outer dimension that we will validate and allow to then trigger this Inner experience.

As you read all this, what hopefully should be starting to occur in your thinking is to realize that it is just as possible to also choose to do something within your head-space. Something which will then allow this Inner state of joy to occur, w*ithout needing that* **outer** *event or situation to be the 'magical' and sole trigger of achieving such an Inner State.* Not easy necessarily, but definitely possible.

Again, it is a sharp reminder to really understand, on a deep, gut level, that this entire human Journey is ultimately about learning to achieve the Inner States, triggered by Inner Shifts of Awareness within us. Much more so than all this endeavoring to achieve or force these Inner States via the *outer* 'reality' of materiality. That's why many of the Eastern Teachers or Gurus call such materiality 'Maya'. Although material things are obviously very solid and real to us here on Earth, nevertheless they are still an Illusion when compared to what we are truly seeking - that Inner State of contentment; fulfillment and peace. All these material objects or situations we so crave for, driven by ego-self are in the end only a *substitute* for that Inner State associated with the Higher Self. And in that sense, they are also the Illusion we so relentlessly chase after, instead of realizing it ultimately is only a shadow of what we really want.

Chapter 11 - Co-creativity - Further Explorations

Importance of 'achieving Inner State of Being' first

Hopefully, a new understanding is dawning, which can help sweep away previous confusions we may have had as to what really gives us satisfaction and fulfillment in life. The mistake or illusion this emergent comprehension is now hopefully bringing to our attention is that the inescapable bottom-line to what we actually desire has more to do with obtaining a certain *Inner State of Being*. When you look more deeply and thoughtfully at the 'desire spirals' we humans are so prone to become entangled in, you'll realize that in the end, it's not really about obtaining any of a myriad of physical manifestations. Yet, it's these external situations, things or objects we so exclusively focus on as the magical *Source* of fulfillment, or that 'State of Being' we're really looking for. *That's* the ironic twist to so much of our human confusion, and our addiction to an endless need to own so much 'stuff'; ultimately a bottomless pit of desires.

Yes, I know... you might need to read these last few paragraphs a few more times to really let it all sink in! The ultimate irony is that if we can achieve this Inner *Shift*, leading to this Inner *State* of already feeling fulfilled and joyful, then that joy will also radiate out from us. In turn, being in such an altered State, inevitably also makes it so much easier to achieve what it is we desire on the outside; certainly through the process of Co-creation. The other interesting phenomenon is that people and situations are more likely to be drawn to us when we are feeling joyful, compared to needy and empty.

You get what you want when you no longer need it

'You get what you want when you no longer need it'. Here we enter into a realm where you get a delicious double-twist to this whole discussion. First, we need to become very clear as to what it is we are really after when wanting to do Co-creation. Then we need to focus on achieving that Inner State... without automatically first having whatever it is we desire. Remember, the mistake we so often make is in thinking that only *it* can catalyze this Inner State of well-being and satisfaction.

In that sense, once you have achieved that Inner State – without needing access or possession of the outer object or situation – then you are also precisely in that Space which is so much more conducive to making any Co-creative venture successful. Simply because now you have been able to achieve that deep Inner sense of *knowingness,* or feeling of already having what it is you desire, before it has manifested; a State of Being which is fundamental to any successful Co-creation. Ironic twist indeed. So now you can draw into your reality precisely what it is you'd *like* - but paradoxically, no longer *need* at this point. It's as if this whole system of Co-creation is guaranteed to work, once the right button is pushed. What's so mind-blowing is how incredibly simple it all is. Not easy; but definitely simple.

Say you feel lonely, and desire a partner. Then even if all the above is nothing more than New Age 'psycho-babble', you can still find yourself in a win:win situation. What's needed here is to choose to deal with your aloneness – and the belief that a partner will be *the only solution* to your loneliness - by first working on creating that Inner shift; in other words, by manufacturing that Inner State of feeling fulfilled and happy – as if you already have that partner. Hence, using this approach whenever we have a desire, becomes a powerful way of progressing on that Consciousness Journey all of us humans are on - whether we know it or not, and whether we want to acknowledge it or not.

You can of course continue to use Co-creation to endlessly manifest a lot of material things into your life. But ultimately, you'll find yourself waking up from this Illusionary approach. Particularly, as the materiality you are manifesting still doesn't seem to truly relieve you of that nagging, Inner sense of continued emptiness and dissatisfaction. We humans have put the cart before the horse as it were, in regard to thinking we know how and where to find ultimate fulfillment and happiness.

Sense of disconnection from Source

Perhaps what drives us so intensely in all our many desires has more to do with a fundamental Inner sense of disconnection from Source; from God, which alone can ultimately be our truest source of joy and fulfillment. It's about 'getting it', on a really fundamental level, how so many of us misguidedly try to resolve this Inner sense of disconnection from Source, solely via these outer, more materialistic means. Such a 'solution' to our Inner emptiness and sense of disconnection can never work in the long run.

Instead, we need to understand a very fundamental aspect to how this reality here on Earth actually operates. First and foremost, we need to learn the skill of creating the State we are searching for - i.e. joy, fulfillment, etc. - on the *Inner* level of who we are. Only then can all these endless manifestations possibly give us the true sense of joy or fulfillment we're seeking. But with an

Chapter 11 - Co-creativity - Further Explorations

interesting twist: we now no longer need such manifestations or things *in order to be happy*. Any manifestations we now draw into our reality only serve to *complement* our happiness, not *create* it for us.

Creating this Inner shift first, does highlight an entirely different spin on Co-creation. But for this to be understood, we need to be willing to see Co-creation within a more Spiritual perspective, rather than just another exciting technique with which to amass further materiality. Instead, we can therefore turn it into a potent Journey through which to increase our level of Consciousness. *That* is actually the true goal of Co-creation. Fulfilling and manifesting your desires is but a happy 'side-effect'!

Bottom-line to why we Co-create

Ultimately, the bottom-line to Co-creation is about skilling ourselves to fully and easily access the Higher Self level of who we are, which is basically a constant state of joy. It's about making that shift of *becoming* that sense of joy, independent of whether we have managed to manifest one of an infinite number of material 'things', supposedly to *give* us joy. In the end, this latter approach is a bottomless pit of need – an addiction of sorts.

It's all about what we choose to make our primary focus. Do we first focus on becoming so clever at being able to manifest absolutely everything we set our minds to? Or do we focus on achieving that Inner State of Being; aligned and actively living our human reality from the Higher Self, rather than ego-self mode? The former gives us much more access to unending joy – never mind our external situation. The latter gives us the potential for endless misery, and still feeling empty – despite all the materiality we may have been able to manifest. Admittedly, it appears easier to find 'joy' via an array of more material things or situations, but ultimately this leads to nothing but an emotional dead-end.

What is this Journey here all about really?

So, from a Higher Consciousness level of reality, what is the primary objective of this Journey here on planet Earth? Perhaps it has more to do with firstly learning to see the necessary differentiation between manifesting that *Inner* State, versus obtaining the *outer* objects... which we're hoping will give us that Inner State. Then, we need to back up this understanding by making the necessary choices within ourselves, allowing for this deep and fundamental Shift to occur.

Next, it is from this new 'platform', created by this Inner Shift, that we subsequently manifest the outer. So the whole thing about Co-Creativity is to keep asking ourselves... 'Why am I so desperately searching for, or trying to manifest XYZ'? If this question isn't answered properly, we are indeed being very unconscious in the way we are going about Co-creation.

Let's look at a solid example to clarify this really very important point. Imagine you strongly want a partner in your life. Absolutely nothing wrong with that. However, let's just briefly step to the side of what is often a deep desire for many people. Let's see if we can get in touch with what it is we are truly after; *beyond* the manifestation of such a person into our lives.

Once we look at this scenario a bit more clearly, we realize that what this person would actually provide us with is a sense of being loved; of being desirable; so we'd no longer feel alone. If they were really handsome or beautiful, some of the attention they receive might just vicariously rub off on us. There would also be someone to help us in our daily Journey, and we wouldn't feel so vulnerable when things got difficult in life, as they often do. We'd feel more fulfilled in our life, having that person there to share our experiences with. And the list goes on.

So what we're really doing when we want to manifest that special partner into our life is actually not so much about the *physical* presence of that person. Yes, there is that too! But it has probably got a lot more to do with these other seemingly ephemeral mental/emotional and Energetic aspects such a person would provide us with, either directly or vicariously. And that's precisely the crunch to this whole issue of Co-creation. In this example, the deeper goal of this process of Co-creating a partner is ironically not necessarily about manifesting that special person into our lives. It's got so much more to do with those *states of being* such a person would vicariously provide us with.

Hence the deeper, more fundamental aim of life and Co-creation has much more to do with achieving that level of Inner Consciousness, Spirit Awareness or Soul maturity. This is where we need to *become* all those *States*, from *within ourselves*, without necessarily having to have that person actually manifest.

Mmmmmm... that certainly puts a twist on it, doesn't it? But interestingly, it's a point that was already brought to our attention, over 2,000 years ago... by Christ, when he taught...' *But seek ye first the Kingdom of God and all his righteousness; and all these things shall be added unto ye*'.[2]

Chapter 11 - Co-creativity - Further Explorations

In other words, we can also read this passage as asserting we first need to seek that Higher State of Being, which in this book and elsewhere has been called the Higher Self. We've also stated that this aspect of who we are exists on a much Higher Realm than the earthly one. The characteristics of this State are those of joy, contentment; fulfillment, etc. Sounds a bit like the proverbial Heaven perhaps?! So if we seek this Level of Reality first, then indeed, whatever else we might like to manifest will happen much more rapidly and easily.

True, it's much more confronting and demanding of *us*, to have to bridge that Inner gap as it were. That requires a lot more Inner work and Inner change from us. Relatively speaking, simply manifesting the *outer* 'thing' we desire, sounds sooooooo much easier - especially when we then expect *it* to provide *us* with what only *we* can ultimately provide for ourselves; in other words, living our lives more from a Higher Self Level of Reality.

Confused?.....Or just upset? It's a bit like having to actually sit for our exams to be able to get our Diploma. Instead, we want to skip those damn exams – after all, they involve far too much study and hard work! It would be so much quicker and easier to have the University hand us that Diploma. Life would be much simpler if we could indeed Co-create our final desire, rather than having to do all that Inner work... and then have our desire manifest. With the final clincher that... we then actually may not desire or need it so much anyway. However, it's not all as hopeless, confusing or weird as it seems at first glance. Be assured, Creative manifestation can definitely occur before we get to these Higher levels of Consciousness.

The good news is that this whole Journey, which at first may seem overwhelming and impossible to achieve, can be done one tiny step at a time. But the bottom line is clear - the more we can manage that deep, Inner Shift to occur, the more spectacularly successful we will become at the art of Co-creation. That's the most fundamental message to take on board.

Do we live our life through ego or Higher Self mode?

Ultimately, it's a matter of who we allow to be in control of our life – ego self or Higher Self? And that is the entire thrust of Co-creation: to increasingly learn to come from the latter. Most New Age books on Creative Visualization tend to only highlight the wonderful *material* things this process can bring to your life. However, it is so much more. But it depends entirely on where you want to come from, when getting involved in this powerful, and potentially very transformative process or technique. Ultimately, it is also important to realize that neither pathway with this technique is inherently better or worse than the other; there are simply different levels from which to live and experience our lives. The reality is that many people do need to initially only focus on the *material* aspect to Co-creation – all that money, property, jobs, and so much more they can now manifest.

Eventually, they will come to realize that although such materiality is not inherently bad, it is also not inherently fulfilling of the deep Inner need or emptiness we, as humans, carry inside. So this is the major difference between the usual New Age angle to Co-creation, or doing it more from the Higher Self Mode. In the former, many of its proponents only advocate coming from the ego level of Co-creation. In the latter however, although exactly the same basic 'recipe' is used, we're also coming from an altogether different level of our Being. It's a bit like trying to manifest our reality purely from the physical plane, with our need to have ego constantly in control. Alternatively, we choose to manifest our reality through the Spiritual Plane, allowing our Higher Self to run the show.

And that's why visualization sometimes seems to work - and sometimes doesn't. We may fluke it, and manage to get to a fairly centered space in the more ego-based physical realm, from which we can also manifest. However, we are much more likely to manifest accurately and cleanly if we do so from the Spiritual Realm. Trying to materialize from the Spiritual Plane has the extra advantage that it's automatically beyond all this ego-related stuff, such as whether we actually deserve having our desire manifest. Do you deserve it? Have you been bad? Have you been good? All that sort of stuff, inevitably associated with ego-baggage, has no sway within the Higher Self Realm.

Ego's role and Higher Self's role – both needed

When Co-creating, the other advantage to coming from the Higher-Self Plane of Reality is that it is the Plane of BEING; not doing. It's from this Higher Level that all need for ego-control disappears. Usually, the ego constantly feels *it* is the one who has to do it all, if manifestation is to occur successfully.

Despite having highlighted our focus so much more on the role of the Higher Self in Co-creation, there is one crucial point we must not overlook. It's very important to understand that we do need to honor the totally valid, as well as crucial role ego is *required* to play when using this process. Ego's

Chapter 11 - Co-creativity - Further Explorations

legitimate and vital role is to outline the desire, set the intention, and then release it *totally* to the Higher Self.

But the two roles need to be clearly delineated and understood, or else the ego self will just end up sabotaging the entire project. What seems to happen far too often is that once the ego has done its basic part of the bargain, it then doesn't know when to stop poking its inquisitive – and often doubting mind – back into the process. Time and again, it retains this lingering sense of doubt about the Higher Self's capacity to now finish the job. It's a bit like being a gardener, planting seedlings into a garden bed, but then every few days, ripping out those poor seedlings to see how far the roots have grown. Do that often enough, and no surprise if those same poor old seedlings wither and die.

So it is with our Co-creation process too. If the ego doesn't trust the Higher Self, and constantly interferes long after it has already released the project out of its hands, this only guarantees to sabotage the manifestation process. It's as if the project is constantly being bled dry of the 'Creativity Credits' initially invested into it. Finally, the 'account' runs dry, and the entire ability to 'finance' the manifestation goes bankrupt.

Where ego can lose the plot

With the smaller desires in life, the stakes are not as high, hence the usual doubts so characteristic of the ego mode of operation are not there. Under these circumstances the ego doesn't have the same urge to still constantly meddle *beyond* its jurisdiction. The end result is less meddling with the Higher Self's aspect to the Co-creative process, and thus a relatively quick, clean and accurate manifestation occurs. However, as the stakes of the desire go up; the more critical and important the manifestation of that desire seems to our mind, so too will we find the ego more likely to meddle where it is no longer wanted.

The ego therefore, has to 'get it' on two major levels. Firstly, *it* is not the one doing the final manifestation. Ego can ever only set the parameters of the desire; set the intention, and then make the choice of releasing it into the Universe – via the Higher Self. *And that is **all** the ego can do in this process.* But here we need to hark back to an earlier comment about the New Age. All too often, remarks from this corner have misguided the ego into believing it *is* actually God.

And when ego enthusiastically takes this on-board, then this is also where we run into big trouble. Such an insinuation is a very misguided perspective of the ego's ultimate importance in the whole Co-creative process. Not so! This may also be the vital missing link to why so many Co-creative failures can occur. As long as the ego thinks, subtly or not, that *it* is doing the manifestation, then the process is inevitably sabotaged to some extent. What needs to happen is for the ego to fully realize the boundaries of its job description, and that if it tries to go beyond those, then the process won't work nearly as well.

So the trick is to train the ego. Whenever it gets anxious, fretful, despairing or into any of those negative spaces most people's ego so often inhabit, then the 'Witness Self' will have to keep re-assuring the ego. It needs to keep reminding ego that it's the job of the *Higher Self* to see all those manifestations do end up occurring. The ego self doesn't have to deal with any of that. It simply isn't its job, and was never meant to be. Ego-self *only* needs to operate as the 'secretarial service' to the Higher Self; that's it. End of story. Ego doesn't have to figure out exactly how it all works on those Higher Levels.

Ego only has to relay the desire – not manifest it

Higher Self however, is that aspect to our incarnational reality which provides the capacity to directly tap into the Universal Source of all that Creative Energy - *through* which to manifest our desires. In order for the ego-self to stop fretting, as well as becoming so confused in its roles, there is one little trick the 'Witness Self' can play at such moments. Any time you feel negative, worried, indecisive, fearful or other typical ego emotional states, just ask yourself... 'Is this an ego-job or responsibility I'm dealing with at the moment'? Or is it in fact a Higher Self job my ego is worrying about?

It's by the ego releasing itself from thinking it has to do all the Higher Self's stuff that it then also doesn't need to fret and worry so much. Ego instead might even feel more joyful in the moment. So the ego self, from now on in should just enjoy the moment by moment experience of running the basics of this human level to life. Getting the breakfast; getting you showered; getting you ready for clients, for instance. But actually organizing the *manifestation* of the clients to consult with; organizing the visualized *manifestation* of that partner; that house, that money to pay the bills... all these are not its jobs. That is the job of the Higher Self, and the latter is totally capable; it doesn't need to be trained.

Chapter 11 - Co-creativity - Further Explorations

The role of Joy in Co-creation

We also need to look at the role of joy in Co-creation. Joy is the key that unlocks the flood-gates, and anything else but joy shuts down the flow of Creative Energy. Joy is the ultimate 'fuel' which drives the Co-creative process. Joy, in a sense, is the 'bricks and mortar' of what it takes to Co-create. So the challenge for the ego-self is to stop feeling it needs to save the world; create everything; organize the whole lot on that Higher Plane of reality. It can't be said often enough... the latter is the Higher Self's job! *All* that the ego self has to do is to run the daily show. *And find joy in that.*

The problem is that the emotion of fear is also a most powerful 'fuel' which activates and drives Co-creation – consciously or unconsciously. Fear is the antithesis of joy – or Love - and every action in our human realm comes from either one or the other of these primal emotional states. As mentioned before, fear is the primary operative of the ego, compared to joy being the primary Energy of the Higher Self.

Certainly, the ego is very much implicated in the Co-creative process. However, using the above ideas it becomes possible for the ego-self to also feel more assured. Simply because it's then much more aware of the boundaries associated with its role within the manifestation process. And if the ego is more comfortable in it's very precisely defined roles for manifestation, then hopefully there will be less instigation of all the usual fears, inadequacies, insecurities, etc. the ego-self is so prone to go into. *But all of which precisely tend to block Co-creative manifestation.*

Hopefully, this discussion has given you a format through which you might find it easier to recognize who is trying to do what. This should make it easier to get out of your own way, while ensuring the ego-self isn't constantly feeling in overwhelm, through unrealistic expectations of what it's supposed to do. No wonder the ego finds it hard to feel joyful. But if ego can simply focus on being present to the jobs it *is* supposed to do, then it will surely feel more capable and proficient, rather than the usual sense of chronic overwhelm which ego tends to experience. It just might be able to feel more joy too.

Co-creativity happens whether we know it or not

Our problem as humans is that Co-creation happens whether we know it or not. This is an absolute, fundamental fact. The only choice we therefore have is to either continue allowing it to occur *unconsciously* or to actively participate in a *Conscious* and *intentional* manner. So all this discussion is about making you as Aware as possible of what's involved in Co-creating, and how you can learn to do it increasingly from a much Higher level of Consciousness.

Visualization – inkpad and stamp metaphor

To start off with, it will be useful to have a basic metaphor through which to get at least some understanding of how this process of Co-creation works. Bring to mind an ink-pad and stamp, and let's work with this as a metaphor. First, we need to have a clear idea of what it is we would like to Co-create. If you like, this is akin to creating the image on a stamp or stencil, which in turn you wish to imprint onto paper. If this stencil is not cut properly or clearly enough, then it also cannot create a clear image, never mind how good the ink or the paper upon which you imprint the stencil design.

Using this metaphor, the 'ink' is the feeling we need to engage in to subsequently allow the thought to manifest into this reality through the Co-creative process. Use too much ink, and the image stamped on the paper will be all smudged and messy. Use too little ink, and the image will be too unclear, and barely visible on that same paper.

The next step in Co-creation involves the use of mental focus. This can be correlated to the concept of how much force is applied to that stencil as you imprint its design onto the paper. Again, if you don't push hard enough, not much of an image will form onto that paper. Press too hard and this equally can lead to distortion or warping of the 'paper'.

The final part of this metaphor is that of the paper. This correlates to our physical dimension here on planet Earth; that level of reality into which we want to manifest our desire.

Our mind is like a movie projector

But there is yet another layer to all of this. It's really important to realize another subtle distinction in regard to that statement 'Thought is Creative'. Firstly, the clarity of the mental and emotional space we come from, when doing Co-creation, determines the extent to which we create accurate manifestations. The less clear we are, the more negative beliefs and programs we harbor within ourselves, the more likely our manifestations will come through either distorted or entirely blocked.

Chapter 11 - Co-creativity - Further Explorations

Let's use another analogy here to elucidate this point. The clarity of our intention, when we're setting ourselves up to do Co-creation, can be likened to the strength of a light source within a slide or movie projector. In other words, the stronger and more focused our intention, the stronger the light source. In turn, our belief systems are like the lens in this projector. The clearer we are about our desire; the less negativity in us, so too the clearer the glass of the lens, and the fewer imperfections found on its surface.

So when the 'light' of our intention shines through the 'lens' of our belief systems, this in turn determines the clarity or sharpness with which the desired 'image' becomes projected onto the 'screen of life'. Unfortunately, there is a problem in our culture with the way we have been brought up to perceive reality. When events occurring on 'the screen of life' – our daily lives - are not to our liking, we go up to that 'screen', and try to alter the 'image' *there*.

This is obviously as useless as trying to alter the focus of a movie being projected out onto the cinema screen, by going up to that screen and demanding that the image focus itself. Where it needs to be changed is *inside* the projector itself; the real source of the problem. So too with us. This analogy again highlights how if things seem to go wrong in our lives – our 'screens' – then the way to truly create change on the *outside* is by going *inside*. And as we thus go more to the heart of the problem, so our Co-creation capabilities and skill will become greatly enhanced.

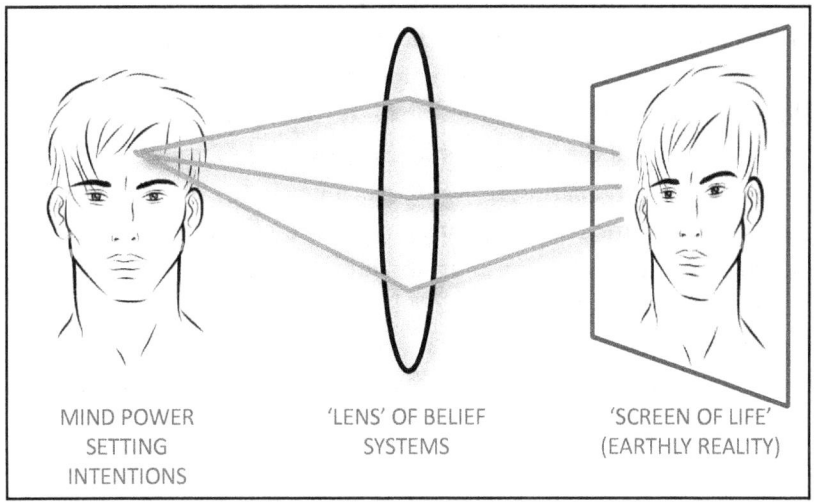

Diagram 3
Our mind as a movie projector

It's not just our various past sufferings that can lead to distorted and usually dysfunctional manifestations, but also the many belief systems we've been exposed to. These include our religious beliefs, political ideologies, social class and so much more that influenced us as we grew up. These can all become major levels to our capacity or incapacity to manifest. Our own Co-creative power is therefore influenced by such factors and many others. For instance, our religion may have taught us that suffering is good; to be rich is evil; to have sex is basically sinful... on and on. Or our cultural beliefs may cause us to have problems if we were to fall in love with someone of the 'wrong' skin color, religion or social class.

Co-creation – the hologram concept

Another important way to look at how Co-creation works is to use the concept of the hologram. Braden explores this powerful metaphor in his book 'The Divine Matrix' (see Appendix 1 for a listing of his books). By its very nature, even the most incredibly tiny part taken from a hologram contains *all* the information of the *entire* hologram. This is no longer science fiction. It is science fact, and can be readily demonstrated nowadays. So it is with us too. Using concepts such as 'The Field', 'The Matrix' or 'The Ether' - or whatever term we wish to use – any of these can be seen as the Primary Hologram. But then, *by accepting we are an integral component of that Totality-Concept*, this also conveniently allows us to use the analogy of the hologram in a very precise and fitting way. It doesn't matter how small we as humans may appear in relation to that 'Totality', nevertheless we do contain within us, *all* that is in the Primary Hologram of the Universe/Matrix/The Field – whatever we choose to call It.

In other words, if the Matrix contains a soup of absolutely *all* possibilities, and we are an integral part of that Field, then precisely like a hologram, we *do* contain *within us* the complete *potentiality* of the Whole. From the human perspective, we seem to be such an insignificantly tiny part of that Whole. Nevertheless, like a hologram, it would seem that via this seemingly minute 'portal' of our humanness, we become a window *through* which to tap into the Infinite possibilities of that Greater Energetic Phenomenon or Whole, Source, 'God,' The Field, The Matrix.

It's as if there is a miniature holographic 'chip'-equivalent of this System, Field or Matrix – the latter usually thought to be 'out there' somewhere – which just as authentically exists within each of us. It appears that this 'chip'

Chapter 11 - Co-creativity - Further Explorations

creates the link between the two fundamentally identical systems – our human system, and that of the Matrix. It's this link, or portal, which seems to allow us to communicate, thus Co-create *from* the Matrix-Field.

Life – hanging onto our pain

For most of us as human beings, we have this nasty habit of hanging onto our pain and suffering, and an almost perverse way of more easily focusing on our pain than focusing on the good in our lives. It's a really dysfunctional way to deal with our reality, and for many people, this inner, unconscious attraction and desire to hang onto pain is perhaps fed by their religious background.

Here, the fundamental belief is that one way or another, suffering is good, and that the more you suffer now, the better your chances to get to heaven and benefit there. One end result is that many people tend to hang onto their pain more than they should. There is also a huge amount of momentum behind such concepts of suffering, which can make it hard to alter – or preferably eradicate. Unfortunately however, the Laws of Co-creativity work in very specific ways… 'what we focus on is what we are more likely to get'. *And this is the reality we really need to entrench deep into our understanding.*

For the average person therefore, getting out of their pain can be quite difficult. We seem to have invested so much into our pain; hanging on to it; somehow having been deluded into believing it is good for us. It may even give us a sense of misguided identity… 'I'm that poor ol' sod who has had to go through so much suffering due to XYZ'. No doubt you know examples of such people from your own life experiences, where their life is a series of disasters, tumbling them along a very bumpy road of life.

Abraham's concept of coherence – or resonance

Let's now take a look at some of the concepts presented by an Energy Being called Abraham. It/he/she is an entity who is channeled through Esther Hicks, and much of what is discussed next comes from their book *'Ask and It Is Given – learning to manifest your desires'*.[3] This is a very powerful book, as are many of the DVD's of their workshops, and it is highly recommended that you do at least obtain this book and read it carefully. However, there may be people who will baulk at accepting anything 'channeled' by some sort of amorphous 'spirit'. Spirits talking through a human: how weird and unreal is that!

Again, the issue is not whether Esther Hicks is indeed in contact with this Spirit entity called Abraham - or whether she could be making it all up herself. The bottom-line is very simple... 'Does the information she comes out with actually hang together'? 'Does it help explain a lot of life's conundrums'? And most importantly... 'Does it empower the reader to deal with their life situations in a more constructive and effective way'? If the answer to such questions is a resounding 'yes', then that is all that actually matters. Forget about whether Abraham actually exists of not; or whether 'he' is just a figment of Esther's imagination. If the information makes sense and is empowering... then use it!

According to this entity 'Abraham', at the very moment of requesting something to manifest, the Universe has already Energetically or vibrationally manifested our desire in what could be called 'CyberSpace Lay-by'. The only thing that now keeps it there - or at bay from *our* reality - is whether we are in 'vibrational resonance' with what it is we have asked for. In other words, if we are totally, utterly *already* in a state, where we completely accept that what it is we desire has already been granted, then we are *resonant* with it, and it can manifest.

When we have doubts, then ironically such doubts keep our desire at bay. It's actually as simple as that. Again, this is where the 'Gratitude Meditation' is so important. If we can place our minds and feelings into a state of Gratefulness - not for the future manifestation of a desire - but rather for *already* having that desire manifested in our lives, then it is done. But more on this 'Gratitude Meditation' later.

Intensity versus integrity of feeling

Remember how we looked earlier at the metaphor of the ink pad and stamp? Within that metaphor, the ink was seen as the 'feeling' component, critical to a successful conclusion of the Co-creation 'recipe'. However, as useful as this metaphor has been in the past, there is a need to clarify some points around this 'feeling' component to the process. It's important to clearly delineate that contrary to what many in the New Age, Creative Visualization fraternity will declare, it's not so much about the *intensity* of the emotion we can generate as the *integrity* of that emotion or feeling. This is an utterly crucial distinction to make.

Chapter 11 - Co-creativity - Further Explorations

Feelingness versus knowingness

The whole thing about using the word 'feeling' within the context of Co-creation is often confusing. What are we supposed to feel? Happy? Angry? Sad? Intense? Hysterical? But if we use the word 'knowingness' instead, this can make all the difference in what is otherwise a bewildering issue. Knowingness is indeed a form of feeling. But by being more specific, also allows us to understand exactly what form of feeling we're trying to engender *within* us, so as to make Co-creation a successful process.

But then you may ask, 'What exactly does this *knowingness* feel like'? Well, it's a very deep, inner still Space one gets to in one's mind. When you find this Space, there is a sense of expandedness, but mostly it's a particularly still, 'solid' or centered feeling that you almost seem to dissolve into. It's like finding the 'eye in the storm' - a deep well of calmness, strength, stability, certainty. Here, there is no need for effort; it truly is a state of Beingness. There's no mental or emotional pushing or pulling; nowhere you need to get to. You simply are experiencing that sense of having arrived in that Space where what you desire truly *does* already exist. It's a Space of 'effortless effort'; indeed, you are no longer 'efforting', but rather are just 'Being'.

Many people initially come across or experience this Space via meditation. Another way of getting there is by using a range of mind-altering CD's which allows you to go into deep states of Alpha and Theta. When you get into these mind states, they have many of the characteristics just described. The CD's certainly can help give you the experience that such 'Spaces' do exist within your mind/Being. From such experiential 'knowingness', you don't have to then rely on hearsay from other meditators... who may have had to meditate for many years to even get a glimpse of this 'Space'.

But after a while of using such CD's, [4] it actually becomes relatively easy to get there on your own, even without the use of such mind-altering techniques which employ specific sound frequencies. Another good time to find yourself a lot closer to such altered mind states is when you first wake up, and still are in that delightful Space of drifty-ness – not fully asleep, but not yet fully awake either.

That Space also contains a lot of the characteristics mentioned earlier. So when you are in that Space it is but an issue of remembering to use this window of mind-state, within which to then do your Co-creation exercises. It does take practise, not only to remember to use this 'portal' before you wake up fully, but to also be able to focus enough on your desires, without this focusing causing your state of mental activity to zoom you up and out of Alpha or Theta, and more towards Beta. This latter brainwave condition occurs when you are fully awake.

Another way to get some idea of what that sense of 'knowingness' is supposed to feel like, is to hark back to a metaphor we used in an earlier chapter. You're leaving for work one day, and as you drive off you have this nagging feeling that you have forgotten something. But you just can't put your finger on it. You run a range of possibilities through your mind; do you have your bag? Your wallet? Your house keys? Your lunch? And so the list goes on. Then all of a sudden you just *know* that you have forgotten your lap-top.

There simply are no ifs and buts about it; no sense of 'is it perhaps that'? You just *know* with every fiber of your being that it is the lap-top you were supposed to bring to work that day. Similarly, it's that sense of absolute knowingness, which you need to be able to access when doing Co-creation. You just *know* – with that same sense of deep inner certainty – that the desire you are Visualizing already exists.

So you don't have to whip yourself into a hysterical frenzy, shouting out your desire. This is in stark contrast to what some books on Creative Visualization do suggest. Too often, they try to get your entire *body* into the act; loudly and vigorously stating your desire; really getting the emotions going - all very much about 'doing' or 'working'. Ironically, on a subtle level it sends the message back to the Matrix that somehow we don't really believe we are going to get this desire manifested, unless we also really work at it. This stands in stark contrast to just BEING in that mind state where we simply *know* that what it is we desire *is* already manifest. That's perhaps a rather subtle, yet vitally important difference between the doing – and just Being.

Torch and laser beam analogy

The crucial point which can determine whether Co-creation will work or not, has more to do with the degree of focus and *integrity* of your 'feeling'. It's not so much about the *intensity* of your feelings. This is a subtle but extraordinarily important difference, establishing either success or failure in Co-creation. Think of light, as used in a torch or a laser beam. Both utilize light, but in a torch, the rays are much more scattered and incoherent, compared to the tight coherence of a laser beam. A torch will definitely help us to see more clearly within a dark space, but the coherence of a laser beam is capable of doing so

Chapter 11 - Co-creativity - Further Explorations

much more - from cutting through steel, to being used in the most delicate of surgeries, to functioning as a channel for transferring information.

So often in our Western culture, there is this perception that 'more is better'. Hence the more feeling, the better the process just has to work. Not so. It's not about working extra hard at this; just smarter. Think again of that laser beam. It's not the actual *pressure* of the light which can allow a laser beam of light to cut through steel. But it has everything to do with how *focused* and coherent the light beam is. So it is with our thoughts when doing Co-creation. And this is where that concept of 'The Moment' – as elucidated by Eckhart Tolle – becomes the most powerful 'portal' *through* which to make those thoughts of ours have as much integrity as possible.

That's what learning to live in the moment is all about. The more we are living in the moment, the less we are distracted by the past or the future, and hence the less we are actually distracting the process of Co-creativity. Therefore, one potent way of learning how to focus that laser beam very tightly is by learning to live in the moment. If we aren't focused on what we are doing now, but rather in other dimensional directions, such as past or future, this results in a diffusing of the beam.

So too we need to be in integrity with the feeling of *already* having what it is we desire, even before it has actually physically manifested. In other words, there needs to be a resonance between our desire and our own Inner, absolute conviction that the desire is definitely *already* granted, and manifest in our physical reality.

It has far more to do with generating a very high level of *coherence* between how we feel, and what we desire, rather than about how loud and hysterically we may shout or express our Inner feelings. In the end, who are we really trying to convince? It's more about the *coherence* of our feeling being in synch with a deep, Inner knowing that what we have asked for has *already* been granted. Not *whether* it will be granted; but that it *has* already been granted!

Radio transmitter analogy

Let's re-visit that analogy of a very powerful radio transmitter and radio set. Here you've got the radio transmitter sending out a very clear signal, but as long as you are off-station with your radio set, you are in static. Let's equate that static with the wide range of distracting emotional states you may be experiencing. But as you twiddle the dial on the radio set, and come closer and closer to the station, so too does the static decrease until you have a crystal clear transmission occurring.

At that point there is a situation of 'resonance'. It's not that the 'static' is bad. It just tells you that you are not yet 'on station'! That's the point of our emotions. If in your daily life you find you're experiencing or playing with a lot of uncomfortable emotions, it's just one way your Higher Self can alert your ego self that you are not yet 'on Station'. Now, you can either keep wallowing around in the 'static' or you can *use* this situation, once you truly understand what this 'static' actually means. In other words, you can use it to become more focused and Conscious about getting closer to the 'Station'.

Another way to look at it is that if you are feeling quite content about a particular Co-creation project, then it basically means you are more likely to be in resonance with the desires you have projected out. This should amplify the ease with which it can now manifest into solid, physical reality. Yet, remain in 'static', and it becomes far less likely that your desire can manifest. Again, this highlights how important it is to become so much more Conscious of how our minds are functioning. What thoughts are we playing with on a regular basis, especially in relation to our desire? Are we in fact resonant with it or are we subtly still keeping it at bay?

Connecting the concept of feelings with that of the Chakras

There is yet another way we can look at this issue of feelings within the context of Co-creation. According to Gregg Braden, the definition of feeling is the union of thought and emotion. He uses the concept of the Chakras to describe how feelings are created by blending the different emotions from these Chakras.

The top three Chakras are seen to be associated with thought. This is where, within our mind, we conceive the idea of what it is we desire. But in the next stage, we have to fuel that thought – to flesh it out or give it life as it were – with those primary emotions generated by the lower three Chakras. The thought and the emotions, blended from these two different groups of Chakras, then combine or meet in the central Chakra, which is the heart Chakra, and from this union we generate the *feeling* of what it is we desire to manifest.

You might well ask… 'But what exactly are these emotions'? We've touched on this before, but due to people usually finding the subtleties associated with emotions difficult to grasp, it's worth re-visiting this concept. As Gregg Braden so eloquently explains, fundamentally the emotions can be broken down into

Chapter 11 - Co-creativity - Further Explorations

two primary states. One is that of Love, and the other is its opposite – fear. It's from those two fundamental *emotions* that all the various *feelings* stem.

For instance, from Love you can generate the feelings of compassion, caring, empathy, gratitude, peace, happiness, sense of knowingness or certainty, etc, while from fear you get anxiety, anger, jealousy, hatred, guilt, shame, doubt, rage, hurt, etc. Yet, keep in mind that on a *primary, fundamental* level we are only dealing with two *emotions* – Love, and its opposite - fear.

So, in Co-creation, when we are unifying our *thought*, image, idea or concept of what it is we desire, empowered or enlivened by our *emotion,* to then generate a *feeling* within the heart Chakra, we ultimately only have two emotion-choices of what to use to *fuel* that Co-creative process. It's either fueled by fear or by Love. In other words, you can have the clearest possible thought of what it is you want; you can do the Co-creative process perfectly, following all the rules, but if you fuel those thoughts with the wrong emotion – fear-driven instead of Love-driven - then you're unlikely to get what it is you want; or more likely, end up with the opposite of you desire, or a very distorted version thereof.

When you look back at the list of feelings which can be generated from that fundamental Love-driven emotion, then gratitude and a sense of knowingness or certainty are the most powerful ones to generate within your system, from which to maximize your ability to Co-create successfully.

It's also important to clarify exactly what a wish is. As Braden explains, a *thought,* lacking that empowerment via our emotions is a *wish*. Remember, it's precisely the *emotions* – fundamentally of Love or fear, and originating from the lower three Chakras – that are the power source for our Co-creativity. Thought can be viewed as the 'guidance system' which directs or moulds this emotional Energy in a specific way, to then physically manifest what was initially just a concept or idea of what we desired... and which originated within our mind. But without that emotional empowerment or activation, our thoughts remain impotent.

This differentiation between thoughts, emotions and feelings are rather subtle, and it may take a while for the crucial differences to really sink in. From that point of view, you may need to re-visit, and chew over the above few paragraphs several more times before they gel.

Co-creativity – need for clarity around desire

Whichever analogy we use, the key point is to be absolutely clear about what it is we desire, as well as what our feelings are around having such a desire manifest into our lives. Something else we do need to keep in mind is that often, over time, it's as if there is a measure of 'drift' in our imagined desire. A house with two bedrooms; no actually make that four. And with a yard and a pool. Well, actually the pool would probably be more trouble than it's worth. And while you're at it, two garage spaces would be better, so you can store all that extra stuff you possess. So yes, you may desire a house – or whatever – but the specifics of that desire keep drifting. However, just as with the light beam described earlier, if we can focus it like a laser, we create immense power. But let that light beam disperse from its laser focus and coherence to the dissipated beam of a normal torch... and this will cause us to lose power.

Similarly with Co-creation. We need to be very clear on specifics – and then once these are formulated, keep to them. Otherwise you may find this constant mental shifting causes you to drift away from being resonant with what you desire. This can certainly slow down or even halt the Co-creative process. So again, there is a phase in Co-creation where you first 'play' with what it is you desire. See it in as many ways as you wish; play with it; change it; expand on it, but eventually it is a good idea to then come to a point where you feel all the specifics are now ready and organized.

Then comes the next phase of Co-creation, where you release it into the Matrix, simultaneously generating that feeling of *already* having what it is you desire. This is the point where you translate your thought or idea of what it is you want from being just a wish into a full-blown, activated and emotionally empowered desire, capable of manifesting into your reality. So the combination of a thought, fueled by the correct emotion to generate those powerful feelings of certainty and gratitude, in turn creates a Force that is truly capable of transforming your reality.

'Effortless effort' most effective

If we *know* something has already manifested, then there should be absolutely no effort in also manifesting a feeling resonant with this sense of *'already having'.* It's a bit like accessing our memory banks about an emotional event that has already occurred. It simply *is* there. No real effort needed to make the feelings associated with that memory come back.

We *know*, with every fiber of our being, that what we are remembering has *already existed*. It becomes an 'effortless effort' to bring back that feeling of knowingness associated with the memory of such an earlier event. Even though it is but a memory from the past, it – and the feelings associated with it - are nevertheless very real to us in the here and now.

Resonance – an example

Let's explore an example of this sense of coherence. Imagine walking down the road, and as you look at someone passing you by, you feel very attracted to them, and think how you'd love to have them as your partner. They're so beautiful; so handsome; whatever....... And yet inside you, beyond the conscious desire of wanting them in your life as a potential partner, there is an internal dialogue going on. Perhaps something along the lines of... 'yes, but they wouldn't want me, because I'm too fat, too thin, too short, too tall, too old, too young, I'm the 'wrong' color - too this, too that.....' So in this situation it is easy enough to see how there is a lack of coherence between what you are in fact *feeling* deep inside yourself, and what it is you *desire*.

We can certainly desire to have that sort of person as our partner, and the process of Co-creativity will work absolutely every time. Abraham claims that the Universe answers our request **the moment we even formulate it in our minds.** So it is definitely there in the Matrix; in 'CyberSpace Lay-by', waiting for us to claim it. *But it can only manifest once we change our internal Energetics to be resonant with already having that sort of person in our lives.* In other words, if we have enough self esteem to feel utterly and completely comfortable with having such a beautiful person in our life, then the resonance is there. Such resonance therefore allows us to draw that person into our life through the process of Co-creation.

Resonance and magnetism

We can also use the metaphor of a magnet. Any negative internal dialogue becomes like the reverse polarity of a magnet, pushing that desire away. It's as if we need to turn something around deep within us, so that we end up using the attractant pole of our magnet. This will then pull our desired objective into our reality. This is actually a powerful metaphor, so let's explore it a bit further.

As you know, magnets have two different poles, and between two magnets you can also generate two different types of reactions. One reaction is where the two poles repel each other, and another where they strongly attract. If we can generate that feeling within us of already having our desire fulfilled, then it is like turning the poles of those two magnets in such a way as to *attract* each other - and hence draw our desire into this reality. This mind-twist does facilitate and accelerate the Co-creative process, even though on one level we are still 'pretending' about it being there for us.

If we don't manage to get to that Inner Space where we can generate a strong feeling of 'already having what it is we want', then we have turned the 'magnet' in such a way that the two poles are in repelling mode. In this situation, our desire is therefore kept at bay by our Inner doubts, and can't manifest. *Even though, according to Abraham, it does already exists – right now - in this Matrix-CyberSpace, only needing to be claimed by us!*

It hasn't gone away. Our desired object or situation – whatever it may be - is still there in the Matrix. But it just can't make it into solid reality, simply because **we** are blocking it from manifesting. Our doubts, inability or lack of skill at imagining the desire as *already* manifested, is what sabotages the process. So we have then turned the 'magnets' into a position where they are repelling each other.

It's true that this is a huge sticking point for people as they first explore the whole concept of Co-creation. All this stuff about 'absolutely knowing that what you desire is already manifested', seems like nothing more than New Age 'double-Dutch'. Yet, as weird and impossible as it all seems, until we can allow this concept to somehow sit comfortably in our minds, the likelihood of being successful at Co-creation is going to be limited, and a pretty hit and miss affair.

We really do have to understand that the point of power for successful Co-creation does lie within us. The blockage is not *out there*. Whatever we have desired, according to Abraham, *is* **instantly a reality** *within the realm of the Matrix*. It's absolutely, completely, definitely wanting to manifest, because that is a fundamental and inherent quality of any desire. But it can only come 'down to Earth' as it were, if we 'turn the magnets' in such an orientation that they are attracting each other; not repelling. That's what Abraham means when he is talking about 'resonance'. That's what is meant when a bit further down, we'll talk in greater depth about 'Attractor Credits'.

So, for many people, they do have to play these 'mind games' for a while. Particularly as they first enter into the arena of Co-creation with only a minimal level of skill. But as you find yourself ever more successful at manifesting your desires, this 'fake it till you make it' is increasingly no longer necessary. A mounting history of successes also provides you with what then becomes

Chapter 11 - Co-creativity - Further Explorations

an automatic sense of *trust*. You now know, deep in every fiber of your being, that this process absolutely does work. At this point, generating that feeling of 'already having' is no longer a problem, and hence there is also no more need to 'fake it till you make it'.

Fantasy or reality?

All this 'fake it till you make it' does brings up a crucial point. To the mind itself, science has now proven that it doesn't seem to matter whether what we imagine *is* real or is just a *fantasy* of what we would like to be real. The effect on our bodies and our reality is the same. That's why 'simulator-training' is as effective as real-life training, and that's also why, in the Co-creative process, it makes no difference to the effectiveness whether that feeling of 'already having what it is we desire' is *actually* real or not. The only thing that matters is how *authentic* we can make that feeling – particularly when our desire has not yet manifested. In a sense, we are indeed fooling the mind. Yet there is no doubt that on another level, this is a crucial component to being successful in Co-creation.

So to manifest with power, there needs to be an easiness of feeling about our desire already being manifested. The easier and more natural this feeling can be generated, the more coherent or resonant we become with its ability to manifest. The more we are 'efforting' to generate this feeling, the less likely we are to actually manifest our desire. Simply because the more we are 'efforting', the less authentic our feelings about 'already having what it is we desire'.

In other words, the more we are 'efforting', the more this implies we are actually still trying to convince an aspect of our mind as to the veracity of our desire being 'already manifest'. In this situation, our mind keeps focusing on the fact that we are still 'acting'. That's also when we have that nagging internal voice saying... 'yes, but this is all just make-believe'; 'the smart part of me knows that my desire has not yet manifested... and this is really nothing but a big con-job'.

We need to become like a superb Hollywood actor. What distinguishes one actor from another is their skill and capacity to play-act a role – *as if it were 200% true and accurate*. That's when we as an audience thrill to the performance, because it is so believable. Not because they are shouting out their lines, hysterically or at the top of their lungs, hoping to impress their audience that they really mean it.

So, if an actor can't get into this 'space', and 'become' the reality of their role, then the movie or play also lacks that X-factor, and we're just not as touched by the performance. These analogies are absolutely, directly translatable to the Co-creation situation. That part of our consciousness which has the desire, and creates the image of that desire, also needs to generate the exact *feelings* associated with already having that desire. We need to become superb, convincing actors, otherwise, when we 'release' that desire into the Matrix, it's almost as if the Matrix knows we are not for-real, and the process simply doesn't work.

Entering Higher Self Space – can't 'effort' into it

So the most important thing to realize is that this Higher Self Space cannot be accessed by effort. The key to entering this domain is 'effortlessness'. The 'cleaner' or easier the 'effortlessness', the deeper one can then enter this Space. It's not a Space we somehow need to Journey to. It is a Space, a dimension that is only a Thought away. An effortless Thought; which goes so against the whole grain of Christian tradition – especially the Protestant 'work ethic' - or the concept so often found on this earthly plane of reality i.e. 'no pain; no gain'. Here the fundamental belief we come from as humans is that we need to work for everything we wish to experience. Especially if this is related to Spiritual matters.

Hence, just starting to understand and accept that we do need to deal with all these apparently confusing issues will already allow for a quantum leap in Co-creative ability. Having a greater clarity about these issues, allows us to shift more easily into BEING on the Higher-Self Level of Reality. In other words, simply seeing how we can get so caught in trying to *do* ourselves into 'Higher Self Mode', already makes it easier to simply get there by Being. After that, all it takes is lots of practise.

Getting to this Higher Spiritual locus is more a matter of almost 'drifting' there, with no effort required. After all, this Spiritual locus is our true Home; it's where we automatically belong. It's where our whole Being-ness exists. It's as if there is an inbuilt system which allows us to automatically go Home, and in that sense we are in fact pre-programmed to go Home. But, as humans, conditioned by our religions and cultures, we have sadly lost the art or skill of BEING, and only know about *doing*. Indeed, we have become very skilled at *doing*. The sad thing is that so many people are *'doing'* with such effort, fervor and devotion in trying to achieve their goals, yet not getting far. So much Energy spent, yet so little achievement of our deep desires.

Chapter 11 - Co-creativity - Further Explorations

But what are we truly focusing on?

Here we come across a very important and often overlooked point. We first need total clarity as to exactly *what* we are financing. In other words, are we focusing solely on our new desire, or are we still mentally and emotionally caught up in – and therefore still investing in - that sense of *'lack of'* what it is we desire?

If we keep harking back to our desire - *from the perspective of **not** having it* - then the bottom-line is that we are actually focusing on the *lack* of what it is we desire. And as per the Law of Co-creation, 'what you focus on is what you get'. Simply because what we *focus* on is what we *finance*. It doesn't matter whether that is our Conscious choice or not. A bit like a computer - garbage in leads to garbage out. We may not have intended to put 'garbage' in, but if we did – even unwittingly – then the computer will give you 'garbage' out. Not because the computer is a mean mongrel of a machine, but simply because that is how it is set up to operate!

Similarly with the Matrix. Hence we need to be very clear and specific about what it is we are desiring, and be very clear as to what we are actually focusing on when we do all these Co-creative processes. Therefore, be very watchful of your mind. Have a clear understanding of where your mind is at, and hence what you are *actually* 'financing' - despite what you may *think* you are 'financing'. You may think you are investing 'Creativity Credits' into your desire – but ironically may end up *maintaining the **lack** of that which you desire*. If we keep focusing on a problem in our lives; this lack of something – then we are also continuing to invest 'Creativity Credits' precisely into the continued presence *of this lack* in our lives.

Unfortunately, there is no way we can wriggle out of the reality that... 'what you focus on is what you get'. Continue to focus on what you are *lacking* in your lives and hey presto... that's exactly what you will then also continue to manifest; never mind how much that may *not* have been your *conscious* intention. Yet, far too often, when Co-creation is being discussed or taught, this subtle but utterly crucial point is not made clear, or simply is not fully understood by the 'teachers'. Remember again, 'what you focus on is what you get'! Not what you may have *meant* to focus on - a totally different scenario. This can't be said often enough.

In this sense, we have to become very dualistic in our thinking. We acknowledge, and know on one level that a lack – of car, money, relationship, job – whatever – does exists in our life. But once we know this – in one wrinkle of our brain – we must also in a sense see *beyond* this all too obvious reality, and keep focusing solely on what it is we desire. It's almost like a banking system. Seeing a zero credit balance in our account can be an incentive to start putting savings into the account. Similarly, from where we presently stand in our life, we can, and need to acknowledge whatever it is we feel we lack, but then *using* this 'state of lack', we now generate a clearer vision of what it is we *do* desire.

In other words, this situation of 'lack' actually helps to clarify what it is we desire. But once this 'lack' has alerted us to what it is we *do* want, then we also need to re-direct our focus away from that 'lack', and move on with the process. Unfortunately, all too often we do the opposite, and nevertheless keep 'investing' in the lack of what it is we desire, via the habitual thoughts and feelings associated with this lack.

This is a crucial point, and yet, so many people seem to find themselves stuck here. Therefore, at the risk of being boringly repetitive, let's hammer it home one more time! So let's say this as clearly as possible.

- A lack in our lives precisely generates a desire.
- Remaining focused on that lack – of partner, of money, of job, of house – whatever - also precisely guarantees the *continuation* of that *lack*.
- Remember, we manifest that which we focus on – *consciously or unconsciously*.
- Hence – once you have done the Co-creation process - it is so fundamentally important to become skilled at then focusing on our desire - *as if it absolutely, definitely, positively, totally, utterly has already manifested.*
- Practise the skill of being Aware of where your mind is at, and if you see yourself constantly going back to dwell on what you feel you are *lacking* in your life, then notice this; acknowledge it... and let it go. Don't feed it!

Co-creation - start small

When we first start using the concepts of Co-creativity, it's important to impress on people that this is about learning a new skill, and as such, it takes time, commitment and practise. It also doesn't make sense to go for the big things first. Don't try to manifest that perfect partner straight away. Instead,

Chapter 11 - Co-creativity - Further Explorations

focus initially on creating parking spaces; finding a specific, but unimportant kitchen item you've been searching for lately, etc. Then as your level of skill goes up – and that can take time – you go for bigger and more complex projects.

The other aspect about starting small, and setting up projects which are actually not all that important to you is that you are automatically more relaxed about 'The Process'. Such a state of mind will in turn be far more conducive to a rapid and successful manifestation of your desire. Then as you see the process does work in these smaller ways, this builds up a confidence about the entire Co-creation concept, making it less daunting to now move on to bigger projects. In turn this generates less doubt or resistance in you – especially on subtle levels.

Every one of us absolutely does have this skill, so it's more an issue of enhancing that skill. This is the case with anything else you may be trying to master in your life too. Aim too high initially, and you virtually doom yourselves to failure. It would be much better to start with the seemingly small and relatively unimportant things. And as you then *do* manifest these, your confidence grows, and your Inner Energetic resistances are less likely to be there to block the process.

Old pattern momentum

In Co-creativity, there is also this issue of 'Momentum'. Keep in mind that we are *all* caught up in patterns of negative thinking. These are precisely the basis for why so much of what we *don't* want has already manifested into our lives. Such negative thought patterns do have quite a lot of 'momentum' energy to them, and it can take a while to turn that around.

So when you first start out with Co-creation, all fired up from your reading, and eager to make change in your life, don't expect instant, miraculous change. It is not only possible, but indeed highly probable that such dysfunctional thinking-energies still do have a strong influence over what it is you are drawing or manifesting into your life. You absolutely need to realize how those old thought patterns you used to play with so much are still in a sense 'creating'. To some extent, they will still be manifesting 'undesired' things into your life, despite your recent big change in view, and despite now working more Consciously via the Co-creative concepts.

If you don't realize that this 'window of dysfunctional manifestation' will continue to occur for a while – guaranteed! - it becomes very easy to give up far too soon. It's exactly the same as deciding to go to the gym, after years of inactivity. You pump iron; run on this insane, endless 'pathway'; sweat your little heart out, and initially nothing much seems to happen. In fact, to begin with you might even feel worse! It takes quite a few weeks before you start to notice more endurance, and that your clothes are starting to feel looser on your body. But if after just one week or so of this gym 'torture', you assessed whether it was all worth it, then based on initial results... absolutely not! Lots of effort and nothing much to tell for it, other than a lot of pain and suffering.

It's yet another reason why during this initial period of time you do need to 'fake it till you make it', as the old energy momentum dissipates. There will be a lag phase before your new vibrational energy patterns, via your new thought patterns, start to kick in. How long this lag-phase lasts depends *totally* on how much you still allow yourself to 'rewind' to those old energy patterns and thoughts, play with them – and hence still investing 'Creativity Credits' into them.

That's why it has been said so many times now that this whole subject of Co-creativity is so much more than just manifesting 'things' into your life. It is far more the beginning of a powerful Journey of self discovery and Inner Consciousness Growth – with manifesting 'things' almost becoming a side issue.

Co-creativity is thankfully not immediate

There is another level to this issue of 'delay' around Co-creativity, which thankfully does exist on this earthly plane of reality. If every single thought we generated was immediately able to manifest, we would end up living in a total nightmare. At our stage of evolution, we actually desperately need some sort of 'delay mechanism', and the density of the Earth plane of reality provides just that; much like 'dampening rods' found in a nuclear reactor.

Think of a nuclear power station. The amount of potential energy inherent in one of these is absolutely frightening. Chernobyl has already given us a taste of what can happen if all that energy is released too quickly. There is a very real similarity which is equally applicable to Co-creation. Just as in a nuclear power station, where we absolutely do need those 'dampening rods' through which to keep the reactor stable, so too with the inherent power we can release via our minds – either constructively or destructively. Hence the amount of Energy which Co-creation could potentially release does need some sense of balance or control - otherwise chaos would ensue.

Chapter 11 - Co-creativity - Further Explorations

Manifestation 'previews' of your desires

When doing your Co-creation projects, you may notice one really interesting phenomenon. As you increasingly become resonant with what it is you desire, you may start to see examples of that desire manifesting into your reality... even if it is not yet quite available to you personally. For instance, your project may entail manifesting that specific partner into your life. Soon, you may well start seeing precisely the sort of person you would like to have as a partner, appearing in situations around you.

Yet, due to idiosyncrasies associated with that particular situation, you'll seem unable to make the desired connection. For instance, let's imagine you are traveling on a train. As your train goes by a particular station, you see someone who perfectly mirrors the sort of person you have specified in your Co-creation. They even make eye contact with you and smile in response. However, you're in the train, pulling out of the station... and they are on the platform looking at you! Not much chance of connecting.

In regard to noticing such situations appearing into your reality, but not quite achievable yet... don't despair. Choose to see it as a 'preview', rather than as... 'there goes my *only* chance to meet the person of my dreams'. Such 'previews' actually mean you are getting pretty good at your Co-creation, and that what you desire has in fact manifested into your reality. However, the fact that it is not quite there yet, in the sense of being able to actually connect with or claim it, also means that you are not yet quite 'on Station'.

There is still some 'static'. There is still something inside you which is preventing full resonance from occurring; and that is O.K. By the same token, it also proves that you are capable of manifesting exactly what it is you want, when using the technique of Co-creation. Even things you desire very much – which are usually the most difficult of all to manifest.

But these are usually also the desires which bring up some of the deepest issues within ourselves, around which we still need to grow and change. Such events are actually a powerful signal telling us we're on-target, but just a little bit more work to do, and soon your Co-creative desire will fully connect into your reality. You're almost there; don't give up. Just keep going a little bit longer, and your desire will be fully manifested.

'Yes, sure you say... nothing but pure coincidence'. O.K, so be skeptical. But remember that it is precisely this sort of internal mind-talk which so efficiently fuels those levels of doubt and negativity. This type of negative 'self-talk' could precisely be the 'static' keeping you 'off-Station' from your desire!

See the episode therefore, as an 'entrée' before the 'main meal'. You might like to take a second look at the 'menu' of what it is you wish to manifest, by comparing it to what *has* already manifested – even if not yet 'claimable'. Assess it carefully, and see if this is in fact exactly what you do want. Is there anything about this pre-manifestation you would like to now alter, so that when it really does manifest completely for your claiming, it is actually precisely what you had wanted? Luckily, at this stage you can still 'tweak' your visualization to make it even more specific.

So be excited and happy. Don't be disappointed. Besides, the happy feeling will be more in resonance with that Mantra we have been hammering home so often now, that... 'we need to create inside ourselves that feeling of *already* having what it is we desire *before* we get it'. Simply latch onto that sense of happiness; how you *have* succeeded... although there is still a little bit of extra work that needs to be done.

Co-creativity - need for much practise

Like all skills, there are stages to becoming increasingly skilled. To become a pilot, initially you need to learn about a whole range of other things besides what buttons or levers to use in the cockpit. There is the need to learn about navigation, engineering, principles of flight, meteorology, and so much more, before you even get into a plane. Similarly, to become a really skilled Co-creator, you do need to become proficient at recognizing which emotional state you are entertaining – and therefore investing in. You need to become increasingly accomplished at being able to shift into a broad range of emotional states with ease and rapidity. You need to become increasingly competent at recognizing Higher Self versus ego self modes of function, and increasingly expert at living from your Higher Self level.

And *then* you practise, practise and practise again, to increasingly define your desire in precisely the correct thought patterns and emotions, before releasing it into the Matrix. Next, you need to focus on creating and maintaining that precise emotional state which is resonant or congruent with what it is you desire to manifest into your life. So you can see that there are a whole series of steps and levels of training you need to put yourself through in this new venture called Conscious Co-creating.

Chapter 11 - Co-creativity - Further Explorations

Too many Creative Visualization books just seem to dive in at the deep end. Somehow they expect all of us to already be masters of these many different stages, which are crucial for effective Co-creation. Yet, for far too many people, even accepting we are capable of Co-creation is already a *huge* shift to make. Such fundamentally new ideas and concepts will need time to get used to, aside from then actually starting to use this power.

Expecting people to be instant experts in Co-creation is a bit like assuming someone who has never encountered a computer, let alone having any understanding of the Web, to somehow miraculously know how to use this technology. Obviously ridiculous. But that's unfortunately what a lot of people espousing Co-creativity do unconsciously expect from those they are teaching. To acquire such computing skills will take time and lots of practise. So too with Co-creativity.

Never give up

It's terribly important in this Co-creativity process, to never give up. It's like any skill; if you give up after the first few attempts, you are *guaranteed* failure, and then the entire process is definitely doomed. If you keep on trying, this at least gives you the potentiality of success. Imagine when you were initially learning to ride your bike. If you had given up the first time you had fallen off your bike, obviously you would never have reached a point where you were finally successful.

It is exactly the same in a sense, when learning how to 'ride your mind'. When you were learning to ride your bike, and in order to stay balanced, you initially had to learn how to co-ordinate your muscles, and a whole lot of other physical and mental aspects of your body. It's the same situation with Co-creation. You need to learn the skill of co-coordinating your mental and emotional, as well as your imagery capacities in order to correctly and effectively visualize what it is you desire. Initially this all takes a lot of Awareness, and a lot of focus. Yet, as with learning to ride a bike, eventually it does get to a point where you can do all this automatically - when you have continued to practise it to that point of perfection.

Exercise
- Explain why it is fundamentally important to make Inner change first if we expect to have any lasting effect on our outer reality.
- Explain the difference between the role the ego and Higher Self play in Co-creation.

Summary of thoughts thus far
- Everyone *can* visualize; it's as easy as closing your eyes, and bringing to mind what your bedroom looks like – for instance.
- We need to focus on creating *Inner* change first, before we can realistically expect long term resolution to problems in our *external* reality.
- As humans, we constantly desire 'things'. Yet if we look for the *underlying* thread that motivates these needs, it would appear what we're really after is a *State of Being* - one where we feel more complete, joyful or fulfilled, deep within ourselves.
- An *outer* person or situation does *trigger* off that Inner experience of joy. But we then make the huge mistake of believing that this *outer* situation is the *source* of, and *fundamental* reason for our *Inner* experience.
- In that sense, all these external, more materially orientated things we seek so relentlessly are in the end nothing but Illusion. We need to realize that such goals are ultimately only the shadow of what we really want.
- 'You get what you want when you no longer need it'. This is based on the reality that we need to create Inner change before we can sort out our outer reality.
- Co-creation can become a potent Journey through which to increase our level of Consciousness. *That* is actually the true goal of Co-creation. Fulfilling and manifesting your desires is but a happy 'side-effect'.
- The entire thrust of Co-creation is to increasingly learn to come from the Higher Self rather than from the ego self.
- Coming from ego mode when Co-creating, inevitably allows for more of the negative ego-based emotions – such as doubt, lack of self-esteem, etc. – to sabotage the process.
- Ego's legitimate and crucial role is to outline the desire, set the intention, and then release it *totally* to the Higher Self.

Chapter 11 - Co-creativity - Further Explorations

- As long as the ego thinks, subtly or not, that *it* is doing the manifestation, then the process is inevitably sabotaged to some extent.
- Higher Self provides the portal and the capacity to directly tap into the Universal Source of all that Creative Energy - *through* which to manifest our desires.
- Joy is the ultimate 'fuel' which drives the Co-creative process. Joy, in a sense, is the 'bricks and mortar' of what it takes to Co-create.
- The problem is that fear is also a most powerful 'fuel' which activates and drives Co-creation – consciously or unconsciously.
- Fear is the primary operative of the ego, compared to joy or Love being the primary Energy of the Higher Self.
- Co-creation happens whether we know it or not. The only choice we therefore have is to either continue to allow it to occur *unconsciously* or to actively participate in a *Conscious* and *intentional* manner.
- Using the concept of the Hologram, we humans can be seen as a window into the Infinite possibilities of that Greater Energetic Phenomenon or Whole, The Field, The Matrix, God – whatever you wish to call it.
- We can visualize all we want, but we need to be in resonance with our desire before it can possibly manifest into physical reality.
- Generating the right feeling is crucial to the success of Co-creation. We need to generate that feeling of already having what it is we desire – even before it has manifested. A bit of a mind-twister!
- When it comes to generating 'feeling' within the Co-creative process, it's not so much about the *intensity* of the feeling we can generate, as the *integrity* of that feeling.
- One potent way of learning how to focus the necessary feeling within Co-creation, is to learn to live in the moment.
- Abraham claims that the Universe provides us with our request **the moment we even formulate it in our minds.**
- However, to manifest it, can only occur *when we change our internal Energetics to be in resonance with already having our desire manifested in our lives.*
- The best way to be successful in Co-creation is to do it from a space of 'effortless effort' – a seeming contradiction in terms.

- Another level to Co-creation is the need to 'save' up enough 'attractor credits', till we have sufficient 'currency' with which to 'buy' or draw our desire from the Matrix, into our reality.

- A primary Law of Co-creation states, 'what you focus on is what you get'. If we therefore keep harking back to our desire - *from the perspective of not having it* - then we are actually focusing on the *lack* of what it is we desire – and that's precisely more of what we'll manifest!

- When first starting Co-creation, it's important to realize that this is about learning a new skill, and as such, it takes time, commitment and practise. It also doesn't make sense to go for the big things first. Start small and build up.

- As you do your Co-creation process, 'Co-created previews' may start occurring in your life. See these as a sign that you are getting close to manifesting the 'full package'.

- With Co-creation, you need to learn many skills, which involve co-coordination of your mental, emotional, as well as your imagery capabilities, before being able to successfully manifest what it is you visualize.

REFERENCES

1. Bible, King James Version, Matthew 7:5.

2. Ibid. Matthew 6:33.

3. Hicks, Esther & Jerry. *Ask and it is Given – learning to manifest your desires,* Hay House, Sydney, 2004.

4. Harris, Bill. *Centerpointe Research Institute,* Beaverton, Oregon. 'Holosync' technology available from: www.centerpoint.com

CHAPTER 12

CO-CREATIVITY – TECHNIQUES

The universe is change; our life is what our thoughts make it

Marcus Aurelius Antoninus

Techniques - step 1 - setting goals

If we want to do Co-creation effectively, we need to clearly focus on what our goals are. Most of us are just flopping around in our day-to-day discomforts and sufferings, without doing anything particularly useful about getting out of our less than optimum situations either.

So the first thing on the agenda is to become very clear as to where we are at; and yet not judging it. We need a starting point, before we can effectively create a destination point. Even if our present life situation, our starting point, is rather full of things and situations which are giving us less than joy, we can be grateful for this, simply because such circumstances can be used most effectively to catalyze us in setting very clear goals about where we *do* want to go. We've already touched on this aspect to Co-creation in the previous chapter, but let's explore it more fully now.

Using our pain to focus on what to manifest.

Abraham discusses this concept a lot in his various communications. It's about understanding that you can actually use your suffering as a spring-board from which to re-orientate yourself. Ask yourself questions like.... 'What is this uncomfortable or painful situation in my life telling me about what I might also be lacking in my life'? 'What is it I really want; don't seem to have, but which is causing me this discomfort'?

In this sense, we initially use our pain or discomfort to become Conscious Witness to where we are at in our lives. Next, we use this Awareness as a means of re-orientating ourselves, and defining more clearly, more Consciously and more specifically, precisely what it is we *do* want in our life. And then we start focusing on *that,* rather than the *lack* of that.

Don't focus on 'fixing what is broke' – just see the alternate state you desire.

When you see something in your life you are not happy with, and would like to change through Co-creation, don't then focus on trying to fix what is broken. This is a critically important point if you want the Co-creative process to work positively for you.

Using Co-creation, it's not so much about trying to *undo* the things in your life you no longer want. Instead, we follow a set of procedures, where we firstly acknowledge, and then allow what is broken or not functioning, or not pleasing, or not happiness-causing, to be there in our life. Don't try to wrestle with it, change it or fix it. Instead, re-orientate your focus, and simply *think* of what it is you *do* want. For instance, if you are ill, don't focus on getting rid of your symptoms. Don't even think about *how* you can become well; *how* this would be done step at a time. Instead, merely visualize yourself as healthy. What would you be doing if you had all the energy you desired? If you had the sense of wellness you are wishing for? Just visualize those *end* points.

Never get involved with the details of *how* you would get to those end points. That is not our business as Co-creators. We need to remember that the mechanisms governing the process of Co-creation are *not* of this plane; they are in a Timeless Plane, and therefore not governed by the same Laws of Time as we know it here. In other words, Co-creation actually occurs *beyond* the Time/Space level of reality.

Change begins within us, but the mechanism for such change lie beyond us.

This is how Eckhart Tolle explains where and how change occurs within the Co-creative process. In other words, *how* your desires are 'manufactured' or

Chapter 12 - Co-creativity - Techniques

created is the function of the Higher realms; the Matrix; the Source. It looks after all such details. Your sole contribution, the only 'thing' you need to do in Co-creation is to clearly define and visualize in as detailed a way as you can, precisely what it is you *do* want. If you're in debt, then *within your process* of visualization, you don't initially figure out *how* all your debts are to be paid. If you don't have a house, you don't try to figure out *how* you are going to find your dream house. Simply see yourself with plenty of money; writing out cheques to pay your bills. See yourself already moving into that house of your dreams.

If you are alone, and wish you had a relationship, don't worry about *how* or *where* you are going to find this special person. Only focus on seeing yourself with the end goal you desire - in this instance, the 'person of your dreams'. Imagine them clearly already in your life. Visualize yourself and them in a whole range of life situations; waking up together in the morning; going to bed together at night; going out to eat at your favorite restaurant; going out to the movies together; visiting friends together.

The hardest part of Co-creation is the reality that the unwanted situations we find ourselves presently in, are also those creating the least resonant emotions capable of manifesting what we *do* want into our life. For example, if you are heavily in debt, and you have a huge pile of bills needing to be paid, you will be frustrated, worried, anxious and possibly fearful. All these emotions will be the *source* for desiring money in your life to pay these bills.

So they will certainly be the *initiating* factor in your reality which then generates the new desires. But the emotional state you are presently in – with all those bills for instance – is also precisely the Energetic state that is least able to allow what it is you *do* want to then manifest into your life. It is *so* important to see this rather ironic twist to Co-creation. In this example, the emotional state you are in is hinged on your *lack* of money. It is all an expression – Energetically – of what you *don't* have in your life at the moment; in this example, having enough money to pay all your bills.

Remember, Co-creation is all about you getting what you focus on. So if you continue – even unconsciously - to remain in these emotional states of 'lack', in turn generating emotions such as anxiety, fear or desperation, then those emotions can only ever keep feeding precisely whatever it is you already have in your life - but *don't* want.

In Co-creation, you truly need to be offering a state which is Energetically resonant with your desire. And this is where it can become difficult, because you need to initially play a game; a mind-game. Firstly, you need to visualize exactly what it is you want; for instance money. You then have to generate precisely those emotional states - *as if you already had the money*. In other words, feeling abundant; feeling enormously relieved; feeling in control of your financial situation; feeling safe from the debt collectors. All because you are now able to pay these piles of bills.

By focusing on your desire, clearly and specifically, and continuing to hold it in your sights, then what you are now focusing on is more likely than not to start manifesting into your life. The Laws of Co-creation guarantee it. Eventually this process will replace whatever it is that is presently causing your discomfort, pain or lack. This will happen – not necessarily in one giant leap – but more likely one step at a time. As you increasingly learn to clearly resonate your Energy from your state of unwellness or sense of 'lack of', to that sense of 'already having what you want', you can't help but be successful. Initially, re-orientating our mindset to such a different way of perceiving our reality can be rather tricky, but as with any skill it is something we can hone with plenty of practise.

Techniques – step 2 – day-dreaming your desire

The next stage in manifesting your desire is to get yourself into a state of day-dreaming about what it is you wish to generate into your reality. Here you wander around in your mind's eye, previewing your wish; playing with the many variables; altering something here; strengthening something there; erasing something else altogether. This part of the process can be time-consuming, but also fun, creative and very dynamic. The *overall* image you are playing with will be in a constant state of flux and change as you wander around and play with ideas. Metaphorically, this is like using your mind as a 'normal' light beam; not as a laser. This is not yet the stage at which you need to focus that light beam. That doesn't happen till later.

The initial process of 'daydreaming' is a really essential component to the overall process of Co-creation. However, it is only a precursor to the real act of Co-creating, where you become focused, and then release your desire into the Higher level of Creativity, or Matrix. Yet, it is amazing how many people doing Co-creation mistake this former process of wandering around in daydreaming, as *the* act of Co-creation.

Chapter 12 - Co-creativity - Techniques

Daydreaming stage – like waiting on the platform for a train

But daydreaming isn't enough. Although it may give you ideas of all the components you'd like to have as part of your ultimate manifestation, nevertheless, by its very nature such daydreaming is also highly *un*focused. Therefore it doesn't have sufficient 'power' behind it, with which to 'connect' into the Metaphysical Dimension or Matrix in any productive way. So a lot of people may be playing around in this initial arena of Co-creation, and then wondering why nothing manifests. It's a bit like sitting on a station platform, waiting for the train to take you to your holiday destination. You may well be sitting there daydreaming of how it will be at your final destination, and what you'll be doing there. But it's not till you actually get onto the train, and travel to your designated destination, that you then really experience it all in its physical reality.

So it is with this Co-creative process too. In the initial stage, you are only playing around in the 'waiting room'. It *is* a very valid and necessary component to the overall process of finally experiencing the reality of being at your 'holiday destination'. However, actually getting onto the train necessitates a very distinct, focused set of actions, in order to do it successfully. So too does Co-creation equally require a moment of 'stepping onto the train', which is likewise a focused, brief moment of activity.

Techniques – step 3 - focused laser beam sent into the Matrix

Enter stage three of the Co-creative process. In stage two you were playing around with a whole set of thoughts, ideas and images. Next, you start to focus or coalesce these individual image components into a more whole or holographic image. Now you create a 'package' as it were, of precisely what it is you desire, climaxing into a very focused 'laser beam' which can be used to shoot your desire into the Higher Metaphysical Dimensions or Matrix.

Co-creation – computer metaphor

Another analogy would be a computer, where you create an essay of exactly what it is you want. You write it out; add and subtract from it; 'cut and paste' to your heart's content, until you're completely happy with the final result. Then you 'save' this 'essay' in a 'zipped' format, prior to then pulsing it - in that brief, focused moment of punching just one key on the keyboard - down into the hard-drive; into the Matrix.

For maximum effect, pulsing it into the Matrix does need to be associated with a strong, undeniable feeling of absolutely *knowing* that what it is you desire *is* already present in your reality. Even if you can't quite see it yet; that's the crucial twist! But with a successful 'launch' also comes the need for a very clean and sharp release. Otherwise, you leave Energy 'siphon-tubes' 'sticking' to your desire-image, distorting the coherency of that pulse, or even totally bleeding it empty. That would be a bit like baking a cake; putting it into the oven, and then every few minutes opening the oven door to see just how far it has already risen. Well, that cake isn't ever going to get cooked!

So to summarize again: in the overall process of Co-creation, initially you:-
- Go through a stage of playing with ideas.
- Then you move easily and smoothly into condensing all those images and ideas into a tight, concise, almost holographic 'package'.
- Next, you send this 'package' into that Metaphysical Dimension - or what Gregg Braden calls The Matrix.
- Finally, you ensure you make a rapid, clear and clean release from that 'package', and get on with your daily life.

Visualization – 'tether your horse '

Having looked at some of the basic mechanics of how to do a Co-creative exercise, we also need to explore a few other vital concepts. Such ideas will ensure your Co-creative projects manifest into your life, in as productive and positive way as possible. There is a saying, mentioned before, which bears repeating... 'Tether your horse and trust in God'. In other words, we need to trust that God will look after us; facilitating certain things to occur in our lives. But the other side of the coin is that we also need to be pro-active in whatever *we* can do on *our* level, to manifest or achieve our goals. Remember the word **CO**-creation. This process or technique is definitely about a *co-operative* venture.

At the end of the day, Co-creativity is an invitation to get beyond our victimness; to grow up from our Spiritual 'childhood'; to become a more Spiritually mature human being. Not always groveling; not belittling ourselves in front of God, but by the same token not aggrandizing ourselves either. Rather, we need to recognize that if Christ's promise is true, and we are indeed made in the image of God, (think back to the Hologram metaphor, where we humans can be seen to contain a small 'chip' inside us, of the Primary Hologram) then this has important repercussions for us.

It is indeed a fine line to tread, and it is equally possible that some will fall off that tight-rope. Either back into victim-hood and self-repression - where a lot of religions would prefer you to be - or into self-deluded aggrandizement or 'god-psychosis'. But that is the nature of life; risk! To sit safely in a corner and to hide our talents, does not serve us as Creations of God either. Again, there is an interesting quote from the Bible, which tends to correlate to this point. In Luke 11:33 it states... *'No one, when he has lit a lamp, puts it in a secret place or under a basket, but on a lamp-stand, that those who come in may see the light'.* [2]

Life is all about risk. Each one of us takes quite big risks on a daily basis; every time we step into our car; onto a bus; a train or plane. Yet this does not cause us as a society to totally ban all these methods of transport. We use these means of getting around with the unspoken understanding that risks are involved. And we accept these risks, because they are far outweighed by the overall benefits. So too with the use of Co-creativity.

It's true that there are some risks involved in playing with this technique, and some people may abuse this process, possibly harming themselves. But this is no reason to then prevent every single human being from accessing this powerful knowledge. Indeed, the harm done by preventing such overall empowerment of humanity far outweighs the possible damage it may do to the un-wise few. Therefore, as in the example of using our various forms of transport, we should use Co-creativity wisely. We also need to understand that it is a very powerful method through which to live our lives, allowing much Consciousness Growth, and many ways through which to improve our lives. Not just personally but most importantly, on a communal level too.

'For my Highest good and through joy'

As with so many other things in life, and certainly with this God-given gift, there also comes a responsibility, not just to 'invest' in this gift, but also to use it wisely. Along those lines, as much as you've been encouraged in this book to empower yourself with this inherent human capacity to Co-create, nevertheless we also need to add a dash of caution here. In accepting that we can manifest *co-operatively*, we also do need to trust in a Higher Level of Awareness; a Source of Wisdom which knows exactly when it's a good time for our desire to manifest - or whether it should even manifest at all.

In this entire game of Co-creation, we need to accept that as clever as we may see ourselves, we are still human. Although made of the same substance, the 'wave' is by no means equal to the 'ocean'. Therefore there is an automatic limit to our ability to fully and comprehensively perceive how our desire may or may not actually be for our Highest good, within the entire context of our lives.

Keeping this important point in mind, we might want to add in an extra step to our Co-creative ventures. To be on the safe side, insert to each Co-creative project, the injunction... *'Be it for my Highest Good, and through joy'*. See this step as a very fundamental, critical and extraordinarily important basis from which to *always* do any Co-creativity project you might wish to engage in. This approach or attitude towards Co-creation does allow you to be more relaxed about it all.

On one level, you can totally believe you have not just the right, but indeed the capacity to be a Co-creator. You can also totally accept that the process of Co-creation does work, if... 'used as directed'. However, you're also acknowledging that there may be aspects to your desire, which you – from your human perspective - are just not Aware enough of, and which could create more harm than good in your life.

High intention - low attachment

As Jack Canfield states in an interview with Barry Goss, [3] it is important to do our utmost in making our Co-creation project come to fruition, but to also have a minimal sense of *attachment* to its manifestation. Similarly, we may need to accept that the 'Source' or 'Universe' may have a better understanding as to what may ultimately be for our Highest good.

The reality is that from a Higher perspective, what it is we desire may actually not be so good for us at all. Now some people may get quite angry about this, reverting to childhood mode, stamping their feet, and demanding that what they want *must* manifest. And it can. But be careful what you wish for! You could end up with a situation in your life which creates more pain and trouble than you had bargained for. Hence the invocation - 'For my Highest Good *and through joy*'; not suffering. If you wish to see this via a Christian perspective, then it gets back to the caveat... *'Thy Will be Done'*.

Let's look at an example to really bring this point home. There was a person who had desperately wanted money – and a lot of it too. So they did their Co-creative process, but ignored the 'For my Highest Good' part of it. Well,

Chapter 12 - Co-creativity - Techniques

they did get their money – and heaps of it, but only after surviving a horrific accident, which put them into hospital for nine months, with the need for multiple surgeries, huge medical expenses and much pain.

Yes, they did finally get a *huge* compensation payout – and again after a lot more strife and stress caused by having to go through the Court system. Mmmmmmm! The slight humbling of attitude; the few seconds it would take to include that strong invocation... 'for my Highest Good', actually looks relatively simple, easy and very sensible! Certainly, when compared to what that person had to go through to finally get what they wanted. Co-creation is an extraordinarily powerful process, and does need to be used with wisdom and care. So do be careful what you wish for... and why not put in that 'safety rider'?

Present versus past tense

A very important point that needs to be understood is that all your Co-creative thoughts and wording need to definitely be in the *Present* tense; not past or future. There is a saying that the 'future never comes', and in regard to Co-creation this is absolutely correct.

So if you are doing your Co-creation with a wording, or even an Energy about getting your desire in the future... *then that is precisely where it will stay.* Unreachable; locked into the future. For instance, we may word our desire along the lines of... 'I would so love to have a good job'; 'It would be great to have good health.....' Such wording however, puts it more in the realm of the future compared to putting it more directly in the present... 'I am enjoying my wonderful new job'; 'it feels so good to be back in excellent health....'

So do be very Aware of what tense you are doing your Co-creation process in. Always keep it in the present tense – even though on logical, rational levels it obviously doesn't make sense, since you are Co-creating for something you don't *yet* have. Nevertheless, rational or not, such a 'mind-twist' is crucial for the Co-creative process to work. In this case, don't try to figure it out; just ensure you always stick to using wording in the present tense, and you can expect it to work.

Many different avenues of communication to Higher Self

When you first start to do Co-creation, there is a whole range of techniques or rituals which can help empower the process, and several of these will be discussed later in this chapter. As you get more experienced, you won't need all these props, and the entire process can be done so much more quickly and efficiently, simply in your mind. By the same token, if you really enjoy some of these 'props' or rituals, then by all means continue using them for as long as you like. They definitely won't detract from the final result. And if they give you a sense of empowerment, they will indeed enhance the process.

It's a bit like being engaged in data transfer between offices across the planet. One way is to write it all down in a letter; type it out; put it in an envelope; go to the Post Office; stand in queue for half an hour; go through all the transactions to buy a stamp; find yourself the Post Box... and then wait god knows how long for that letter to go through the Postal sorting system. Finally it gets sent to the airport; loaded onto a plane... you're getting the idea no doubt! Or you simply pick up the phone, dial the international number directly to your boss at Head Office and simply tell them – quickly and efficiently – the contents of what is in your letter. Sooooo much easier and efficient! But either way, the information still gets to your boss at Head Office.

In the same way, ultimately you don't have to go through all the various rituals and routines, to manifest what it is you desire in your reality. You will become so skillful that you can take the safety wheels off the bike and ride without them. Ultimately one gets to the point where a person can then manifest like the Eastern Guru, Sai Baba for instance, who is reputed to be able to manifest a number of physical things instantly, and out of so-called 'thin air'. However, don't necessarily expect this level of proficiency to happen overnight; perhaps not even in your lifetime. Nevertheless, 'go for it'... and see what happens. As Jack Canfield explains, it's better to come from a mind-space where you have high intentions, but low attachment to the outcome.

Co-creation – still a need to remain realistic

In that saying of 'tether your horse and trust in God', it may be more appropriate to actually reverse it, with the emphasis being more on trusting *first* in God and *then* tethering your 'horse'. By the same token, we also need to do our little bit, especially in the field of Healing, for instance. Health issues are definitely an arena where Co-creation can be surprisingly successful. Here, we invoke Healing on the Higher level, from where we can subsequently alter our present 'reality' of ill-health. This can happen even to the point of tumors disappearing – a more frequent phenomenon than medicine will acknowledge. However, we also need to back up this Metaphysical approach to the problem – cancer

Chapter 12 - Co-creativity -Techniques

for instance - by more earthly or physical levels of intervention, be that naturopathic, medical or a bit of both.

There is no point in continuing to live a life that is fundamentally very unhealthy, and thus understandably the basis of a present health issue... and then expect a magical, quick-fix Healing. Or doing your Co-creative work, but then once Healed, expecting to be able to maintain that former unhealthy approach to life, and get away with it further down the line. The reality is that without an accompanying Inner change to our beliefs or perspectives on how to be healthy, we're just as likely to manifest a relapse. Or in time to come, to generate another disease, still driven by the previous Inner dynamic.

So we do need to 'tether our horse'. In this example, where we are discussing health issues, it would involve backing up our Metaphysical, Co-creative approach with an equally active program of altering diet, taking certain nutrients, herbs, or whatever is seen as necessary. You need to ensure that you are at least also doing something pro-actively and materially to maintain future good health.

Gratefulness as a powerful way to connect to Source.

One point to be Aware of is that having a sense of gratitude for things in your life is one of the quickest, easiest, most powerful ways to connect with Source Energy; to Higher Self Mode or to the Matrix – however you want to conceptualize it. Hence, before even starting to practise manifesting things in your life, it would be a really good idea to initially spend some time – be that several weeks or even several months - just learning how to become grateful for so many things in your life. Through such activity, this raises your own vibrational status to a closer alignment with Source. Such a greater sense of resonance then automatically allows what it is you wish to manifest more powerfully, quickly and accurately.

How to do the Gratitude Meditation

Using this concept of gratitude can be done via a form of meditation or ritual. For instance, you can set aside some time to focus, and go through whole lists of what you are grateful for. However, another very useful technique is to become Conscious and focused enough during the day, to give thanks... as you are going through your daily activities. You can start to incorporate this practice into many areas of your life. It's not even that you have to set aside a specific five or ten minutes of your precious daily life schedule to do this.

For instance, as you are cooking dinner, this provides a wonderful opportunity to internally voice your gratitude - that you have a house; within which you have a kitchen; within which you have a stove; on which you can cook food; that you have pots and pans *within* which to cook the meal; that you have a fridge to store your food; that you have a table at which you can sit to eat your meal; that you have easy access to electricity with which to light, heat or cool the room, etc. So many good things we just take for granted in our affluent, Western culture!

If you are brushing your teeth, give thanks for the fact that you live in a country or situation where you have running water; that you have access to good dental care; that you still have your teeth. If not... be grateful that you live in a country where it's possible to get a good set of false teeth! If you are cleaning the house, give thanks that you have a house; a vacuum cleaner; an electrical supply – and so much more. It's actually not all that hard to find things to be grateful for. It's just that in the West we take far too much for granted – as if everyone else in the entire world also has these things. The reality is that the majority don't.

Another opportunity is when you are in the car sitting at the lights, which provides some odd, free moments. When you are standing in the queue at the supermarket or the bank, you've got a few moments of otherwise 'wasted time'. When you are doing a range of routine, daily chores which don't really need your full focused, conscious attention, you can be elsewhere in your mind, going through a list of things you can be grateful for.

Some people have commented that surely such a daily procedure would become unbearably boring. Indeed it could! One way to help keep the process fresh is to be as fully 'present' in the Moment as possible, while giving thanks, rather than just rattling through a list of things. Another angle to keep in mind is that we can be grateful for even having another day within which we still have all these lists of things to be thankful for! Remember, nothing is automatically guaranteed in life – other than death; but far too often we tend to live our lives as if what we have is guaranteed to continue.

Another twist to the 'Gratitude Meditation' is to go through the list of all the things we feel we are genuinely grateful for. Then right at the end, when you have really got yourself into the swing of it, and you have a bit of momentum going, now also start affirming and giving thanks for the things you are Consciously desiring and visualizing for; even though they have not yet manifested! Because at this point, you will already have built up an enormous sense of *genuine* gratefulness *for what you really do have*. Hopefully, by tying this in with your Co-creative projects, this genuine sense of gratefulness from the Gratitude Meditation will then spill over to those things you *expect* to manifest into your life.

Nothing to be grateful for? Try the local hospital wards!

And if you truly can state that there is nothing much in your life you can find to be grateful for, or you generally feel so terribly hard done by, then you're hereby challenged to go to any ward in any hospital. Just walk around, and see the many things people are going through in *their* life - which you don't. Simply by dint of the fact that you were able, more likely than not, to freely *walk* there, while they are *stuck* there. In no time at all, you may find yourself with quite a long list of things to be grateful for. Or you'll realize that life hasn't been so harsh with you afterall.

Sometimes we can become very pre-occupied with our own miseries, to the point where it seems we're the only ones who are suffering so dreadfully. But ultimately, everything is relative, and using this technique will quickly allow us to find even a few things for which we can indeed be grateful. Perhaps as simple as the fact that you still have sight, can walk, can talk, still have all your limbs – despite the joints aching.

It is easy enough therefore, to start incorporating this technique or practice into your daily life, even if initially it's only in those occasional moments, scattered throughout the day. But as time goes by, you'll find that you will actually want to set aside five or ten minutes of quiet, focused, meditative time. During such quiet moments, it becomes much easier to focus your entire mental attention and Energy into this 'Gratitude Meditation' practice. This in turn will allow you to raise your vibration to the inherent and most primary quality engendered by Source; by Higher Self – which is a Vibration of Love itself.

The 'Gratitude Meditation' can thus become an on-going daily prayer of sorts, but one which is also constantly shifting our Energy point into a Higher vibration or pattern. It does so simply because a positive and grateful focus automatically raises our Energy, whereas being critical and negative automatically decreases our Energy. If you want to look at it in the sense of

'Energy credits', being non-critical, being grateful, increases the Energetic 'bank balance' of 'credits'. This in turn then provides you with a lot more to 'invest' or spend on Co-creative projects.

However, if you are constantly critical; constantly miserable, then in a sense you are going more into an 'over-draft' situation with your Co-creative 'credit account'. In this way it becomes a lot harder, not just to 'finance' your Co-creative projects, but also to Energetically drawn them into your reality, via the concept of Energetic resonance. Critical, negative emotional states are like a repelling magnetic force, keeping what it is we want at bay. Being in a positive, non-critical state is turning the 'magnet' into a more attracting Energy status. This therefore allows for a greater ability to be in resonance with what we want, and thereby allows it to manifest.

Service as a means to get to Higher Self mode

Service to humanity in one form or another is a powerful technique through which to increasingly live from Higher Self mode. It works by helping to move us beyond the ego mode, with its endless critical analysis of anything and everything, as well as its tendency to be self-absorbed with our own 'problems'. Service forces us to step beyond all this self-focus and absorption, giving our full attention instead to the 'other' needing our help. Service to others is about a selfless, voluntary giving of care, by action or just by listening and being present for another, rather than being of service because of the 'brownie points' we feel we might score as people see us do all these 'good deeds'. 'Gee whiz, aren't I good to do this for Johnnie' or 'I hope they appreciate what I'm doing for them'. Or the power-tripper's version... 'they sure owe me big-time now'!

Often these latter ways of doing 'Service' have strings attached – if not ropes. So coming from a genuinely caring perspective of Service allows us to shift our focus away from ourselves, and any possible ego-driven sense of self-pity or over-focus on our own life issues. It's certainly not about invalidating whatever problems and sufferings may be occurring in our own life. However, if we find that we have a tendency to get rather too self-absorbed in our own problems, and wish to distract ourselves from this pattern, then Service can be a powerful means to do so. The bottom-line is that the more we can focus our attention away from ego-driven issues; opening our heart with compassion, the more we will find ourselves operating from Higher Self Mode.

Chapter 12 - Co-creativity -Techniques

Gratitude as a powerful energy converter

Doing the 'Gratitude Meditation' is not just about rattling off a list of things we can be thankful for. It's about changing the dynamics of our internal Energy status, which in turn creates a much more powerful and productive platform from which to do our Co-creation. So it's about using every tiny scrap of something good we feel we can genuinely be grateful for, as a way to start re-orientating our Energy, away from anger, bitterness, disappointment, disillusionment, fear or whatever it might be. By keeping focused on what we *can* be grateful for, we start to invest in and pile up our 'positive credits', which then start to create – like any investment – a return in a positive way as well. But it takes time; it takes effort; it takes focus; it takes commitment; it takes perseverance.

But if we keep that concept in mind, step by step, we can then walk our way out of what may seem to be an impasse, tragedy or other painful situation. In this way, you can move yourself – albeit slowly – into a brighter life situation and reality. In the end it's all about 'balancing the books', via our 'inputs' versus our 'outputs'. Continuing to fight, and in a sense hang onto the pain of where you may be at, ironically also becomes exactly what you keep drawing into your reality.

There's that damn basic Law of Co-creation poking its nose in – again! So it's not about denying where you are at. You definitely need to honor that - but also focus on coming to a Space of being at peace with it, rather than constantly fighting it. In this way you can start focusing on turning your Energy around, an inch at a time, to crawl your way out of your present dilemma. But nevertheless you are then moving – and moving increasingly *away* from your pain or suffering. Coming to a Space of peace in regard to whatever is ailing you in life at least provides a crack in the door from which the possibility of escaping your suffering becomes more probable.

Simple? Perhaps just too plain basic to deal with the magnitude of your pain or suffering? Well, so it may seem. But don't underestimate the power of simple gratitude, done as a daily 'prayer' or affirmation. From such humble beginnings, you actually create a powerful platform from which the good things you wish for can more easily manifest into your reality.

Subtle mind-speak negating the 'Gratitude Meditation'

However, there is one delicate point with which we do need to conclude, in regard to the 'Gratitude Meditation'. Be really Aware of subtle Inner 'mind-speak' which can go on in the periphery of your mind. For instance, you may be giving thanks for having a car or a house. Then very sneakily and very subtly – in the background – there is this little inner voice that says 'yeah… till the car breaks down… or gets stolen… or someone crashes into it and writes it off'.

So be aware that there can be this negating Energy which can sneak in from the peripheries of your consciousness, and in a sense sabotage the 'Gratitude Meditation' process. As you become clear and sensitive enough to perhaps notice this going on, don't despair. Just observe it; don't process it; don't fight it. Just let it be, thereby not feeding it either, and with time it will fade away. Remember, what you fight… you feed. Certainly within the mental sphere.

'Delete' button

There is a powerful technique which can come in very handy in such above situations. On your computer, you have a 'Delete' key. Simply hit that, and whatever you have on your screen is deleted. So too within your mind. Every time you notice certain negative or less-than-constructive thoughts entering where you don't want them, then don't automatically go into 'fight mode' as your first and only response. All you have to do is to acknowledge, and then 'Delete' such thoughts. So easy! Then refocus on something else. Take the attention away from it; don't struggle with it.

Yellow rose technique

The Metaphysical teacher Louise Hay has an interesting technique she uses to help refocus her attention away from thoughts or feelings she chooses not to engage in. For her, a yellow rose is apparently the epitome of beauty. She finds it a powerful focal point upon which to turn her conscious mind, in order to distract her from other negative mind states she wishes to avoid, and thus not empower. So if she found herself in certain feeling or thought patterns, and wished to break from them, she would simply switch her mind onto the mental image of a beautiful yellow rose. The interesting thing is that for the average human, it is quite difficult to remain simultaneously fully focused on two separate mental patterns, thoughts or feelings. So it is either the negative situation or the 'yellow rose' – in Louise Hay's case.

But it doesn't matter at all what you choose as your 'distracting focus' or 'yellow rose' alternative. It could be to place your attention into some part of your body, really feeling the stretch of muscles there; sense of air on the skin – or whatever. Or in your mind, you latch onto a piece of your favorite tune. Or, if convenient, do a few Tai Chi or Yoga movements. Or you bring to mind your favorite spot somewhere on this Earth: a beautiful mountain top, watching the sunset; or sitting on that tropical island, drink in hand, enjoying the movement of the palm leaves in the gentle breeze. Whatever serves you; but you're sure to be able to conjure up some pleasant and powerful memory which you can use as your alternative to a 'yellow rose'.

For those who are more kinesthetic, you may be able to distract your mind better by going into your body, via Tai Chi or similar activities. For those who are more auditory, you may find yourself choosing the music option as the positive distraction. For you visual people out there, no doubt you'll bring to mind that favorite scene. Whatever works for you is fine.

But it is important to create that mental distraction 'vignette' ahead of time. Once you're in the middle of a mental pattern you wish to divert yourself from, it's not going to work to *then* figure out what you're going to use to distract yourself. Do spend some time beforehand to generate the ideal image, sounds or body focus which you can then instantly 'download' into your Awareness as you become conscious of the negative mental pattern you find yourself in. As you start using this technique, you'll find you can access your 'distraction vignette', quickly, clearly and without any mental fumbling.

Another way to use a Mantra

However, another very useful technique with which to control or by-pass an excessively chattering mind, whirling with endless thoughts you just can't seem to get rid of, is to use a Mantra.

As discussed in chapter 9, normally this is a 'tool' which is used in meditation, through which to focus the mind. In this situation of wanting to distract the mind, we can use a Mantra as an alternative 'yellow rose'. As mentioned earlier, the mind finds it hard to focus on more than one thing at a time. Hence, by using your favorite Mantra in a focused way; repeating it in your mind, you can help break a spiral of mental over-activity.

Certain Eastern Mantras - by the very 'sounding' of the word or phrase within your mind - have an inherent ability to calm the mind too. For some people, repeating a word or phrase such as a Mantra is an easier way of sidetracking the mind than imagining a specific scene or to focus on particular areas of the body. If you are more an auditory type, you might want to give this technique a go. For many people, using a Mantra in this way has been a real breakthrough in gaining a more peaceful mental state.

Need for Healing past wounds in your life

All of us have areas of trauma and pain in our lives, and it is important to start Healing such old wounds. Inevitably they are associated with much negative Energy, which may still be actively circulating through us, as it were. Abraham, who we have mentioned before, [1] recommends that you first make peace with where you are at. Now, that may be very difficult when you are in deep suffering or keep harking back to old wounds inflicted even decades ago. However, keeping the 'Gratitude Meditation' in mind, you could argue that if you look broadly and deeply enough, you *will* find things to be grateful for.

On the other hand, it's a totally different issue whether you *choose* to allow yourself to look for what may seem like minuscule little grains of goodness in your life. This is especially so when you are being swamped by much pain and suffering.

Pain can be addictive

Looking back at the concepts of the Pain Body, as put forward by Eckhart Tolle, [4] we can see that pain loves to feed off pain. Once pain is firmly established in our consciousness, especially over long periods of time, it seems almost a 'betrayal' of sorts to now start seeking out those 'good' things in life. This is particularly true when there is a very solid case to be made that our suffering is so real – a broken marriage; death of a loved one, or some other tragedy. It almost feels as if allowing in the 'good', might in some way negate the validity of our suffering. For some people there may even be a rather bizarre twist to this situation, in that it would also mean giving up their 'pay-off' for the suffering – the sympathy it earns them for instance.

Initially, when some sort of suffering strikes, it is very valid – and healthy – to allow ourselves to feel the pain, and be with it. We need to process it in whatever way we can. Yet, there also comes a time when legitimate pain and suffering, endured beyond its 'due by date', starts to become a real saboteur Energy within our life. It's almost as if we can become - strangely enough – addicted to our suffering. The problem is that holding on to such chronic pain also has its consequences, in that it can cause a sense of disconnection or numbness to so many of the more joyful feelings equally available in life.

This can progress to the point where for some people, their suffering creates for them a 24/7 hell. But here we do have a choice, a choice which does validate that our suffering is real, and that awful things may truly have happened to us. However, there also comes a point where either we remain unconscious to the situation's dynamics, and continue to wallow in our pain, or we consciously choose to say 'enough already'! Time to move on with our life.

It may be that despite being in a really horrible job; living in a dreadful flat; having the most awful partner; having gone bankrupt... nevertheless, you may still have your mind. You still have your capacity to think and plan; you still have friends; you still have eyes that can see; legs that can walk you around; a bed to sleep in each night - rather than a park bench; food on your table. If we look around hard enough, most people can still find something in their lives for which they can give thanks.

Now, being grateful about these seemingly small or irrelevant things may not appear like much when compared to the suffering you are going through. They may seem very insignificant under the circumstances, *but it is not the 'size' of what you can be grateful for that counts*. It's the simple fact that you can use them as a type of 'anchor' to steady your 'boat' when you are being tossed about on the stormy 'ocean' of life. And from that point of 'anchorage', rather than being wildly thrown around in the storm, you can start to get your 'engines' going again; plotting a new course which will get you out of the 'storm area'.

How to deal with suffering when you're mortally ill

When a person is seriously ill, and particularly when they are trying to manage a wide range of symptoms as well, it is so easy to remain seduced in a cycle of just focusing on one's – very real – suffering. However, the problem is that what you focus on is what you manifest. Rather inconvenient, but unfortunately that is how it is! So there comes a moment in the Journey of illness, even if you are desperately ill, when nevertheless a very clear, intentional decision has to be made. At this point, if you truly want to try to get well, you then also do need to simply un-hook yourself from this merry-go-round of only focusing on pain and suffering, and set a very firm intention to start visualizing healthy states of body instead. Admittedly, when the body is truly feeling so ill, this can be a most challenging thing to do.

That turning point is a difficult moment in the Journey of Healing, as the momentum behind the pain and suffering is still so enormous. The pain and suffering can easily swamp one's efforts at focusing more on health rather than ill-health. This is where it is really important to do two things; honor the fact that you are still ill, but also keep a commitment to that intention to start focusing on wellness instead. Initially, something very fundamental needs to shift within your mind, and it is not until you can turn that corner – internally - that there will be any hope for true Healing to occur. This is where it may be useful to have people around you who can help you in this process, by gently reminding you to do your affirmations, or to help you visualize the body starting to heal.

Indeed, just as I finished the first draft of this manuscript, I became severely ill, and had to really 'walk the talk'. What needs to be understood and acknowledged however is that when you are truly ill, with the mind and body feeling completely out of whack, this is the most difficult time to then start being 'Metaphysical'. All you may be able to achieve at this point is to crawl your way to the bathroom for basic body-function needs, hope to keep a mouthful of food or water down, all the while feeling like death-warmed-up.

Yet, if you want to engage in some of these more esoteric ways of trying to Heal your situation, there comes a point where you simply have no other option but to re-orientate your mental chatter. If you focus on your mind-talk, you'll no doubt soon find that it's one long monologue of negativity... 'why is this happening to me'; 'ooh...I feel so sick'; 'god... I'm going to throw up... again'! 'I can't stand the pain anymore'; 'A human shouldn't have to put up with so much suffering'. Endlessly on....

So where to start in turning around this incessant stream of negative self-talk? Most of the Metaphysical tools and exercises may be completely beyond you at this stage, but one thing you can do is to mentally start making a list of things in your life you can truly be grateful for. At first this suggestion may sound utterly ludicrous, and even cruel. Afterall, with this level of illness, how could there possibly be anything in your life to be grateful for... other than a swift release from your present misery! However, despite the many symptoms and suffering you may be enduring, there will almost always be something in your life or present circumstance for which you can be grateful.

Chapter 12 - Co-creativity - Techniques

There may be friends who are caring for you; dropping by with food and shopping items; offering to make the bed with fresh linen, and washing that pile of dirty laundry which has accumulated lately; cooking up some soup or other 'nibblies' you feel you could handle without throwing up. You may be in your own home; have a roof over your head; a bed to lie in; access to medicine; hot and cold running water with which to bathe; hopefully you still have your sight; you can still walk; you may have minimal pain – or access to effective drugs to help control the pain.

Although there may be many things occurring right now for which you would *not* feel grateful, nevertheless there will equally inevitably be some things you *can* be grateful for. Ignore all the negative stuff you could very validly complain about. Just start to focus on those things you can equally validly be grateful for – as minimal as they may seem for now. Yet, within the Metaphysical realm, focusing on these positive things in your present situation, and giving thanks for them, definitely does initiate a more constructive Energetic change.

Somewhere along the Journey with your illness, if your deep intention is to get well again, a point has to be reached where you start to turn a corner – at least within your mind initially. Your outer and bodily reality will follow, as this book has already explored in much detail. The main thing is to set an *intention* to get well, deep within your mind, even if you're not sure how this is exactly going to work out or manifest itself.

Then trust! Know that the mind is unbelievably powerful, and that science has now fully vindicated this fact in endless experiments and studies. Know and accept that you can make a difference by how you use your mind, especially in regard to what sort of internal mental chatter you allow to corrode your mind - and therefore your body.

Start with just one symptom, and tune in to the negative self-talk around it. Then create a positive affirmation to counteract this negativity, and say it frequently and with conviction. For instance, if you have a severe pain in your left leg, your affirmation may be along the lines of...'my left leg now feels completely comfortable'.

At first, making up an affirmation which counteracts a present situation of suffering may seem ludicrous, when you obviously are still in such suffering. For instance, you may be in a lot of pain, and to now go and tell your mind that you are not in pain seems not just weird, but blatantly untrue. In that case, if your mind comes up with such strong objections to using any affirmations which seem too unrealistic, then lace those affirmations with words like 'my body is *increasingly* feeling more comfortable'. Yes, you are still in pain, but you're affirming that things are definitely *improving*. That's something one *can* hope for, and which will perhaps also sound more realistic to your mind.

The main point is to make a start somewhere – never mind how small or seemingly insignificant. But set that intention, and then back it up by frequently saying your affirmations, especially as you see your mind going into 'negative internal speak'.

So there are three critical points to this process. First, become aware of your internal 'mind-speak' – far too often heavily laced with negativity. Don't judge it; simply acknowledge it, and then go to the next point which is to set that deep, internal intention that you wish to change this negative mental chatter. Thirdly, select even one aspect of this mind chatter, or focus on just one symptom you're presently suffering, and make up appropriate affirmations which assert a positive outcome to what is presently going on.

Also be careful in the wording of your affirmations. Do not use any words which acknowledge or describe your present suffering. For instance, if you are in a lot of pain, then don't make your affirmation 'the pain in my leg is decreasing'. Instead, focus on its opposite, putting this into words – e.g. 'my leg is increasingly feeling more comfortable and normal'.

Change won't necessarily come instantly, but change can occur over time; one thought; one affirmation at a time. And as your health improves, you can start using some of the many other Healing suggestions and concepts we've explored in this book, or which can be accessed in other publications.

How the role of the critic can sabotage healing

Criticism can be such a corrosive force in our lives, and yet so many of us walk around in 'critic mode' far too often. Things we see; people we see; situations we hear about, may cause us to jump into a critical analysis or judgment of these scenarios. This only helps foster a sense of negativity, capable of acting as a potent repeller-Energy when it comes to the overall Co-creation process. It would be so much more constructive to ourselves - let alone to others – if we could work on breaking this mental pattern. 'They're too fat, too thin, too tall, too short, they're not the right color... endlessly'. Just become Witness to your criticism, and in that moment you see yourself in 'critic mode', send that person a bubble of Healing or Loving Light instead.

Chapter 12 - Co-creativity -Techniques

This relates to situations too; not just individual people. So if you see a situation that you feel critical about, then again visualize a bubble of Light, and direct it to that situation as a counteractive measure. Such situations may be a group of people having an argument; seeing a group of Muslims bowing down to prayer – when, some people have irrational beliefs that all Muslims are potentially terrorists, or may have other biased perspectives about Islam; a group of indigenous people walking into your favorite club; a bunch of teenagers with multi-colored Mohawks. One is sure to find even a few such situations where the internal critic jumps into full alert and 'lets rip'!

On an Energetic level, these judgmental states of mind only help to strongly pollute our own Energies, which is the basic 'currency' with which we Co-create. So being in, or nourishing the 'critic mode', certainly doesn't help you in your Co-creation endeavors. Neither does projecting such negative Energies onto others serve them. On one level of reality, these negative projections are actually 'wounding' them – albeit on a subtle and unspoken Energetic level. Remember, as we discussed in a much earlier chapter, we are ultimately all One.

So, becoming more Aware of your Inner Critic is a very powerful tool, which can start changing your own internal Energy set points. Ironically, it may alert you to just how critical you may be of yourself. Inevitably, the externally directed critic is but a projection of our own *internal* lack of self-esteem or acceptance. But it's important to realize that it is O.K. to see faults in ourselves; to just acknowledge them, and then choose to change them. Yet far too many of us are caught in a spiral of useless self-criticism, driven by that low self-esteem. This can only keep damaging us. It would be much better to acknowledge where we are at, and then try to build ourselves up.

So these are all ways that ultimately can have a profound effect on changing your own Energy. In turn, this changes the dynamics through which you can be 'in resonance' with your Co-created desires, thus allowing you to manifest them more powerfully into your life.

Telepathic process through which to communicate to people or events

In helping to Heal some of these old wounds, there is an amazingly powerful, yet simple technique you might like to try. It will cost you nothing but a few moments of your time. It can be done from the privacy of your own space, and no-one needs to know about it. If nothing else, it can serve as a 'dry run' before perhaps dealing with someone face-to-face.

Firstly, find yourself a quiet area where you won't be intruded upon. Take the phone off the hook, throw the cat or dog out the room, and set up two chairs - one opposite the other. Sit yourself in the first chair, and then allow yourself to go into a deep, meditative or prayerful Space. Once you feel comfortable and Centered, *imagine* the person with whom you need to do some Healing work as sitting in the empty chair opposite you. As soon as you have a sense that they are there – Energetically - imagine a powerful beam of Light going from your heart to theirs – if this is comfortable for you. Also, see another beam from your mind to their mind. If that is simply asking too much, just imagine a cocoon of Light around them – as a symbol of your intention to transact something positive and Healing between the two of you.

Then, in your mind, open your heart to them. Remember, this is *all* happening strictly within your own mind and your 'imagination'. However, in this part of the process, you can really let them 'have it', if you feel this will help the Healing process from your perspective. You may indeed have some very valid and justifiable anger towards this other person, for what they may have done to you.

So, you can be as blunt and to the point as you wish when 'speaking' to them – in your mind. The reality is that you're not having to deal directly with their ego-mode self, which would only respond in a typically defensive – if not offensive – manner. This communication can go on for as short or long as you choose. But the essence of such a communication, for maximal efficiency, is best broken down into several components or steps.

Firstly, you may need to un-load and vocalize – within your mind – whatever emotions you may have been sitting on for ages; unable to express face-to-face. Tell them how you feel about what happened; what it did to you; how it wounded you in some way. Be clear, concise, honest and accurate. Next, state what it is you wish for yourself as well as from them, as you conclude this process. Perhaps you wish to re-connect with them again.

This was certainly so for many of my AIDS clients in years gone by, when they had often been thrown out of home; disowned by their family for being gay – let alone having HIV. Now that many of them were coming close to their death, they often desperately wanted resolution to a wound which had been festering, frequently for years.

Chapter 12 - Co-creativity - Techniques

So, whatever *your* desired resolution may be, state it clearly. Then, create a small mental vignette in which you see yourself in that state of resolution. This may be in the form of seeing you both having a cup of tea together; walking along the beach together; receiving a caring letter from them.

To end such a Telepathic session, it is very important to disconnect Energetically, in the correct manner. You might first like to offer them forgiveness or ask for forgiveness – if you are ready for this step. Next, create a powerful cocoon of Energy, which you place around them, as a symbol of your Love or Compassion – or simply well-meaning towards them. Then see those 'beams of Light' you may have connected to their mind and heart simply *dissolve*. No need to cut them or break them, or anything quite so aggressive. Once you've done these steps, get up, and do whatever is next on your list of things to do that day.

One point needs to be emphasized, as it is so crucial to achieving a positive outcome from this process. It is *absolutely critical* to ensure the session is ended on a Loving – or Compassionate note, never mind how heated or vitriolic your communication may have been in the earlier phase, and as much as you have an absolute right to voice your own pain. If not, the process will seriously backfire, and only be more likely to fuel further negative Energy around whatever the original issue was.

The wounded inevitably create further wounds to others

The problem is that for some people the wounds are so deep, that to even think of Loving the other, makes them feel physically ill. If this is the case, there is another way to look at such situations. Go to that Higher Self Space we've already talked about so much, *from* which to then ask the question... 'Why is this person so dysfunctional; so damaged'? You may already know of something which happened to them, creating their own wound. It was this wounding which then generated their dysfunction, in turn aimed at you, causing *your* wound. Whether you can or can't figure out what damaged them is actually beside the point.

It would be absolutely safe to say that everyone has had events happen to them, creating wounding. And anyone who is themselves a 'wound*er*', can be guaranteed to have been wound*ed*. In this way, we *choose* to allow ourselves to go to a Space, from which it becomes perhaps a bit easier to understand why they did what they did.

However, this has absolutely nothing to do with *validating* what they did. Please understand and recognize this vital distinction. Using this perspective of a person is only about trying to formulate an *understanding* as to why they may have done whatever they did. In the same way as we explored the process of forgiveness, discussed in earlier chapters, this act of trying to understand *their* woundedness is *not* one of automatically *condoning* what has occurred. Quite the contrary. But it is a healthy step towards allowing a Healing and a resolution to occur in *your* life.

If you are entwined in a painful 'dance' with someone – or even a group of people – then you choosing to walk off the 'dance-floor' does end that 'dance'. Certainly on Energetic levels, such a choice, and power do lie with *you*. Strangely, not everyone necessarily wants to accept that power. Some are just too addicted to the drama associated with their woundedness. But hopefully, in the overall Journey towards our own Healing, it becomes possible to engender an alternative perspective, one where we can see that as with just about every human on Earth, we are *all* flawed and 'damaged goods'. Accepting this may also make it a bit easier to feel Compassion for them, even if we can't Love them.

But back to what can be called the 'Telepathic Technique'. This is aptly named, because ultimately, the form of communication you have just engaged in - with whoever was 'sitting' in that chair opposite you - was really a telepathic one. Many clients, on initially hearing this suggestion, simply snorted in disbelief that something so 'airy-fairy' could possibly be asked of them. How could anything as irrational and obviously stupid as talking to a figment of your imagination - 'sitting' in an empty chair opposite you no less - possibly work?

Over the several decades of working as a clinician, and in the hundreds of clients who did 'give it a go', it has never ceased to amaze me, how powerfully this process *has* worked. As mentioned earlier, there is actually nothing to lose – except your wounding or whatever the problem may be. No-one needs to know that you have been talking in your mind to an empty chair, somehow hoping this would solve what have often been complex and long-standing, painful scenarios.

Yet, the number of times the 'other' did in fact pick up the phone; or pen or made contact in some way is utterly astounding... 'I know it's been a long time, but you have been so much on my mind lately – [interesting that!] – and I felt I should perhaps make contact'. Finally a chink in the armor; the door slightly opened. But from such early tentative steps, often great Healing did occur. Not necessarily easily and painlessly; that would be expecting too much in a lot of cases, but with both parties now at least communicating, often a resolution was achieved.

This process is powerful; it does work. Too many individual situations have utterly vindicated that something is communicated via this process or technique. You can do this process on a one-on-one level. You can do it with a group of people you have some issue with. It can even be done with someone who has in fact 'died' – perhaps years ago. Since this is an Energy technique, it is not beholden to the Laws of Time and Space, and so will very much still work in cases of people who are no longer on Earth. And for the ultimate skeptic... what's lost for the person doing this process, if it allows them a greater sense of resolution to a problem they may long have struggled with? Also, in a lot of relationship issues, such a process – if nothing else – does provide an opportunity to at least practise what and how they might like to communicate to someone, once they do get to sit face-to-face.

Finally, we are assuming in the above description and examples, that we have been the aggrieved one. It could equally be that perhaps *we* were the one who did the wounding, and now want to ask for forgiveness, yet know that the 'other' absolutely refuses to meet with us. This Telepathic Technique has often allowed for a reversal in this stance, thereby allowing for an opportunity to personally put things right again.

You can engage in this process as often as you like; certainly at least once daily for a while is recommended. The more intransigent the situation you have been locked into, the longer it may take to get some 'movement' going. So don't give up too easily or quickly. But results with many of my clients, friends and myself, vindicate that change can often happen - almost overnight.

Also understand that there is a significant difference in doing such a process in this very specific, structured and focused manner, compared to having mental conversations with someone while you're doing the dishes or mowing the lawn. This is far less likely to be effective. Keep in mind that analogy of the light beam of a torch, and that of a laser. For a really effective result, you do need to use the 'laser light' option of communication. Torch-beam light is just too scattered, and much more likely to only give a hit-or-miss result.

Telepathy – sending Healing back to past traumatic events

This next process requires some time and a good memory. Go back to childhood or to your first memories, and list all the people and events that were painful or caused you suffering. Then one by one go through this list, and do the Telepathic process to each of them – dead or alive. The basics of this process are exactly as discussed above for the Telepathic Process. Set up the two chairs; link in Energetically; communicate your feelings; state the desired result you want now; give or ask for forgiveness; dissolve – not *sever* – the Energy connection... let go, and get on with your day.

Despite doing this technique, as described above, you may still have various memories or thoughts come back to mind around the issue you're working on. These could also indicate new layers or angles to the situation which were not so obvious before, but now offer another viewpoint from which to do even deeper Healing. Just observe them, name them, work with them via the Telepathic Process... and let them go. Don't necessarily fight or wrestle, as this only feeds them.

You can go through the list in any order, but keep the list, and mark it off as you do this process. We always want the magical 'quick-fix', whereas this technique is a relatively slow and fairly labor-intensive process. So be patient, because the benefits you can gain in shedding internal 'baggage' you may have hung onto for decades, are enormous. Remember the 'hot-air balloon' analogy we used in chapter 6? Truly, such internal mental and emotional 'ballast' only serves to make it harder to get to your Higher Self Mode of Being, which in turn makes it all that much harder to do your Co-creation cleanly and efficiently.

Realize that all of these seemingly unrelated discussions inevitably do come back and tie in with your ability to do Co-creation!

Music as a technique to uplift us

Music is a very powerful way in which to enhance a feeling of wellness within you, just as the 'Gratitude Meditation' can do. Music is a magical stimulator of a wide range of emotions, from utter despair and sadness to ecstatic heights of joy, and a sense of potent aliveness. So it's a matter of going through your music library, and consciously choosing music that inspires and uplifts you; that allows you to feel centered, calm, or just very much alive and happy to be alive.

And if you haven't been playing music lately, make this a conscious part of your life. Ensure that every day, or at least every week, you play some of this music or allow yourself some time to just sit, and become uplifted and feeling more positive about life. This way, day by day, you practise coming to a Space of calmness, centeredness or feeling uplifted, positive and well. In a sense, it's another form of meditation, and you might want to use the music routine as a variation-on-a-theme to meditation. Sometimes, it can be easy to become bored with doing the one process day in, day out. Adding some variety can be most productive.

Stepping into your visualization

Another powerful and indeed critical technique in the Co-creative process is not just to image what it is you want, but to actively see yourself *in* that image too. This is very important, because when you do that, and thereby become part of it, you're also making a statement... 'yes, this is what you desire; this is a signal of your acceptance that you are resonant with your desire, and really do want it to manifest'. Remember, your mind can't tell whether you imagining yourself in your visualization represents *actual* reality or *imagined* reality.

But if you do it genuinely enough, along with the generation of the appropriate feelings, your mind will believe that what you're imagining is real. Therefore, it will be all the more likely to produce it. Seems weird, but this is how the mind works. So you need to see yourself step into all these Co-creative visualizations. It's saying that you don't just want to 'see' or 'watch' that event happen in *other* people's lives or as something *outside* of *your* reality. You want it to be an integral component of your reality; you want to *be* that. On one level it is going from a stage of *doing* this process to *being* it.

Cross-linking visualizations

There can also be great value in cross-linking projects or visualizations. For example, connecting the visualization you're doing about having that wonderful partner in your life, with also having that special house you've always wanted. Here you can definitely continue to Co-creatively visualize for each one separately, but also think of connecting the two. See you and your special partner in that special house – together - in as many variations and different 'scenes' as you can imagine. Working in the garden together; lounging on the settee watching TV together; helping each other making dinner or washing up. This adds an extra 'oomph' to the entire process, which is worth thinking about.

Rajneesh approach to help break through the Maya – or Illusion

Some of you may find this next discussion most disturbing and controversial, especially if you come from a strong, religious background. However, this dialogue is based on the understanding that it comes with a major stipulation of limitation, which acts as a safety net towards others. As outrageous as this proposal may appear on initial presentation, you may find upon further reflection that it does have inherent value after all – even if at first it does throw your mind into an absolute loop.

As stated earlier in this book, the fact that most people using Co-creativity will do so as a way of accumulating or experiencing even more materiality is not something that should be condemned out of hand. Strange as it may seem, it actually is a life process that needs to be encouraged. Along those lines, Rajneesh, the former 'Rolls Royce' Guru, as abhorrent as a lot of his actions were, nevertheless did seem to get it right on at least one level. The reality is that in the quest towards spirituality, certain aspects to the human Journey of life are seldom eradicated by denial and repression – techniques so readily suggested and used by most religions.

A much more effective way to get beyond such obsession with our materialistic or physical issues is to do as Rajneesh recommends, which is to dive into whatever we are so enamored with. However, he does stipulate several very important restrictions. Firstly, this does not mean open slather to do absolutely anything you desire, without regard of the consequences – especially to others. This concept absolutely does not give carte blanche to now go and kill, rape, pillage and commit other forms of mayhem! The concept has to be totally under-pinned by that Caveat we've spoken of before i.e. 'do what you desire – *as long as it does not impinge negatively on the well-being of others, physically, mentally, emotionally or Spiritually*'.

Secondly, understand that for 'every action there is a reaction'. Doing the Rajneesh approach, even if in the name of being part of your Spiritual Journey, does not suddenly give you immunity from this fact, and the consequences of one's actions. For instance, in areas such as sexuality, if this is an area that has been particularly stifled for an individual, they may decide to dive in, and experience it in all its myriad facets. No problems. But by the same token, there can be serious consequences to this. Not only are there all sorts of STI's one can catch, but there can also be much heart-break.

The Rajneesh approach, in certain circumscribed areas of Life, does have a controversial validity. All the same, it is a potentially hazardous 'side-track' to take on the overall Path of Life. The Rajneesh approach can be a most productive Journey, but be warned that there may be many dangers on that particular Path. Any Journey taken here must not be taken lightly. Rajneesh

Chapter 12 - Co-creativity -Techniques

does also stipulate such a Journey should always be undertaken with one fundamental concept kept foremost in mind, which is that ultimately one is playing with Maya – or Illusion. In the end, such Maya can never fulfill what the soul is really looking for. It cannot become the answer to any particular dilemma in one's Life.

This is definitely not a course that would be generally recommended for the majority of people. This is a path that would appeal and suit only a very select sub-group of people. But for them, it can indeed be a life-altering, transformative, Spiritually enhancing Journey to take, which needs to be done with as much Consciousness as possible. Often, you can only truly leave such temptations for the physical behind you, when the *heart* has understood what an Illusion your 'urge' is. Just having a cerebral 'knowingness' about it is not enough; it's too shallow.

The primary issue here is that denial or repression of your urges doesn't automatically or magically get rid of those urges. More often than not, it only drives them underground, and puts them on hold. Even after many years of seemingly successful repression, it can take but a word, a situation or some apparently insignificant stimulus, and suddenly that urge can be brought back in full force. This can happen despite having felt absolutely convinced that you had no more attachment to such desires.

This is because there were inevitably still some residual cords of attachment – much like elastic bands, stretched ever more tightly as time went by. Till one day, with a big 'twang', they suddenly can snap you back into your urge, full-on, and with a lot of pent-up energy to now drive them too. An interesting book which discusses this phenomenon is called 'Initiation' by Elizabeth Haich; [5] a must-read if you're interested in this Rajneesh approach.

Now, it is absolutely true that the Rajneesh approach is a very challenging and controversial perspective to propose on a whole range of human 'urges', from wanting to amass huge fortunes; to playing with power; to fully diving into sexuality and more. Once again, it needs to be reiterated that such a proposed way of dealing with 'urges', nevertheless needs to come with that powerful Caveat mentioned earlier. This point needs to be hammered home repeatedly! The 'Rajneesh approach' is not some blank cheque with which to now go and impinge on the freedoms of others or do them harm.

Rajneesh's view was that in a wide range of materialistically orientated desires, if a person felt strongly attracted to experiencing them, then it may serve them better to 'dive in'. His view was that you would only be able to truly release yourself from the pull and seduction of your 'urge', by fully living through such situations - indeed, to the point where you realize on a deep, almost cellular level, that playing with such Maya is ultimately not giving you the satisfaction you thought it would.

Often, as humans, we live with a sense of internal emptiness. In the end this deep sense of emptiness is inevitably associated with our sense of disconnection from Source. And a very human way of trying to 'fill that emptiness' is to accumulate an endless array of material or other 'distractions' - be that sex, money, power, work; or material goods like cars, yachts, holidays and so much more.

However, there will come a time in such a Journey, where we realize – on a deep, core level – that although none of these things are in themselves inherently evil or bad, they also are not that ultimate 'something' we are often so desperately searching for. This is where the Rajneesh view of 'diving' right into one's 'stuff' - with Consciousness – can make sense.

It is true that the Christian view of fighting the 'temptation' may indeed develop a sense of inner power or control over our 'stuff'. However, from observation, it doesn't automatically result in actually getting *rid* of the issue being suppressed. It may *appear* to be under control, but usually remains festering below the conscious surface. Even after years of such apparent success, a life situation can recur which brings it back to life in no uncertain terms. In fact, often with much more of a vengeance, because it now also has many years' worth of accumulated, repressed Energy added to it.

A final thought

In a book like this, you might easily feel overwhelmed by all the different exercises you can play with, through which to enhance this Journey or deal with 'stuff' in your life. So, one way to manage this sense of being overwhelmed is to first make a list of what all that 'stuff' is. Then choose just *one* issue you most want to deal with, and next choose the appropriate 'tools' as discussed here - or from other sources - to focus solely on this one issue alone. Choose a time-frame – say 1-2 months. Put this in your diary, and at the end of this period, re-assess how well you feel you have done in working through that issue.

Then choose the next problem on your list; choose the tools, and again set aside a period of time over which to hone the skills in this arena. Life is not about somehow 'quantum-leaping' through your allotted years to some final goal. It is a step-by-step Journey, where the focus needs to be more on those steps in that Journey, rather than on the goal itself. Trying to live your life the other way round is guaranteed to make that Journey rather empty, and inevitably very frustrating. It will also more likely make you blind to the many wonderful day-to-day events, while only looking towards your aspired goal – which you may never reach. Far better to instead live each day as fully as possible.

Exercise
- Explain how pain and suffering can be productively used in Co-creation.
- Why is it so important to put in a caveat of 'for my Highest Good and through joy', when doing Co-creation?

Summary of thoughts thus far
- Never get involved with the details of *how* your desire is to manifest. That is not our business as Co-creators.
- The origin for change lies *within* us, but the mechanism for such change lie *beyond* us.
- Co-creative technique - step 1 - setting goals.
- Co-creative technique - step 2 - day-dreaming your desire.
- Co-creative technique – step 3 - focused 'laser beam' sent into the Matrix.
- In Co-creation, we also do need to trust in a Higher Level of Awareness, which knows exactly when it's a good time for our desire to manifest - *or even if it should manifest at all.*
- To be on the safe side, you might want to add in to each Co-creative project, the injunction *'Be it for my Highest Good and through joy'*.
- All your Co-creative thoughts and wording need to be in the *present* tense; not past or future.
- When dealing with health issues, by all means use your Co-creative visualizations, but do also use more earthly means to get well – medical, naturopathic or a mix of both.
- Being grateful for the things in your life is one of the quickest, easiest, most powerful ways to connect with Source Energy; to Higher Self Mode, or to the Matrix.

- Being grateful increases the Energetic 'bank balance' of 'Co-creative credits'. This in turn provides you with a lot more to 'invest' or spend on Co-creative projects.
- If you are constantly critical or constantly miserable, then in a sense you are going more into an 'over-draft' of your Co-creative 'credit account'.
- When you are desperately ill, all you might be able to manage is to stop the internal, negative mental chatter, and start with the 'Gratitude Meditation'.
- The 'Telepathic Technique' is a very powerful way in which to help heal old wounds or bring resolution to difficult situations.
- Understand that these Telepathic sessions *absolutely* must end on a Loving, or at least a Compassionate note.
- Anyone who is themselves a 'wound*er*', can be guaranteed to have been wound*ed*. This understanding allows us to become more compassionate towards others.
- For the brave or adventurous, there is always the 'Rajneesh Approach'.

REFERENCES

1. Hicks, Esther & Jerry. *Ask and it is Given – learning to manifest your desires*, Hay House Inc, 2004.

2. Bible, King James Version, Luke 11:33.

3. Canfield, Jack in interview with Barry Goss, available at:- (http://mastersoft-hesecret.com/ebooktmp/talkingebook.pdf, p. 15)

4. Tolle, Eckhart. *The Power of Now – a guide to spiritual enlightenment*, Hodder Headline Group, Australia/NZ, 2000.

5. Hicks, Esther & Jerry. *Ask and it is Given – learning to manifest your desires*, Hay House Inc. 2004. pp. 149-153.

6. Haich, Elizabeth. *Initiation*, Aurora Press, USA, 2000.

CHAPTER 13

BLOCKAGES TO CO-CREATIVITY

The most handicapped person in the world is a negative thinker.

Heather Whitestone, former Miss America

Let's take a look at a range of issues which can unfortunately act very effectively in blocking our ability to Co-create. These may range from religious perceptions; to cultural beliefs; to incorrect use of words; to our internal dialogue; to impatience... and much more. Exploring these one at a time should help break through such creativity barriers.

Belief that 'desire' is not spiritual can be a powerful saboteur

Probably one of the biggest blocks associated with trying to do Co-creation is the belief that 'desire', fundamentally and intrinsically is 'un-spiritual' – if not evil. Many people believe that spirituality and desires are mutually exclusive concepts, and that the only way they are going to attain spiritual perfection is by releasing all desires.

What they've forgotten is that *the desire to have no desire... is itself a desire.*

It would seem that desire is one emotion which we as humans just cannot avoid. The tendency to have desires is simply a fundamentally hard-wired aspect to us as humans. Those who believe that desires are inherently evil will find this situation to be incompatible with life as a human. The very nature of existing in a flesh and blood 'vehicle', entails a plethora of desires.

It would be more practical to just accept that desire is a built-in facet of the human experience, and as such is not the problem. The problems start when we use our desires to substitute for something they never can be – which is a full, Conscious, experiential sense of Connection to our Source; our Real 'Home'. There is also another layer, or a more Buddhist perspective to desire, which is to see it becoming a problem when we become *attached* to our desires.

Cultural and ideological blocks – 4 minute mile

Our ability to Co-create so-called miracles into our lives is also dependent on our cultural belief system. Blindly accepting some of those beliefs can be very effective at sabotaging our ability to Co-create. Yet once one person breaks through that cultural conditioning, suddenly it becomes possible for many others to do the 'impossible' too. However, someone had to break through that barrier first. One potent example is that of the 4 minute mile. Such a feat was thought to be a total impossibility until 1954 when Roger Bannister, a 25 year old medical student, became the first man to run a mile in less than 4 minutes.

His time was 3 minutes, 59.4 seconds. Within a month, the Australian John Landy broke this magical record with his own result of 3 minutes, 57.9 seconds. But it took Bannister to initially break what had thus far been perceived as the impossible. From there on in, many others were soon able to break through this previously impossible hurdle to 'reality'. Another, more biological example is that of an experiment in which fish were placed in an aquarium, which had been partitioned off by a glass wall. After some time, the fish became used to not being able to swim beyond this point. When the glass was subsequently removed, the fish still didn't swim beyond this point. They had become conditioned to there being a barrier at that spot, and it was now so 'self-evident' that they didn't even venture to challenge this perception. Fish are not the only ones to get caught up in such ironic situations! Most of humanity finds itself in similar situations all too frequently.

As humans, we tend to limit ourselves in many ways, and this tendency is particularly applicable to anyone first coming across the concept that 'thought can create reality'. This idea goes against the grain of everything we may have been taught, making it very difficult to accept.

Ego trying to figure out how desire will manifest

Another way we can very effectively block the results of our Co-creation from manifesting into this reality is to constantly try and figure out *how* our desire

Chapter 13 - Blockages to Co-creativity

could possibly manifest. Here you are, absolutely broke; piles of unpaid bills and no job. So how on earth could the $20,000 you desperately need possibly come to you in such a predicament, with no rich friends or recently deceased family to hopefully leave you something in their Will?

This is a classic example of where the ego puts its nose into an arena that should absolutely not concern it. Ego *only* has to set up the details of what it is you desire. The Matrix, via the Higher Self, *knows precisely* what It needs to do to allow your desire to manifest. But constantly having ego interfering with this aspect of the Co-creative process, will only slow it down, if not sabotage it altogether.

Become pro-active after doing visualization & really augment the process

By the same token, this does not mean you just do your visualizations ... and then lay back, become a 'couch-potato', and wait for someone to magically dump a $20K wad of notes in your letterbox. In the above example for instance, do your visualization, and even though on one level you truly believe your desire has already manifested – as per the Co-creative principles – on the other hand start becoming proactive around this project. Be open to reading or hearing about ways to make money; look around for a job; ask friends for any leads. Let your imagination go wild as you explore the talents you have which could make you money – and be game to try them out. Often, what at first glance seems impossible, if looked at more closely can be seen to have viability.

So, on one level you do your Co-creative technique with gusto and skill, and yet on a concurrent level you start playing with practical ideas that could augment the mind or Energetic aspect to Co-creation. Here, it truly helps to act in this dualistic way. Once we engage in this parallel approach, amazing 'synchronicities' usually start to occur. You 'happen' to meet just the right person who can help in some way; you 'happen' to see an ad – in a magazine you never usually buy. Magic can start to occur, but it is less likely to come about if we do our visualization, and then just hang around the house all day, doing nothing. Getting active in the desired directions allows for opportunities to occur.

Co-creativity – don't use the word 'no' in your affirmations

Although this point has been made before, it's really important to remember that when you choose the words of an affirmation, which encapsulate the intentions of your Co-creation, that you do not use the word 'no' in that wording. Always ensure that the desire is stated in its most positive form. Remember that central Law within Co-creativity, where 'what you focus on is what you will draw into your life'. Let's look at a few examples.

For instance, your desire may be to have good health, when at present you are in ill-health. Yet, if you word your Co-creative affirmation along the lines of... 'I do not want to be sick'; 'I choose not to have headaches....' then unfortunately you will more likely end up drawing further ill-health or headaches into your life. Just read those sentences again, but leaving out the 'no' or 'not'. Bit of a shock isn't it?

In your heart and mind your intention is to be healthy; understood. But the Matrix is very literal in how it responds to your instructions, and in these examples, all it hears is... 'I want to be sick' or 'I choose to have headaches'! By stating it in this opposite or negative sense, by using words like 'no', you definitely end up sending the wrong message, as well as manifesting more of precisely what you *don't* want.

This occurs because you are in fact still *focusing* on what it is you don't want i.e. ill-health or headaches. So, firstly look at what it is in your life you wish to change. Next, carefully choose the wording which only focuses on the positive aspect of what it is you desire, and then use those words in the Co-creative process. For instance, in these examples, something along the lines of... 'I choose to be healthy' or 'my head now feels completely comfortable'... is more likely to work.

The Laws governing this Co-creative process are incredibly literal. Like a computer – rubbish in leads to rubbish out. The dynamics of Co-creation won't tease out for you that ill-health is actually not what you meant. You put in the word 'ill-health' - or more importantly - your focus was on avoiding 'ill-health', *rather than on creating 'health'.* The Co-creative process just got the message about ill-health... and thus manifested more for you. The process was only 'doing its job'.

This may all seem rather pedantic, but unfortunately is simply how it works. It's very much like writing a web or email address on your computer. Leave out one tiny letter, or even put in a comma versus a full-stop, and this unfortunately will be enough to incapacitate your ability to access that web address or get your email to the right person. You may say... 'yes, but it was just a *tiny* mistake – a comma instead of a full-stop, for heaven's sake'! And yes, you're right - but

Chapter 13 - Blockages to Co-creativity

that's how literal a computer system is in its workings. The computer doesn't know you really meant to type in a full-stop instead of a comma, and thereby automatically change it for you. That's just not how these machines work – well, at least not yet.

Hence it is important to *always* ensure your desires are couched in terms *directly* related to what it is you desire, and to not even subtly allude to or allow any focus on what you don't want. It's actually a very straightforward and simple process, but as with using a computer, it needs to be absolutely clear and concise to get the system to do as you wish. Accepting this reality allows you to work within the Laws of Co-creativity. Fighting against it, because you feel it should be otherwise, is just not going to work. Instead, you'll end up walking away from an amazingly powerful process, declaring it to be useless. But instead, it was your inability to work within the Laws governing this process, which was the problem.

Over-desiring something throttles the energy

Deepak Chopra spoke of the way in which the things we desire the most are also usually the hardest to manifest into our reality. It's almost as if desiring something too much seems to throttle off the flow of Creative Energy. Or put another way, the more we desire something with a sense of urgency or desperation, the more we need to look at where our head-space is really at, when doing the Co-creation process. If your Energy is one of desperation, then you are also automatically tainting that Co-creative Energy with a quality of being in a state of 'lack of'. Remember, there is one fundamental principle under-pinning all of Co-creation, which is the need to generate a sense within yourself of 'already having what it is you desire... before it has even manifested'.

Attachment, desperation, urgency, craving – having any of these feelings only contaminates the process. They automatically are the antithesis of trusting, and *absolutely knowing* that what you desire is already there for you. Allowing such negative feelings to creep into your Co-creation can therefore only have one effect - a blockage of your manifestation on a very deep and fundamental level. Such feelings precisely give the strongest message of what we feel we *don't* have. Desperation is a powerful, negative, and yet very Co-creative Energy. Instead, engaging in visualization with a light sense of playfulness allows the Energy to flow in a more unobstructed way, and thereby allows things to manifest more easily.

Compliments – how easily can we accept them?

There is also the related issue of compliments. Someone compliments us, and immediately we shrug it off or denigrate it. On one level we may feel that we are being modest – after all, being egotistical is bad. But actually, such avoidance of compliments only represents how closed off we might be to letting nice things come into our life. By the same token, so many of us, so many times, will scream to the Universe how we desperately want a particular thing. Yet deep down – as shown by our inability to even accept a compliment – we simply aren't willing or capable of letting our desires manifest into our reality either. Fending off compliments is a classic sign of how closed we actually may be to letting good things come into our reality.

By such actions, we are basically saying either 'yes' or 'no' to the Universe. First we beseech the Universe – on bended knee – to give us something we really want or need. However, despite our most earnest pleadings, seemingly small actions, such as the inability to accept a compliment graciously, also betray us. It would appear from such clues that we may not be capable of letting into our lives even a minuscule version of what we so urgently want. No wonder the Universe often seems to be ignoring our requests!

Visualization – impatience a major blocker

Another way we can impair or cancel our 'order with the Universe' is to become impatient with the process. If we have an expectation that 'it should arrive within the week', but then it hasn't, we start to automatically doubt the process. This in turn very effectively blocks any further possibility of that manifestation coming through. 'We get what we focus on'. So if we focus on or play with doubt about the timing of the manifestation, then it's precisely this sense of doubt, which will influence our ability to manifest the desired Co-creation. Hence, the moral of the story is... 'don't put a dead-line on your Co-creation'. Allow it to manifest in its own good time.

Despite the Co-creative process being a well established, reliable, workable phenomenon, as real and 'workable' as the Laws of Gravity or Time, sometimes it seems as if Co-creation just won't work, never mind how hard you tried. Let's examine some of the reasons why this could be so.

The most likely explanation may be in not having used the 'recipe' correctly or skillfully enough, especially when it comes to the generation of the appropriate feelings. If you have used the 'recipe' correctly and with skill, the process actually has no choice but to work. Doing the Co-creative protocol in the correct manner automatically guarantees that the Matrix will respond by manifesting your desire. It's as direct and simple as that. However, where the stumbling blocks can occur are inside your own mind, through your doubts or negative, subconscious beliefs about yourself or your reality.

Then there is another very important reason why your manifestation may not have occurred. Remember that Caveat of... 'for my Highest Good and through joy'? This may be the other point which caused the manifestation process to become side-tracked or deleted. If you have asked Source/God/Universe – whatever you want to call that Supreme Being - to only allow your desire to manifest if it will indeed be for your Highest good, then Source may have decided this desire wasn't appropriate for your life at this point.

So if we can truly accept these points, while also being as relaxed as possible about the whole process, then the sooner our desire is likely to manifest. In this regard, we truly need to live out this earthly plane's deeply engrained sense of duality. On one level, we trust *utterly*, that the process works, and will 'deliver the goods'. By the same token, we also allow for the fact that the Universe/God knows better than we do whether the manifestation of our desire is actually going to be for our Highest good. This Source of Higher Wisdom may decide to protect us from ourselves – particularly when we have asked It to do so with the Caveat of... 'for my Highest good and through joy'.

Either way, trusting fully in both these seemingly contradictory levels to the equation, also allows us to get on with our lives, relaxed and confident that what needs to happen, will happen. So in this way, the process remains light and playful, rather than grim, demanding and urgent.

As within; so without – consciously or unconsciously

Along the lines of the above, we need to fully grasp that the Laws of Co-creation work perfectly every time – whether instigated by conscious or unconscious desires. So when we look at our lives with all its good and bad things, we need to understand that on many levels it may well be a 'perfect' reflection of what sort of thoughts and beliefs we've been playing with in our minds to date.

On first glance, this may seem terribly unfair, and from one point of view this is indeed the case, especially when seen from the perspective that various powers have for so long with-held these crucial concepts from the general population. The problem is that humans are always Co-creating – consciously or unconsciously; it's something that as humans we simply can't avoid doing. However, it is precisely because this vital knowledge about Co-creation has been withheld for so long, that our Co-creations are mostly occurring from an *unconscious* and inevitably more negative stance. No wonder the world is in such a mess! We need to remember that the Laws of Co-creation don't 'take a break' because we are not aware of them.

This is why it is important to finally get this sort of information out to the wider community. People have for too long been caught in an unconscious cycle of churning out many unwanted realities. What needs to change therefore is the way this inherent human phenomenon has inevitably manifested so *unconsciously*. Co-creation now needs to be done via a more fully understood, and therefore Conscious perspective.

So it is high time this unconsciousness is reversed. And the first level to such a reversal is to understand and acknowledge that the phenomenon of Co-creation is absolutely real, and is constantly in operation – with or without our conscious participation. Next, we can use our *present*, and inevitably less than perfect life situation, to get at least some inkling as to where our own *internal* negativities are perhaps most active. Yet again, let's immediately also stress that this needs to be done *without blame!* Instead, just use our present situation in a non-judgmental way, to understand where we need to start the work of restoring our life to a higher level of perfection.

With such increased Consciousness, we can at least begin manifesting a greater number of more 'perfect' situations into our lives. No, this won't happen overnight, just as you don't renovate a really broken-down house overnight. Before you can even commence rebuilding, it will take a lot of work simply to get rid of the 'rubbish' and 'debris'.

Internal dialogue sabotage

In chapter 11 we explored how we can sabotage our 'Gratitude Meditation' with negative, internal 'chatter', and we can do exactly the same with our Co-creative process. Once more, it becomes very important to look at, and attend to our internal dialogue. We may have a very clear and conscious intention of what it is we want to manifest, but if we also persist with a lot of old-pattern, negative, background 'chatter' inside our mind, this can still powerfully sabotage our *conscious* attempts at Co-creation. This happens, simply because

Chapter 13 - Blockages to Co-creativity

such 'chatter' is still creating an Energy which is often the opposite of what we consciously want to create in our reality.

For instance, you want some extra money for a much needed holiday. So, you do your Co-creative processes, but if you were to pay close attention to your 'internal chatter', you might find that it goes along the lines of... 'the boss would never dream of giving me a raise'. Or... 'even if I got the money, there's no-one I couldn't leave the kids with, so as to get a real break'. Can you see that each one of these 'internal dialogues' is not exactly coherent with what you desire? What effect do you suppose such thoughts would have on your Co-creative project?

Since these negative, background patterns have been there for a long time, they've also accumulated an enormous amount of momentum. The fact that this negative Energy is being created in such an unconscious manner, doesn't detract from the very real, sabotaging affect it will have on our Co-creation process. Initially, what may therefore win out in this process is not the clear, *conscious* intention we may have, but this background, negative 'chatter' instead.

And so we can find ourselves in an interesting dilemma. On the one hand we are quite clear about what it is we want, and would like to manifest. On the other hand, we're creating a mental tug-of-war, due to not attending to this internal, negative, and destructive prattle. One part of us wants to go one way, and another part of us is unconsciously dragging us back the other way. End result? We basically stand still and end up going nowhere.

EFT for dealing with ego sabotage – and more

There is an incredibly powerful process called EFT (Emotional Freedom Technique), which can become a potent tool in the process of Co-creation, particularly as we become aware of our negative internal dialogue. This is especially the case in regard to the important stipulation within the Co-creative process of having to conjure up the feelings of *already* having what it is we desire. This situation seems like such a 'mind-twist', and can certainly generate a lot of unwanted, negative mental dialogue, in turn capable of sabotaging our Co-creative attempts. This is a situation for which EFT was almost tailor-made.

Fundamentally, EFT is a relatively simple and easy technique, but it's beyond the scope of this book to go into any more than just mentioning it here. A basic explanation of this powerful process is provided in Appendix

III, as well as some web-links. Please do investigate and start playing with this amazing tool, which can truly help transform your life on so many levels.

Finally - keeping the process light and playful

When dealing with Co-creativity, it's important to emphasize the need for keeping it all light and playful. Becoming too earnest, or desiring something too urgently, actually tends to come more from a state of 'lack'. Instead, if we can come from a space where it isn't the end of the world if we don't get our desire fulfilled, then the whole Energy is lighter, and the process more likely to be successful. The procedure encounters less internally driven resistance, and your manifestations should enter your physical reality so much more quickly and easily.

Exercise

- Why is it important to avoid using the word 'no' in your Co-creation projects or affirmations?
- Why is it so important to watch your internal, mental dialogue if you wish to be successful in Co-creation?

Summary of thoughts thus far

- One of the biggest blocks associated with trying to do Co-creation is the belief that 'desire', fundamentally and intrinsically is 'un-spiritual' – if not evil.
- A desire to have no desire is itself a desire. In other words, life without desire is impossible.
- Desires only become a problem if we use them to substitute for something they never can – which is a full, Conscious, experiential sense of Connection to our Source.
- The ideological barrier of the '4 minute mile' is a good example of how we as humans limit ourselves via beliefs.

Chapter 13 - Blockages to Co-creativity

- An effective way to block the manifestation of our Co-creation into this reality is to constantly try and figure out *how* our desire could possibly manifest. Leave that to the Higher Self.

- Use your external reality as a mirror to give you a sense of what may be going on in that mind of yours. But remember... no blame! Simply, Awareness.

- Avoid using the word 'no' in your Co-creation affirmations e.g. 'I no longer want to be poor'. The Matrix will only hear...'I want to be poor'.

- Enhance your Co-creative projects by being pro-active. On one level, do your Co-creative technique with gusto and skill, yet on another level, you start playing with practical ideas that could augment the mind aspect to Co-creation.

- Fending off compliments is a classic sign of how closed we actually are to letting good things come into our reality. This has important ramifications for our ability to Co-create successfully.

- What we desire most is inevitably what eludes us the most too, especially if we desire with a sense of desperation or urgency.

- Impatience to have our desire manifest can become a major blocking energy.

- Watch that subtle, internal, negative mental chatter, which is quite capable of derailing your Co-creative projects.

- EFT can be a potent technique for dealing with such disruptive mental chatter.

- Finally - keep the process of Co-creation light and playful.

Lifenotes - A user's guide to making sense of life on planet Earth

CHAPTER 14

MULTIPLE REALITIES GIVE HOPE

None of us can change our yesterdays, but all of us can change our tomorrows.

Colin Powell

It doesn't take a genius to figure out that from so many angles, we as a species are in a truly desperate situation. If Global Warming doesn't get us, it will be terrorism; and if that doesn't get us, it's the dreadful poisons accumulating in our environment, food and water. And so the list goes on. Such a wonderful array of dreadful deaths to choose from! But the problem is that this is all far too real. Nor can these realities be relegated to the science fiction basket any longer, just as they can't be dismissed as the ravings of various fringe groups any more either.

Under such circumstances, it becomes easy to feel powerless. It seems we have no option but to be dragged along by the momentum of our inherently destructive human tendencies, to a precipice from which there is virtually no survival. Not if... but when we finally topple over the edge - an edge we are already desperately close to.

What makes it so much worse is that far too many people remain, or choose to remain blind to these possibilities. This is so despite the clear and detailed warnings from eminent scientists and other knowledgeable people. Sadly, a lot of people within the human family are still in deep denial, or they repeatedly come up with an array of excuses as to why they or their country should be exempt from any proposed solutions, while merrily continuing in their destructive habits. All such responses can only guarantee that we will then end up precisely with what we are trying so hard to ignore.

Prophecy and multiple realities

Then along came a really powerful book called 'The Isaiah Effect – decoding the lost science of prayer and prophecy', by Gregg Braden. [1] It gives enormous hope for the future - for us as individuals as well as a species. In this book Braden talks about an apparent discrepancy which repeatedly occurs within the various biblical prophecies. On one level they talk about hell and damnation occurring on this planet, but then they also talk about an amazing time of human co-operation, compassion, an era of happiness and no more sorrow. Almost sounds too good to be true, and one does wonder if a bodily death is necessary for this latter experience to occur.

But according to Braden, these prophecies seem to suggest that this beautiful and positive description of a potential human scenario *is* possible within the human experience, while still incarnate on planet Earth. He has a fascinating take on these sort of discrepancies of doom and gloom on the one hand, and then this heavenly picture on the other. Braden suggests that a really good prophet is capable of tapping into *multiple,* alternate time-lines... simultaneously. The most likely time-line they primarily end up focusing on is determined more by what humans are doing and thinking *at the time of prophesying.*

If we briefly look at Rupert Sheldrake's 'Morphogenetic Field' again, remember, it is supposed to consist of every iota of humanity's thinking, feeling and learning. From that perspective, all thinking and doing by us humans, does create a sort of Energetic momentum, compelling us along a particular course.

This in turn will tend to orientate us towards specific end-points. Imagine two different scenarios. One in which all humans are compassionate, respectful and caring of each other, thereby greatly decreasing the chances of constant wars and other miseries. And then there is another earthly possibility, where we are constantly bickering and fighting; relentlessly competing against and trying to outdo each other. Sounds more like the Earth I know! It doesn't take a prophet to figure out that these two different human settings would also result in quite marked dissimilar endings. The former, an end-point of peace and prosperity for all; the latter, a situation where humanity is more likely to finish up with constant wars, and other forms of social unrest.

Chapter 14 - Multiple Realities Give Hope

Which multiple reality will you choose?

However, as Braden strongly points out, this human experience here on Earth, is only *one* of many dimensional possibilities for us to be engaged in. In other words, via the science of Quantum Physics, he is invoking the strong likelihood that the human experience is in fact occurring in a *multi*-dimensional fashion. Which dimension you - i.e. *this* one particular aspect of 'you' - ends up experiencing, is dependent on where *your* focus is at. What sort of thoughts are *you* constantly playing with? How do *you* live those out? What are *your* fears, etc?

As has been endlessly stated now, we experience the reality we are constantly Co-creating - consciously or unconsciously. Well, from all our previous discussion, we already know this anyway, don't we? So why the sudden fuss about Braden's take on prophecy? But let's tap into the fascinating twist which his perspective on this concept of multiple realities does present us with. The power of this alternate view of reality is that it allows for a wonderful, new and influential way to alter where *you* might end up in the future. Which alternate future time-line would you prefer to be part of?

As Braden explains in his book 'The Isaiah Effect', [1] Quantum Physics strongly indicates that we live in a reality with the potential for many futures emanating *from any one moment in time*. Which future we end up experiencing seems to be dependent on how we think and choose in that 'Now' moment, which Eckhart Tolle talks so much about.

Braden bases his insights on the Isaiah Scroll, the only one found intact amongst the Dead Sea Scrolls. The fascinating point however, is that this Isaiah Scroll appears to contain information which backs up the relatively recent discoveries by Quantum Physics about the possibility of such alternate realities.

Diagram IV may help make more sense of this part of the discussion by giving a visual description of these various Time-line realities. It is from all these alternate Time-lines that a genuine prophet would then tend to tap into the most likely 'life-trajectory', as fueled by the cumulative 'thought-mass' generated by humanity at any one moment in time.

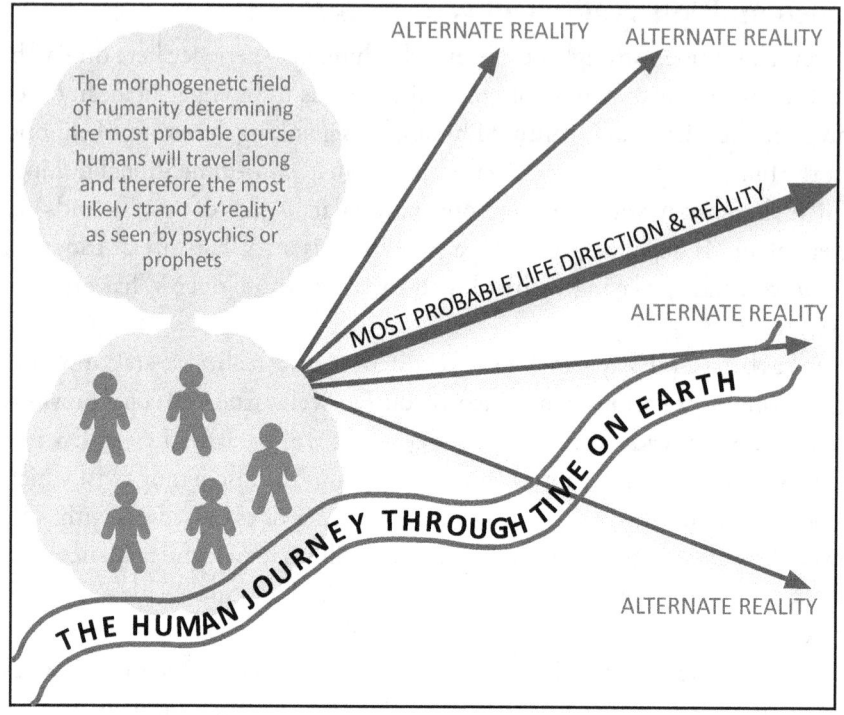

Diagram 4
Humanity's thoughts and beliefs determining the most probable reality from a range of multiple realities.

As we sow, so shall we reap

What Braden's concept suggest is that at any one point in time, humanity is traveling along a particular Time:Space route, dictated by the cumulative thoughts and beliefs we humans collectively engage in. These thoughts, powered by humanity's beliefs are Co-creating consciously or unconsciously all the time, creating a form of Energetic 'momentum' which then drives us along a specific and almost predictable course.

It shouldn't come as a surprise, that the most likely path into our future may be heading into a very challenging and difficult direction – a path beset with many problems and suffering. This would seem the most likely future outcome if we accept that 'Thought Creates Reality', and if we then consider what the collective 'thought-mass' or 'thought-field', engaged in by humanity is presently generating.

What Braden proposes in his book is that when a prophet peers into the future, what they tend to tap into is the most *likely* future. Not a one and *only* future. They're tapping into that future which has been most energized by the cumulative and combined thought patterns and beliefs of humanity at *that* point of doing the reading. Assuming of course that they are an accurate prophet, what they are seeing is indeed very much a reality, but only the one which stands out the most from all the other 'future-options'.

The point of power is now

However, where it gets exciting is when we can grasp the *essence* of what Braden is proposing.

What we need to understand is the very real possibility of the multiple futures we can and do have access to.

So, it is really important to understand that although a good prophet may have picked up on the most *likely* future, this does *not* automatically mean this is the *only* future available to us. But then comes the next crucial line of reasoning. The point of power, as Seth repeatedly says in the Jane Roberts books (see Appendix I)... is right *NOW*! In any moment of time, we as humans *can* choose an alternate reality, through the type of *consistent* thought patterns we choose to play with. Not that such an alternate reality somehow just magically jumps into our experience, simply because we wish it to be so. Rather, by a dedicated, unswerving and focused choice, repeated day in and day out, we can, on personal levels, choose an alternate reality we wish to be part of. Surely this would seem a better option than remaining disempowered and stuck on the present path we're on, heading for the cliff edge like a pack of lemmings?

Braden explains that even a small shift in one's Awareness at *this* point in time – personally or collectively – can, over time result in quite a large divergence from the direction we were initially heading into. So what we can legitimately conclude from his concepts so far is an incredible sense of empowerment; a sense of hope again.

Take a close look at diagram V, and see if this pictorial representation helps elucidate the above discussion.

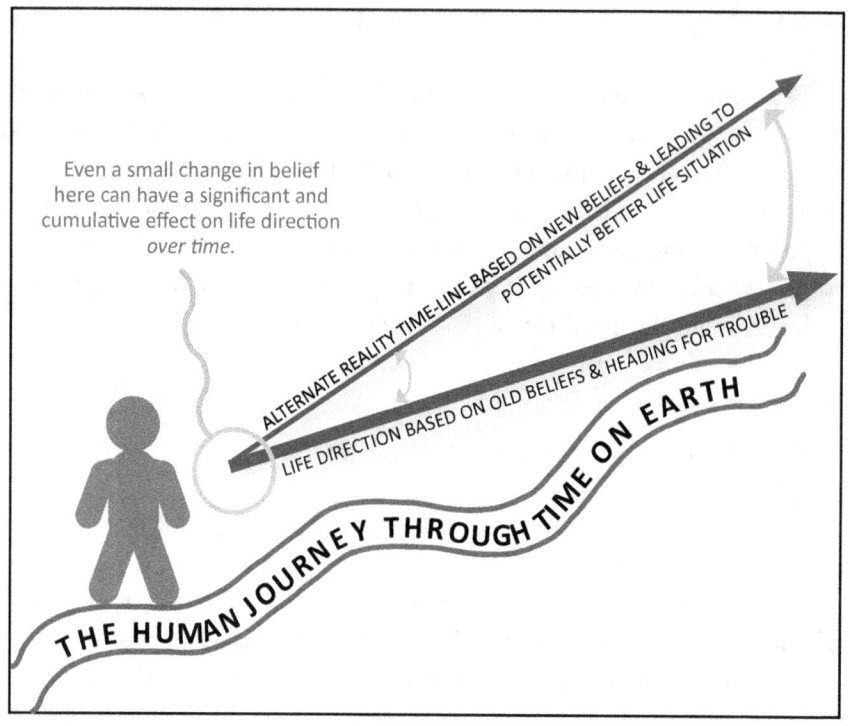

Diagram 5
How small changes in belief can result in considerable change in life-direction, over time.

Specific religions have had few qualms about laying bare the horrors awaiting mankind in the future, one example being the Apocalypse so many Christian religions believe we still have to endure in the near future, and possibly even in this present lifetime. If one buys into this perspective of humanity's prospect, then from our present stance, such predictions don't necessarily seem all that 'far-out'. Especially, if we look at what is happening on the world stage, and then tie it in with what has already been predicted, many centuries ago.

The future could be a bumpy ride

It would appear from even a cursory glance at the present state of affairs on this planet, that as a species we are indeed in for a very bumpy ride over the next 50-100 years or more, especially if you also accept what those 'old prophets', as

Chapter 14 - Multiple Realities Give Hope

well as some of the more 'modern' ones such as Nostradamus had to say about our possible future.

Already, many animal species have perished, due to what we as humans have done to this Earth. Such extinctions are being driven by Climate Change, as well as the massive poisoning we've created of the sea, air and land, as we march ever faster to the mesmerizing drumbeat of our economic masters, and the mantra of... 'increased economic growth and prosperity above all else'. Unfortunately, constant and maximal economic growth seems to have become the only valid and worthwhile yardstick of human success, driven by our obsession and greed for materiality and the Western 'quality of life'. The recent world-wide economic melt-down would strongly suggest however, that the wanton ways of our past can no longer be sustained, and require an urgent, fundamental overhaul.

The future need not be one of 'doom and gloom'

However, after reading Braden's books, we can once more gain a strong sense of hope. We are not necessarily locked into a 'doom and gloom' future. Far from it. We do have choices; especially in how we choose to think and accept certain foundational concepts of what life on planet Earth is all about.

Hopefully, what this discussion has allowed is for you to travel along a series of stepping-stones, each one designed to lead you a bit higher up that 'Mountain' we discussed in chapter 2. With any luck, the 'view' you now have of your 'horizon' is much changed compared to when you were viewing it from the 'valley'. Each changed perspective should now increasingly enable you to make more empowered choices in your daily life.

Quantum Physics validates these perceptions

What is particularly exciting about Braden's perspective of the future, and our ability to make other choices, is the *fact* that Quantum Physics now vindicates such speculations. The concept of multiple realities truly is no longer in the realm of the absurd. However, do understand that this is not about just making one single choice in one single moment along the time-line of our human Journey. It is about a moment-by-moment re-focusing on what is important to our lives. What sort of reality is it you truly desire to be part of? You need to set that intention, not just here and there, but as often as you can; certainly many times daily.

This is why so much of the previous discussion in this book has focused on our need to become skilled at being Witness to the thoughts we entertain in our minds. We also need to be keenly Aware of what we allow ourselves to get drawn into. This is especially so from the point of view of what society may choose to accept as a real or valid foundation from which to live our lives. In other words, it would appear from this discussion that we don't automatically and necessarily have to remain a participant in *this* particular version of the human or 'me' experience; the one we are presently aware of living in.

The bottom-line is that ultimately, nothing particularly revolutionary is being proposed here. What Braden has unquestionably done, however, is to 'connect the dots' from seemingly disparate sources, in turn creating quite a different 'picture' of how this reality can be managed when it comes to the future. It's highly recommended you do read his books, especially the 'Isaiah Effect' [1] and the 'Divine Matrix', [2] which will greatly expand your perceptions of reality.

Perhaps we do have some degree of free will

Various religions have made much of our supposed 'Free Will'. Many people, however, claim this belief in 'Free Will' to be one of the major con-jobs of religion. Nevertheless, perhaps we do have at least more Free Will than may have seemed possible at first, particularly if we look at Braden's ideas in the light of... 'thoughts are creative'. It's precisely our thoughts which do drive the reality of Co-creation, in turn providing the potential to transform our lives – for good or bad.

In that sense, there is this amazing *choice*-capacity to our human Journey. Through the thoughts we allow ourselves to 'play' with inside our minds, we do have the capacity and the power to *choose* to diverge out of this present reality we otherwise seem so 'locked' into. And the key to this divergence is indeed via the power of our thoughts – *but in each Moment NOW*.

Multiple realities and the power of thought

In other words, we can be part of a reality in which Peace and Love *are* the predominant Energies ruling our existence as a human species and as individuals. But then we also need to *create* a trajectory out of this present, rather difficult and challenging reality, and into the one we desire to be part of. We can do this by ensuring we create *within* ourselves precisely what it is we wish to be part of - *externally*.

Chapter 14 - Multiple Realities Give Hope

If we want to be part of a human reality living out our existence via the fundamentals of Peace and Love, then there is one, underlying point which does need to be deeply grasped, right down to the very core of our being. In other words, *those qualities we so desire to experience in our external reality, must first be created within our daily thoughts -* **moment by moment.**

If we desire to 'leave' this present reality of suffering, stupidity, greed, destructiveness, and so much more, then we will need to anchor those values of Peace and Love deeply within our day to day experience of the human Journey. Not just as some 'nice mental philosophy', but rather, as a total *Beingness*, where every cell in our body; our very genes, are living this alternate and desired reality. This means increasingly living our lives from Higher Self vs ego-self, the former being primarily fueled by that Love and Peace Energy, compared to fear which drives the ego state.

This change in *where* we live our lives from creates an 'attractor' Energy, as discussed previously, which slowly but surely starts to pull you from this reality into the one you wish to be part of. Just like two magnets being strongly pulled together. On one level it may all sound like science fiction... 'Yeah, right, you're gonna change dimensional realities are you'? 'Good luck'! 'Why not get a good sci-fi DVD instead - much more practical'.

Dimension-hopping only needs your mind & thoughts – not necessarily a 'gizmo'

But as you focus on and explore these ideas further, it seems increasingly feasible that these concepts are no longer in the realm of Sci-fi, especially if you're willing to look deeper and further into reality than simply what society or religion has presented it to be. Quantum Physics supports the idea that there are multi-dimensions to the human experience, and that it is actually possible to 'dimension-hop' under certain circumstances. Physicists may be waiting for the invention of various gizmos which would allow us to do such dimension hopping, but the irony is that all we need is our minds, directed by our intentions, and careful, consistent use of our moment by moment thoughts.

This really is no longer New Age fantasy and wishful thinking. We need to understand that what we perceive as our present, seemingly very real human experience, is but one of **many** *alternative dimensional options.*

And the way to achieve this very real possibility of shifting dimensions is via our state of mind. That seems to be the key. And the primary state of mind to facilitate such a dimensional hop is being as much as possible in a state of Peace and Love. Our every thought, feeling, judgments and our choices - **moment by moment** - all need to be strongly colored by these fundamental states of Peace and Love.

Again, fundamentally, we already know this; most religions have espoused these ideas for centuries, and so you might be wondering why all the excitement about something we have seen as a possible 'truth' for eons. What is new and exciting is the manner in which to change our reality – externally and internally – through these fundamental concepts of Co-creation, and all its Spiritual ramifications. After reading these books by Braden, you'll hopefully grasp that this 'dimension-hoping' is no longer just a possibility... it's very much an actuality.

Strangely enough, the irony is that this is something we are doing all the time anyway, through the fundamental Laws of 'Thought is Creative'. It's just that humanity has rarely cottoned on to the fact that as humans, we are constantly engaged in Co-creating our reality, albeit with little Consciousness of this phenomenon, which is such an essential part of the human experience within this earthly realm.

But the bottom line is that the power to make such dimensional shifts lies not *outside* of you; but *inside* you. How incredibly empowering!

But what it does take, is to BE what it is we *wish* to experience. You might like to read that a few times, even though it is a point raised many times now in this book. So the nitty-gritty of it all is as follows:-

- We don't necessarily have to be dragged kicking and screaming into our all too obvious and likely future reality, as indicated by the way we as a species are presently living our collective lives. And you definitely don't need to be a genius to predict the most likely outcome of where we are currently heading - especially in the West.
- You can personally *choose* to 'dimension-hop/slide/whatever' into an alternative dimensional version of what you are presently engaged in.
- The key is simple - although challenging.

Chapter 14 - Multiple Realities Give Hope

But first... that Inner shift

An alternative does exist, despite where we as a species, and you as a member of that human species, are presently so collectively stuck, heading for the gurgler. The major point to be taken on board here is to look completely *beyond* the 'reality' you are presently in. You need to make a fundamental *Inner* shift, where you literally *become* Peace and as much Lovingness as possible. This needs to be done so powerfully that it automatically, and over time, draws you into this alternative dimension - *reflecting your new Inner shift*. However, this is a day by day, thought by thought process of focusing on the alternate reality you wish to draw into your life.

Challenging? Yes. Impossible? No! It's also important to back this up as much as possible, by starting to do daily actions which are resonant with this desire. In other words, at this point, constructive actions need to back up our new thought patterns. Start focusing on all the many, already existent inventions which can turn the tide of Global Warming. Focus your Awareness and Energy on the increasing number of organizations setting themselves up to make positive change in our reality. Some examples of those using the power of the Internet include 'Getup' and 'Avaaz'.[3]

Nothing to lose

And if this is all a huge load of New Age nonsense, what would be the very worst that could happen? Actually, nothing would be lost and indeed, so much gained. At the very least, we would be attempting to increase the sense of positivity in our own lives. This in turn can only allow for more positive changes to occur in our personal spheres of influence. We might find ourselves more motivated to put in solar hot water systems; solar cells for our electricity supplies; not to automatically use the electric wash-drier when there is sunshine and wind outside; ensure we diligently re-cycle; become aware of how much water we use. We could make a list of the names and addresses of key politicians and other people in power, and write letters or emails to them on a frequent basis. Let them know *you* know there are alternate ways of dealing with our various crises. Do the daily 'Fountaining' visualization - to be described later in this chapter.

But before we even think of creating all these changes on the *outside*, yet again, understand that we first need to look at fundamental shifts *inside* us.

Only then will there be any chance of true change occurring in our external world. Out of such a new focus, strong intention, and backed up by action as well as daily visualizations of success, we can allow positive and Healing change to occur on this plane of reality. So even if this is all New Age hype, such a lot of good can still come out of this turn of mind – if for no-one else but you. But do also remember, it can help to engage others into this process too.

Such changes of perception as have been discussed, if passed on to others, can hopefully still allow for an instigation of powerful change within humanity. This is especially so if we use the power and magic of electronic, instant information sharing. Perhaps we shouldn't under-estimate the capacity for humans to change. Just look at how relatively quickly the reality of global Warming did sink in. No longer are these concepts just some wacky theory of dooms-dayers. Instead, they present valid, scientific realities we desperately need to pay attention to.

However... don't ram these ideas down others' throats

But absolutely no proselytizing. Firstly, make the changes yourself; 'walk-the-talk' as it were. Using the power of the Internet, pass on snippets of empowering ideas. The worst that can happen is the recipient deletes those emails... or asks you to stop sending them; hardly like facing a firing squad. Be willing to discuss it further if they wish to know more. But *definitely* don't force others to your vision - or judge them if they see things differently. Such attitudes are precisely what have caused so much of humanity's woes in the first place. So, don't get caught up in a 'blame-game' or 'we-have-to-change-*them*' game.

Hope is always a crucial ingredient to life

Hopelessness is never as strong as when we feel we cannot act. It's been interesting to note recently that there is a new phenomenon of hopelessness occurring within many who feel overwhelmed by issues of Global Warming, and the recent planetary economic melt-down. They hear the constant discussions on the News and elsewhere, and feel paralyzed by the enormity of it all.

Yet the above ideas, as proposed by Braden, and explored in this chapter, *do* give us very reasonable, simple and yet *individually* powerful ways of dealing with the many human crises we always appear to be in.

Chapter 14 - Multiple Realities Give Hope

The power of one... and one percent!

In 'The Isaiah Effect',[1] Braden also discusses various research projects which examine the power of meditation and prayer on communities, through what scientists call the 'field effect'. Maharishi Mahesh Yogi, the founder of Transcendental Meditation, believed that there was a direct correlation between the buildup of stress in the collective human Morphogenetic Field, and its expression as a range of negative human emotionally driven actions, such as violence, conflict, crisis or other sociological problems.

This suggests an interesting conclusion. When the amount of 'stress' or internalized conflict in any group of people is allowed to build up to a certain critical point, it can then erupt into more generalized and externalized violence, such as war, and other disruptive phenomenon. The Maharishi's insight was to understand that there was a powerful link between the previously mentioned 'Field Effect' and meditation. Much the same sort of link as is seen between the Matrix, and Co-creation, and much along the lines of the Hologram concept, discussed earlier in this book, where we humans can be seen as a 'chip' off the Larger Hologram. When this 'Field' was actively engaged, through group visualization, meditation or prayer, then as the 'stress' in the meditation group fell, so too was there a reflex effect in the wider community.

Several studies of these effects have been conducted, which measured various community parameters, such as violence, criminal events, fires, suicides, traffic accidents and so on. Again and again, these parameters would improve in a positive manner, when as little as the square root of 1% within any particular city or population engaged in this *specific* form of focused meditation. Serious statistical study eliminated any aspect of chance to these documented changes.

One study set up in Jerusalem in 1983, during the then conflict with Lebanon, placed groups of TM meditators in various key areas of this city. The results were astounding, as they again verified a direct link between the number of people engaged in the *focused* meditation exercises, and a drop in diverse societal end-points used to measure effectiveness. This was called the 'Maharishi Effect'. This range of studies indicated that this effect first started to make itself felt when the number of people engaged in collective meditation was greater than the square root of one percent of a population.

When you work this out, it amounts to a ridiculously small number. As calculated by Braden,[4] just 100 individuals would be needed in a city of a million to start having some positive and measurable effect on that community's quality of life. This is an astounding piece of information, especially when considered within the context of the *total* world population, where that square root result of 1% would be just on... 8,000 people!

According to the many serious, scientific studies already done, that's all it would take to start catalyzing positive and powerful change on a *global* level, if people combined in a *specifically* focused meditation and *unified* agenda.

Science has vindicated the power of thought

Firstly therefore, scientific studies by different people, at different times, in different parts of the world have vindicated, again and again, what a staggeringly low number of people are needed to create positive and measurable effects on the general community. This is mind-blowing, and incredibly exciting news. It provides us with concrete evidence that we *can* change our reality for the better on this seemingly doomed planet of ours.

Nowadays it is very possible and easy to connect such relatively small numbers of people into a 'one-mind' group, and for such a group to then focus on *specific* goals in their meditation, directed to *precise* targets within humanity. This is particularly possible through the power of the Internet.

The power of the mustard seed

It is of course true that many religions have always talked about the power of prayer, but now we actually have the scientific proof, backed up by Quantum Physics, that this is no longer just church gibberish, or New Age hog-wash for that matter. This phenomenal power of the mind is real, and whether we use it via prayer, or Co-creation, or visualization, or whatever you wish to call it... it works. Interesting, how that parable of the 'mustard seed' now makes a lot more sense. Let's take a look at the wording of that passage in Matthew 17:20 [5]

.......'If ye have faith as a grain of mustard seed, ye shall say unto this mountain, remove hence to yonder place; and it shall remove; and nothing shall be impossible to you'.

This Biblical quote is ultimately a statement about the power of the mind, and the capacity we as humans do have to alter our reality. Remember this bit of information was given to humanity over 2,000 years ago. Yet it is only now, through the amalgamation of Quantum Physics and Eastern mysticism, that we may be really starting to understand what was offered way back then.

This parable would seem appropriate and prophetic within today's greater understanding of the power of the mind.

It's not just some literary metaphor, but the actual reality behind a powerful human phenomenon: a power and ability which humanity has been disconnected from for such a long time. In a sense, only half the recipe was provided in previous times. We were told we could create miracles, but we were not adequately taught *how* to make this process work. The further development of science, backed up by actual field trials using statistics, and various other scientific methods of validation, now does help us to connect more deeply with this process. It is science itself which is currently providing a solid foundation to what may formerly have been seen as 'religious nonsense'. As Braden suggest, by tapping into this new understanding of how reality seems to work, perhaps it is high time we engage in more than just political or military solutions to the wide range of societal ills experienced in just about every country on Earth.

'Fountaining' – a powerful tool to change the world

It is also interesting that there was a meditation concept which started in 1981, called the 'Fountain Groups'. Briefly, it originated in Brighton, UK, where groups of people would come together at set times to focus their attention upon the local city or town fountain. The aim was to have a collective meditation, on the theme of sending Light or 'positive Energy' to the designated city or town focal point; in these cases, always the local town fountain. From there, it was visualized as radiating out into the general community of that town or city.

Over the many years these Fountain Groups were doing their meditations, a range of statistics were gathered and analyzed. Again, positive and statistically verifiable correlations were found to occur between such regular meditations and a wide range of quality-of-life measures. Now, with the power of the Internet, this can be done on a much more global level, easily recruiting potentially millions of people to conduct a similar practice on a daily and regular basis.

Enter a variation on a theme called 'Fountaining'. This is a process where mind power is utilized to heal the planet of its sufferings, on so many levels. There are no organizations to join; no fees to pay; no dogmas to believe, nor group politics to contend with. Just you and your Mind Power linked in with millions of others. Sounds interesting?

If you regularly watch the News, horrified by what you see, feeling impotent to do anything much about it as an *individual*, then know you can make a difference on a *personal* level. There is a way in which it is possible to link your mind with many others, creating a massive Healing Force, capable of changing your reality. And all it will involve is three minutes of your time, once daily.

Simply apply your Mind Power, in synch with millions of others, for just three minutes at noon your local time. That's it! *Individually*, that power may seem trivial and impotent to change World events. However, by consciously visualizing your mind synergistically connected to many other minds, tremendously increases our *collective* ability to influence reality. Quantum science, and the above discussion show how this is no longer some optimist's fantasy!

Imagine: it's 12 noon where you live. Use your mobile phone or wrist-watch alarm to alert you to this set time. Now take just three minutes out of your busy schedule. Disconnect from what's happening around you by finding yourself a nice quiet spot, even if this means excusing yourself to go to the bathroom for a few moments of privacy. Now focus on a quiet Space within yourself. When you feel centered, imagine your mind linking in with everyone else who at that point in your time zone is also choosing to do the same, for those brief three minutes. By using your local or international News, choose those trouble spots presently most in the News, e.g. Iraq, Iran, Palestine, Pakistan, Burma, North Korea, etc. - and focus your mind power there.

Now visualize sending Healing, Loving Energy to that trouble spot. Visualize this in whatever way works for you. Don't worry about details. In other words, don't get caught up in *how* Peace or Healing change might come about. Simply visualize the end result. Peace and harmony; people being respectful, kind and more understanding towards each other.

Never mind how impossible it may seem, just visualize the desired end result as clearly as you can. Letting your mind become distracted by the potentially thousands of 'ifs', 'buts' and 'hows', will only sabotage the entire process. Just see this exercise as a fantasy game where you can set the parameters, and make whatever constructive, Healing changes you wish to your present reality.

And that is basically all there is to it. Hold your focus as clearly as you can for just three minutes; of course, longer if you wish. But the idea is to make this all as easy as possible, without minimizing the effectiveness of what many minds linked together can achieve in catalyzing powerful and positive change.

Chapter 14 - Multiple Realities Give Hope

Twelve noon may not suit your schedule. Then consider this reality - as vindicated by what Quantum Physics is now proving about Time - **Time is not static; it is in fact quite plastic.** So, if 12 noon doesn't work for you, just use your *intention* to ensure your session of Visualization – never mind what actual time you might end up doing it - is *warped* back or forward to 12 noon of your day. Sounds crazy... but studies have shown this to be scientific fact. Plus it still allows you to co-ordinate with the millions of others Visualizing for Peace at 12 noon.

O.K. You've just done a strong, focused visualization of Peace and Healing, linking in with whoever else knows about this concept in your time zone. Now imagine the 12 noon time zone marching across the entire planet as it revolves. As it becomes 12 noon in the next cities or town on the Globe, more people in turn link in with all the others in *their* time zone. Together, they're all sending a united Visualization-Image of Peace and Healing to various trouble spots.

In this fashion, using this simple, easy concept, a 24 hour-a-day wave of Healing visualization is being constantly generated, and sent to where it is most needed.

This is an exquisitely simple concept, capable of running itself once set into motion, yet how powerful in its potential to truly alter or positively influence various negative realities occurring at any one particular time on the planet. The only thing needed to make this concept work is for the idea to become commonly known, and for people to truly incorporate this concept into their daily schedule. And three minutes once daily is surely not a big demand.

Working *collectively* in this way, by linking in Consciousness with the many others who know about this concept, can therefore empower us *individually* to nevertheless help Heal humanity *generally*. You don't need to know who all those others are. *Intention* is the primary key to successfully using Mind Power. Simply imagine or visualize yourself - in whatever way works for you - connected to these other minds in your time zone. Then allow your personal visualization for Peace and Healing to unite with the collective image.

Obviously, the more people who know about this simple concept and choose to participate, the more effective the process will be. But remember, using Braden's calculations, based on experimental evidence, only a minimum of the square root of 1% of the population are needed to create societal change. For the entire current planetary population, that figure again, was an unbelievably low 8,000 people! Surely this is not an overwhelming or impossible target to achieve? To that end, you might like to share this concept with as many others as you feel may be interested and open to the concept.

Every single person, actively participating in this enormous potential to help influence a much needed Healing on this planet, *can* make a truly significant difference. Through the power of the Internet, the concept can be rapidly spread across the entire Globe, like a strong ripple affecting the Awareness of millions. This information has been presented in one of the appendices, where it is easy to tear out the page, scan it into your computer, and then pass it on via email. By the same token, don't proselytize, never mind how enthusiastic you might be about this idea.

Fountaining is a very powerful concept which can empower *you* as an individual to be truly effective in helping catalyze Healing changes to humanity and the planet. No longer do you have to continue observing humanity's suffering, while feeling powerless to personally do anything about changing it.

The process would cost you nothing more than three minutes of your time daily. It is a self-running process once people have been made Aware of it. All you need to do is to remember to do it! Simply use your local and international News sources as the means to determine which areas of humanity or the planet need our collective focus of visualization, at any particular time. Hence no need to check in with anyone as to who or where to send your Healing Energies to.

At the very worst, it means three minutes of your life wasted daily. But if there is any substance to what is presented above, *how can we afford not to do the process?* Any opportunity to help humanity through such a simple, quick process, is surely worth three minutes of your time? And god knows we as a species need all the help and Healing we can get.

But here comes the crunch; what are *you* now going to do with this information? 'Oh, that was quite interesting actually... must do that "sometime"'. Or will you commit *yourself* to now making this a regular and consistent feature of your daily life?

But there are already millions praying... and still we have suffering

Many people, when they hear about the relatively small number of people needed to make change via mind-power, find it hard to believe these figures. In their minds, there are already so many people praying, meditating and

Chapter 14 - Multiple Realities Give Hope

visualizing for peace and harmony – and yet look at the mess the world seems to be in. This skepticism is indeed valid, but there are at least two possible answers to this potential dilemma. Firstly, we need to hark back to the concept of light, as used in two very different ways – via a torch or via a laser. Remember, in the former the light was dispersed, while in the latter it was far more coherent. Such a dispersed beam of light from a torch is fine to light a room, but no good for cutting through steel.

In a similar fashion, perhaps all this praying and meditating that has indeed been going on for a very long time is overall being done in far too dispersed, or just not enough of a *coherent*, specifically focused manner to give maximal effectiveness. Remember, in these various studies mentioned earlier, a very clear, specific and intentional target was set up upon which to focus mind power.

Secondly, anyone wanting to dismiss the power of the mind in changing world events may simply be assuming that nothing has happened; that no change has occurred to our human condition. However, one could equally argue that our human condition just might have been a whole lot worse if we hadn't had all those people praying and meditating!

Perhaps the Cuban Missile Crisis *would* have jump-started World War III; perhaps the various other stand-offs we've lived through during the Cold War – and since – may have equally sparked off much more conflict and chaos than did occur. Perhaps the various Stock Market crises we've had over the last few decades would have ended up in a much more serious situation, much sooner than it occurred end 2008.

Ultimately, it is true that neither side to these arguments can prove their stance beyond a shadow of doubt. However, these 'mind-power' ideas – such as 'Fountaining' – are so simple, user-friendly and potentially capable of doing so much good... why would we not want to at least try them? Again, three minutes of our time, once a day, to use a bit of focused mind-power surely is not an overwhelming burden in anyone's life? Never mind how busy we think we are! The major – and very real obstacle – to doing this simple process is to... actually remember to do it.

What will the changes look like

As we increasingly focus on creating this new *Inner* dimension of Peace and Love, how can we hope to see these anticipated changes actualize, on a very mundane, daily-life level? Events should start occurring where politicians, religious leaders and others are getting together, and making the necessary changes to how we live and treat each other. For instance, it's interesting to see the Pope some time ago opening a dialogue of reconciliation and better understanding towards key leaders of Islam – a very significant step forward. Similarly, moves have been made by President Obama towards Iran and other countries of the Middle-East. Very recently, at a world meeting of leaders, a resolution was passed to rid the world of nuclear arms. Even Russia and China signed on.

We should see additional situations of reconciliation occurring, as happened in South Africa after Apartheid crumbled, as well as more recently in Ireland. We could equally still hope for a true and lasting peace in the Middle-East between Israel and Palestine. Hopefully, peace, or at least an effective 'cease-fire' situation, may even become possible between so-called 'terrorists' and the 'rest of us'. Sounds impossible now, yet once upon a time it was also thought impossible for the Berlin Wall to ever come down. But it did.

So, as you make this Inner shift of choosing to live in an alternative time-line of this reality, expect to increasingly see us humans listening to each other, and realizing how we have truly harmed others through our greed and ignorance. We should start to see humans acknowledging and rectifying these things; appreciating how we can rejoice in each other's differences, and most importantly, acknowledging that there are many ways to God. In fact, it actually would be a wondrous thing to have such diversity in these Paths, with no need for competition, comparison or judgment between them.

Change – we can instigate it now

As dark as the future seems at times, there may still be time to make a difference to where we are heading. And for this to happen, we don't need to wait for religion, or politicians, or any *outer* force, groups or organizations to get it together first. We can start that process *right now*. From *this* moment on. All it will take is to see the possibility, and to truly understand that reality-altering and dimension-hopping are now scientifically viable realities. Each of these realities is possible via the power of the mind, and through the various techniques already explored. We can also feel secure in *knowing* that the power to do so lies not *without*, but *within*. It's about being Conscious of where our minds and souls are at, *moment by moment*. Equally, it's not about ignoring our present reality. Acknowledge and honor it – but also don't buy into it being the *only* reality we have access to.

Visualize for peace – but also anchoring it via action

The need to Visualize for Peace and Healing on this planet does however need to also be anchored into our daily lives – by actions. It's no good just to think 'nice thoughts', but then act out the opposite towards situations or people, via anger, judgment, irritability, etc. Working on aligning our Inner and outer Energy, so as to be more resonant with a state of peace is also more likely to align us with Alternate Dimensions or Realities where greater harmony and peace are a fundamental factor.

We need to focus on the peace and harmony that automatically flows from being able to live our daily lives more from our Higher Self perspective. It is *the* key. We need to anchor these qualities into our physical, human sphere, making them a part of every living moment of our lives.

As much as some people believe an Apocalypse to be coming, we also need to remember that peaceful life options *can* be drawn into our present reality. Certainly this is possible if we tap into, and use Gregg Braden's concepts of multiple Realities. But this does involve us remaining focused on being peaceful in everything we do and think. It's that old adage of 'being in the world but not *of* it'.

In other words, we acknowledge where our human reality seems to be heading, but then we also don't lose hope because of what we see and sense all around us. We need to keep reminding ourselves that this is not the *only* reality ahead of us. Depending on our focus, and constancy of that focus, we are able to split off from this general reality into more positive, alternate realities. But this does require of us an incredibly focused sense of where we want to end up, and to hold that focus day in, day out; moment by moment. No mean task - but possible, yes.

Choices & solutions need not always be limited to an either/or response

Another fundamental and important point we need to explore is the way we humans normally respond to crises or problems in far too unilateral a manner. True, we live in a reality of duality – dark/light; good/bad; right/wrong; up/

down, etc. But the problem is that we've then also allowed this situation to prejudice the way we respond to life. The majority of humanity tends to see their life situations – and their solutions – needing an either/or response. This approach can work, but inevitably only provides for a limited response.

Humanity needs to realize that life simply isn't so much about black and white situations, as it is about a vast range of choices between shades of grey. Hence, many of our solutions to life's problems can be made more powerful and productive if we look at them, not from an either/or stance, but rather as a 'bit-of-both' response.

Treating illness provides a good example of how this different and more inclusive approach also offers a much more effective therapy, inevitably with enhanced outcomes. At present, if we get ill, most people still only think in terms of an orthodox medical solution to their health issue. Instead, we can also choose to incorporate a more natural medical intervention, such as the use of a good diet; some antioxidants or other nutrients, medicinal herbs, and so on.

Far too many people still believe it has to be an either/or choice, yet a truly healthy and balanced response would be to realize that *both* approaches can be used, concurrently, safely and effectively. We need to realize that using such a bi-lateral – or complementary – approach to our ill-health issues is not inherently incompatible or mutually exclusive. Quite the contrary; and such a revised and more inclusive approach to dealing with life's challenges extends to all realms of human endeavor too.

Our present energy crisis is another example, where the solution is not just to go for one other option, such as nuclear alone, or wave power alone. The most powerful and sustainable solution would be to include a wide range of alternate and complementing natural energy resources, simultaneously.

Within the religious sphere, we need to understand that it's not as if one religious path alone leads to salvation and all others to damnation, despite what certain religious leaders and their followers may think! Life just isn't that black and white. There are as many roads to salvation as humans on this Earth. One path is not inherently better than another, yet this belief that it is, remains a primary point of contention amongst humans, simply because we still choose to see such life options as an either/or situation.

Chapter 14 - Multiple Realities Give Hope

Such narrow and restrictive perspectives in this arena of life are important to look at, precisely because they are also still the basis of so much prejudice and suffering we humans cause each other.

Exercise
- Make a choice to do the daily three minute 'Fountaining Meditation'. Set your mobile or wrist watch alarm – right now – for 12 noon.
- Set the intention that the next time you go on-line, you also sign up to 'GetUp' or 'Avaaz'.[3] This allows for the power of 'one', multiplied by 'many', to equal great change.

Summary of thoughts thus far
- Quantum science suggests the existence of many possible futures which extend outwards from each moment of our lives. In turn, there are ways we can choose which future we wish to be part of.
- Gregg Braden dubs this the 'Isaiah Effect'.
- We can choose to change our future by re-focusing, moment-by-moment, day-by-day, on what is fundamentally important to us in our lives.
- If we want to be part of a human reality, living out our existence via the core principles of Peace and Love, *we must first create these qualities in our daily thoughts and actions -* **moment by moment.**
- All occurrences of violence, negativity, conflicts and crisis in any society are the expression of stress in the collective consciousness.
- Studies have confirmed that when a group meditates on *specific*, focused, coherent goals, huge changes can occur in the target population or situation.
- Many religions have always talked about the power of prayer, but now we have scientific proof, backed by Quantum Physics, that this is no longer just church gibberish or New Age hog-wash.
- Using the 'Fountain Meditation' concept is a very powerful way in which individuals can positively influence global reality.

- Despite this earthly realm being one of duality, our responses to life's challenges don't automatically have to be an either/or choice. A 'bit-of-both' approach can be more empowering and productive.
- This is a fundamental and crucial shift in thinking that we as humans need to make before we can more powerfully resolve our many human dilemmas.

REFERENCES

1. Braden, Gregg. *The Isaiah Effect – decoding the lost science of prayer and prophecy*, Hay House, 2000.

2. Braden, Braden. *The Divine Matrix – bridging Time, Space, Miracles and Belief*, HayHouse Inc, 2007.

3. Avaaz, www.avaaz.org/ . Getup, www.getup.org.au

4. Braden, Gregg. *The Isaiah Effect – decoding the lost science of prayer and prophecy*, Hay House, 2000. p. 237.

5. Matthew 17:20. *Bible, King James Version.*

CHAPTER 15

ONCE YOU'VE OPENED PANDORA'S BOX....

Take the first step in faith. You don't have to see the whole staircase. Just take the first step.

Martin Luther King. Jr.

So here you are; you've made it to the last chapter! Congratulations - unless you are like a dear friend of mine, who always cheats when he starts a new book... by reading the final chapter first.

Having opened Pandora's box

Reading this book may have been a bit like opening Pandora's Box. What you now need to realize is that once opened, and as soon as you start to explore alternate perspective of life here on planet Earth, things may never be quite the same again. Old patterns of thinking and doing may no longer work for you. Things you might previously have found to be irresistible or indispensable to your life, may now seem quite unimportant. Issues and ideas you had never conceived of may instead become central to how you want to now live. Initially, this can be experienced as rather chaotic; a bit like a butterfly having to break out of its cocoon.

Breaking free from a formerly restrictive environment does involve some struggle. The cocoon itself needs to be broken before release is possible, and a new phase of life begins. So too with us humans. Before we can fly free, old ideas and concepts need to be reassessed, as they may now seem rather limiting. Initially, the butterfly may have been quite content to crawl around on plants, ferociously gobbling anything in sight - a bit like us Westerners, overly focused on our materialistic way of life.

Once free from the cocoon, however, the butterfly finds itself inhabiting a seemingly alien environment – the free air. And once in the air, the butterfly can truly fly free in all its glory and beauty. That transformation of the caterpillar from the pupae into the butterfly is an accurate metaphor of our human Journey too. Nothing less than total transformation is required for us to be able to move into the next phase of that trip.

Concluding thoughts

We have looked at our reality here on planet Earth in some lateral, and possibly challenging ways. We've looked at the role of religion, and the fact that for many people religion is still a very viable structure or format through which to facilitate their continued growth. However, for those who have been feeling stifled or disempowered by their religion, what's equally important to know is that there are other valid options.

Religion - you <u>are</u> allowed to expand the boundaries

One such choice is for people to expand *within* the structure of their present religion, while giving much more credit to their *own* sense of what is right or wrong, rather than what dogma demands they believe. But another option is to step out of the 'Bonsai Pot' altogether, as discussed via that metaphor used in chapter 5, and make their Journey through an alternate paradigm. It's extremely important, however, to understand that the Journey this book may have taken you on does not mean you now have to automatically leave your religion. This step may happen – *if* it needs to happen – in its own good time, and not before. You will definitely know if that time arrives, and this is not something you should allow yourself to be pushed into before you are ready.

Suffering – a 'hard-wired' aspect to 'Planet Earth School'

A major theme covered in this book was that of suffering: how we first of all need to acknowledge that this seems to be an inherent and possibly hard-wired aspect to 'Planet Earth School'. This latter concept hopefully provides for a shift in focus when dealing with suffering, so that we can *choose* to work with suffering. It's about doing so in a positive manner, and to our advantage, rather

Chapter 15 - Once You've Opened Pandora's Box...

than running away from it or trying to cover it up with materiality, as we are so wont to do in the West.

We also looked at alternative ways of dealing with pain and suffering through Eckhart Tolle's concept of the 'Pain Body'. His perspective provides an empowering way of managing pain, rather than feeling overwhelmed into hopelessness by it.

We looked at the basic concept of 'Thought Creates Reality', as well as exploring a lot of Co-creative techniques through which we can use this fundamental fact to our benefit.

Spiritualizing our lives

The need to shift our human focus more into a Spiritual slant towards life was also explored, with many suggestions as to how we can achieve this in our daily lives. This shift allows us to live our lives differently and more productively on mental, emotional, physical as well as Spiritual levels. Perhaps for many, the idea of bringing back a 'Sabbath' of our own making, and our own timing – a day to rest and re-connect with deeper aspects to who we are - could provide huge rewards on many levels of our life, both physically and Spiritually.

Along with this concept comes the issue of really needing to scale down our way of life. Our modern, Western economic system thrives on consumerism and constant growth, but these are precisely the factors driving so many Westerners into debt and bankruptcy, on both dollar and Spiritual levels. Just take a look around your home now, and see how much material 'stuff' you have accumulated.

All very nice, and there's also nothing intrinsically evil about it. That point is most important to get clear. It's not about now having to sell everything, and start living like a monk or nun. But do you actually *need* it all? Are you even using it much or is it just sitting there? These are important questions you might like to ask yourself before going on your next spending spree.

Do we need all this material 'stuff'?

An interesting exercise would be to sit down, and go through all the material goods you already have, never mind what you also still have on your 'wish list'. Then start to really look at how much of it you truly *need* – compared to just *want*. There is also a great necessity and urgency to start asking questions such as 'what emotional or Inner void is all this materiality actually trying to fill'? 'And has it'? 'Are you really so much more at Peace in your life because of all this material 'stuff'? 'Are you feeling truly fulfilled on some deep level for having all this materiality'? As we have explored in previous chapters, it just might serve us better to figure out what we are *really* desiring, and then go for this more directly, rather than via all the materialistically orientated 'stuff' so ubiquitously part of our Western lives.

This consumerist conveyor-belt promises us all sorts of things – happiness, success, power, envy, being seen as sexy and desirable, and so much more. Yet it is also driving us into family breakdown, burnout and sometimes bankruptcy. Perhaps the more we can release ourselves from this form of slavery, the better; definitely on an Energetic and Spiritual level. If we could do this, and not have to work so hard on acquiring all these consumer goods, we might just find that extra time to be with our kids or our friends; to be able to sit and watch a sunset; to have more time for Inner reflection and Spiritual Growth via a range of practices – such as meditation, which we explored in chapter 9.

Life is a series of cycles

In both West and East, we commonly break up the life Journey into several different stages. There is our childhood stage, leading to early adulthood, and for many, parent-hood. For most people, then comes that stage where the kids have 'grown and flown', thus giving back to parents an ability to concentrate on themselves to a greater extent. In the East, there is an additional possibility to the last stage, where life's focus can be more on contemplation, Spiritual exploration and Growth; much like a 'priest' or 'monk/nun'. By the same token, this doesn't mean you all have to join a monastery or nunnery once your kids have flown the coop!

But it does mean the extra time you should now have on your hands may be better invested into some Spiritually-orientated things, rather than simply accumulating or experiencing further materiality. In the West, we mostly seem to have lost this perspective of how life can be seen to be made up of different stages or cycles. Interestingly though, the various 'sea-changes' which so many retired couples are lately embarking on, is at least a signal that people – post-parenthood – are looking for something more. Just sitting around at home, 'dusting and cleaning' all those material goods they have accumulated over their lifetime... and waiting to die... isn't cutting it any longer.

Again, it needs to be emphasized that there is absolutely nothing inherently bad or wrong with materiality. Far from it! But what we as Westerners may have done is become too enamored with this side of life. Too often, we also expect such materiality to be the answer to our sense of Inner emptiness, our loneliness, our despondency with life itself. Yet, this emptiness may have more to do with the way we have lost touch with our Energy-related or Spiritual dimension. This is an important aspect of life which is invariably dismissed by science, or generally under-rated by Western culture. Nevertheless, that sense of lost Connection with these Higher Dimensions, which is such an inherent aspect to who we are as humans, also causes us so much more pain than we need to endure.

Alternate realities and dimension-hopping

We also looked at Gregg Braden's ideas of alternate Time:Space trajectories within Reality. We need to realize that despite a vast array of dire prophesies, we are not automatically locked into such future realities, unless we continue to make ourselves resonant to the negative Energies which so frequently drive humanity. Braden's mathematical analysis as to how relatively few people it would take for major shifts to occur in our human direction of life, is truly inspiring. We just need to grab that fact by the horns, and activate the ideas behind this paradigm.

Alternate realities can definitely be manifested, and we have looked at a range of tools through which to empower us to do so. The 'Fountaining' concept, via the power of the News and the Internet is a really quick, easy, yet mind-blowingly powerful way to engage us all into making change occur. But such change needs to first come from a Space where we have looked deeply inside ourselves, and made the biggest changes there. Before we can realistically expect to see external changes, it is crucial that new perceptions and beliefs on life need to enter and guide our personal realities first.

Calling on Higher Dimensions for help with our human journey

In an earlier chapter, we spoke of the reality that nothing much *fundamentally* seems to ever change within the human realm, despite the eons that have gone by. Technologically, we have definitely advanced, but as far as human beings are concerned, we are still living and dealing with our basic, primordial emotions, many of which are very destructive – to ourselves and to others.

Within the Metaphysical Realms, there is, however, the much discussed, but controversial concept that human beings have Free Will. Apparently, this concept also implies that such Free Will is not to be interfered with - even by the Higher Realms of Spirit. On the other hand, there appears to be a slant to this latter situation. Here, Spirits from Higher Realms may intervene, if enough human beings show, not just by their intentions, but by their actions, that they really do desire an important shift within their reality, and need outside help to do so.

Such intentions, backed by actions, could include becoming involved in various Metaphysical exercises; for instance, group meditations or 'Fountaining', as discussed previously. In such scenarios, Spirit Beings then do have a right to slot in with such ventures, empowering us Energetically way beyond what we ourselves could do.

In other words, it seems as if human beings, by themselves, are unable to pull themselves out of their own hole – by their own boot-laces, as it were. Indeed, history tends to vindicate this perspective. But if we initiate attempts to help ourselves, and then invite Spirit to help us too, apparent miracles can happen. Through such combined efforts, we do open a powerful window of opportunity for real and meaningful change to occur in our physical dimension.

We're not alone in our life tasks

What we need to know and take on board, is that we are not so alone as we may feel. We definitely do have the ability to choose to ask for help from the Spirit Realms. We also do have affirming concepts such as multiple realities, vindicated by Quantum Physics, and you also now have a range of 'tools' such as Co-creation and 'Fountaining'.

Combining all these tools, backed by our intention and actions, does provide for a powerful platform from which to start manifesting positive change in our personal Journeys, as well as for humanity as a whole.

One of the biggest hurdles to change, especially on psychological levels, is our almost inherent sense of limitation as to what we can achieve alone. Religions have not necessarily helped here. Many philosophies, and even numerous political systems haven't helped either, because all seem to have had vested interests in keeping the power of the individual pretty much suppressed.

Chapter 15 - Once You've Opened Pandora's Box...

So hopefully, what this book has done is to alert you to how much more you as an individual human being *can* do, especially when this is combined with the co-operation of others. Then change will be possible, not just in a linear, but rather in an exponential manner. If on top of that we also invite Spirit from Higher Realms to add *their* input into our efforts or projects, we might just be able to create a major transformation and shifting of the human condition into its next level of Consciousness evolution.

Humanity on a tight-rope

But there seem to be some inherent dangers associated with these progressive 'jumps' in Consciousness. When we look at the example of atoms and electrons, it's as if the electron needs to build up its energy to a certain critical point before it can make that quantum leap to the next energetic orbit. Perhaps as human beings, we too need to incrementally accumulate a higher and higher level of vibration or Consciousness, before we can jump to the next phase of homo sapiens' evolutionary Journey. But the danger lies in how much of our fairly primitive, primordial and more animal based level of consciousness we keep hanging onto during such a transition.

If our spiritual maturity or level of Consciousness is outstripped by our technical sophistication – as it would appear to be at the moment - there is still a real risk of misusing whatever Consciousness-Energy we have accumulated. We are presently in a time where humanity is potentially teetering on a dangerous tight-rope. If such increased Energy or Vibrational Consciousness does end up being used in a dysfunctional and immature way, this could implode us with horrendous force into barbarity, chaos and destruction. It's a bit like an elastic band in a catapult, progressively stretched to a point where it can be used to propel something like a stone. If all goes well, that stone will be launched towards its target. If the elastic band snaps however, it can snap back in a very destructive manner.

It's also a bit like a male teenager who is maturing, and now has reached a stage where he does need to learn how to drive a car. Hopefully he learns this in a safe and sensible manner. However, time and again the vigor of youth, driven by powerful surges of testosterone, and often a lack of sufficient maturity can cause such youths to spin out of control – and to their destruction. It would appear from even a cursory glance that humanity is presently in this 'immature teenager' phase, and in real danger of 'crashing the system'!

So the Energetic increase that happens on this Consciousness Journey can go either way. It's ultimately a form of stored Energy. When released for that 'quantum leap', it all depends on our own internal 'direction' as to where we will then land as a species. If too much of our focus is still involved with old style consciousness, driven more by ego than Higher Self, then we're guaranteed to be heading for trouble.

Instead of 'financing' our jump to the next level of Consciousness, it's as if this increased source of Energy we as a species have been accumulating then ends up being used instead to 'finance' our dysfunctionality. In this latter case there will be so much more potential for chaos and destruction, simply because we now also have so much more Energy with which to 'play'. However, if we can come from a clearer, Higher-Self Mode of function, we should also be able to make that quantum leap upwards to a Higher Level of Consciousness, safely and successfully.

It's a bit like those Space rockets used for the various Moon missions. The capsule, right on top of the rocket is sitting on an unbelievable amount of potential energy - the fuel tanks. If released in a controlled way, this stored energy is enough to hurtle that capsule thousands of miles into the totally different dimension of Space. Yet, many things could go wrong, as has happened in the past, and with horrendous consequences. Unfortunately, this can happen within the human condition too.

Certain writers within the Metaphysical realm claim that humanity is now at that point, ready to 'blast off'. But the safety of our 'blast off' will really be determined by how much we have our own act together; how coordinated we can be amongst ourselves. Similarly, in any rocket launch, a huge number of things need to be planned and synchronized together, if that fuel-energy is to be transformed into a safe and effective blast-off, rather than an explosion. So too with us humans: we are going to need an enormous amount of fine-tuned co-ordination and co-operation within ourselves and between ourselves. Otherwise the very fact that we have achieved such incredible technical sophistication, but with its equal potential for destructiveness, will probably also become our undoing.

Perhaps, we as a species are still too much like that adolescent teenager. We're placing ourselves into a high-powered 'racing car', but with debatable levels of maturity to handle the astonishing power of that 'car'.

Chapter 15 - Once You've Opened Pandora's Box...

That's why, at this imminent point of 'lift-off', we do need to be so careful how we interact with each other, to ensure that this 'blast-off' doesn't turn into a catastrophic scenario. This is also why all this Metaphysical discussion is so terribly important. There is an urgent need for us to understand ourselves more fully; what drives us; why we are so inherently destructive to ourselves and others. We have to see those aspects within us, of both saint and sinner. We need to learn to re-direct our destructive urges; to manage and transmute them in more constructive ways.

This is why the 'philosophical niceties', as discussed in this and so many others books, are in fact crucial points we have to not only take on board, but fit into our own lives first. That's where the most fundamental and surest change can ever happen. Each component of the 'lift-off program' has to be as mature, strong and functional as possible. Only then is there any real hope that our next evolutionary step will work.

In a Space rocket, it only takes one tiny component to fail for the entire project to explode. It's the same for us in our human Journey. It may take only one political party, or one country to not really play their part appropriately, for our entire human system to go into catastrophic melt-down, if as a species we don't have the appropriate level of Consciousness with which to handle the crisis. One interesting book which discusses these sort of ideas, using the medium of fiction, is Elizabeth Haich's 'Initiation'. [3]

This is now a very important as well as a potentially dangerous time for the human race. But with focused dedication, effort, commitment, as well as inviting the Higher Realms to join us in this Journey towards our next level of Consciousness... perhaps we just might make it!

We are primarily Energy 'morphers'

Perhaps a major part of our human experience here on planet Earth, is to become firstly Aware, and secondly skilled at managing Energy - from *within* the physical reality of a human life. Let's use the metaphor of a gigantic Generator producing huge amounts of electricity. Electricity is just pure energy. It is also pure potential, capable of being converted into an endless number of different functions. But that electrical energy, in and of itself seems to have no particular or specific agenda other than to be utilized in some way.

It's simply there. But remaining just as electricity is really a bit of a waste of all that potential - it needs to be specifically directed and focused into some form of creative outlet. Normally this is achieved via electrical 'gadgets', which then create sound, light, heat, and all the other things we are able to create from electricity. It's the same for us humans. There's this Infinite Source of Energy out there, which in Itself, and on one level, may not have any direct agenda other than to be used creatively in as many ways as possible. It needs an expression. Just the 'Is-ness' of that Energy may not be enough. Actually, It may need to be able to generate something *from* its 'Is-ness' in order to experience Itself.

As human beings, we are perhaps just one of many tiny links between that Infinite Source of Energy or Creativity *Potential*, and the creative *manifestations* from and through that Energy. However, our ability to make choices, to imagine and to create - which is such a special capacity of our human Consciousness - allows for an infinite number of creative events to be materialized, from what was previously just 'potential'.

So, as humans, we are actually 'Energy-morphers' or Energy transmuters. We are doing it all the time as human beings, but it is just that we are mostly so unaware of what we are truly capable of.

Hence, a major part of the human Journey is to first of all become Aware of exactly what it is we are actually implementing. Moment by moment; day by day. Yet, so much of what we are usually doing is done on 'auto-pilot', without any genuine Awareness of what's really happening. It's a bit like someone who has driven cars for decades, and now finds themselves able to drive home safely, along the same route, but basically in auto-pilot mode. Then they realize, once having arrived at their destination, that they actually have no recollection of any part of the entire trip. It was all carried out in 'automatic mode'.

Using another analogy, it's as if we suddenly learn we have just received a *huge* inheritance. With that news comes the capacity to transmute all those millions of individual banknotes – 'commercial energy' – into a huge array of physical things and experiences. But if you haven't been told you have this inheritance, then all this 'money-energy' sitting quietly in an account somewhere is utterly inert. All the myriad of things and experiences which it could activate, never occur.

All that potential remains just that - potential. Bank notes in a bank are just bank notes in a bank. At least till a Consciousness comes along with an agenda, and an intention to transmute those bank notes into a range of creative end

Chapter 15 - Once You've Opened Pandora's Box...

products or experiences. An endless array of creative things can be fashioned from that potentiality, both good and bad.

And this is where we as human beings do have a choice as to how we use that Energy. But first we need to know that in fact this Energy exists, and is there *to be used*. Unfortunately, this knowledge is something which most religions and social systems have rather actively deflected us from connecting with. This is simply because it is too empowering of *the individual* and therefore takes away from the power of the *organization*.

Is this book meant to be the 'Final Answer'?

Is this book meant to be the final answer on how to achieve perfect happiness and harmony in one's life? The answer is a resounding NO! Is this book providing a recipe for some sort of Utopian style of life? Again, a resounding NO!

I think we have to go back to the fundamental concept set out right at the beginning of this book. If it is true that our human experience here has more to do with this being planet 'Earth School', then along the lines of that paradigm, the fundamental parameters of that 'School' have already been well and truly hard-wired into position. This is precisely so as to provide the greatest capacity for learning to any Spirit incarnating onto this human plane. It's almost as if the system is rigged – on one level – to generate some degree of suffering, or rather... challenge.

If this is indeed so, then the answer to a happier, calmer, more fulfilling life may be more dependent on firstly acknowledging this reality for what it is, and secondly, we need to stop trying to change the fundamental hard-wired nature of this planet Earth School. What we might want to focus on instead is how we can change *our* ability to deal with this reality, and thereby deal with our own suffering in the most empowering, nurturing and transformative way possible. But this also needs to happen in a way which doesn't impinge on the freedoms and rights of others, thus giving everyone else the Space to make their own Journey too.

I for one am still very much on this Journey of trying to understand what this human life is all about; how this earthly plane really works, as well as trying to manage my own life in as positive and empowering way as I can. I also acknowledge that there is still a huge amount of learning to be done, leaving me still very unskilled in so many areas of life. But ultimately we need to let go of this obsession with goals, which we in the West are particularly prone to, learning instead to focus more on the moment-by-moment Journey itself.

Striving for excellence rather than perfection
What this book hopefully does provide is not some magical formula for achieving an ultimate state of Enlightenment or a Utopian Earth. Instead, it's about allowing us to Journey along our own individual Path through this reality, as positively as we can, and with as much insight as we can garner. In turn, we can thus choose to create as much Love and harmony as possibly, rather than adding further strife to the already overwhelming amounts of pain and suffering on Earth.

Perhaps that's ultimately what the process of 'Enlightenment' is all about. Not so much *one* sudden burst of blinding Light engulfing us, after which life is all 'bliss and bubbles'. Rather, it's about the day to day addition to this dark realm, of a bit more 'Light', as created and generated via our own incremental bits of increased Awareness or Consciousness. It's from this Higher Level of Consciousness that we then respond to our life, and that of others, in a more Loving and Compassionate way.

We should also clearly understand that Enlightenment is no magical solution to the human dilemma. As Jack Kornfield discusses in his book 'After the Ecstasy, the Laundry',[1] achieving Enlightenment within the human experience does *not* automatically mean the end of life's ups and downs. To the contrary! As he says, after the ecstasy of the Enlightenment process, there are always still the daily chores of laundry, cooking, cleaning, etc. to contend with. But what does change dramatically is *how* we deal with these life situations. It's not the activities of life which change, but rather the *Consciousness* with which these activities are able to be carried out which changes.

Another vital point to take on board is how we judge success. In the final analysis, the aim is not so much to have changed our outer reality before we leave - as much as we nevertheless do validly need to focus on that too. Again, it's that issue of not making life into such an either/or situation. Instead, we need to see to what extent we have been able to alter our *Inner* reality, using the events and circumstances of our individual human Journey here on planet Earth School. And ironically it's precisely by changing our *Inner* reality; our level of Consciousness, that we can have a definite effect on our *outer* reality. By increasing our level of Consciousness, and even though we are still on 'planet

Chapter 15 - Once You've Opened Pandora's Box...

Earth School', it now becomes a 'school' where learning can occur increasingly through joy, rather than through suffering alone. All this is associated with the concept of simply striving for excellence as much as possible, rather than trying to have been 'perfect' in all we've attempted.

Perhaps it's as simple as striving to be happy

Perhaps the Dalai Lama has it right after all. He basically believes that a major component of any human incarnation is to experience happiness. Plain and simple. Or at least try and achieve as much happiness within an incarnation as possible. Not just for our own experience of joy, but to also allow this to then spill over onto others. In this way, we are at least working on decreasing the totality of pain on this plane, rather than the more Christian tradition of seeing suffering as somehow inherently 'good'. In fact, by living our lives from this latter platform, we can only end up contributing *more* pain and suffering to a reality already bursting at the seams with those emotional states of being.

Living in the moment

A major aim or priority of a human life should be to increasingly live in the Moment. Not in a wanton manner, or to the exclusion of being able to access memories of the past or hopes for the future, but rather in a more focused and balanced way. This opens a portal to 'Being' in Higher Self Mode, and in turn to experiencing joy – the primary state of Higher Self. Being constantly out of the Now, drowning in our daily routines, and excessive amounts of materiality, means we are living our lives from ego mode.

So the fundamental aim of our lives could be seen as one of constantly choosing to move our point of Awareness from ego self to Higher Self. And in that shifting, we increasingly start to live our lives less from fear-based, and more from Love-based actions. The ramifications of such a simple shift – individually as well as collectively – are huge. The most important outcome is a greater ability to truly be in joy, never mind what our circumstances; whether we have all the things we would like to creatively manifest or whether we don't.

Although the primary goal of life could be put in very simplistic terms, i.e. making a choice whether to live life through ego or Higher Self mode, actually *making* those choices amidst our busy, distracting and often chaotic lives is far from easy. Frequently, there is so much confusion about how to achieve this, let alone the nonsense surrounding the supposed 'true' or 'correct' way to do it. Everyone seems to have *the* answer. And unless we can see the illusion of this 'Truth Trap', we will constantly be caught in an endless battle between validating *our* sense of 'The Truth', compared to everyone else's. This is a recipe for strife and lots of suffering; a quick look at life only vindicates this prospect.

So the choice in life is simple; the ways to get there are multitudinous, confusing and not necessarily easy. But hopefully, what this book has done is to question a lot of the illusions we as human beings so easily buy into, and to set out at least some of the primary issues needing to be addressed or explored during a human incarnation. And if what you explore and discover resonates as true to *you*, then play with it. See where it leads you. But remember that major Caveat we've spoken about so often now – *'think what you like; believe what you like, and do what you like. Just don't allow such actions to impinge on the rights and freedoms of any other individual or group, on physical, mental, emotional or Spiritual levels'.*

It is with this frame of mind and intention that I offer you, the reader, this book and the Journey it has taken you on. Hopefully it is a journey that has empowered you more than confused you... or at least provided you a few more 'pixels' from which to create a clearer 'picture' of where you are going in your life. If the book has achieved this for you, then my work has indeed been done.

Remember too, that ultimately the aim of this volume is not to provide you with yet another recipe book, where, through using Co-creative concepts you can now increasingly manifest further materiality into your life. Yes, indulge and enjoy to your heart's content! But realize that ultimately the essence of what Co-creation is *really* about: its most fundamental characteristic, has more to do with a Journey of Growth in Consciousness. In turn, such Growth hopefully provides us with an increased ability to live closer to, and through our 'Source' – however you wish to label or perceive that.

Ultimately then, the book offers Co-creative concepts as the 'vehicle' through which to eventually experience greater and deeper levels of Consciousness and Spirituality.

Nelson Mandela encapsulates it all

I'd like to give Nelson Mandela the last words, as per his presidential inauguration speech. Here's a true saint if there ever was one; a person who has obviously found a way of living much of his life from Higher Self. In that

Chapter 15 - Once You've Opened Pandora's Box...

speech, he speaks so eloquently about some major issues associated with being on the human Journey...

Our deepest fear is not that we are inadequate.
Our deepest fear is that we are powerful beyond measure.

It is our Light, not our darkness that most frightens us.
We ask ourselves, who am I to be brilliant, gorgeous, talented and fabulous?

Actually, who are you not to be?
You are a child of God.

Your playing small doesn't serve the world.
There is nothing enlightened about shrinking so that other people won't feel insecure around you.

We are born to make manifest the glory of God that is within us.
It is not just within some of us: it is in everyone!
And as we let our own Light shine,
We unconsciously give other people permission to do the same.

As we are liberated from our own fear, our presence automatically liberates others!

Exercise

- make a list of all the material 'stuff' you already own, and then categorize the items as 'stuff' you truly *need* – compared to just *want*.
- choose a Co-creative goal in which you specifically request the Energetic help from Higher Realms.

Final summary of thoughts

- Once the Metaphysical Journey is engaged in, our lives do inevitably start to change on deep and fundamental levels.
- At times this can be unsettling and confronting, till we get used to our new state - much like a caterpillar, now exiting the cocoon as a butterfly.
- For many people, religion is still a very viable structure or format through which to facilitate their own further growth. However, many other equally valid and alternative options do exist.
- Suffering is an inescapable and ubiquitous phenomenon on Earth, but there are powerful and productive ways in which to use suffering to our advantage. The concept of Tolle's 'Pain Body' is one such option.
- If humanity is to make it, there is a great need to increasingly Spiritualize our lives. Co-creation is one powerful technique in this direction.
- Rampant consumerism and the constant need for economic growth are also major factors driving so many Westerners into debt and bankruptcy, on both dollar and Spiritual levels.
- A challenging question to ask yourself is:- 'what emotional or Inner void is all this materiality actually trying to fill'? 'And has it'? 'Are you really so much more at Peace in your life because of all this material 'stuff'?
- In our endeavor to make change on personal as well as global levels, we should not forget that the Spirit Realms can be invited to assist in these goals.
- Humanity is presently on a potentially dangerous 'tight-rope', as it gets ready to make the next quantum leap in our human, Metaphysical evolution.
- Perhaps the Dalai Lama has it right after all. He believes that a major component of any human incarnation is to simply experience happiness.

- A major priority in life should be to increasingly live in the Moment. This opens a portal to Being in Higher Self Mode, and in turn to experiencing joy – the primary state of Higher Self
- Another fundamental aim of our lives could be seen as one of constantly choosing to move our point of Awareness from ego self to Higher Self.

REFERENCES
1. Kornfield, Jack. *After the Ecstasy – the laundry,* Rider, U,. 2000.

Lifenotes - A user's guide to making sense of life on planet Earth

APPENDIX I

RECOMMENDED READING LIST

- Anderson, U. *The Magic in Your Mind*, Wilshire Book Co., Hollywood, USA, 1961.
- Bailes, Frederick. *Hidden Power for Human Problems*, Prentice-Hall, Eaglewood Cliffs, USA, 1957.
- Bailes, Frederick. *Your Mind Can Heal You*, DeVorss & Co., Marina del Rey, USA, 1971.
- Bartholomew. *I Come as a Brother*, High Mesa Press, Taos, 1986.
- Braden, Gregg. *The Divine Matrix – bridging Time, Space, Miracles and Belief*, Hay House Inc, 2007.
- Braden, Gregg. *The Isaiah Effect – decoding the lost science of prayer and prophecy*, Hay House Inc. Sydney, 2000.
- Bristol, C. *The Magic of Believing*, Prentice-Hall, New York, USA, 1986.
- Chopra, Deepak. *Quantum Healing*, Bantam, New York, 1989.
- Dethlefsen, Thorwald. *The Healing Power of Illness*, Element, Sydney, 1993.
- Gawain, Shakti. *Creative Visualization*, Bantam, 1982.
- Harrison, John. *Love Your Disease*, Angus & Robertson, London, 1984.
- King, Petrea. *Quest for Life*, Equinox, Sydney, 1988.
- King, Serge. *Imagineering for Health*, The Theosophical Publishing House, Wheaton, USA, 1985.
- Levine, Stephen. *Meetings at the Edge*, Anchor Press, New York, 1984.

- Levine, Stephen. *Who Dies?*, Anchor Books, New York, 1982.
- McTaggart, Lynne. *The Field*. Element (Harper Collins) U.K, 2003.
- Rinpoche, Sogyal. *The Tibetan Book of Living and Dying*, Harper, San Francisco, 1992.
- Roberts, Jane. *Seth Speaks*, Bantam Books, NY, USA, 1972.
- Roberts, Jane. *The 'Unknown' Reality –Volume 2*, Prentice-Hall, Inc, Englewood Cliffs, New Jersey. USA, 1978.
- Roberts, Jane. *The Individual and the Nature of Mass Events,*, Prentice-Hall, Inc, Englewood Cliffs, New Jersey. USA, 1981.
- Roberts, Jane. *The Nature of personal Reality: a Seth Book,*, Prentice-Hall, Inc, Englewood Cliffs, New Jersey. USA, 1974.
- Roberts, Jane. *The Nature of the Psyche – its Human Expression,*, Prentice-Hall, Inc, Englewood Cliffs, New Jersey. USA, 1979.
- Siegel, Bernie. *Peace, Love & Healing*, Rider, London, 1990.
- Smith, Shirley. *Set Yourself Free*, Bantam, Sydney, 1990.
- Stanley, Arthur. *Mind Your Own Health*, Nacson & Sons, Sydney, 1993.

APPENDIX II

YOUR MIND POWER CAN HELP HEAL THIS PLANET OF ITS SUFFERING

There are no organizations to join; no fees to pay; no dogmas to believe, nor group politics to contend with.

Just you and your Mind Power linked in with millions of others.

Sounds interesting? Then do read a bit further. Do you watch the news, disturbed by what you see, yet feeling impotent to do anything much about it as an **individual**? Yes? Then know that you **personally** can make a difference. There is a way in which it is possible to link your mind in with many others, creating a massive Healing Force, capable of changing our reality. And all it will involve is 3 minutes of your time, once daily.

Simply by applying your Mind Power - in concert with millions of others - for 3 minutes at noon your local time. That's it! Sounds too fantastic? Not really; and here's why.

The basis to this concept is that our Minds, through the process of Creative Visualization, have great Power to at least *influence* our reality.

Individually, that power may seem trivial and impotent in changing World events. However, consciously visualizing your Mind connected synergistically with many other Minds, tremendously increases our **collective** ability to influence reality.

Imagine. It's 12 noon where you live. You now take just 3 minutes out of your busy schedule; disconnect from what's happening around you (finding yourself a nice quiet spot would be ideal even if this means excusing yourself to go to the bathroom for a few moments of privacy!) - and now focus on a quiet Space within you.

When you feel centered, imagine your Mind linking in with everyone else who at that point in your time zone is also choosing to do the same, for those brief 3 minutes.

Focus on whatever trouble spot on the planet, locally or internationally, is presently most in the news, e.g. Iraq, Palestine; Pakistan, etc.

Now visualize sending - in whatever way works for you - Healing, Loving Energy to that trouble spot. Don't worry about details i.e. don't get caught up in how Peace or Healing change might come about. Simply visualize the end result; Peace, Harmony; people being respectful, kind and more understanding towards each other.

Never mind how impossible it may seem, just visualize the desired end result as clearly as you can. Allowing your Mind to become distracted by the potentially thousands of "ifs," "buts" and "hows" will only sabotage the entire process. Just see this exercise as a fantasy game where you can set the parameters and make whatever constructive, Healing changes you wish to our present reality.

Another variation-on-a-theme is to set an Inner intention of sending an Energy of Compassion and Love to every single political, religious and secular leader on this planet; anyone who has a role of power and decision-making affecting the lives and wellbeing of many other people. Send that Energy with the intention that all such power-brokers increasingly come from a more Compassionate and Caring Space when making their decisions. You don't need to actually know who all these people are, nor do you need to somehow figure out how to connect that Energy to them all. Just set the Intention, and send out that wave of Energy, trusting It knows exactly how and where to connect.

And that is basically all there is to it! Hold your focus as clearly as you can for just 3 minutes; off course, longer if you wish. But the idea is to make this all as easy as possible, without minimizing the effectiveness of what many Minds linked together can achieve in catalyzing powerful and positive change.

Twelve noon may not suit your schedule. Then consider this reality - as vindicated by what Quantum Physics is now proving about Time. **Time is not static; it is in fact quite plastic.** So, if 12 noon doesn't work for you, simply use your **Intention** to ensure your session of Visualization – whatever time you do it – is *warped* back or forward to 12 noon of your day. Sounds crazy.... but this

Appendix II - Your Mind Power Can Help Heal This Planet Of Its Suffering

is now scientific fact ... and still allows you to co-ordinate with the millions of others Visualizing for Peace at 12 noon!

O.K. You've just done a strong, focused visualization of Peace and Healing, linked in with whoever else knows about this concept in your time zone. Now imagine the 12 noon time zone marching across the entire planet as it revolves, and as it becomes 12 noon at the next spot on the Globe, more people in turn link in with all the others in that time zone, together sending a united Visualization Image of Peace and Healing to various trouble spots or to all those leaders in positions of influence.

In this fashion, using this simple, easy concept, a 24 hour a day wave of Healing visualization is being constantly generated and sent to where it is needed.

An exquisitely simple concept, capable of running itself once set into motion. Yet, how powerful in its potential to truly alter or positively influence various negative realities occurring at any one particular time on the planet! The only thing that is needed to make this concept work is for the idea to become commonly known, and for people to truly incorporate the concept into their daily schedule. And 3 minutes once daily is surely not a big demand.

Working **collectively** in this way, by linking in Consciousness with the many others who know about this concept, can therefore empower us **individually** to nevertheless help Heal humanity.

You don't need to know who all those others are. **Intention** is the primary key to successfully using Mind Power. Simply imagine/visualize yourself - in whatever way works for you - connected to these other Minds in your time zone, and then allow your personal visualization for Peace and Healing to unite with the collective Image.

Obviously, the more people who know about this simple concept and choose to participate, the more effective the process will be. To that end, send this entire message to as many others as you feel may be interested in the concept, and open to actively participating in the enormous potential to truly help influence a much needed Healing on this planet. Through the power of the Internet, the concept can be rapidly spread across the entire globe, like a strong ripple affecting the awareness of millions.

In closing, this is a very powerful concept which can empower **you** as an individual to be truly effective in helping catalyze Healing changes to humanity and the planet. No longer do you have to continue observing humanity's suffering, but feeling powerless to personally do anything about changing it.

The process would cost you nothing more than 3 minutes of your time daily. No clubs to join, no fees, etc, etc. It is a self-running process once people have been made aware of it

Use your local and international news sources as the means to determine which areas of humanity or the planet need our collective focus of visualization, at any particular time. Hence no need to check in with anyone as to who or where to send your Healing Energies to.

At the very worst - *if* this is all nonsense - it means 3 minutes of your life wasted daily. But if there is any substance to what is presented above, *how can we afford not to do the process?*

Any opportunity to help humanity through such a simple, quick process, is surely worth 3 minutes of your time?

And god knows, we as a species need all the help and Healing we can get!

REFERENCES ON CREATIVE VISUALISATION.

- Anderson, U. *The Magic in Your Mind*, Wilshire Book Co., Hollywood, 1961.
- Bailes, Frederick, *Hidden Power for Human Problems*, Prentice-Hall, Eaglewood Cliffs, 1957.
- Bailes, Frederick, *Your Mind Can Heal You*, DeVorss & Co., Marina del Rey, 1971.
- Braden, Gregg. *The Isaiah Effect - decoding the lost science of prayer and prophecy*, Hay House, Aust, 2000.
- Bristol, C. *The Magic of Believing*, Prentice-Hall, New York, 1986.
- Gawain, Shakti. *Creative Visualization*, Bantam Books, 1978.
- King, Serge, *Imagineering for Health*, The Theosophical Publishing House, Wheaton, 1985.
- McTaggart, Lynne. *The Field*. *Element* (Harper Collins) U.K, 2003.

If you agree with the above, please feel free to pass it on to as many others/groups as possible.

APPENDIX III

T.F.T. - THOUGHT FIELD THERAPY

(Please note that the following information is based on the books and Website indicated in the Bibliography)

Various people have pioneered the concept of TFT, with Dr. Callahan, a psychologist, being one of the original workers in this field. He developed TFT theory based on direct observations of replicable, first-hand experiments with his patients. It is a process which is able – in a high percentage of cases – to totally eliminate all traces of psychological distress, of recent or long-standing origin. It doesn't do anything directly to the brain or its biochemistry, nor does it consciously change core beliefs. One of the most attractive components of Energy Psychology or TFT is that you don't necessarily need to understand why you have a problem before you can treat it.

Although results can be achieved very rapidly, and in a seemingly simplistic manner, this doesn't detract from the reality that people achieve long-standing cures from many emotional issues, such as phobias, shame, anger, anxiety, depression, panic, obsessions, etc.

A formal definition of TFT is... 'a treatment for psychological disturbances, providing a code (algorithm), which when applied to a psychological problem that the individual is attuned to (i.e. is able to actually *feel* in their emotional being) will eliminate perturbations in the Thought Field, which is seen as the fundamental cause of all negative emotions'.

'The cause of all negative emotions is a disruption in the body's energy system'.

In some circles, it is the accepted practice to 'treat the memory' - seen as the basis to the emotional problem - and, in the process, ask the client to repeatedly relive some emotionally painful event in an effort to relieve it. EFT, by contrast, respects the memory but addresses the true cause... a disruption in the body's energy system.

A 'perturbation' in turn can be defined as a disturbance within the body's Energy system, which can be isolated, and which is responsible for triggering and controlling all negative emotions. The perturbation is the generating 'structure' in the mind, which in turn determines the biochemical, hormonal, nervous system, cognitive and brain activity, all commonly associated with, and an intrinsic part of negative emotions. Perturbations contain 'active information' which is activated when a Thought Field is tuned into, simply by asking a person to think about their problem, thus stimulating an emotional feeling associated with that issue.

It's like an electrical system, where there is a short-circuit happening amongst the wires, causing an electrical 'zzzzzt'. In the same manner, when our energy systems become imbalanced, we have an electrical 'zzzzzt' effect going on inside us. Straighten out this 'zzzzzt' (by Tapping) and the negative emotion goes away. It's that simple.

Although Thought Fields and perturbations are not energy in and of themselves, they require energy for activation, and this occurs when a person tunes into the emotional problem.

These perturbations can be isolated as it were, within the mind, by bringing up the associated emotions, or by the use of specifically worded affirmations, and then treated or 'collapsed' - along with all the information it contains - by stimulation of energy meridian points. This in turn results in the presenting problem being resolved, *without* removing the memory of the experience itself or anything the person may have learnt as a result of that experience. So it is *not* the memory of the trauma that is causing a person's resultant problems. It is rather that when a perturbation is activated, by voluntarily or involuntarily focusing on the problem, that this sets off a chain of biochemical and psychological events, causing the range of experienced symptoms, such as shame, fear, anxiety, etc.

The treatment itself consists of 'algorithms' i.e. specific sequences of energy meridian points which are stimulated in a pre-determined manner. Much like specific sequences of numbers being needed to unlock a combination lock, so too the correct sequence of meridian points is crucial to the success of this style of treatment using TFT (this is not the case when using EFT – discussed later).

Appendix III - T.F.T. Thought Field Therapy

These algorithms were developed through work with thousands of clients over many years during the 1980's. They are easy to apply to others or to use personally, resulting in painless, non-invasive and highly effective treatments. Results are usually seen 'on the spot', but sometimes it may take a day or two before symptoms are fully removed. For other situations, especially addictions, the appropriate algorithm may – in some cases - have to be applied several times daily over a number of weeks to be fully effective.

After a successful TFT treatment, the person can think about a previously upsetting or traumatic event or situation, without any trace of emotional upset. In some cases, the memory can become even more clear and detailed than it was prior to treatment, but without the distress. Clinical results have shown that most successful treatments hold for years and don't relapse. If they do, further treatment with the appropriate algorithm will provide success again, but it would also be wise to check for what set off the relapse. Dr. Callahan found that the cause of such relapses was inevitably an exposure to a substance which the person reacts negatively to, at an energy level. This could include such things as various environmental toxins/chemicals or triggering items like wheat, eggs, perfumes, solvents, etc.

WHAT THEN IS 'EFT?'

Although Dr. Callahan's TFT provides a very successful way of dealing with a wide range of emotional as well as physical issues, inevitably someone else came along and refined the process. Gary Craig is the next link in that evolution, and he calls his version EFT (Emotional Freedom Technique). The major difference is that whereas Dr. Callahan believed it was essential to use a highly specific sequence - or algorithm of tapping points - to be used for any particular issue e.g. anger; fear; anxiety, sorrow, etc, Gary Craig found from his experience that such specificity was not necessary, and that tapping the points in one universal sequence still allowed for profound healing to regularly and reliably occur.

His 'tapping points' are the same as those used by Dr. Callahan, but Gary starts the tapping process from the top of the body, working down the various points, and ending up with the hand points.

The other major difference between the two systems is that whereas Dr. Callahan insisted that it was crucial to be able to bring up the emotion wanting to be worked on, during the tapping procedure, Gary Craig had noticed that for many people, they found it very difficult to bring up a full-on experience of a specific emotion 'on demand'. To overcome this problem, he found that it was still possible to 'tune-in' to the specific issue needing to be addressed, by using affirmations. There are many ways of using such affirmations.

The tapping process is best done just before you go to bed, because then the subconscious has at least 6-8 hours in which to consolidate and manifest the inner changes stimulated by the EFT.

EFT can be a very literal process, in that some problems have a range of separate layers to them, and it may be necessary to deal with each layer separately before the entire problem resolves itself. For instance, if someone got bashed, there may have been the layer of the shouting and abusive language they first had to suffer, followed by the pushing and being thrown onto the ground. Then the kicking, followed by the being hit by a stick. Then the taste of blood in the mouth may have left a strong impression, as well as the pain in a particular body part, etc. etc.

Sometimes it becomes necessary to EFT each separate component before the entire trauma is once and for all resolved.

Gary Craig provides a website for his EFT process as well as regular emails one can subscribe to, which provide an enormous amount of further information about EFT; how it continues to evolve; experiences of other people in dealing with specific problems, etc. I highly recommend you access this invaluable resource at:-

www.emofree.com/email.htm

To view past newsletters in these archives, go to:-

www.emofree.com/archives.htm

BIBLIOGRAPHY

Callahan, Roger. *"Tapping the Healer Within."* Contemporary Books, 2001.

Gallo, Fred & Vincenzi, Harry. *"Energy Tapping."* New harbinger Publications. Inc, 2000.

INDEX

4 minute mile 352, 360

A
Abraham 117, 269, 295, 296, 303, 304, 315, 317, 334
Akashic Records 255, 277
Anti-Christ 114
Apartheid 82, 83, 382
Archbishop Desmond Tutu 82

B
Roger Bannister 352
Beliefs 32, 34, 66
Bible 115, 116, 117, 124, 194, 246, 249, 278, 316, 323, 350, 386
Big Bang 33
Blame 55
Bonsai 125, 388
Gregg Braden 386, 405
Buddhism 74, 120, 121, 126, 226

C
Caveat 116, 124, 126, 127, 128, 129, 131, 346, 347, 357, 400
Chakras 300, 301
Christ 21, 25, 114, 118, 177, 246, 247, 276, 286, 322
Christianity 73, 74, 75, 110, 117, 120, 187, 226, 280
Co-creation 55, 59, 166, 208, 239, 244, 245, 246, 247, 248, 249, 250, 252, 253, 254, 255, 256, 257, 258, 259, 260, 261, 266, 267, 268, 272, 274, 275, 276, 277, 280, 281, 283, 284, 285, 286, 287, 288, 289, 291, 292, 293, 294, 296, 297, 298, 299, 300, 301, 302, 303, 304, 305, 306, 307, 308, 309, 310, 311, 313, 314, 315, 316, 317, 318, 319, 320, 321, 322, 324, 325, 326, 331, 338, 339, 344, 349, 351, 352, 353, 354, 355, 356, 357, 358, 359, 360, 361, 370, 372, 375, 376, 392, 400, 402
Coherence 279
Compliments 356
Copenhagen 34
Council of Trent 75
Cross-linking 345
CyberGame 79

D
Dalai Lama 164, 165, 399, 402
Dead Sea Scrolls 365
Dimension-hopping 371
Dimension I 51, 52, 53, 69
Dimension II 51, 52, 53, 255, 277
Dogmatism 119

E
Earth School 61, 69, 75, 78, 80, 86, 93, 95, 107, 108, 110, 111, 245, 265, 388, 397, 398, 399
Earth stage 98
EFT 160, 359, 361, 412, 413, 414
Ego 140, 141, 142, 144, 145, 149, 151, 160, 171, 172, 222, 288, 289, 290, 314, 352, 353
Ego self 141, 145, 171
Einstein 14
Emotional distress check-list 159
Emoto, Masaru 278
Enlightenment 10, 18, 157, 162, 169, 173, 221, 222, 223, 224, 225, 234, 239, 240, 398
Evil 261

F
Faith 119, 121, 124, 125, 131, 251
Feelingness 297
Forgiveness 97, 98, 99, 112
Fountain Groups 377
Fountaining 6, 373, 377, 380, 381, 385, 391, 392
Free Will 47, 120, 214, 370, 392

G
God 22, 24, 25, 27, 33, 57, 58, 59, 61, 62, 65, 78, 103, 113, 114, 117, 118, 120, 121, 127, 131, 133, 134, 135, 141, 151, 166, 173, 176, 185, 229, 233, 234, 243, 244, 245, 247, 248, 250, 251, 255, 259, 272, 273, 274, 275, 276, 277, 284, 286, 289, 294, 315, 322, 323, 326, 357, 382, 401
Peter Gomes 112
Gravity 14, 59, 60, 61, 184, 257, 266, 356
Guidelines 21

H
Elizabeth Haich 350
Esther Hicks 278, 316, 350
Higher Self 12, 24, 67, 88, 89, 92, 102, 103, 104, 140, 141, 142, 144, 145, 146, 147, 148, 149, 150, 151, 153, 154, 155, 156, 157, 158, 160, 161, 162, 165, 171, 172, 177, 183, 186, 187, 191, 192, 193, 200, 201, 212, 215, 219, 221, 222, 223, 231, 232, 234, 240, 241, 243, 261, 270, 282, 285, 287, 288, 289, 290, 291, 300, 306, 312, 314, 315, 325, 327, 329, 330, 341, 344, 349, 353, 361, 371, 383, 394, 399, 400, 403
Highest good 323, 324, 357
HIV ii, 3, 4, 36, 340
Hologram 294, 315, 322, 323, 375

I
Illusion 79, 99, 135, 143, 161, 191, 215, 216, 219, 282, 314, 345, 347
Impatience 361
Inner change 23, 28, 48, 84, 87, 111, 287, 314, 327
Internal dialogue 358
Intuition 14
Isaiah Effect 364, 365, 370, 375, 385, 386, 405

Index

Isaiah Scroll 365
Islam 74, 93, 95, 117, 128, 226, 339, 382

J

J.C. 236, 247, 251, 280
Jesus 21, 29, 85, 112, 246, 251, 276
Joy in Co-creation 291
Jung 46

K

Karma 60, 61, 189, 190, 191, 192, 193
Knowingness 143, 161, 297

L

Laws of Co-creation 247, 258, 259, 320, 357, 358
Left brain 51
Life is perfect 134

M

Maharishi 237, 375
Mantra 74, 208, 227, 229, 230, 232, 240, 259, 312, 333, 334
Matrix 24, 251, 253, 254, 255, 256, 257, 258, 267, 269, 275, 277, 279, 294, 295, 298, 302, 303, 304, 306, 307, 312, 315, 316, 319, 320, 321, 322, 327, 349, 353, 354, 357, 361, 370, 375, 386, 405
Maya 79, 99, 143, 145, 282, 345, 347, 348
Medicine 44
Meditation 104, 148, 149, 168, 202, 221, 225, 227, 229, 232, 233, 237, 238, 239, 240, 241, 270, 296, 327, 328, 329, 331, 332, 334, 344, 350, 358, 375, 385
Metaphysical 26, 33, 41, 42, 43, 46, 52, 63, 109, 112, 135, 184, 195, 259, 268, 274, 321, 322, 326, 327, 332, 336, 337, 392, 394, 395, 402
Molecules of emotion 36
Morphogenetic Field 46, 49, 51, 68, 128, 129, 137, 269, 364, 375
Mother Nature 45
Multiple realities 370
Muslim 115, 118, 121, 128, 130, 227

N

Nazi 123, 260
New Age 10, 12, 18, 24, 28, 63, 114, 128, 129, 134, 135, 139, 140, 141, 142, 145, 146, 157, 162, 170, 171, 175, 182, 187, 213, 222, 223, 226, 240, 243, 244, 258, 259, 275, 284, 287, 288, 289, 296, 304, 371, 373, 374, 376, 385
Michael Newton 112, 194

O

Oversoul 6, 12, 141, 177, 180, 181, 182, 183, 186, 187, 188, 189, 193, 213, 223, 240, 264, 265

P

Pain body 158, 231
Pandora's Box 6, 101, 387
Pavlov 211
Candice Pert 44
Planet Earth School 69, 75, 78, 80, 86, 93, 107, 110, 111, 388
PNI 48
Point of power 213
Present tense 325
Prophecy 364
Proselytizing 63

Q

Quantum Physics 34, 43, 176, 185, 255, 365, 369, 371, 376, 379, 385, 392, 408

R

Radio transmitter 299
Rajneesh 345, 346, 347, 348, 350
Reality 5, 24, 41, 43, 71, 80, 84, 136, 145, 146, 148, 162, 171, 178, 179, 180, 183, 223, 255, 259, 287, 288, 306, 366, 389, 391, 406
Rebirthing 187, 188
Religion 86, 126, 388
Resonance 279, 303
Jane Roberts 406
Rosary 227

S

Science 3, 14, 17, 32, 52, 70, 278, 376
Service 330
Setting limits 210
Somalian woman 93, 94, 95
Source 24, 25, 27, 45, 46, 127, 131, 165, 166, 177, 178, 179, 193, 215, 233, 234, 243, 246, 251, 254, 263, 276, 277, 283, 284, 290, 294, 315, 319, 323, 324, 327, 329, 348, 349, 352, 357, 360, 396, 400
South Africa 3, 82, 83, 382
Suffering 80, 111, 133, 167, 170, 172, 388, 402
Surrender 152, 155, 156, 172

T

Techno-intrusion 197
Technology 84, 196, 217, 236
Telepathic process 339, 344
Tether your horse 322
The Field 255, 277, 294, 315, 406
Thought is Creative 54, 55, 62, 64, 65, 66, 69, 252, 253, 260, 275, 292, 372
Time-lines 365
TM 229, 237, 375

Index

Eckhart Tolle 112, 173, 220, 350
Torch 298, 343
Truth 10, 15, 28, 33, 37, 38, 41, 57, 72, 74, 82, 115, 118, 119, 121, 122, 124, 125, 127, 184, 185, 260, 400

U
Ultrasoul 141

V
Visualization 11, 12, 22, 23, 24, 25, 28, 51, 52, 57, 59, 60, 61, 63, 64, 65, 66, 69, 87, 137, 170, 171, 180, 208, 212, 213, 221, 234, 235, 243, 275, 287, 292, 296, 298, 313, 322, 356, 379, 405, 407, 408, 409
Visualize 319, 378, 383
Voice dialogue 50

W
Western life 200, 203, 234
Witness State 50, 140, 146, 147, 149, 152, 153, 154, 156, 158, 159, 161, 171, 190, 193, 225, 239, 240, 270

Y
Yellow rose technique 332, 415

BOOK ORDERING DETAILS

To order additional copies of this book, please contact the following suppliers:

Australia and New Zealand

- Peter de Ruyter
  P.O. Box 701
  Randwick NSW 2031
  Email: peterderuyter@optusnet.com.au

- BookPOD (ship worldwide)
  On-line Store at www.bookstore.bookpod.com.au
  Phone: (03) 9803 4481

- 'Bayside Health Food Store'
  30-36 Bay Street
  Double Bay NSW 2028
  Phone: (02) 9327-8043

www.ingramcontent.com/pod-product-compliance
Lightning Source LLC
Chambersburg PA
CBHW060937230426

43665CB00015B/1972